From 1400 to 1750 Asian capital cities were often ruled in such a way that they became symbols of the power and influence their emperors extended over their states at large. These 'sovereign cities' became the empire in miniature.

Shahjahanabad: the sovereign city in Mughal India, 1639–1739 is the first study of a pre-modern Indian city as a sovereign city. Stephen Blake demonstrates how all aspects of life centred around the emperors and their nobles in Shahjahanabad (Old Delhi) between 1639 and 1739. He explores the way in which their palaces and mansions dominated the landscape; how cultural life revolved around that of the emperors and their families; and how the households of the great men also dominated the urban economy and controlled a large percentage of state revenue. This study thus illuminates how Asian capitals were not the great amorphous agglomerations described by Marx and Weber. Instead they were urban communities with their own distinctive style and character, dependent on a particular kind of state organization.

The author's analysis is based on a wealth of sources. These include chronicles, archival manuscripts, biographies and memoirs, newsletters, poems and administrative manuals. Shahjahanabad: the sovereign city in Mughal India, 1639–1739 makes an important contribution to Mughal history and the history of urban development in India. It will be of interest to students and specialists of South Asian studies, anthropologists and geographers.

CAMBRIDGE SOUTH ASIAN STUDIES

SHAHJAHANABAD: THE SOVEREIGN CITY IN MUGHAL INDIA, 1639–1739

SHAHJAHANABAD: THE SOVEREIGN CITY IN MUGHAL INDIA, 1639–1739

STEPHEN P. BLAKE

*Department of History, St. Olaf College,
Northfield, Minnesota*

CAMBRIDGE UNIVERSITY PRESS

CAMBRIDGE

NEW YORK PORT CHESTER

MELBOURNE SYDNEY

PUBLISHED BY THE PRESS SYNDICATE OF THE UNIVERSITY OF CAMBRIDGE
The Pitt Building, Trumpington Street, Cambridge, United Kingdom

CAMBRIDGE UNIVERSITY PRESS
The Edinburgh Building, Cambridge CB2 2RU, UK
40 West 20th Street, New York NY 10011–4211, USA
477 Williamstown Road, Port Melbourne, VIC 3207, Australia
Ruiz de Alarcón 13, 28014 Madrid, Spain
Dock House, The Waterfront, Cape Town 8001, South Africa

http://www.cambridge.org

First published 1991
First paperback edition 2002

A catalogue record for this book is available from the British Library

Library of Congress Cataloguing in Publication data
Blake, Stephen P.
Shahjahanabad: the sovereign city in Mughal India, 1639–1739 / by
Stephen P. Blake.
        p.   cm. – (Cambridge South Asian studies)
Includes bibliographical references.
ISBN 0 521 39045 1
1. Delhi (India) – History.   2. Mogul Empire – History.
3. Urbanization – India – History.   I. Title.   II. Series.
DS486.D3855   1990   89-77373
954′.56025–dc20   CIP

ISBN 0 521 39045 1 hardback
ISBN 0 521 52299 4 paperback

For Meg, who made the whole thing worthwhile.

CONTENTS

List of figures, maps and tables   *page* x
Preface   xi

1 City and Empire   1
2 Cityscape   26
3 Society   83
4 Economy   104
5 Courtly and popular culture   122
6 Aftermath of imperium, 1739–1857   161
7 Comparison and conclusion   183

  Select glossary   212
  Select bibliography   213
  Index   223

FIGURES, MAPS AND TABLES

FIGURES

1   Hall of Ordinary Audience   *page* 91
2   The Emperor's establishment in the imperial camp   95

MAPS

1   Cities of Delhi   8
2   Palace fortress   37
3   Mansion of Qamar Al-Din Khan   46
4   Suburbs of Shahjahanabad, 1739   59
5   Mansions and mosques in Shahjahanabad, 1739   72–3

TABLES

1   The cities of Delhi   7
2   Mosques constructed in Shahjahanabad 1639–1857   53
3   Central place hierarchy of mosques in Shahjahanabad   53
4   Population of the Imperial camp in 1650   100
5   Great Amirs (2500–7000 zat): 1658–78   126
6   Population of Shahjahanabad   174
7   Mosques and temples in Shahjahanabad   181

PREFACE

Its towers are the resting place of the sun... Its avenues are
so full of pleasure that its lanes are like the roads of paradise.
Its climate is beautiful and pleasant...[1]

So wrote Chandar Bhan Brahman of Shahjahanabad, the new capital of
the Mughal Empire. A noble at the court of the Emperor Shahjahan,
Chandar Bhan composed these lines in 1648/9 to commemorate the
inauguration of the imperial palace-fortress. The new city, built between
1639 and 1648, sprawled along the banks of the river Jamuna in the
southeastern sector of the Delhi triangle. While Shahjahanabad remained
the home of the Mughal emperor until 1858, it probably ceased to be an
imperial capital after 1739 – the year Nadir Shah and his Persians
captured, burned, and ransacked the city.

This study of Shahjahanabad focuses on the period 1639–1739 and fills
an important gap in the history of premodern urbanization. Although
there have been sophisticated treatments of premodern cities in West
Asia, China, and Japan,[2] there has been, up to now, no serious analysis of

[1] Chandar Bhan Brahman, "Chahar Chaman Brahman," Persian Manuscript Collection,
Or. 1892, British Museum, London, fols. 141–2.
[2] Paul Wheatley and Thomas See, *From Court to Capital: A Tentative Interpretation of the
Origins of the Japanese Urban Tradition* (Chicago and London: University of Chicago
Press, 1978); Paul Wheatley, *The Pivot of the Four Corners* (Chicago: University of
Chicago Press, 1971); Ira M. Lapidus, *Muslim Cities in the Middle Ages* (Cambridge,
Mass.: Harvard University Press, 1967); R.W. Bulliet, *The Patricians of Nishapur*
(Cambridge, Mass.: Harvard University Press, 1972); Edward Farmer, *Early Ming
Government: The Evolution of Dual Capitals* (Cambridge Mass.: East Asia Research
Center, 1976); Gilbert Rozman, *Urban Networks in Ch'ing China and Tokuqawa Japan*
(Princeton: Princeton University Press, 1973); Gilbert Rozman, *Urban Networks in
Russia, 1750–1800, and Premodern Periodization* (Princeton: Princeton University Press,
1976); and Gilbert Rozman, *Population and Marketing Settlements in Ch'ing China*
(Cambridge: Cambridge University Press, 1982); and William Skinner, ed., *The City in
Late Imperial China* (Stanford, Calif.: Stanford University Press, 1977).

premodern Indian cities. The works that are available are descriptive and diffuse, showing little awareness of either urban theory or contemporary social-science techniques.[3]

In addition to its contributions to the fields of Mughal Indian history and the history of urban development in India, this analysis sheds light on the field of premodern urbanization generally. The sovereign city model, of which Shahjahanabad is the examplar, seems to fit the capital cities of several other roughly contemporaneous Asian empires as well. Accordingly, the final chapter consists of brief analyses of Istanbul, Isfahan, Edo (Tokyo), and Peking, capitals of the Ottoman, Safavid, Tokugawa, and Ming states respectively.

The sovereign city was the capital of the patrimonial–bureaucratic empire, a type of state which characterized the Asian empires from about 1400 to 1750. In developing this type, the work of Max Weber is of great importance. Weber's description of the genesis, organization, and decline of the patrimonial state is the most fully realized attempt yet to analyze traditional polities. The controlling metaphor in the patrimonial state is the patriarchal family and the central element the imperial household. The patrimonial ruler tried to assimilate state to household: he attempted to administer, control, and finance the entire realm as if it were part of his own private domain. Rulers of smaller states could hope perhaps to approach the ideal represented by the patrimonial state. For rulers of larger and more complex entities, however, the ambition to organize and govern their states as a patriarch would control his extended household, was clearly utopian. Thus, the patrimonial–bureaucratic empire was a compromise of the patrimonial ideal, an expedient forced on rulers of the great premodern Asian states by the realities of population, resources, area, and technology.[4]

The metaphor which controls this analysis of Shahjahanabad and the other cities, is city as imperial mansion. The patrimonial–bureaucratic emperor dominated the social, economic, and cultural life of the city, and he dominated its built form as well. From the micro-perspective, the sovereign city was an enormously extended patriarchal household, the imperial palace-fortress writ large. The arrangement of mansions, mosques, shops, and gardens in the city copied the layout of buildings within the palace complex; the organization of production and exchange

[3] See Hameed Katoon Naqvi, *Urban Centres and Industries in Upper India: 1556–1803* (London: Asia Publishing House, 1968); Hameed Katoon Naqvi, *Urbanisation and Urban Centres Under the Great Mughals: 1556–1707* (Simla: Indian Institute of Advanced Studies, 1972). For a further discussion see Howard Spodek, "Studying the History of Urbanization in India," *Journal of Urban History* 6 (1980) p. 252.

[4] For a complete discussion see Stephen P. Blake, "The Patrimonial–Bureaucratic Empire of the Mughals," *Journal of Asian Studies* 39 (1979) pp. 77–94.

in the city followed, by and large, that of the palace; and the structure of social interaction among the residents of the imperial palace set the pattern for the inhabitants of the city.

From the macro-perspective, the sovereign city was the kingdom in miniature. The palace-fortress stood for the city, and the mansions of great nobles for the provinces, districts, and other subdivisions of the state. The emperor intended that his command of the city – the power he exerted, the obedience he received, the resources he extracted, and the influence he radiated – be symbolic and paradigmatic of the control and influence he and his subordinates exerted over the empire.

The cityscapes of Shahjahanabad and the other sovereign cities – Istanbul, Isfahan, Edo, and Peking – were dominated by the palaces and mansions of the emperors and their nobles. The imperial palace-fortresses were enormous structures, covering between 125 and 2,700 acres, and containing from 60,000 to 100,000 persons. In addition to the household troops of the emperor, they held merchants, artisans, servants, poets, painters, musicians, clerks, and administrators. They also contained workshops, stables, stores, treasuries, state records, mints, and weapons. They were the most important neighborhoods or quarters in these cities and set the pattern for the mansions of princes and nobles. The residential complexes of the great men ordered the urban system, the palace-fortress directing the life of the city as a whole and the noble mansions the affairs of their sectors.

The structure of society in the sovereign cities followed that of the imperial palace. The patron–client ties between the emperor and the great nobles and between them and the members of their households bound the city together in a kind of vast extended family. In the daily ritual in the imperial palace-fortress these ties were renewed and reinvigorated and the bond between the emperor as patriarch and the other inhabitants of the city as sons was strengthened.

The households of the great men also dominated the urban economy. The palace-fortresses and the great mansions contained workshops that accounted for a substantial proportion of urban production. Urban markets were, in many ways, captive centers of exchange, either manned by client merchants who provided goods and services to fellow house-holders or overwhelmed by the wealth of the great patrons. And, because they controlled a large percentage of state revenues, the great households dominated the process of consumption as well.

Cultural life in the sovereign cities revolved about the households of the emperors, princes, and great nobles. In the Mughal Empire the great men of court were expected to be expert in the arts both of peace and of war and their households contained poets, musicians, dancers, painters, calligraphers, historians, and architects. In the other states as well emperors and nobles were sophisticated patrons of the arts and their palaces and mansions were centers for cultural and artistic activity.

Like the other sovereign cities, Shahjahanabad was a sacred center. The Mughals conceived of the city as an *axis mundi*, the meeting place of heaven and earth. The palace-fortress was the center not only of the city and the empire but also of the universe. According to the traditional theories of Islamic architecture, the city lay between the two major poles of man and the cosmos and incorporated the principles of both. On the one hand, the city was understood in terms of the body and an organic analogy controlled the plan and functioning of the urban system. On the other hand, the city was thought to encompass both the empire and the universe. The emperor in the palace-fortress was the symbolic center of a nested hierarchy: city, empire, and universe. The control he exercised over his household was paradigmatic for the order he hoped to impose on both city and empire.

Although Max Weber wrote a good deal about the patrimo-nial–bureaucratic empire, he did not have a lot to say about the urban organization of such states. Like Marx before him Weber worked with a series of assumptions about the importance of private property, capital-ism, and the industrial revolution. According to Weber, a true urban community depended upon a predominance of trade–commercial rel-ations, a form of merchant association, and partial autonomy. By this definition cities in patrimonial–bureaucratic empires were not urban communities. The great cities of Mughal India, Weber stated on the evidence of Bernier, were merely princely camps. In Europe, cities had become independent corporate units, breaking down the ties of clan, family, and village but in the Orient family ties remained strong and the countryside retained its hold over the city. Unlike European cities Asian cities were joint settlements, aggregates of subcommunities that were not socially unified.[5]

What this study shows is that the Asian capitals were not the great amorphous agglomerations that Marx, Weber, and others described.[6] Rather, the sovereign city, arising out of different circumstances and conditions, had a logic and structure all its own. The Asian cities were no

---

[5] See Max Weber, *The City*, trans. and ed., Don Martindale and Gertrud Neuwirth (Glencoe, Ill.: Free Press, 1958), pp. 66–9, 80–1; and Byron S. Turner, *Weber and Islam: A Critical Study* (London: Routledge and Kegan Paul, 1974), pp. 75–8.

[6] See Karl Marx, *Pre-Capitalist Economic Formations*, trans. Jack Cohen, ed. E.J. Hobsbawm (New York: International Publishers, 1965), pp. 77–8; Henry Sumner Maine, *Village Communities in the East and West* (New York: Henry Holt and Company, 1889), pp. 118–19; and W.H. Moreland, *India at The Death of Akbar* (London: Macmillan and Co., 1920; reprint edn, New Delhi: Atma Ram and Sons, 1962), pp. 12–14.

doubt different from the cities of medieval Europe but they were not formless, undifferentiated globs of villagers, ready to dissolve at a moment. They were urban communities with their own distinctive style and character.

The sovereign city is a distinctive model of urban structure dependent on a particular kind of state organization. A number of authors have written about the autocratic or absolutist state in Asia but they have not had much to say about cities.[7] To define that state more exactly and to trace out its implications for urban organization is the aim of this study. What kind of a capital city governed the absolutist state in Asia?

In Mughal India historians wrote to win the patronage of powerful men. Ornamented according to convention and sensitive to the interests of the great, a skillful narrative could gain for its author a pension, a purse of gold, or a position at court. Although historians can no longer hope for such rewards, they are often moved by a similar spirit. In part at least, I write to win the approval of a circle of patrons, to repay in kind those who taught, supported, and encouraged me.

At the University of California at Berkeley Ellen McDonald Gumperz introduced me to history as a social science and the city as a topic of research. A stimulating teacher and an imaginative scholar, her tragic death deprived students and scholars of a rich source of insight and inspiration. Philip Calkins guided me over the uneven terrain of Mughal India. Although he had many reservations about my project, he restrained his own enthusiasm and displayed an open and receptive attitude towards my work. Ronald Inden read several early drafts of this manuscript. His criticisms and suggestions were incisive and thought-provoking and he continually argued for a cultural, indigenous perspective. Paul Wheatley pointed to similarities between cities in Mughal India and in other premodern civilizations and sparked my interest in comparative analysis. Gilbert Rozman read several parts of the manuscript and also stressed the need for a comparative perspective. Bernard Cohn led me to explore the relationship between Shahjahanabad, the Mughal capital of the late seventeenth and early eighteenth centuries, and Delhi, the British–Indian city of the early nineteenth century. All of these people provided advice and support at critical times during the years of research and writing and to all of them I am deeply grateful.

[7] For Marx see above. See also S.N. Eisenstadt, *The Political Systems of Empires* (New York: The Free Press, 1969); Arnold Toynbee, *A Study of History*, 12 vols. (London: Oxford University Press, 1935–64), 7, pt. 4; Marshall G.S. Hodgson, *The Venture of Islam*, 3 vols. (Chicago and London: University of Chicago Press, 1974), 3; Max Weber, *Economy and Society*, ed. Guenther Roth and Claus Wittich, 3 vols. (New York: Bedminster Press, 1968), 3; Perry Anderson, *Lineages of the Absolutist State*, (London: N.L.B., 1974); and Karl Wittfogel, *Oriental Despotism* (New Haven: Yale University Press, 1959).

I examined Persian manuscripts in a number of libraries in England and India and was saved by the kindness, patience, and understanding of their staffs from the fate of Mr. Thorowgood, a member of the English mission to Aurangzeb's court, whose

too close application to the Persian language disordered his brains so far that he has made himself incapable of business, and unfit for conversation, and indeed is a melancholy object. He attempted to commit suicide.[8]

I pay tribute to the people at the Oriental Printed Books and Manuscript Room of the British Museum, the India Office Library, the National Archives of India, New Delhi, the library of the Central Archeological Museum, New Delhi, and the Aligarh Muslim University Library, Aligarh, Uttar Pradesh.

Finally, to my wife Meg I owe the greatest debt. Without her patience, support, and understanding this book would never have been completed.

---

[8] Harirar Das, *The Norris Embassy to Auranqzeb (1699–1702)*, condensed and arranged by S.C. Sarkar (Calcutta: Firma K.L. Mukhopadhyay, 1959), pp. 171–72.

1

City and Empire

Shahjahanabad, the capital city of the Mughal Empire, occupied a prominent spot in the Delhi triangle. Within the watersheds of both the Jamuna and Indus rivers, the Delhi triangle had been the preeminent site for the capitals of North India empires for over six hundred years. It was an area steeped in the glorious traditions of the past and Shahjahanabad was the last in a long line of premodern capital cities. The Mughal capital was the culmination of a period of urban development that began to the north in the Indus Valley about 2000 B.C. and continued until about A.D. 1750, when both Shahjahanabad and the Mughal Empire collapsed. In the almost unbroken succession of urban settlements in the Delhi area, Shahjahanabad was the crown jewel, the climax of the premodern urban process in the Indian subcontinent.

The Mughal Empire (1526–1739) was the last of the great premodern Indian empires. It was direct heir to the Mauryan and Gupta Empires, earlier states that had also aspired to subcontinental dominance. The Mughals, however, surpassed all other premodern Indian polities in the efficiency and extent of their rule and in the strength of the order which they imposed. The British followed the Mughals and, for many years, saw themselves as successors, attempting to rebuild the rotten imperial structure which they had so easily toppled. As a patrimonial–bureaucratic empire, the Mughal state was an intermediate structure, situated somewhere between the personal, household-based polities of earlier traditional rulers and the great bureaucratic, nation-states of the nineteenth and twentieth centuries.

The subcontinent of India drops from the Eurasian land mass into the Indian Ocean like the submerged section of a great iceberg. Walled off from the rest of Asia by the Himalayas in the North, the mountains and jungles of Assam in the East, and the ranges and deserts of Baluchistan in the West, this triangular tapering piece of land constitutes a separate

1

geographical entity. Physical geographers distinguish three major geomorphological components: the Himalayas and their flanking ranges to
the east and west, the peninsula of South India and, between these two,
the flat expanse of the Indo-Gangetic Plains.[1]

The Indo-Gangetic Plains are divided into three parts. The Punjab
Plains, the northern section, are composed primarily of the *doabs* (area
between two rivers) of the five rivers that feed the Indus – the Sutlej,
Beas, Ravi, Chenab, and Jhelum. The Ganges Plains, the southeastern
section, extends from the upper Jamuna to the Bay of Bengal, and
includes most of present-day Uttar Pradesh, Bihar, and Bengal. The two
rivers (the Ganges and the Jamuna) and the moist climate combine to
make this area one of the most productive and populous in the
subcontinent. The third part of this central region, the Indo-Gangetic
Divide, lies between the deltas of the Indus and the Ganges. It
encompasses the area between the Sutlej and the Jamuna and marks the
shift from the dryer environment of the Northwest to the more humid
climate of the lower Delta.[2] For the Mughals and, in fact, for most
premodern Indian empires, the primary geomorphological region was the
Indo-Gangetic Plains. This was the core of all Indo-Muslim empires and
Delhi (or Shahjahanabad), the capital of most of these states, lay within
the Indo-Gangetic Divide.

Urbanism in India

The emergence of urban life in the Indian subcontinent dates to about
2150 B.C.[3] This first appearance of cities seems an indigenous pheno-
menon, unrelated to the earlier beginnings at Sumer in West Asia.
Because scholars have yet to decipher the script of the Indus Valley
civilization, however, less is known about the origins of urban life in India
than in China, West Asia, or Middle America. The two principal cities,
Mohenjo-Daro and Harappa, are thought to have been the capitals of a
civilization spread along the Indus and its tributaries, covering about
500,000 square miles in northwestern India.

Each city was divided into two areas: an elevated citadel surrounded by
a high brick wall and a lower residential area where the main body of
inhabitants lived. The citadel contained a great bath, a granary, and a
small number of houses, and it has been argued that the citadel was

[1] O.H.K. Spate and A.T.A. Learmonth, *India and Pakistan: A Regional Geography*
(London: Methuen and Co., 1967), pp. 176–7.
[2] Ibid., pp. 513–18.
[3] See Bridget and Raymond Allchin, *The Birth of Indian Civilization* (Baltimore: Penguin
Books, 1968), pp. 126–55, 238–311.

controlled by a group of priests who ruled both city and state, somewhat on the West Asian model. The cities featured gridiron street patterns, elaborate drainage systems, barracks-like blocks of houses, and buildings for shops and crafts. The population of Mohenjo-Daro, the best preserved site, is estimated at 35,000 persons. The demise of the civilization has been dated to c. 1750 B.C. A number of theories have been put forward but, without deciphering the script or excavating more thoroughly, no definitive answers can be given. It seems likely, however, that the downfall of the civilization was due to one or more of the following factors: flooding, desiccation due to a shift in the course of the Indus, lake formation and silting, or invasion.

The Aryans, a semi-nomadic tribe of hunters and herders who entered India in the early centuries of the second millennium B.C., may or may not have attacked and destroyed Harappa and Mohenjo-Daro. They did, however, lead an unsettled, uncited existence, living mainly in camps. During the first half of the first millennium B.C., with the emergence of kingship and territorial states, permanent settlements of size and complexity began to reappear. By c. 500 B.C., the capitals of the largest of these territorial states (called *mahajanapadas*) were cities of considerable size.[4]

Magadha, the mahajanapada that came to dominate the Indo-Gangetic plains, had its center in northeastern India on the lower Ganges delta. In c. 321 B.C. Chandragupta Maurya, an adventurer of uncertain origin, collected a body of troops, marched down the Ganges, and defeated the Magadhan ruler. Taking over the army and resources of the state, Chandragupta and his successors extended Mauryan rule to all of the subcontinent north of the Narbada river, leaving out only the southern half of the peninsula. Under Asoka (c. 272–232 B.C.), perhaps the greatest Indian ruler before Akbar, the empire represented an imperial achievement unmatched until the time of the Mughals. After Asoka, however, the strains of size and scale began to tell; decline set in, and the empire lasted only until 183 B.C., when the last Mauryan ruler was slain.

The period between the decline of the Mauryans and the arrival of the Ghurid Turks in c. A.D. 1200 is not one of particular interest for students of Indian urbanization. Broken into a mosaic of small states by the attacks of feuding rivals and the invasions of Central Asian armies, the subcontinent offered an inhospitable soil for urban growth. The last

---

[4] For a discussion of urban development after the fall of the Indus Valley civilization see A. Ghosh, *The City in Early Historical India* (Simla: Indian Institute of Advanced Study, 1973), pp. 1–53; Amitya Ray, *Villages, Towns, and Secular Buildings in Ancient India* (Calcutta: Firma K.L. Mukyopadhyay, 1964), pp. 1–47; B.B. Dutt, *Townplanning in Ancient India* (London: Thacker, Spink, and Co., 1925), *passim*.

Mauryan ruler was overthrown by his commander-in-chief, a Hindu warrior who established the brief Shunga dynasty (*c.* 183–173 B.C.). With the downfall of the Shungas began a period of nearly five hundred years in which the ruling dynasties in North India were largely foreign.

Under the Guptas, the first indigenous ruling group since the Mauryans, a revival of urban activity took place. Chandra Gupta (r. A.D. 320–328), the founder of the dynasty, established himself in eastern India and slowly extended the area under his control. With the pacification of North India, trade flourished, and cities and towns prospered and grew. Under Kumara Gupta (r. 415–455) the rate of urbanization probably reached a level not seen since the end of Mauryan rule. The attacks of the Huns in the latter half of the fifth century, however, and their subsequent and repeated depredations over the next century or so, forestalled further growth. Even Harsha (r. 606–48), the North Indian ruler who rekindled the blaze of Gupta glory, could not reverse the trend of urban decline. For the next six hundred years, the subcontinent remained disunited and unsettled.

With the arrival in *c.* A.D. 1200 of the Ghurid Turks, the first Muslim dynasty of the subcontinent, a new and different era begins. The rapid expansion of Muslim rule in the early thirteenth century brought peace and stability to large portions of North India for the first time in centuries. Secure borders and safe roads encouraged expansion of trade. A routinized system of administration led to the founding of a network of administrative centers. Often sited in the hierarchy of market towns that grew up to service the newly expanded trade in grain (that stimulated by the revenue demands of the new rulers), these centers attracted converts, merchants, artisans, bureaucrats, soldiers, and others dependent on the new regime.

There were other reasons for the revival of urban activity after 1200. Islam, unlike Hinduism, was congenial to city life. A Muslim had to worship once a week in a congregational mosque in the company of fellow believers. In India a great many of the foreign nobility settled in cities and towns. After the Mongol conquest of Eurasia in the middle decades of the thirteenth century, a conquest in which city after city was razed and ploughed under, India received a good number of immigrant Muslims from urban West Asia. In addition, the rapid increase in the number of converts served to swell the urban population. By the beginning of the sixteenth century, on the eve of Mughal conquest, the level of urbanization in India had never been greater.

Urban expansion continued under Mughal rule. The Mughals extended their sway from the Indo-Gangetic heartland in North India to the west, south, and east, establishing a zone of peace and prosperity. Within this zone, which each emperor tried his best to enlarge, an administrative system of unprecedented reach and complexity was established. The primary task of the system was to collect the taxes due the state, taxes which were, for the most part, levied on food grains and denominated in cash. In an environment of stability, prosperity, and governmental expansion, a new generation of urban centers was born. Rooted in the past, their origins in the older, smaller, administrative and economic centers of the pre-Mughal period, these new settlements were the outcome of a dramatic transformation. The periodic marketplaces and sluggish towns of the fourteenth and fifteenth centuries were transformed into thriving, populous centers of economic, social, and political activity during the sixteenth and seventeenth centuries.

Cities of Delhi

For nearly a thousand years the rulers of North Indian states established their capitals in the Delhi area. The Delhi triangle, a sixty-square-mile area bounded by the Aravalli hills on the west and south and the Jamuna river on the east, occupied a strategic position in upper India. It commanded the 115-mile wide corridor that, on the one hand, separated the Deccan tableland and the Thar desert from the Himalayas and, on the other, separated the Punjab and the lands of the Northwest from the rich unbroken flood plain of the Ganges. Touching the Jamuna at its northernmost point of year-round navigation, the Delhi triangle encompassed the major break in transportation between the two great river systems of the subcontinent, the Ganges and the Indus.[5]

Much has been written about the historic cities of Delhi, but there has not yet been a comprehensive attempt to interpret the archeological findings in light of the historical evidence and what is known about the organization of premodern states. Earlier treatments err by treating as historic cities ancient sites that cannot be reliably identified, by failing to distinguish between palaces or palace-complexes and cities, and by not separating temporary settlements and local headquarters from cities. In this account of the cities constructed in the Delhi area a distinction is drawn between those for which there is solid evidence, both archeological and literary, and those for which there is little or none. Table 1 and map 1 summarize the results of this investigation.[6]

---

[5] For more information on the geography of the area see Ujagir Singh, "New Delhi: Its Site and Situation," *National Geographical Journal of India* 4 (September 1959): pp. 113–20; and Spate and Learmonth, *India and Pakistan*, pp. 541–5.

[6] Y.D. Sharma, *Delhi and Its Neighborhood*, 2nd. edn (New Delhi: Director General – Archeological Survey of India, 1974) is the best single source. It has the most

The first appearance of the name Delhi is impossible to pinpoint. According to one tradition a certain Raja Dilipa, mentioned in the *Vishnu Purana*, founded a city named Dili before the time of the *Mahabharata*.[7] A second tradition names Raja Dillu or Dhilu as the founder of Dilli or Dhilli sometime around the beginning of the first millennium A.D.[8] According to the most popular theory, however, the first city was built about the middle of the eighth century A.D. by the Tomar Rajputs and was called Dilli or Dhilli or Dhillika.[9] The earliest documentable use of the name is in an inscription of A.D. 1170 that refers to the capture of Dhillika. An inscription dated 1276 mentions Dhilli of the Hariyanaka region and another of 1316 names Dhilli of Haritana.[10] Delhi is the modern Hindi equivalent of the Sanskrit Dhilli or Dilli.

The first evidence of settled habitation in the area dates to *c*. 1000 B.C. Excavations in 1955 at a site near *Purana Qila* (Old Fort) turned up shards of painted gray pottery, but further exploration during 1969–73 failed to discover a regular painted gray ware strata. According to local tradition this was the site of *Indraprastha* (Indra's District), the capital of the Pandavas, the great heroes of the Mahabharata. The arguments put forward – that painted gray ware had been found at other sites associated

up-to-date and sophisticated discussion of the archeological evidence. J. Burton-Page in *Encyclopaedia of Islam*, 2nd edn, "Dihli" presents a lucid and well-illustrated account of the settlements in the area. However, new archeological finds (reported by Sharma) have rendered his treatment of some of the earlier sites inadequate. Alexander Cunningham's report – *Archeological Survey of India: Four Reports Made During the Years 1862, 63-64-65* (New Delhi: Indological Bookhouse, 1972), 1, pp. 131–231 – was the first serious study in English and is still of interest. It has, of course, been superseded in a number of ways, but many of its conclusions and judgements have not been disturbed and its presentation of the literary evidence is excellent. The earliest systematic look at the area is Sayyid Ahmad Khan's *Asrar al-Sanadid* (Delhi: n.p., 1854; reprint edn, Delhi: Central Book Depot, 1965). His overall treatment is uneven, but it does throw light on the premutiny remains, the historical literature, and certain local traditions. The Archeological Survey's exhaustive catalogue – Archeological Survey of India, *List of Muhammadan and Hindu Monuments in Delhi Zail*, 4 vols. (Calcutta: Superintendent of Government Printing, 1915–22) – is the basic reference for the remains at each site. Bashir al-Din Ahmad's *Waqiat-i Dar al-Hukumat-i Dilhi*, 3 vols. (Delhi Muhammad Bashir al-Din Khan and Muhammad Shams al-Din Khan, 1919) is, for the most part, an Urdu translation of the Archeological Survey's four-volume report. It does, however, include a number of maps and local traditions. The following sources provide supplementary information. Archeological Survey of India, *Report for the Year 1871–72* (Varanasi: Indological Bookhouse, 1966), pp. 1–91; M.P. Thakore, "Sixteen Sites of Delhi," *The Indian Geographer*, 8(1963) pp. 84–91; and M. Aziz, "The Origin and Growth of Delhi," *The Geographer* 14(1967) pp. 101–17; R.E. Frykenberg, ed., *Delhi Through The Ages: Essays in Urban History* (Delhi: Oxford University Press, 1986).

[7] *Archeological Survey: 1871–72*, 4 pp. 4–5.
[8] Aziz, "Origin and Growth," p. 103; Cunningham, *Archeological Survey: 1862–65*, 1 p. 137.
[9] Sharma, *Delhi*, p. 15; Cunningham, *Archeological Survey: 1862–65*, 1 p. 141.
[10] Sharma, *Delhi*, p. 15.

Table 1 *The cities of Delhi*

Name	Builder	Dynasty	Date
1. Lal Kot	Anang Pal	Tomar Rajputs	*c.* 1052 AD
2. Qila Rai Pithora	Prithviraj (*c.* 1170–92)	Chauhan Rajputs	*c.* 1180 AD
3. Siri	Ala al-Din Khalji (1296–1316)	Khalji Turks (1290–1321)	*c.* 1303
4. Tughlaqabad	Ghiyas al-Din Tughluq (1321–25)	Tughluq Turks (1321–1414)	*c.* 1321
5. Jahanpanah	Muhammad ibn Tughluq (1325–51)	Tughluq Turks	*c.* 1325
6. Firuzabad	Firuz Shah Tughluq (1351–88)	Tughluq Turks	*c.* 1354
7. Din Panah	Humayun (1530–55)	Mughals (1526–1739)	*c.* 1533
8. Shergah	Sher Shah (1540–5)	Sur Afghans (1540–55)	*c.* 1540
9. Shahjahanabad	Shahjahan (1628–58)	Mughals	1639
10. New Delhi	Lord Hardinge (1910–16)	British (1803–1947)	1911

with the Mahabharata, that the epic mentioned Indarpat as one of the prasthas or districts demanded by the Pandavas, that a Sanskrit inscription of A.D. 1329 placed a nearby village in the district of Indraprastha, and that a village named Indarpat occupied the site until about 1900 – are no more than suggestive. They cannot support the statement that Indraprastha was the first city of the area.[11]

A strata containing northern black polished ware and punch-marked coins and dated *c.* 300 B.C. is evidence of a settlement during the Mauryan period (322–185 B.C.). In fact, the recent discovery on a rock in the nearby hills of a shorter version of the Minor Rock Edicts establishes an unmistakable tie between Delhi and the great Mauryan Emperor Asoka (*c.* 269–232 B.C.).[12] Coins, pottery, terracotta sealings, and figurines indicate settlements at the site during the Sunga (*c.* 185–173 B.C.), Kushana (*c.* A.D. 48–220), Gupta (*c.* A.D. 320–510), post-Gupta (*c.* A.D. 500–700), Rajput (*c.* A.D. 700–1200), and Sultanate (A.D. 1206–1526) periods.

A clan of Rajput warriors, the Tomars, settled in the Aravalli hills south of the Delhi triangle toward the end of the first millennium A.D. An early ruler named Surajpal, whom we know only from later tradition, is

[11] For a review of the evidence see ibid., pp. 8–9 and Cunningham, *Archeological Survey: 1862–65*, 1 p. 135.
[12] Sharma, *Delhi*, p. 10.

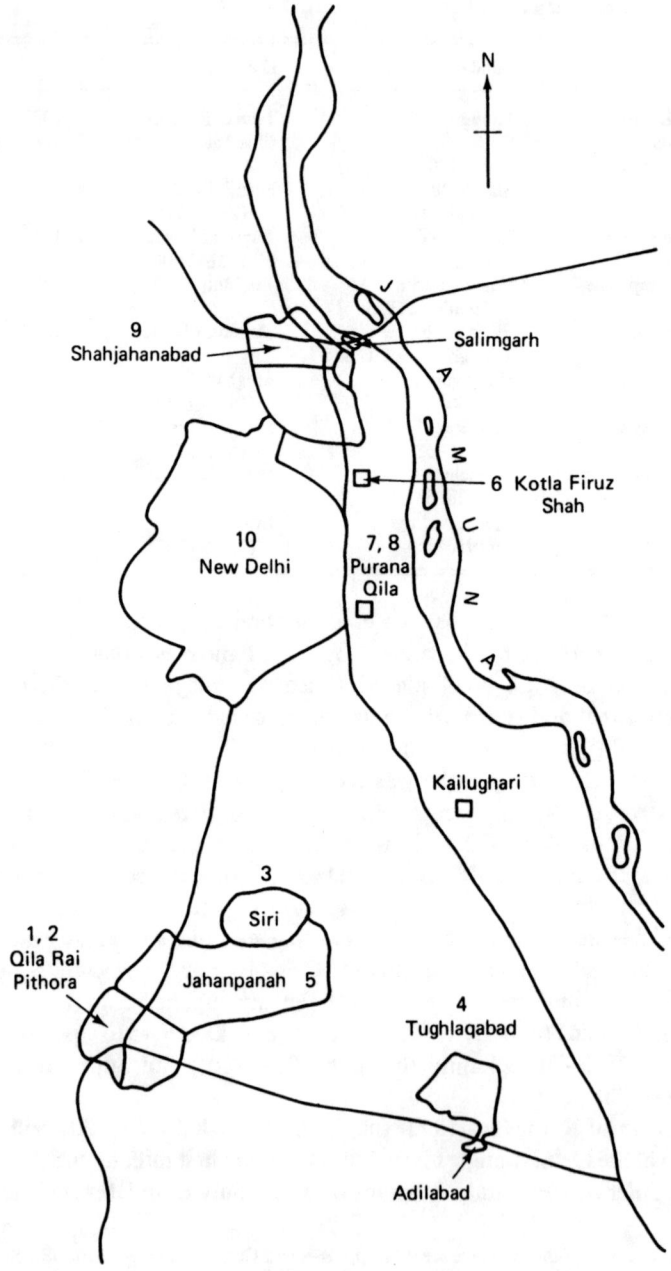

Map 1   Cities of Delhi (source: J. Burton-Page, *Encyclopedia of Islam*, 2nd edn, 'Dihli', p. 261.

said to have constructed a large reservoir called Surajkund in the area. Scattered here and there about the reservoir are ruins of houses, temples, walls, dams, and other buildings – evidence of a Tomar settlement of sorts.[13]

The Tomar ruler Anangpal, a shadowy figure mentioned in a much later history of Prithviraj, is said to have built the first identifiable city in the Delhi area. *Lal Kot* (Red Fort) is the first site with remains substantial and extensive enough to be called a city. Neither the dates for Anangpal nor the date of the city are known with certainty but Cunningham's estimate of A.D. 1052 seems reasonable.[14] A little over a century later (according to an inscription dated A.D. 1163–4) another clan of Rajput warriors, the Chauhans, defeated the Tomars. The most famous Chauhan ruler, Prithviraj or Rai Pithora, established a new city for his followers by expanding Lal Kot. He raised a great wall that enclosed not only the old city but a much larger area besides. Called *Qila Rai Pithora* (Fort of Rai Pithora), the city is thought to have been founded around A.D. 1180 in response to attacks from the northwest by Muhammad Ghuri.[15]

Prithviraj was given little time to enjoy his new capital. In 1192 he met the Afghan warriors of Muhammad Ghuri outside Delhi and was soundly defeated. In 1193 Qutb al-Din Aibak, the Turkish slave general left in charge of Muhammad's army, captured Delhi. The Muslim conquerors, however, did not build a new city. Content to settle within the walls of Qila Rai Pithora, Qutb al-Din and his immediate successors confined their building activities to renovation and reconstruction within the Rajput city. From the materials of twenty-seven Hindu and Jain temples, Qutb al-Din erected a great congregational mosque called *Quwwat al-Islam* (Strength of Islam). He also founded the famous minaret, *Qutb Minar* (Qutb's Minaret), that was finished by Shams al-Din Iltutmish, his successor.[16]

Until the reign of Mu'izz al-Din Kaiqubad (1287–90), the Muslim rulers of northern India kept their headquarters in Qila Rai Pithora. *Qila Marzqhan* (Fort of Refuge), built by Ghiyas al-Din Balban (1266–87) near the the tomb of Nizam al-Din Auliya, was an asylum for debtors and not a separate citadel or city.[17] In 1287, soon after his accession, Sultan

---

[13] Ibid., pp. 12–13. Cunningham, *Archeological Survey: 1862–65*, 1 pp. 141–52 and Burton-Page, "Dihli," p. 256 present accounts that differ from Sharma and one another. Sharma's discussion seems to me the most persuasive.

[14] Sharma, *Delhi*, p. 10; Cunningham, *Archeological Survey: 1862–65*, 1 p. 151.

[15] Sharma, *Delhi*, pp. 13–14; Cunningham, *Archeological Survey: 1862–65*, 1 pp. 183–4; and Burton-Page, "Dihli," p. 256.

[16] Sharma, *Delhi*, pp. 14–15, 18; Burton-Page, "Dihli," p. 256; Cunningham, *Archeological Survey: 1862–65*, 1 p. 133.

[17] Cunningham, *Archeological Survey: 1862–65*, 1 p. 133.

Kaiqubad began work on a new palace-fortress on the banks of the Jamuna at a place called Kailughari. Kailughari was primarily a place of residence for the emperor, a few nobles, and their servants and retainers; it did not replace Qila Rai Pithora. In fact, Kaiqubad's successor, Jalal al-Din Khalji (1290–6), though crowned in Kailughari, soon moved back to the old Rajput city.[18]

Siri, the first complete Muslim city of the area, was finished by Ala al-Din Khalji (1296–1316) in about A.D. 1303. An enthusiastic builder and one of the greatest Muslim rulers of India, Ala al-Din erected or renovated a great many structures in Qila Rai Pithora. Siri, the new city, began as military camp on a plain north of the old capital, a response to the threat of Mongol invasion. Having successfully defended the area, Ala al-Din walled the camp and ordered the building of permanent structures.[19]

Ghiyas al-Din Tughluq (1320–25), founder of the Turkish dynasty that followed the Khaljis, threw up a walled enclosure called *Tughluqabad* (Home of the Tughluqs) on a site about 8 km. east of Qila Rai Pithora. Erected soon after his accession to the throne in 1321, this fortified city was divided into a citadel or palace-fortress for the ruler, his family, and retainers; an area for the houses of nobles and others; and a business-commercial sector laid out in a gridiron pattern. In one corner of the city Muhammad bin Tughluq (1325–51), Ghiyas al-Din's successor, built a palace-fortress named '*Adilabad* (Home of Justice).[20]

Muhammad, however, returned to the area around the original Rajput city for the major building project of his reign. Since the Mongols had plundered the heavily built-up area between Qila Rai Pithora and Siri several times, Muhammad ordered a wall to be erected around the suburbs separating the two cities. The enclosure, called *Jahanpanah* (World-Protector), soon became a thriving center of urban life. During this period Muhammad remained with his family and followers in Tughlugabad. In 1328–9 he led a large part of the Muslim population of the city to Devagiri (renamed Daulatabad) in South India and spent over two years there. He returned in 1330–1 and was followed in 1335–7 by the rest of his North Indian followers.[21]

[18] Sharma, *Delhi*, pp. 18–19; Burton-Page, "Dihli," p. 256; and Mohammad Habib and Khaliq Ahmad Nizami, eds., *The Delhi Sultanat (1206–1526)*, *A Comprehensive History of India*, 5 (Delhi: Peoples' Publishing House, 1970), pp. 304–11.

[19] Sharma, *Delhi*, p. 23; Burton-Page, "Dihli," pp. 256–7; Habib and Nizami, *Delhi Sultanat*, p. 372.

[20] Sharma, *Delhi*, pp. 24, 101–4; Burton-Page, "Dihli," pp. 257–8; Cunningham, *Archeological Survey: 1862–65*, 1 pp. 212–17; and A. Waddington, "Adilabad: A Part of the Fourth Delhi," *Ancient India*, 1 (1946) pp. 60–76.

[21] Sharma, *Delhi*, pp. 25, 73; Cunningham, *Archeological Survey: 1862–65*, 1 pp. 217–18; Burton-Page, "Dihli," p. 258; Habib and Nizami, *Delhi Sultanat*, pp. 487–514; and C. Defremory and B.R. Sanquinett, eds., *The Travels of Ibn Battuta: 1325–54*, trans. H.A.R. Gibb, 3 vols. (Cambridge: Hakluyt Society, 1958–71), 3 pp. 619–21.

Firuz Shah (1351–88), the last Tughluq ruler of note and a great builder, founded his new capital *Firuzabad* (Home of Firuz) in an area remote from the southern sites of the previous centers. Begun *c.* 1354 on the banks of the river Jamuna, this city appears to have covered a large area. Although no walls now remain, the city is said to have been about twelve miles in diameter and to have included the entire site of Shahjahanabad. *Kotla Firuz Shah* (Palace of Firuz Shah), near the Akbarabadi gate of Shahjahanabad and one of the few substantial structures remaining, was the palace-fortress of the emperor.[22] After the death of Firuz in 1388, the Delhi area fell on hard times. Timur, the great Central Asian ruler, invaded North India in 1398–9 and plundered, sacked, and burned Siri, Jahanpanah, and Firuzabad.[23]

Two Afghan dynasties, the Sayyids (1414–51) and Lodis (1451–1526), followed the Tughluqs to the throne of Delhi. After the invasion of Timur, however, Delhi no longer commanded a state of any size. The North Indian empire of the Khaljis and Tughluqs shrank under the Sayyids to an area around Delhi of about two hundred square miles. Khizr Khan (1414–21), founder of the dynasty, defeated the last Tughluq ruler and established himself in the imperial palace in Siri. He spent most of his reign battling his neighbors, defending, and trying to enlarge, the boundaries of his small kingdom.[24]

Mubarak Shah (1421–33) succeeded his father and spent the early years of his reign putting down rebels and rejuvenating Lahore, a city which had yet to recover from the effects of Timur's attack. On 1 November 1433 Mubarak Shah laid the foundations of a new city called *Mubarakabad* (Home of Mubarak) in the Delhi area. Mubarak was assassinated just over three and one-half months later and, as a result, not much work appears to have been done on the new capital. Since no archeological remains have been found at the site (south of Shahjahanabad along the banks of the Jamuna), there is good reason to suppose that the city was never finished.[25]

The building activities in the Delhi area of the Lodis, the Afghan dynasty that followed the Sayyids, were confined almost entirely to tombs. Bahlul Lodi (1451–89), founder of the dynasty, ruled his small

---

[22] *List of Monuments*, 2 pp. 69–80; Sharma, *Delhi*, pp. 25–6, 129–30; Cunningham, *Archeological Survey: 1862–65*, 1 pp. 218–20; Burton-Page, "Dihli," p. 258; Habib and Nizami, *Delhi Sultanat*, pp. 585–9.

[23] Habib and Nizami, *Delhi Sultanat*, pp. 120–3.

[24] Ibid., pp. 630–5. Some writers state that Khizr Khan built a city named Khizrabad on the banks of the Jamuna. See Burton-Page, "Dihli," p. 258 and Thakore, "Sixteen Sites," p. 100. Since, however, there is no reliable literary or archeological evidence of the city, I have not included it in the table. See Sharma, *Delhi*, p. 28.

[25] Habib and Nizami, *Delhi Sultanat*, pp. 643–56 and Sharma, *Delhi*, p. 29. Other authors assume that a city was built and populated. See Burton-Page, "Dihli," p. 258; Thakore, "Sixteen Sites," p. 100; and Cunningham, *Archeological Survey: 1862–65*, 1 p. 134.

North Indian principality from Delhi. Like his Afghan predecessors, Bahlul had to contend with insubordination and rebellion among his tribal followers and with attacks and invasions from the rulers of surrounding kingdoms. In 1506, in order to govern more effectively, Bahlul's successor, Sikander Lodi (1489–1517), decided to shift his headquarters to Agra. From there the Afghan leaders could deploy their forces to greater advantage in dealing with predatory Mewatis, rebellious zamindars, and ambitious rajahs.[26]

The Mughals (1526–1739), the dynasty that succeeded the Lodis, displayed an intense interest in architecture. The emperor Babur (1526–30) laid out several gardens during his short four-year reign while Akbar and Shahjahan erected some of the most magnificent examples of Muslim architecture in India. Humayun (1530–56), Babur's son and successor, founded a modest city called *Din Panah* (Refuge of Religion) on the banks of the Jamuna in 1533. Using bricks and stone from the remains of Siri, the walls and gates of the city were put up in about ten months. No trace of Humayun's city remains, however, since Sher Shah Sur (1540–5), his successor, plundered and razed the settlement.[27]

In 1540, having defeated Humayan and driven him and his Mughal followers from India, Sher Shah began a new city. Called *Shergah* (Sher's Place) or Delhi Sher Shah and located near the site of Din Panah, this city appears to have covered a considerable area. Sher Shah's palace-fortress, known later as Purana Qila, contained a mosque and the tower from which Humayun, after he had defeated the Surs and captured the city, tumbled to his death.[28] Islam Shah (1545–54), Sher Shah's son and successor, built a palace-fortress called *Salimgarh* (Residence of Salim) for his family and retainers on the banks of the Jamuna north of Shergah. Erected sometime between 1546 and 1550 and only three-quarters of a mile around, the fort was intended, it seems clear, as a residence for Islam Shah and not as the nucleus of a new city.[29]

In 1639 the Mughals began work on another city in the Delhi area. In the northern sector of the triangle, on a piece of ground overlooking the river, the Emperor Shahjahan founded a completely new city called *Shahjahanabad* (Abode of Shahjahan). When finally completed in 1648,

---

[26] Habib and Nizami, *Delhi Sultanat*, pp. 666–95; Sharma, *Delhi*, pp. 30–2.

[27] I follow Sharma, *Delhi*, pp. 37, 122–3 and *List of Monuments* 2 pp. 85–7 here. Both Cunningham, *Archeological Survey: 1862–65*, pp. 221–2 and Burton-Page, "Dihli," p. 259 differ slightly in their accounts of the relationship between the cities of Humayun and Sher Shah.

[28] Sharma, *Delhi*, pp. 34–6, 122–3; Burton-Page, "Dihli," p. 259; and Cunningham, *Archeological Survey: 1862–65*, p. 221–3.

[29] Sharma, *Delhi*, pp. 36, 148; Cunningham, *Archeological Survey: 1862–65*, p. 223; and Burton-Page, "Dihli," p. 259.

this new center contained two imposing structures of red sandstone – the imperial palace-fortress and the Jami' Masjid – and a number of very fine but smaller buildings of marble, sandstone, and brick. Shahjahanabad served as the Mughal capital from 1648 until the effective demise of the empire in 1739.

The last city in the area was built by the British. On 12 December 1911 King George V announced that the center of government would shift from Calcutta, longtime capital of British rule in India, to Delhi. Lord Hardinge (1910–16) chose a site to the southwest of Shahjahanabad, and Edward Luytens and Herbert Baker drew up plans for a magnificent city that took years to complete. The wide, carefully planned streets of New Delhi, the great monuments, and the imposing government buildings spoke eloquently of the imperial impulse to dominate and order.

The Mughal Empire

Muhammad Zahir al-Din Babur, a Chaghtai Turk from Ferghana in Central Asia, was the founder of the Mughal Empire (1526–1739). Although Babur could trace a connection to Chaghatai Khan, the second son of Chinghiz, through his mother, it is by no means accurate to call him or his successors Mongol. Mughal, the name of the dynasty, is a variant of Mongol and was used in India to distinguish immigrants or the recently immigrated from local Muslims. It was applied to Persians, Turks, and Arabs as well as to descendants of Chinghiz Khan. European travellers, who misunderstood the meaning of the word, thought it denoted the descendants of Babur exclusively. This meaning gained currency in Europe and soon Mughal became the accepted name of the dynasty. However, since Babur's father, Umar Shaikh Mirza, had been fourth in a direct line of descent from Timur (the great Central Asian empire builder), it is more accurate to call the dynasty Timurid, the name by which it was known to Indians of the period.

In 1526 Babur, at that time ruler of a city state centered on Kabul, was invited to the Punjab by a group of Afghan nobles dissatisfied with the rule of their chief Ibrahim Lodi. Meeting Ibrahim at Panipat, Babur decisively defeated the Afghans and inaugurated Mughal rule in the subcontinent. Following his victory Babur and his men moved quickly down the Ganges, capturing Delhi, Agra, Gwalior, Kanauj, and Jaunpur in the space of a few months. In 1527 he defeated the massed armies of the Rajput ruler, Rana Sangha, and by 1529 was master of the Indo-Gangetic Plains all the way to Patna. In 1530, at the height of his power, he died.

Humayun, Babur's son and successor, faced a difficult task. He had to mold territories in Afghanistan, Punjab, and the Gangetic Plains into a functioning state, and he had to do it against the opposition both of his own followers and of the recently defeated Afghans of Ibrahim Lodi. It is no wonder that he failed and was forced to seek refuge with the Safavid ruler of Iran. From 1540 until Humayun's return to India in 1556 Afghans ruled North India. In 1554 succession quarrels opened the way for Humayun. Several years before, he had defeated his brother Kamran and had collected a substantial fighting force in Afghanistan. With these men he quickly overran Lahore and Delhi and seemed on the verge of reconquering the territory left him by his father. In 1556, however, he died in a freak accident and bequeathed his young son Akbar a situation fraught with uncertainty and danger.

At the age of thirteen, and newly crowned, Akbar was hardly prepared to assume command of the Mughal armies. In a time of peace the task would have been difficult; in the uncertain period following Humayun's return to India the task was simply too much for an inexperienced adolescent, even one of genius like Akbar. On Humayun's death the Mughals held only Punjab, Agra, and Delhi. Under the Hindu general Hemu, the Afghans quickly reconquered Agra and Delhi and soon threatened to drive Akbar and his men from the subcontinent altogether. At this juncture Bairam Khan, one of the most loyal and successful of Humayun's generals, took over direction of the Mughal forces. He defeated Hemu at Panipat near Delhi in late 1556 and over the next four years gradually reestablished Mughal supremacy in Hindustan. In 1560 at the age of eighteen, Akabar dismissed Bairam Khan. He had grown increasingly impatient of all restraints and in 1562, having rid himself of the influence of his foster-mother and her family, became his own man entirely.

For the remainder of his reign Akbar sought to extend the boundaries of the empire; his goal, like that of so many Indian rulers before and after him, was to make the boundaries of state and subcontinent coincide. In 1560 he conquered Malwa and in 1564 Gondwara, both in Central India. In 1567 Akbar began a campaign to subdue the Rajputs, the Hindu warrior caste of North Central India and the most formidable threat to Mughal hegemony. Several years before he had taken a Rajput wife, had abolished the tax on Hindu pilgrims, and had accepted several Rajput chieftains into Mughal service. These inducements, however, were not enough. Some Rajputs remained recalcitrant, and it took several years of hard fighting to reduce them. In 1573 Gujarat was annexed and in 1574 campaigns against Bengal, a stronghold of Afghan influence, were begun. In 1585 Akbar moved to Lahore. Babur's old enemies, the Uzbegs, the warrior tribesmen who had driven him from his homeland over fifty years before, threatened Mughal possessions in the Northwest. From his headquarters in Lahore, Akbar not only repulsed Uzbeg attacks, but also added Kashmir, Sind, Baluchistan, and Qandahar to the empire. In 1598 the Uzbegs withdrew, and Akbar was free to shift troops to South India. In 1601, after several years of hard fighting, the Mughals drew the Deccan states of Ahmadnagar and Khandesh into the empire. Akbar's achievement was to establish a governing structure for India and to put Mughal rule on a sound footing for the first time.

In 1605 Jahangir (1605–27), Akbar's only surviving son, assumed the throne. Jahangir was the least forceful of the four great emperors, and he has usually been seen as weak and uncertain, failing to build on Akbar's successes and ceding much of his authority to his wife Nur Jahan. While this is not a complete or accurate characterization of Jahangir's rule – a time to pause and consolidate was probably in order after the whirlwind expansion and innovation under Akbar – no reassessment of his reign and its significance has yet been made.

During Jahangir's reign no serious attempt was made to extend Mughal dominion in the Deccan and South India, and Qandahar in central Afghanistan was lost to the Persians. On the other hand, Mughal rule in the province of Bengal was reorganized and put on a peaceful and more stable footing. During Jahangir's rule also the number of nobles in imperial service expanded from about eight hundred to nearly three thousand. This proved to be a major burden on the treasury and the percentage of state revenues controlled by the imperial household dropped precipitously during this period.

The Emperor Shahjahan (1628–58), the builder of Shahjahanabad, was a different man altogether. He was energetic and bold, a skilled general, and he had the inclination and resources to patronize the arts. As a prince he had led the Mughal armies in a number of important battles and as emperor he readopted Akbar's policy of vigorous expansion. His first move was to reestablish Mughal rule in the Deccan, and he spent several years reconquering states, defeating others for the first time, and reorganizing the Mughal administration. He was also responsible for the last serious attempt by the Mughals to recover Qandahar – winning it briefly, losing it to the Persians, and then failing on three separate occasions to regain it. By the middle of his reign, he had consolidated Mughal rule in most of the subcontinent, and had appointed men of talent and experience to administer the revenue system.

All of this meant that he was free to patronize the arts – poetry, music, painting, and especially architecture. Shahjahan is best known as the builder of the Taj Mahal, that beautiful memorial to his wife in Agra, but he also renovated the palace-fortresses in Agra and Lahore and planned and built the new capital city in the Delhi area.

Aurangzeb (1658–1707), the last of the four great emperors, is an enigma. Possessed of energy, talent, experience, and discipline, he should have been the perfect ruler, presiding over a reign of peace and prosperity. Yet there is almost universal agreement that Aurangzeb was a failure and that his reign marked the beginning of the end for the Mughals. Like other Mughal princes before him, Aurangzeb had grown discontented and had revolted against his father. He differed from his predecessors, however, in his success. In 1658 Shahjahan fell ill and Aurangzeb, fearing that his brother Dara Shikoh would capture the throne, allied himself with his two other brothers and attacked and defeated Dara. Outwitting his allies, he crowned himself emperor, notwithstanding the fact that Shahjahan had in the meantime recovered.

Aurangzeb had always been a skillful general and a careful administrator, and he moved quickly to reinvigorate and expand the empire. He brought Assam and Eastern India into the state, put down a revolt among the Afghan tribesmen of the Northwest, and subdued the Sikhs, a militant, newly founded religious movement centered in the Punjab. He also moved against the Marathas, a group of people located in Western India who were restless and dissatisfied under Mughal rule. At first he was successful, defeating the Marathas and assimilating them to the Mughal system much as Akbar had done with the Rajputs earlier. Soon, however, this strategy began to fail and Aurangzeb decided to leave North India and to direct the campaign in person. In 1679 he left Shahjahanabad and for the next twenty-eight years, until his death in 1707, he pursued the Marathas from place to place, conquering and reconquering small forts, fighting innumerable skirmishes, but always failing to entice them into the one major battle that would have decided the issue. This effort so bled the Mughals of men, resources, and will that Bahadur Shah, Aurangzeb's successor, found it impossible to reestablish the old imperial structure on his return to North India in 1707.

Because Aurangzeb had ruled for so long, Bahadur Shah (1707–12) was an old man when he finally came to the throne. On his death the usual succession struggle broke out but this time the imperial princes were pawns rather than principals. Competing factions among the nobility supported rival candidates and, after a short rule by one particularly undistinguished prince, Farrukhsiyar (1713–19) was put on the throne. His reign was short and he made no attempt to assert himself against his supporters. In 1719 he was removed from the throne and replaced by Muhammad Shah (1719–48). Like his immediate predecessors, Muhammad Shah had no interest in generalship or administration. He hunted in the area around Delhi, amused himself in his palace, and refused to support efforts to reform the state.

In 1739 Nadir Shah, the newly crowned ruler of Iran, took Qandahar and Kabul from the Afghans and entered the subcontinent. Easily defeating the disorganized and badly led troops of the emperor, he occupied Shahjahanabad. The initial intentions of the Persians were peaceful but when a group of young men from the city attacked and killed some nine hundred Persian soldiers, Nadir ordered a general massacre. Thousands of persons were killed, many areas of the city were burned, and bazaars and mansions were looted. When Nadir and his men finally left, the city lay devastated and the Mughal Empire was, in any meaningful sense, at an end. It is true that Mughal emperors remained on the throne until 1858, but these men had few troops, little money, and limited authority. They did, however, retain a symbolic importance for the subcontinent at large: a number of successor states considered the emperor a source of legitimacy and new rulers generally asked for his sanction.

Patrimonial-bureaucratic empire

The Mughal Empire is an example of a type of premodern state which I call the patrimonial-bureaucratic empire.[30] In discussing the political framework of this type I draw heavily on Max Weber's work concerning the patrimonial state. The rulers of such states govern on the basis of a personal kind of traditional authority whose model is the patriarchal family. Patrimonial domination orginates in the patriarch's authority over his household; it entails obedience to a person, not an office; it depends on the loyalty between subject and master; and it is limited only by the ruler's discretion. Patrimonial states arise, according to Weber, when lords and princes extend their sway over extrahousehold subjects in areas beyond the patriarchal domain. Expansion, however, does not limit the ruler's ambition. Within the larger realm, conceived as a huge household, the ruler/master exercises military and judicial power of an unrestrained nature.

One can distinguish two variants within the patrimonial type of political organization. The first, the patrimonial kingdom, is the smaller entity and is closer in organization and government to the ideal represented by the patriarchal family. The second, the patrimonial-bureaucratic empire, is larger and more diffuse. Rulers of such empires developed strategies and techniques which allowed personal, household-dominated rule of an attenuated kind within realms of considerable area, population, and complexity.

---

[30] For an extended discussion see Blake, "Patrimonial-Bureaucratic Empire," *JAS* 39 (1979) pp 77–94.

To govern successfully a patrimonial ruler must have at his disposal a body of loyal, disciplined soldiers. Patrimonial armies were made up of troops whose primary allegiance was to an individual rather than to a dynasty or an office. In patrimonial kingdoms the military forces consisted, for the most part, of the household troops of the ruler. In patrimonial-bureaucratic empires, on the other hand, armies grew large and complex. To conquer and order states of such size required a collection of soldiers too great for the imperial household to manage and maintain. As a result, the armies of patrimonial-bureaucratic emperors split into two groups; one, private household troops of the emperor and, two, soldiers of major subordinates, the bulk of the army, men who were bound more to their commanders than to the emperor.

Patrimonial administration followed a similar pattern. In the limited compass of the patrimonial kingdom the private domain of the ruler was virtually coterminous with the realm itself, and there was little or no difference between state and household officials. In patrimonial-bureaucratic empires, however, these groups were not the same. Extension of control beyond the household domain called forth extra-patrimonial officials who administered, for the most part, the collection of taxes and the settlement of a limited number of disputes. Such officials, neither dependants nor bureaucrats, worked in an organization inter-mediate between the household apparatus of the patrimonial kingdom and the highly bureaucratized system of the modern state. For example, patrimonial-bureaucratic officials filled positions that were loosely de-fined and imperfectly ordered – a situation very different from the articulated hierarchy of precisely circumscribed offices in modern bureaucracies. Candidates for posts in patrimonial-bureaucratic admini-strations had to demonstrate personal qualifications – loyalty, family, and position – in addition to technical qualifications such as reading and writing. Whereas modern bureaucrats are given fixed salaries in money, members of these administrations were often assigned prebends or benefices, such as rights to certain of the fees, taxes, or goods due the state. In a modern bureaucracy a job is a career, and is the primary occupation of the jobholder; in patrimonial-bureaucratic administr-ations, on the other hand, officeholders served at the pleasure of the ruler and often performed tasks unrelated to their appointments. Finally, while modern bureaucrats are subject to an official, impersonal authority, patrimonial-bureaucratic emperors demanded personal loyalty and all-egiance of their officials. Such rulers ignored the modern distinction between private and official, or personal and professional, and tried to make household dependants of their subordinates.

In the smallest and most intimate patrimonial kingdoms, officials received compensation for their services directly from the ruler's household – they ate at his table, clothed themselves from his wardrobe, and rode horses from his stables. Beyond that, however, they had no claim on the resources of the realm. In the larger, more complex situation of the patrimonial-bureaucratic empire, on the other hand, rulers found it impossible to maintain personally all members of their expanded administrations; thus they began more and more to give officials benefices or prebends. In time this led to a situation in which the greater portion of state revenues was assigned to soldiers and officials. Since these revenues bypassed the ruler entirely, and since the assigned lands were often at considerable distances from the capital, this arrangement meant a loosening of the emperor's control over his officials. Under such conditions the strength of personal, patrimonial authority began to wane, and officials began to appropriate prebends and declare their independence.

As a result, patrimonial-bureaucratic emperors began to devise strategies that would replace, to some extent at least, the traditional sources of control. In order to maintain their hold and prevent appropriation, emperors travelled widely and frequently, renewing in countless face-to-face meetings the personal bond between master and subject on which the state was founded; they demanded of all soldiers and officials regular attendance at court and, on their departure, often required that a son or relative be left behind as hostage; they periodically rotated officials from post to post, allowing no one to keep his job for more than a few years running; they maintained a network of newswriters or intelligence gatherers outside the regular administrative structure who reported directly to them; and, finally, in an effort to check the power of subordinates, rulers of partimonial-bureaucratic empires created provincial and district offices with overlapping responsibilities.[31]

It is important to remember that the patrimonial-bureaucratic empire is a model and that one cannot expect to find a perfect example in the governmental organization of any historical state. What one can find though is a number of states that approximate the model more or less

---

[31] The most complete discussion of the patrimonial state and its variants is found in Weber, *Economy and Society*, 1 pp. 229–57, 263–4; 3 pp. 966–72, 1006–69, 1086–92. Weber's remarks on the patrimonial-bureaucratic empire are scattered and fragmentary, not at all easy to integrate and interpret. His style is to construct pure types – the patrimonial state and the modern bureaucratic state – and contrast them. No historical state, as Weber himself points out, exactly matches either type. All present and past state systems are combinations of elements from several types; the patrimonial-bureaucratic empire is a mixture of the modern bureaucratic and patrimonial states. Actual historical examples of the model differ as they approach closer to one or the other pure type.

closely. The Mughal Empire belongs to the number, as do the Ottoman, Safavid, Tokugawa, and Ming empires.[32]

The *A'in-i Akbari* of Abu al-Fazl is the major text on Mughal government: it is a manual that reveals Akbar's conception of the state and his plans for ordering and administering it. The structure developed by Akbar and described in the *A'in* by Abu al-Fazl endured. Succeeding emperors left it pretty much alone, and it survived in its basic form down to the early eighteenth century. In his preface to the *A'in*, Abu al-Fazl states that the art of governing comprises three topics:

I shall explain the regulations (*a'in*) of the household (*manzil*), the army (*sipah*), and the empire (*mulk*), since these three constitute the work of a ruler.[33]

The divisions of the text reflect this view of state organization. Book One discusses the imperial household, Book Two the army, Book Three the empire at large, Book Four Hindu religious, social, and intellectual activities, and Book Five the sayings of Akbar.

Household

The dominating presence in Book One and, indeed, in the text as a whole (two of the five books center on him) is Akbar, the emperor. A major theme in the first book, one that is treated from a variety of perspectives, is the relationship between the emperor and his subjects. Abu al-Fazl defines a ruler as a man touched by God, a person ennobled by divine inspiration.

Royalty (*padshahi*) is a light from God... Without a mediator it appears as a holy form to the holders of power and at the sight of it everyone bends the forehead of praise to the ground of submission.[34]

On receipt of this illumination a ruler acquires the qualities and virtues needed to govern successfully. These include trust in God, prayer, and devotion, a large heart, and, first and most important, a paternal love for the people – the ideal ruler governs as a father.[35] Such a ruler, and Abu al-Fazl uses Akbar as the exemplar, is presented as a perfect man (*insan-i*

---

[32] This is, as far as I know, the first serious attempt to analyze the Mughal empire in terms of the patrimonial-bureaucratic model. Both Michael Pearson, *Merchants and Rulers in Gujarat* (Berkeley and Los Angeles: University of California Press, 1976), p. 62 and Peter Hardy, *The Muslims of British India* (Cambridge: Cambridge University Press, 1972), pp. 12–14 mention Weber's work. Neither, however, writes at any length on the application of the model to Mughal India.

[33] Abu al-Fazl, *The A'in-Akbari*, ed. H. Blochmann, 2 vols. (Calcutta: Asiatic Society of Bengal, 1972–77), 1 p. 7.

[34] *A'in*, 1 p. 2. For a similar statement see *A'in*, 1 p. 158.

[35] Ibid., 1 p. 2.

kamil), a Sufi phrase which describes a person who enjoys a special and intimate relationship with God.[36]

A second theme – the mixing of household and state – surfaces in Abu al-Fazl's discussion of this first branch of government. In the imperial household departments dealing with purely domestic matters coexist side by side with departments of wider reach and significance. In Book One there are regulations for the harem, the wardrobe, the kitchen, and the perfumery; there are also directives on the care and keeping of the emperor's elephants, horses, cows, camels, and mules. Several *a'in* touch on matters of construction – on styles, materials, and workmen – while others discuss the imperial mint, the state arsenal, and the departments of the treasury.

All of this suggests close similarities between the Mughal and patrimonial-bureaucratic empires. The centrality and importance of the imperial household in the organization of Akbar's empire parallels the position of the ruler's establishment in the ideal type. Abu al-Fazl's portrayal of Akbar as a divinely aided father to his people recalls the traditional, family-rooted authority of the patrimonial-bureaucratic emperor. And the inclusion of state offices and officials in the imperial household, the combination there of personal and official, brings to mind the thwarted ambition of patrimonial-bureaucratic emperors to absorb state into household and to rule the realm as one great extended family.

Army

In Book Two of the *A'in-i Akbari*, Abu al-Fazl discusses the army. He divides this second branch of Mughal government into four classes: *mansabdars* (officeholders) and their men, *ahadis* (single troopers), other soldiers, and infantry. Men with mounted followers became mansabdars only after an interview with Akbar. In the meeting between emperor and applicant, Akbar had an opportunity to size up the candidate and to inquire into his background and experience. With his divinely aided insight and judgment, Akbar was, according to Abu al-Fazl, consistently able to choose superior men.

According to his knowledge of the temper of the times... he evaluated many [candidates] immediately and gave them high rank at once.[37]

---

[36] For a discussion of the term see *The Encyclopaedia of Islam*, 2nd edn, "al-insan al-kamil." Hodgson, *Venture*, 3 p. 75–80 and Srivastava, *Akbar*, 2 p. 309 both argue that Abu al-Fazl presented Akbar in such a light throughout his writings. A'in 77 provides perhaps the best example of Abu al-Fazl's approach. See *A'in*, 1 p. 158–60.

[37] *A'in*, 1 p. 179. For another example of Akbar's penchant for making quick decisions on mansabdari candidates see *A'in*, 1 p. 191. According to Francois Bernier, the Emperor

Ahadis, the second class of the Mughal army, were single men who had no mounted military following, and so could not be given mansabdari rank. Since they were often men of talent and birth, however, and skilled in fighting and administration, the emperor decided it was better to keep them nearby as a body of personal servants than to assign them to mansabdari contingents. Ahadis, like mansabdars, had to maintain a certain number of horses in proper condition.[38]

The third class of the Mughal army included all those horsemen who were neither ahadis nor members of mansabdari contingents. Since these men were usually too poor to own horses, the Mughals gave them lands or cash to buy mounts and to support themselves.[39]

The dominance of the cavalry in Mughal military thought and organization is reflected in the rag-tag character of the fourth class of the Mughal army, the footsoldiers. Of the nine groups listed under A'in 6, only one, matchlock bearers, participated in actual combat. Porters, runners, guards, gladiators, wrestlers, slaves, bearers, and laborers worked as miscellaneous support personnel.[40]

A large group of regulations in Book Two appears at first glance to have little to do with the army. A'ins 16–19 treat Akbar's charitable contributions; A'in 22 discusses feasts; A'in 23, fancy bazars, A'in 24, marriage; and A'in 25, education. If these regulations are read carefully and in context, however, a common theme links them all: namely, the emperor's effort to influence, order, and shape the lives of his subordinates. Thus, the a'ins on Akbar's gifts to the needy and deserving are intended to give mansabdars examples of meritorious activity.[41] The regulations on feasts and fancy bazaars are also exemplary, since feasts provide opportunities to dispense charity, and bazaars are occasions for hearing the grievances of local shopkeepers and inspecting the productions of household workshops.[42] Akbar's intention to regulate the private lives of his nobles is even more evident in the a'ins covering marriage and education. In A'in 24 Akbar established rules for the size of dowries, the age of consent, and the permitted degrees of consanguinity; he also appointed two officials to see that the rules were followed. Finally, in A'in 25 Akbar suggested reforms in the traditional system of education; he wanted the method of instruction simplified and its pace increased, and urged that the curriculum be expanded to include subjects of practical interest, like arithmetic, arithmetical notation, agriculture, household

Aurangzeb knew all his mansabdars personally. *Travels in the Mogul Empire, 1656–68*, trans. Irving Brock, ed. Archibald Constable (1892; rpt. Delhi: S. Chand and Co., 1972), p. 262.
[38] *A'in*, 1 p. 187.   [39] Ibid., 1 pp. 175, 187–8.   [40] Ibid., 1 pp. 188–90.
[41] Ibid., 1 pp. 197–9.   [42] Ibid., 1 p. 200–1.

management, rules of government, and physiognomy, in addition to the traditional religious topics.[43]

No chain of command separated emperor and officeholders; all mansabdars reported directly to the ruler. In addition, mansabdars had to spend a good deal of time in the presence of the emperor. They were called to court on change of assignment and for promotion, and had to stand three separate guard duties in the imperial household. The personnel of the Mughal army, like soldiers in patrimonial-bureaucratic empires, could not be contained entirely within the imperial household. As a result, the Mughal army functioned in two parts. One part was headquartered in the imperial household. It included ahadis, imperial foot-soldiers, and the mansabdars who had been assigned duty at court. The other part, on campaign or stationed in posts around the realm, comprised the mansabdars outside court, their cavalry, and the extra horsemen and infantry assigned them. All of this suggests that the Mughal army followed a patrimonial-bureaucratic pattern; in Abu al-Fazl's discussion, it appears as the adjunct of a household-dominated patrimonial-bureaucratic empire.

Empire

The designation of the Empire as the third aspect of governance indicates a progressive widening in the range of the ruler's responsibility. A'in 1 of Book Three lays out the duties of the *sipah salar* (army commander), the man in general charge of provincial affairs.[44] A'in 2 discusses the major military subordinate of the sipah salar, the *faujdar* (army captain).[45] A'in 3 outlines the duties of the imperial subordinates (*qazi* and *mir 'adl*) responsible for the administration of justice in the provinces. A'in 4 takes up the duties of the *kotwal* (magistrate), the chief urban official in Mughal India, and A'ins 5, 6, and 7 describe the responsibilities of revenue collectors. The rest of Book Three deals with matters of land revenue. A'ins 8–13 look at the classification and measurement of agricultural lands and A'ins 14 (The Nineteen Years' Rate) and 15 (The Ten Years' Settlement) deal with the assessment of the land tax. In A'in 15 there is a general account of the fifteen provinces of the empire. Included in these descriptions are revenue figures for each *mahal* (revenue subdivision) of each *sarkar* (district) of each province.

The seven officials of Book Three are not links in an administrative chain joining individual villages – by way of revenue circle, district, and provincial offices – to central departments in the capital. Rather, an

---

[43] Ibid., 1 pp. 201–2.   [44] *A'in*, 1 pp. 280–3.   [45] Ibid., 1 p. 283.

official's responsibility often cut across several of these essentially fiscal divisions; individual men were not posted at each separate level. In this arrangement Mughal officials, unlike modern bureaucrats, were expected to deal not only with those nearest them in the organization – immediate superiors and subordinates – but with others as well. In fact, the expectation seems to have been that most officials would report directly to the emperor. A passage in A'in 7 suggests the Mughal view:

All of the work, from that of the sipah salar to that of this person [khizanadar], is primarily in the charge of the emperor. And since the strength of one person is not sufficient, he appointed a deputy for each task and gave the necessary threads [of government] extra strength.[46]

In the same vein, Chandar Bhan Brahman described the emperor Shahjahan's intimate knowledge of and control over the affairs of government. He was kept informed day and night of everything that happened in the empire and was able to draft financial and administrative orders without need of a secretary. In fact, when Sa'adullah Khan, the wazir, died Shahjahan took over his duties and handled all of the financial affairs of state until his replacement had arrived from the Deccan.[47]

Book Three, like Books One and Two, describes an empire quite similar to the model. Although the Mughal state was too large to be absorbed into the household and administered as the emperor's private domain, the Mughal policy of dividing the realm for purposes of land-revenue administration into two types – household lands and assignable lands – enabled the Mughal ruler to control a large part of state revenues personally, as did the patrimonial-bureaucratic emperor. In the area of the imperial domain, supplementary officers from the imperial establishment were assigned to district and subdistrict levels to help the regular officials with tax collection. Officials at court, whose responsibilities covered both household and empire, directed the activities of all administrative personnel in the lands of the imperial domain.

The organization of officials also followed a patrimonial-bureaucratic pattern. In Mughal India the great men of the state were not expected to specialize in either the civil or military branches of government; high-ranking officials came from one class and were deemed capable of handling both kinds of responsibility. For the Mughals, there was no clear relationship between mansabdari rank and position in government; high-ranking officials sometimes held provincial or subprovincial posts, and middling ranks often filled central level offices in the household. For Mughal officials, promotion depended as much on being present at court

⁴⁶ Ibid.   ⁴⁷ Chandar Bhan Brahman, "Chahar Chaman," fols. 41–5.

for birthday, New Year, and '*Id* (Islamic holiday) celebrations and on the quality of gifts given the emperor, as it did on performance in office. Finally, Mughal officials usually reported directly to officers in the imperial household rather than to officials of lesser responsibility outside the capital. In the Mughal method of government there were no clear-cut lines of authority, no separate departments at successive levels of administration, and no tables of organization. To the contrary, men of the imperial household oversaw, on behalf of the emperor, provincial and subprovincial officials, who in turn exercised military, financial, or legal power within jurisdictions of varying scope.

As a sovereign city, Shahjahanabad must be seen in the context of the patrimonial-bureaucratic character of the Mughal Empire. The city was inextricably bound up with the state, and it was the personal, household-oriented character of the state that determined the order and style of the city. The imperial household was the central institution in both city and empire but it was in the smaller, more manageable arena that the emperor was able to realize his ambition. While it might be impossible to rule the empire like a great household, to transform the city into something like a patriarchal compound was conceivable. In the city the imperial household loomed large and the emperor was able to stamp his mark in a way he could not on the state as a whole. Shahjahanabad was the urban conclusion to the patrimonial-bureaucratic premises of the state, the city as mansion an inescapable implication of the state as household.

2

Cityscape

Urban historians have too often ignored plan and build in their studies of towns and cities. This is unfortunate for, as a number of scholars have shown, the shape of architectural space is often suggestive of political, social, and economic relationships.[1] For a city like Shahjahanabad that suffered long years of pillage and anarchy, years in which records, diaries, memoirs, and other written materials were destroyed, remains of the urban fabric constitute a major form of evidence.

The Mughal Emperors were interested, as practitioners and patrons, in all of the arts, including architecture. Babur was a poet, a prose writer of distinction, and a man who took delight in a skillfully designed and well-stocked garden. Akbar maintained poets, musicians, calligraphers, painters, and architects in his household. He built the palace-fortresses in Agra and Lahore and encouraged the rejuvenation of both cities, and he constructed Fathpur Sikri, that magnificent but short-lived capital near Agra. Like Babur, Jahangir was an accomplished prose stylist and exhibited an acute appreciation of painting.

Of all the Mughal rulers, however, the one who displayed the most intense and sophisticated interest in architecture was Shahjahan. He had decided opinions on style and once told the faujdar of Sirhind to build his mansion with a garden on one side and a pool on the other.[2] During his daily *darbar* (audience) nobles and princes exhibited their plans for

---

[1] E.A.J. Johnson, *The Organization of Space in Developing Countries* (Cambridge: Harvard University Press, 1970), pp. 3–5 and David Harvey, *Social Justice and the City* (Baltimore: The Johns Hopkins University Press, 1973), pp. 31–4, argue that the organization of urban space is of great significance. E. Baldwin Smith examines this aspect of urban structure in his book on imperial Rome, *The Architectural Symbolism of Imperial Rome and the Middle Ages* (Princeton: Princeton University Press, 1956).

[2] 'Abd al-Hamid Lahauri, *Badshah Namah*, ed. Maulavi Kabir al-Din Ahmad and Maulavi 'Abd al-Rahim, 2 vols. (Calcutta: Asiatic Society of Bengal, 1866–72), 1, pt 2, p. 9.

buildings and gardens, and often in the evenings he would look at maps of the provinces and the designs of buildings under construction.[3] When they had finished structures they were proud of, men like Afzal Khan and Dara Shikoh invited Shahjahan for a visit.[4]

Shahjahan's interest in architecture was not limited to Shahjahanabad. Soon after assuming office, he began redoing the buildings of his predecessors. In the palace-fortress at Agra he replaced many of Akbar's structures in sandstone with those of his own design in marble.[5] In the imperial residence at Lahore he reconstructed Jahangir's Hall of Private Audience.[6] In both palaces he added a *Shah Burj* (King's Tower)[7] and a Hall of Forty Pillars in front of the Balcony of Public Audience.[8]

Thus, in 1639, Shahjahan was ready to found a new capital. The desire to distinguish himself from his predecessors, to stamp on his era an individual and lasting mark was one reason for his decision. The author of *Ma'asir al-Umara*, an eighteenth-century biographical work, wrote: "exalted sultans always had it in mind to cause the world to remember [their reigns] by a permanent monument."[9]

The other reason was the increasing unsuitability of Agra, the capital Shahjahan had inherited from his father. A long thin strip of a city sprawled along the banks of the river Jamuna, Agra had long suffered from erosion. The action of the river had cut deep ravines that extended nearly to the heart of the city into both banks and had caused many structures along the water's edge to collapse. The main gate of the palace-fortress had become too small for the crowds that gathered on court days and festivals, and many persons had been bruised or crushed as they had tried to squeeze inside. Mansions, shops, and other structures had encroached on lanes and thoroughfares, rendering safe and orderly transit difficult or impossible.[10]

Shifting the capital to Lahore, a city that had served as the seat of government under both Akbar and Jahangir, was considered and rejected. Like Agra, Lahore was crowded and unattractive. It could no

[3] Muhammad Salih Kanbo Lahauri, *'Amal-i Salih*, ed. G. Yazdani, 3 vols. (Calcutta: Asiatic Society of Bengal, 1912–46), 1 p. 248.
[4] For Afzal Khan see Nawab Samsam al-Daulah Shah Nawaz Khan and Abd al-Hakk, *Ma'asir al-Umara*, ed. Maulavi Mirza Ashraf Ali and Maulavi Abd al-Rahim, 3 vols. (Calcutta: Asiatic Society of Bengal, 1887–91), 1 pp. 145–51. For Dara Shikoh see *Badshahnamah*, 2 p. 474.
[5] Lahauri, *Badshah Namah*, 1, pt 1, pp. 221–2; 1, pt 2, pp. 235–41.
[6] Ibid, 1, pt 2, pp. 12–13.
[7] Muhammad Salih, *'Amal-i Salih*, 1 pp. 248–9.
[8] Muhammad Salih, *'Amal-i Salih*, 1 pp. 310–11.
[9] Shah Nawaz Khan, *Ma'asir al-Umara*, 3 pp. 462–3.
[10] Muhammad Salih, *'Amal-i Salih*, 3 pp. 26–7.

longer house the emperor and his court and its plan and build were
jumbled and haphazard.[11]

In 1639 Shahjahan instructed the *muhandis* (architect-planners) and
astrologers of his household to select a site for the new capital, a place
somewhere in North India between Agra and Lahore.[12] Soon after, a spot
in the Delhi triangle on a high bluff overlooking the river Jamuna was
selected. At this point Delhi had served as the capital of one North Indian
state or the other for almost five hundred years. From about A.D.
1000–1200 it had been the home of Hindu rulers and from about A.D.
1200–1500, of Muslim rulers. Although it had been nearly one hundred
and fifty years since Delhi had had a real capital, its role as principal center
of Muslim rule in India had not been forgotten.

In 1609 an English visitor to the court of Jahangir described Delhi as
"the chief city or seat royal of the Kings of India";[13] in 1614 two English
travellers wrote of it as "a Citie ... which is great and ancient, in times
past the Seat of the Kings";[14] and in 1615 an English merchant reported
that Jahangir kept the city in good repair because of its position as a
former capital and as the birthplace of emperors.[15]

For Muslims of the mid-seventeenth century Delhi was a religious
center as well. A place of pilgrimage, it held the tombs and graves of
saints, shaikhs, pirs, and holy men and was one of the most important sites
in the subcontinent for pious Muslims. Sujan Rai, author of the late
seventeenth-century history "Khulasat al-Tawarikh," wrote: "There
are so many saints' tombs ... that their number can't be expressed in
writing."[16] To these centers came thousands of pilgrims seeking advice,
comfort, and help.[17] Akbar's visit in 1576 – "he went to the tombs of the
great [holy men] and shaikhs";[18] and Shahjahan's in 1633–4 – "he

---

[11] Ibid., 3 p. 27.
[12] Ibid.
[13] William Foster, ed., *Early Travels in India: 1583–1619* (London: Humphrey Milford, 1921), p. 100.
[14] Richard Steel and John Crowther, "A Journal of Richard Steel and John Crowther," in Samuel Purchas, ed., *Hakluytus Posthumus or Purchas His Pilgrims*, 21 vols. (Glasgow: Janus Maclehose and Sons, 1905), p. 164.
[15] John Jourdain, *The Journal of John Jourdain: 1608–17*, ed. William Foster (Cambridge: Cambridge University Press, 1905), p. 164.
[16] Sujan Rai, "Khulasat al-Tawarikh," Persian Manuscript Collection, Or. 1625, London, British Museum, fol. 26a.
[17] There are description of such celebrations in Shahjahanabad during 1737–40. For Bakhtiyar Kaki see Nawab Dargah Quli Khan Salar Jang, "Risalah-i Salar Jang," Persian Manuscript Collection, Add. 26,237, British Museum, fols. 80a–1b; for Nizam al-Din Auliya see fols. 80a–1b; for Chiragh-i Dihli see fols. 81b–2b; for Baqi Billah see fol. 80b.
[18] Nizam al-Din Harawi, *Tabaqat-i Akbari*, ed. B. De and Muhammad Hidayat Husain, 3 vols. (Calcutta Asiatic Society of Bengal, 1913–40), 2 p. 299.

completed . . . a pilgrimage to the tomb of Nizam al-Din. He supplied the keepers of that place with five thousand rupees for good works"[19] – are examples.

As a pilgrimage center, Delhi acquired an aura of sanctity. A mid-eighteenth-century historian described the city as "one of the old holy places."[20] And Ghulam Muhammad Khan, who visited near the end of the eighteenth century, wrote "Hasrat [revered, respected] Delhi is the guardian of religion and justice."[21]

To fully understand the founding of Shahjahanabad, however, it is necessary to look at what Mircea Eliade calls the symbolism of the center and to explore the concept of the capital city as an *axis mundi* or center of the world. In many premodern civilizations capital cities were thought to be situated at the center of the world. The center was the zone of the sacred, the meeting place of heaven, hell, and earth where rulers and priests communicated with the divine. Every creation was thought to repeat the original act of creation and since creation took place at the center of the world, whatever was founded or created was by that very fact at the center.[22]

There is no doubt that such ideas permeated Hindu thinking. In ancient India the capital city, home of the king and site of the Brahmanic ritual, was sacred. The king was himself the *axis mundi*, the center of the universe. The capital city was located at the center of the kingdom, the palace-fortress at the center of the city, and the throne of the king at the center of the universe.[23] Among Hindu architects and builders (many of whom worked on Shahjahanabad) such ideas survived well into the Mughal period. Banaras was considered to be at the center of the earth, and Jaipur, founded in 1728 by Rajah Jai Singh, was laid out as a microcosm of the universe, symbolic of the sacred, cosmic order.[24]

Rites of construction testify to the belief that capital cities are sacred centers. In 1639 Shahjahan's household astrologers specified the day, hour, and second of the laying of the cornerstone and prepared a

[19] Lahauri, *Badshah Namah*, 1, pt 2, p. 6.

[20] Chaturman Rai, "Chahar Gulshan," fol. 33b.

[21] Ghulam Muhammad Khan, "Navad al-Qisas," Persian Manuscript Collection, Or. 1866, British Museum, fol. 15b.

[22] Mircea Eliade, *Myth of the Eternal Return*, trans. William R. Trask, Bollingen Series, 46 (New York: Pantheon Books, 1954), pp. 14–18. See also Paul Wheatley, *City as Symbol* (London: H.K. Lewis and Company, 1969).

[23] Ronald Inden, "Ritual, Authority, and Cyclic Time," in John F. Richards, ed., *Kingship and Authority in South Asia* (Madison, Wisconsin: University of Wisconsin–Madison Publication Series, no. 3, 1978), p. 33.

[24] Shri Bijit Ghosh, "The Palace-Complex of Jaipur," *Urban and Rural Planning Thought* 8 (1965) pp. 87–127; Diana Eck, *Banaras: City of Light* (New York: Alfred A. Knopf, 1982), p. 6.

horoscope for the city, to determine auspicious times for ceremonies and celebrations.[25] At the beginning of construction a lark was sacrificed and the bodies of several freshly beheaded criminals were put in the trenches round the cornerstone.[26] Underlying these sacrifices, according to Eliade, are the beliefs that nothing can endure without a soul and that the original creation involved a sacrifice.[27]

Descriptions of seventeenth- and eighteenth-century writers suggest that the Mughals conceived of Shahjahanabad as an *axis mundi*. One man wrote "[the city is]...a garden of Eden that is populated"[28] and Muhammad Salih described it as "the foundation of the eighth heaven."[29] In the early eighteenth century a geographer wrote:

[Shahjahanabad] was always the *dar al-mulk* [seat of the empire] of the great sultans and the center of the circle of Islam [*markaz-i-dairah Islam*].[30]

And Muhammad Salih wrote "its four walls... enclosed the center of the earth [*markaz-i khak*]."[31]

Having settled on a site Shahjahan was eager to begin work. On 29 April 1639 Ghairat Khan (subahdar of Delhi) ordered the two expert builders of his establishment, Ustad Ahmad and Ustad Hamid, to begin digging.[32] In two weeks (12 May 1639) initial spadework was completed. Princes and high-ranking amirs, having received plots of land about the site, ordered plans drawn up and work begun on their mansions. Work on the imperial structures was carried out under the supervision of three subahdars. In the four months of his tenure Ghairat Khan completed the

[25] Muhammad Salih, *'Amal-i Salih*, 3 p. 27; Muhammad Waris, "Padshah Namah," Persian Manuscript Collection, Add. 6556, British Museum, fol. 402a. An elaborate horoscope was drawn for Ahmadabad. See Ali Muhammad Khan, *Mirat-i Ahmadi Supplement*, trans. Syed Nawab Ali and Charles Norman Seddon (Baroda, India: Oriental Institute, Gaekwad's Oriental Series, n. 43, 1924; reissued and corrected, Baroda, India: Oriental Institute, 1928), pp. 1–3.

[26] Waris, "Padshah Namah," fol. 402a. Niccolao Manucci, *Storia Moqor*, trans. William Irvine, 4 vols. (reprinted edn, Calcutta: Editions Indian, 1965), 1 pp. 177.

[27] Eliade, *Myth of the Eternal Return*, pp. 18–20.

[28] Ghulam Muhammad Khan, "Navad al-Qisas," fol. 15b.

[29] Muhammad Salih, *'Amal-i Salih*, 3 p. 30.

[30] Hakim Maharat Khan Isfahani, "Bahjat al-'Alam," Persian Manuscript Collection, Ethe 729, Indian Office Library, fol. 34a.

[31] Muhammad Salih, "Bahar-i Sukhan," Persian Manuscript Collection, Or. 178, British Museum, fol. 203b.

[32] Ustad Ahmad seems to have been a favorite of Shahjahan's. According to a poem of his son, Lutfullah Muhandis, Ahmad had been put in charge of the work on the Taj Mahal. See M. Abdullah Chaghtai, "A Great Family of Mughal Architects," *Islamic Culture* 9 (April 1937), pp. 200–9. It seems likely then that Ahmad was a member of Shahjahan's, not Ghairat Khan's, household. Shahjahan probably sent him to Shahjahanabad to oversee the construction under Ghairat Khan's supervision. In all likelihood, this is the reason both court historians placed Ahmad in the establishment of the subahdar.

excavation and collected building materials. Under Allah Vardi Khan the palace walls fronting the river were erected. And Makramat Khan, who replaced Allah Vardi Khan, presided over the completion of the walls, buildings, and gardens of the palace-fortress.[33]

When the palace-fortress was finished Shahjahan was notified. The household astrologers declared 19 April 1648 auspicious and on that day Shahjahan entered the *Daulat Khanah-i Khas* (Hall of Special Audience) by the gate fronting the river. To commemorate the occasion and to inaugurate the new capital, Shahjahan ordered a great celebration. Singers from Iran, Turan, Kashmir, and Hindustan performed, and dancers and clowns cavorted here and there.[34] The palace-fortress was splendidly turned out. As *pishkash* (a ceremonial offering) Sa'adullah Khan furnished the Hall of Special Audience with carpets worth Rs. 60,000 and Ali Mardan Khan provided carpets for the *Aramgah* or *Khwabgah* (Place of Rest or Sleep). Sa'adullah Khan composed a verse and had it inscribed on the wall of the Aramgah.[35] The roof, walls, and columns of the Hall of Ordinary Audience (*Daulat Khanah-i Khas-o' Am*) were hung with brocaded velvet from Turkey and silk from China. A great canopy of embroidered velvet prepared by artisans in the imperial workshop in Ahmadabad was raised on four silver pillars in the courtyard of the Hall of Ordinary Audience. It measured 219 feet by 135 and stood nearly 70 feet high. It was surrounded by a silver railing and held over one thousand people. The emperor sat on a special throne enclosed by a golden railing. Before him the princes and great nobles sat on smaller thrones. Shahjahan held a general audience (*bar-i 'am*) and distributed gifts and honors to the great men of state. Dara Shikoh, the heir-apparent, received a special *khil'at* (ceremonial robe), an elephant, two hundred thousand rupees, and an increase in rank of two thousand zat; Sa'adullah Khan received a special khil'at and a promotion to seven thousand zat and seven thousand suwar; and Makramat Khan was given a special khil'at and was elevated to the rank of five thousand zat and five thousand suwar.[36]

Plan and build

A massive stone wall 27 feet high, 12 feet thick, and 3.8 miles long encircled Shahjahanabad, enclosing an area of about 1500 acres. Erected

---

[33] Muhammad Salih, *'Amal-i Salih*, 3 p. 29.
[34] Muhammad Waris, "Padshah Namah," fol. 156b.
[35] Ibid., fol. 404a.
[36] Muhammad Salih, *'Amal-i Salih*, 3 pp. 56–7; Muhammad Waris, "Padshah Namah," fols. 406a–7.

during the years 1651-8, this was not the first attempt to enclose the city. A wall of stone and mud had been thrown up in four months during the latter part of 1650 and had promptly collapsed in the monsoon rains of the following year.[37] The wall was surmounted by twenty-seven towers and broken in numerous places by gates and entryways, both large and small. Although it is impossible now to distinguish all the original openings, it is fairly easy to determine the major gateways (see map 5).

Set at regular intervals around the wall were the seven large gates that handled the bulk of the mounted, vehicular, and pedestrian traffic: the Kashmiri, Mori, Kabuli, Lahori, Ajmiri, Turkomani, and Akbarabadi gates. The wall fronting the river was interrupted by the Raja Ghat, Qila Ghat, and Nigambodh gates. These three provided Hindus of the city access to the riverside platforms (*ghats*) upon which they burned their dead. Interspersed among the large gateways were a number of smaller entries that allowed pedestrians quick and easy passage to and from the city. Some of these were located near mansions while others stood near places of public importance. Examples include the Zinat al-Masajid gate on the Jamuna, the *Farrashkhanah* (Wardrobe) gate, and the gates of Ghazi al-Din Khan and Ahmad Baksh Khan.[38]

There were two hillocks within the area enclosed by the great walls. *Jhujalal Pahari* (Jhujalal Hill), near the northwestern wall of the city, held nothing of significance but *Bhujalal Pahari* (Bhujalal Hill), near the center of the city, held the Jami' Masjid.[39]

The plan of Shahjahanabad reflects both Hindu and Islamic influences. The street plan seems to have followed a design from the ancient Hindu texts on architecture, the *vastu sastras* (rules for architecture). These texts contain directions for constructing buildings, and for laying out and dividing settlements of different kinds. The *Manasara*, a vastu sastra dating to about A.D. 400–600, contains a semielliptical design called karmuka or bow for a site fronting a river or seashore.[40] This design seems to have influenced Shahjahan's architects and engineers. The north–south road that connected the Akbarabadi and Kashmiri Gates of the city and which includes Faiz Bazar represents the bow string. The streets running from south to east and connecting the Turkomani and Ajmiri gates with the Lahori Gate and that running northeast and

[37] *List of Monuments*, 1 p. 187.
[38] For a discussion of the gates see Sayyid Ahmad Khan, *Asar*, p. 133 and Bashir al-Din Ahmad, *Waqiat*, 2 pp. 93–4.
[39] Bashir al-Din Ahmad, *Waqiat*, 2 p. 9.
[40] Prasana Kumar Acharya, *Indian Architecture According to the Mansara Silpa Sastra* (London: Oxford University Press, 1927), p. 88. See also Binode Behari Dutt, *Town Planning in Ancient India* (London: Thacker, Spink, and Co., 1925), pp. 237–9.

connecting the Mori and Lahori gates represent, along with the outer
wall of the city, the curved shaft of the bow. Chandni Chawk, which ran
from the Lahori Gate of the fort to the Lahori Gate of the city, was the
arm of the archer. In the karmuka plan the most auspicious spot was the
juncture of the two main streets. In the Hindu settlement this held a
temple to Vishnu or Shiva; in Shahjahanabad it held the imperial
palace-fortress.

The influence of Islamic ideas can also be seen in the plan of
Shahjahanabad. The source for these ideas, as for most of the other arts of
the Indo-Islamic style, was Iran. In painting, poetry, music, and dance as
well as in architecture and city planning the Persian influence was
predominant. The Emperor Humayun, the father of Akbar, spent twelve
years (1543–55) in exile in Iran and was heavily exposed to Shi'ism and
the Safavid court. In addition, the five Islamic kingdoms of the Deccan
had all been Shi'i from before the time of Akbar and had maintained
close diplomatic and cultural ties with Iran through the fifteenth and
sixteenth centuries. Their conquest by the Mughals in the early
seventeenth century increased the Persian, Shi'i influence at court.

In the minds of the rest of the Islamic world Mughal India was a land of
great wealth (it had two harvests a year), and the Mughal courts were the
richest and most generous of the time. A steady influx of Iranis seeking
fortune and position made that group the largest of the foreign
contingents during the Mughal period. Under Shahjahan many of the
great men of state were from Iran; Shaista Khan, Asaf Khan, Jafar Khan,
Makaramat Khan and, most importantly, Ali Mardan Khan who, as
commander of the fort at Qandahar, defected to the Mughals in 1638.

In addition to Safavid nobles, administrators, and soldiers, there were
poets, painters, architects, musicians, philosophers, and physicians who
immigrated to India. The first poets returned with Humayun and the
exodus continued throughout the sixteenth, seventeenth, and eighteenth
centuries. The historian Badauni, writing at the end of the sixteenth
century, listed 170 immigrant poets, and almost all of the great poets of
Safavid Iran came to India at some point during their careers.[41] Persian
painters founded the Indo-Islamic school of Indian painting, and
immigrant architects and engineers influenced the design and build of
palaces, mansions, mosques, tombs, and gardens in Shahjahanabad and
other cities as well. Abd-al Rahim Khan-i Khanan, for example, had in
his household an Iranian architect named Baruli who had worked for the
Safavid emperors and had fled to India. He knew the techniques and styles
of royal buildings in Iran, Iraq, and Khurasan. He designed and built

[41] Aziz Ahmad, "Safavid Poets and India," *Iran* 14 (1976) pp. 17–32.

several bathhouses and was responsible for the markets and streets of a mahallah named Jahangirpura in Burhanpur.[42] In addition, the tile-work on the Lahore fort was the work of Iranian architects and craftsmen. An example of another kind of immigrant was Mir Abdul Kasim. A member of a distinguished family of Sayyids from Astrabad, he was the most eminent philosopher of his time. Although he was held in great esteem by Shah Abbas, he spent many years in India and was twice introduced to Shahjahan by Asaf Khan, the wazir. He finally returned to Iran and died there in the reign of Shah Safi.[43]

To understand the cosmological context in which the Iranian architects of Shahjahan's court worked it is necessary to consider the *Rasail* (Epistles) of the *Ikhwan al-Safa* (Brothers of Purity). These are a collection of fifty-two letters probably written during the tenth and eleventh centuries by a group of scholars who were Shi'i (probably Ismaili) and who had pronounced Sufi leanings. The Rasail present a conception of the universe accepted by a large portion of both the Sunni and Shi'i worlds for over a 1000 years. They have been widely translated into Persian, Hindustani, and Turkish and have been part of the libraries of educated men for centuries.[44]

There are two cosmological principles central to the *Rasail*: the analogy between the microcosm and the macrocosm (man and the universe) and the great chain of being. The counterparts of these ideas can be found in other Asian traditions as well: the Sufi concept of the universal man is paralleled by the Hindu idea of the Purusha and the Chinese notion of the Chen-jen. Nearly every chapter of the *Rasail* is informed by the analogy between man and the universe.[45]

The relationship between man and the universe is the basis of traditional Islamic architecture. Within the ordered world of traditional society man moves between the macrocosmic conception of the universe and the microcosmic view of self. The concept of the city lies between the two poles, incorporating the symbolic principles of both. Man, as microcosm, is the mirror image of the macrocosm and contains all the possibilities of the universe within himself. He is the last stage of creation and occupies the central position in the universe, at the intersection

---

[42] Abd al-Baqi b. Baba-i Kurd Nihawandi, *Ma'asir-i Rahimi*, ed. Maulavi Muhammad Hidayat Husain, 3 vols. (Calcutta: Asiatic Society of Bengal, 1910–31), 2 pp. 607–10.

[43] Mir Abd al-Kasim, "Ma'rifat al-Sanai," (Persian Manuscript Collection, Add. 16,839, London, British Museum) is one of his works that had some influence in India. It is a philosophical treatise on the relationship among and relative importance of the various arts and crafts.

[44] Sayyed Hossein Nasr, *An Introduction to Islamic Cosmological Doctrines* (Cambridge, Mass: Belknap Press, 1964), pp. 25–7.

[45] Ibid., pp. 63–7.

between the divine and the temporal. The model is the universal man, whose perfect manifestation was Muhammad, the prophet of Islam.[46]

The cosmos is composed of a macrocosm (universe) and a microcosm (man) and each has three divisions: body (*jism*), soul (*nafs*), and spirit (*ruh*). From the macrocosmic point of view, God is seen as external or manifest (*zahir*). From within the concentric circles of the macrocosm, there is an outward movement from the earth (the body) through the all-pervading soul to the heavens, the seat of the divine spirit. From the microcosmic point of view God is hidden (*batin*) within man, and the movement is from the body through the soul to the spiritual center. These two schemes correspond to one another as mirror images. There were other similarities between man and the universe. The movement of the heavenly spheres – north, south, east, west, up, and down – corresponded, according to Ibn Sina, to the movements of the human body: left, right, front, back, up, and down. Using numerological and cosmological principles, the authors of the *Rasail* drew fourteen parallels between man and the cosmos.[47]

As man and the cosmos were defined so also was the city. All three scales were viewed as determined, persistent, and complete, perfect in archetypical existence. Although the actual city only approached the ideal, the significance of the archetype lay in the sense of ordered place which it gave the urban inhabitants. The artifacts of man were temporal forms reflecting heavenly archetypes. Thus, the conceptual synthesis that produced the miniature, the garden, the carpet, arabesques in metalcraft, and the city followed analogous paths tempered only by the mode of expression and that which was expressed. The world of similitudes guided the ultimate formation of the city. Within the articulated space of the cityscape man, the microcosm, contained all that made up the macrocosm. As a symbolic form, the city drew on the images of both man and cosmos.[48]

Man lives best, it was thought, in a physical environment analogous to him. Thus, the plan of the city was seen to emulate the anatomy of man. The central bazaar (the backbone) began at the palace (the head), grew toward the Jami' Masjid (the heart), and continued to the city gate. The smaller streets inserted themselves into the body proper as ribs and the vital organs – bathhouses, schools, sarais, bakeries, water cisterns, teahouses, and shops – developed in proximity to the skeletal center. The city walls and gates defined and protected the volume of the body proper.[49]

---

[46] Nader Ardalan and Laleh Bakhtiar, *The Sense of Unity: The Sufi Tradition in Persian Architecture* (Chicago and London: University of Chicago Press, 1973), pp. 3–9.
[47] Ibid., pp. 11–12, 26. [48] Ibid., p. 79. [49] Ibid., p. 93.

Not only was the city understood in terms of human anatomy but the body was often pictured as an urban center. Its four parts corresponded to the four gates and both recalled the four elements of the universe. The authors of the *Rasail* wrote:

The body of man was constructed by the Creator like a city. Its anatomical elements resemble stones, bricks, trunks of trees, and metals which enter into the construction of the city. The body is composed of different parts and consists of several biological systems like the quarters of a city and its buildings. The members and organs are connected by diverse joints like the streets with respect to the quarters.[50]

Elements of the traditional Islamic city plan were found in Shahjahanabad. Chandni Chawk, the central bazaar and backbone, began at the Shahjahan's palace-fortress, the head, ran to the Jami' Masjid, the heart, and exited at the Kashmiri gate. The palace-fortress faced west toward Mecca, Chandni Chawk, the principal bazaar, ran west and the Jami' Masjid also opened toward the sacred city. The eight large city gates (the seven major ones on the landward side plus the special riverfront gate leading to the Hall of Special Audience) carried symbolic significance: the walled city symbolized the cosmos and the eight gates the four cardinal directions plus the four gates of heaven.[51] The mixed character of the plan reflected the nature of the city. Shahjahanabad was a predominantly Hindu city governed by Muslims, the capital of a Muslim dynasty in an overwhelmingly Hindu subcontinent.

Palace-fortress

The palace-fortress of Shahjahan, called the *Qila' Mubark* (Auspicious Fortress) in court documents and official histories, was an overpowering structure. Constructed of red sandstone quarried near Fathpur Sikri, it occupied a bluff above the Jamuna along the eastern wall of the city. The walls of the structure traced an irregular octagon nearly two miles around. Its basic dimensions were 3100 feet by 1650 feet and it enclosed an area of about 125 acres: a piece of ground, the sources are careful to point out, twice the size of Akbar's fort in Agra. The walls ranged in height from 60 feet along the river to 75 feet on the landward side and in width from 45 feet at the base to 30 feet at the top.[52]

---

[50] Rasail in Nasr, *Cosmological Doctrines*, p. 99.
[51] G.E. von Grunebau, *Islam: Essays on the Nature and Growth of a Cultural Tradition*, Comparative Studies of Cultures and Civilizations, no. 4 (New York: American Anthropological Society, memoir 81, 1955), pp. 141–58; Ardalan and Bakhtiar, *The Sense of Unity*, p. 15.
[52] Muhammad Salih, *'Amal-i Salih*, 3 p. 32; Muhammad Waris, "Padshah Namah," fol. 402.

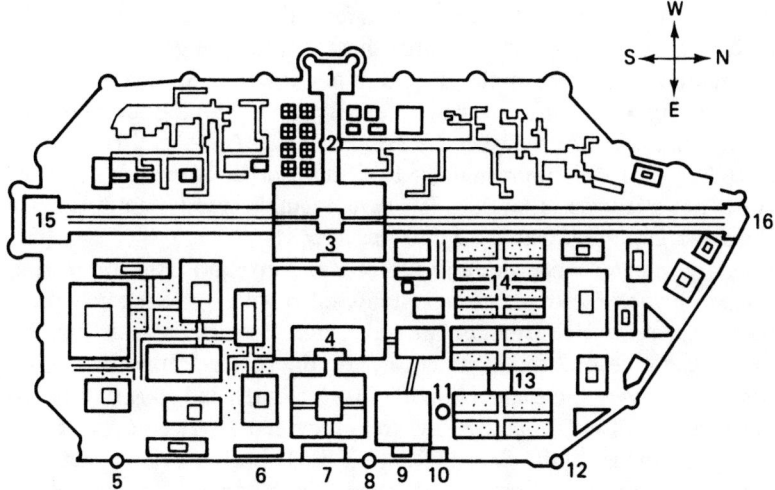

1. Lahori Gate
2. Covered bazaar
3. Naqqar Khanah (Drum room)
4. Daulat Khanah-i khas-o-'am (Hall of Ordinary Audience)
5. Asad Burj (Lion Tower)
6. Jahanara Begum's mansion
7. Imtiaz Mahal (Distinguished Palace)
8. Jharokah-i Darshan (Balcony of Audience)
9. Daulat Khanah-i Khas (Hall of Special Audience)
10. Hammam (bath)
11. Moti Masjid (Pearl Mosque)
12. Shah Burj (King's Tower)
13. Hayat Baksh Garden (Life-giving Garden)
14. Mahtab Bagh Garden (Moonlight Garden)
15. Akbarabadi Gate
16. Salimgarh Gate

Map 2 Palace-fortress (source: Gordon Sanderson, 'Shahjahan's Fort, Delhi', *Archeological Survey of India: Annual Report 1911–12*, plate 11).

Four large gateways, two small entrances, and twenty-one towers, (seven round and fourteen octagonal) broke the monotony of the expanse. The Lahori and Akbarabadi gates (numbers 1 and 15 on map 2) were the chief entryways. In front of both gates Shahjahan constructed a pair of life-size elephants to stand guard. The Emperor Aurangzeb regarded such images as sacrilegious and had them pulled down in the early part of his reign.[53] To strengthen the outworks Aurangzeb put up

---

[53] Muhammad Salih, *'Amal-i Salih*, 3 p. 44; Bernier, *Travels*, p. 256; and Muhammad Saqi Musta'idd Khan, *Ma'asir-i 'Alamgiri* (Calcutta: Asiatic Society of Bengal, 1873–5), p. 78. There has been a good deal of confusion about the number and location of the

barbicans in front of the two principal gates and made the Lahori gate the
headquarters of the *Qila'dar* (Fort Commander). The gateway toward
Salimgarh and the gate on the riverfront to the Hall of Special Audience
were the third and fourth. One of the small gates was on the northeastern
slant of the octagon, between the Salimgarh gate (number 16) and the
Shah Burj (King's Tower, number 12) and the other one was at the base
of the fort a few yards south of Jahanara Begum's mansion (number 6).
From it a large drain emptied into the river.[54]

A large moat, 75 feet wide and 30 feet deep, surrounded the fort on the
landward side. Faced with rough stone, filled with water, and stocked
with fish, it served to further isolate and protect the imperial household.[55]
Immediately beyond the moat, separating the palace-fortress from the
city proper, were the *Buland* (High), *Gulabi* (Rose), and *Anguri* (Grape)
Gardens. This swath of flowers and trees provided a stark contrast to the
great red expanse of the walls.[56] Between the Lahori gate of the fort and
the intersection of the two great thoroughfares was a large square. Here
Rajput amirs camped with their troops while standing guard, grooms
from the imperial household exercised horses, and officials inspected the
contingents of newly admitted mansabdars.[57] Before the eastern wall of
the fort on the riverfront was a wide sandy beach. Early each morning
people gathered to glimpse the emperor at his daily *darshan* (showing).
Later in the day elephant fights were staged for the emperor and his
family and contingents of amirs and rajahs passed in review.[58]

The arrangement of buildings and the distribution of persons illustrate
the mixed domestic–official character of patrimonial-bureaucratic rule.
For Shahjahan and his successors the palace-fortress was both home and
office. The north–south road connecting the Akbarabadi and Salimgarh
gates divided the interior into two rectangles. The larger, to which access
was limited, fronted the river and contained quarters for both domestic
and governmental activities.

elephants. For a discussion see Gordon Sanderson, "Shahjahan's Fort, Delhi,"
Archeological Survey of India: Annual Report 1911–12 (Calcutta: Government Press,
1915), pp. 26–7; Gordon Sanderson, *Delhi Fort; A Guide to The Buildings and Gardens*,
ed. Zafar Hasan (Calcutta: Superintendent of Government Printing, 1932), pp. 9–10;
and J.H. Marshal, "Restoration of Two Elephant Statues at the Fort of Delhi,"
Archeological Survey of India: Annual Report 1905–6 (Calcutta: Superintendent of
Government Printing, 1909), pp. 33–42.

54 Muhammad Waris, "Padshah Namah," fols. 402–2a.
55 Bernier, *Travels*, p. 243; and Muhammad Waris, "Padshah Namah," fol., 402a.
56 Muhammad Salih, *'Amal-i Salih*, 3 p. 46; Muhammad Waris, "Padshah Namah," fol.
404; Bernier, *Travels*, p. 243; Sangin Beg, "Sair al-Manazil," Persian Manuscript
Collection, Or. 1762, British Museum, fol. 59.
57 Bernier, *Travels*, p. 243.
58 Ibid.

The southern half of this area contained the mansions of the wives, sisters, widows, and concubines of the imperial household. This was the harem and no men other than the emperor, his sons, and the household servants could enter. Because of the secrecy surrounding this area and because many buildings were destroyed during the eighteenth and nineteenth centuries, information is available on only a few individual structures. The largest building in the area and the chief center of communal activity was the *Imtiaz* or *Mumtaz Mahal* (Distinguished Palace) or, as it was later called, the *Rang Mahal* (Colored Palace). The ceiling of this mansion was brightly colored and inlaid with gold. At the four corners were small enclosures, lined with swatches of wet, sweet-smelling reeds, called *Khas Khanahs* (Reed Houses). Small domes with golden knobs topped the four corners of the roof and in front of the building was a large garden with a pool and a marble basin. A stairway led from the back of Shahjahan's throne in the Hall of Ordinary Audience of the western edge of this garden. Following his daily audience Shahjahan made his way through the garden to the comfort of the Imtiaz Mahal. There he listened to music, played with his children, watched dancing girls, and enjoyed the offerings of poets and storytellers.[59]

Immediately north of the Imtiaz Mahal was a beautifully carved marble building called the *Aramgah* or *Khwabgah* (Place of Rest or Sleep). Protruding from its eastern wall and hanging out over the beach was an octagonal marble balcony called the *Jharokah-i Darshan* (Balcony of Audience) and later the *Mussaman Burj* (Octagonal Tower). Its interior walls were brightly painted and its spires were flecked with gold. Around the open five-sided balcony facing the river a low screen of finely worked marble had been placed.[60] Early each morning from this balcony Shahjahan received the petitions and heard the complaints of any of his subjects who cared to come. Any person who felt he had been mistreated in the lower courts could seek redress here.[61]

South of the Imtiaz Mahal lay the living quarters of the harem. Gold-inlay work and bright paint decorated rooms and apartments and lanes paved with colored stones separated dwellings. In the courtyards were small gardens laid out around central pools. Flowers and trees sprang from the carefully tended earth. An offshoot of the *Nahr-i Bihisht* (Paradise Canal) wound through the area feeding the pools and gardens while fountains sent jets of water high into the air, creating rainbows in

[59] Muhammad Salih, *'Amal-i-Salih*, 3 p. 41; Muhammad Waris, "Padshah Namah," fol. 405–5a.
[60] Muhammad Salih, *'Amal-i Salih*, 3 pp. 41–2; Muhammad Waris, "Padshah Namah," fols. 404a–5. Similar balconies can be found in the forts at Agra and Lahore.
[61] Muhammad Salih, *'Amal-i Salih*, 3 p. 243.

the hanging spray.[62] The largest apartment, erroneously called Mumtaz Mahal by later scholars (the name properly belongs to the other building), belonged to Jahanara Begum, favorite daughter of Shahjahan. This structure had a delicately carved marble screen facing the river and its walls and ceiling were painted and encrusted with small pieces of glass. *Khwaspura* (Special Quarter), a place for the widows and dependants of former emperors, was here also.[63]

The northern half of this inner rectangle contained the public, official buildings of the imperial household. West of the Imtiaz Mahal stood the Hall of Ordinary Audience. A marble baldachino set into a niche about six feet above the floor covered the balcony where Shahjahan sat during the hours of public audience. The niche was painted and inlaid with precious stones. Immediately below was a marble platform where nobles stood while handing petitions and other papers to the emperor. The hall itself was a large open pavilion of forty pillars. The three sides of the courtyard surrounding the pavilion were lined with beautifully decorated apartments for the amirs of the standing guard. At the western end of the courtyard stood the *Naqqar Khanah* (Drum Room, number three). This great gate was the principal entrance to the Hall of Ordinary Audience and housed musicians who played martial music during audiences. A small passageway led through the north wall of the courtyard to the Hall of Special Audience.[64]

In the Hall of Ordinary Audience Shahjahan handled the routine military, administrative, and financial matters of state. He granted promotions to mansabdars, received reports from administrative officers in the field, and examined papers relating to offices, land grants, and cash salaries.[65]

To the east of the Hall of Ordinary Audience stood the Hall of Special Audience, also called the *Shah Mahal* (King's Palace) and *Ghusl Khanah* (Bathhouse). The most elegant building in the palace-fortress, it was built of pure white marble. Its lower walls were studded with agates, pearls, and other precious stones and its upper walls were painted with colorful intricate designs of flowers and fruit trees. Sheets of gold in trefoil pattern decorated the ceiling and tiny pieces of glass in the walls and ceiling bounced sparks of light across the hall. Four gold domes marked the corners of the roof. In the middle of the room stood a magnificent throne covered with rubies, diamonds, pearls, and emeralds. The two jeweled

[62] Ibid., 3 pp. 33–4.
[63] Muhammad Waris, "Padshah Namah," fol. 406.
[64] Muhammad Salih, *'Amal-i Salih*, 3 pp. 42–3; Muhammad Waris, "Padshah Namah," fols. 405–6; Bernier, *Travels*, pp. 259–63.
[65] Muhammad Salih, *'Amal-i- Salih*, 1 pp. 244–6, 2 p. 42.

peacocks perched on the canopy gave the throne its later name of Peacock Throne.

Before the hall was a large courtyard, and around the courtyard was an arcade divided into small rooms. At the western end of the courtyard a door, hung with a red curtain, opened on to a passageway from the Hall of Ordinary Audience. Anyone who desired to enter the hall had to do special obeisance on the far side of the curtain. The location of this hall deep within the living quarters of the imperial family indicated its special character. With the help of few trusted advisors the emperor dealt with the sensitive, secret, and most important affairs of state in the Hall of Special Audience.[66]

North of the Hall of Special Audience lay the *Hammam* (bath). An integral part of Islamic life, the bath, along with the congregational mosque and the market, were required to transform a settlement into a full-fledged urban community.[67] Like the other buildings in the palace-fortress, the bath was built of marble, decorated with mosaics and pieces of glass, and brightly painted. The structure had three stories: one given over to a dressing room and the other two dispensing hot and cold water respectively.[68]

At the northeastern corner of the palace-fortress stood the *Shah Burj* (King's Tower, number twelve). Constructed of specially polished marble from Gujarat, this octagonal tower had three stories. The lower walls were decorated with mosaics and the upper walls and ceiling with gold inlay work. A small pool lay in the middle of the lower room and sheaves of wetted reeds placed in the windows cooled the air in summer.[69]

Near the Hall of Special Audience was a small, delicate, beautifully wrought mosque of marble. Called *Moti Masjid* (Pearl Mosque, number eleven), it was the only building in the palace constructed by Aurangzeb. Although Shahjahan had been content to use the Jami' Masjid, his pious brother wanted a more convenient sanctuary for this devotions. It took five years and one hundred and sixty thousand rupees to complete.[70]

[66] Ibid., 3 p. 35; Muhammad Waris, "Padshah Namah," fols. 404–4a; Abd al-Hamid, *Badshah Namah*, 1, pt 2, pp. 78–81; Jean-Baptiste Tavernier, *Travels in India*, ed. William Crooke, trans. V. Ball, 2 vols. (London: Humphrey Milford, 1925), 1 pp. 381–4. Sanderson's account of this hall is flawed. The passage from the *Badshah Namah* ("Shahjahan's Fort," pp. 17–19) describes the Peacock Throne in the Hall of Ordinary Audience in Akbarabad not in the Hall of Special Audience in Shahjahanabad. This explains Sanderson's puzzlement in fn. 1, p. 17 over the location of the throne.
[67] von Grunebaum, *Islam*, pp. 141–58.
[68] Muhammad Salih, *'Amal-i-Salih*, 3 p. 35; Muhammad Waris, "Padshah Namah," fol. 404a.
[69] Muhammad Waris, "Padshah," fols. 402a–3.
[70] Muhammad Kazim b. Muhammad Amin, *'Alamgir Namah*, ed. Maulavi Khadim Husain and Maulavi 'Abd al-Hai, 2 vols. (Calcutta: Asiatic Society of Bengal, 1865–73), 1 pp. 467–81.

The Hayat Baksh and Mahtab gardens in the northern sector of the palace-fortress were some of the most beautiful in the city. Hayat Baksh, the larger of the two, featured a rectangular pool with an open summer house surrounded and partly hidden by the spray from forty-nine silver fountains. Around the pool another one hundred and twelve fountains sent spurts of glistening water into the air. Avenues split by canals containing thirty silver fountains led from the four sides of the central pool to the surrounding wall. Pavilions called Bahadun and Sawan after the monsoon months of the Hindu year stood at the ends of the north–south avenues. Built entirely of marble, these had offshoots of the Paradise Canal cascading water to and from open pools. Flowers of all kinds bordered the avenues and pools and fruit trees grew in such profusion that their tangled branches nearly shut out the sky.[71] A coffee tree stood near one wall.[72]

Less is known about the smaller garden to the west. It seems not have been laid out with the care and extravagance of the other. The major structure in this garden was a summer house of red stone called the *Balal Mahal* (Water Palace). The Paradise Canal flowed through its center.[73]

North of the two gardens was a large triangular area which contained the mansions and households of the younger princes. Princes of the position and wealth of Dara Shikoh and Aurangzeb had mansions outside the palace-fortress.

To the west of this inner rectangle lay another roughly rectangular area which held the bulk of the population of the palace-fortress. Before the Naqqar Khanah was a large open square (the Jilau Khanah or Forecourt) where the amirs, ministers, ambassadors, officials, and petitioners who attended the daily audience assembled. Only royal princes could pass through the Naqqar Khanah on horseback; all others had to dismount and walk. The sides of this square were lined with small rooms under an arcade and housed the amirs of the daily guard and their men. In the southwestern corner of the courtyard stood several buildings where the *Nazir* (Superintendent) of the imperial household conducted business. A large rectangular pool lay in the middle of the courtyard.[74]

A covered bazaar (*bazaar-i mussaqaf*, number two) led from the Lahori gate of the fort to the western edge of the Jilau Khanah. Two hundred and

[71] Muhammad Salih, '*Amal-i Salih*, 3 pp. 36–7; Muhammad Waris, "Padshah Namah," fols. 403a–4.

[72] Anand Ram Mukhlis, "Mir'at al-Istilah," Persian Manuscript Collection, Or. 1813, British Museum, London, fol. 218a.

[73] Muhammad Waris, "Padshah Namah," fol. 404.

[74] Muhammad Waris, 'Padshah Namah,' fol. 406; Muhammad Salih, '*Amal-i Salih*, 3 p. 43.

seventy feet long, 27 feet wide, and two stories high, this bazaar contained arcaded shops on both levels and both sides of the street. Near its middle a section had been cut from the roof, letting air and light in on an octagonal court. Although roofed bazaars were usual in Iran and West Asia they were rare in India.

a building like the covered bazaar, which the people of Hindustan had never before seen, was a new idea produced by the ruler of the seven lands with effortless attention and unique building talent.[75]

Running through the pool of the Jilau Khanah and down the middle of the wide avenue linking the Salimgarh and Akbarabadi gates was a branch of the Paradise Canal. After watering the houses and shops in the part of the fort, it emptied into the moat. Rooms under arcades set on ledges four feet wide and five or six feet high bordered the avenue. Tax collectors and the clerks who maintained the financial and military records of the government transacted business toward the southern end of the avenue. At the northwestern end were stables for the horses, elephants, camels, and cows of the imperial establishment. Other rooms held workshops where weapons, carpets, fine cloth, gold work, and jewelry were manufactured; storerooms where clothing, food, books, and candlesticks were kept; and buildings for the treasuries and mints. The remainder of this area was given over to dwellings for the soldiers, clerks, merchants, artisans, physicians, poets, scholars, religious specialists, and astrologers of the imperial household.[76]

A period of just under nine years elapsed between groundbreaking and Shahjahan's inaugural entry. During that time thousands of stone-cutters, masons, stone-carvers, carpenters, garden-designers, and other builders labored over the palace-fortress. The total cost was six million rupees. Two million eight hundred thousand rupees were spent on the buildings in the public half of the household sector; one million four hundred thousand on the Hal of Special Audience; five hundred and fifty thousand on the Imtiaz Mahal and Aramgah; two hundred and fifty thousand on the Hall of Ordinary Audience; and six hundred thousand on the Hayat Baksh garden and the bath. Jahanara Begum and the other ladies of the harem spent seven hundred thousand rupees on their buildings. Four hundred thousand rupees went for the bazaars, houses, chawks, workshops, offices, and stables in the other rectangle, and two

[75] Muhammad Salih, '*Amal-i Salih*, 3 p. 44. Shahjahan saw a covered octagonal bazaar in Peshawar that he greatly admired. He sent a plan of the structure to Makramat Khan with orders to model the bazaar in the palace-fortress after it. Ibid., 2 pp. 471-2.
[76] Muhammad Waris, "Padshah Namah," fols. 402a, 406; Bernier, *Travels*, p. 257; Muhammad Salih, '*Amal-i-Salih*, 3 p. 43.

million one hundred thousand rupees were spent on the walls and moat.[77]
The craftsmanship was of such an order that 'a sharp nail could not be
pushed between the stones of the buildings.'[78]

To the men of Shahjahan's day the palace-fortress was a wonder.
Muhammad Waris confessed that his pen was lame and helpless,
inadequate to the task of description. Only the words of the poet Amir
Khusrau (d. 1324–5), inscribed on the north and south arches of the Hall
of Special Audience, would suffice:

If there is a paradise on the face of the earth.
It is this, it is this, it is this.[79]

Mansions

The people of Shahjahanabad inhabited a variety of dwellings. The large
walled mansions of princes and great amirs contained gardens, watercourses, and beautiful apartments. Lower-ranking amirs and rich
merchants had smaller houses constructed of burnt tile and lime, stone, or
brick. Although some well-to-do Hindu or Armenian merchants may
have lived in houses as tall as six or seven stories,[80] their homes were on
average more modest than those of the nobles. They were not elaborately
carved and decorated and didn't boast large gardens. Ordinary merchants
often lived in quarters behind their shops. Soldiers, servants, craftsmen,
small traders, and others lived inside the palace-fortress or the great
mansions or in straw-thatched mud huts scattered about.[81] As the
population increased these small dwellings gobbled up much of the open
space in the city and encroached on lanes and thoroughfares. An early-
eighteenth-century resident, for example, reported great difficulty
negotiating the clogged passageways near his home.[82] The inhabitants of

---

[77] Muhammad Waris, "Padshah Namah," fol. 406. The other contemporary
   source – *'Amal-i Salih*, 3 p. 32 – gives a different and less detailed reckoning. Muhammad Salih simply says that five million rupees were spent on the walls and moat and
   five million on the buildings within. An inscription on the northern arch of the Aramgah
   gives five million rupees as the cost of the structure. Gordon Sanderson's accounting
   ("Shahjahan's Fort," pp. 3–4) is seriously mistaken. He and his translator misunderstood the organization of the imperial household and the Mughal state and, as a result,
   misinterpreted the passage from *Mirat al-'Alam*. Bakhtawar Khan, the author of *Mirat-
   al-'Alam*, lifted this passage word for word from the "Padshah Namah."

[78] Muhammad Salih, *'Amal-i Salih*, 3 p. 32.

[79] Muhammad Waris, "Padshah Namah," fol. 406. The lines probably describe Siri, the
   capital of Ala al-Din Khalji and the Delhi of Khusrao's day. This same inscription is also
   found in the Shalimar garden in Kashmir, built by the Emperor Jahangir in the early part
   of his reign.

[80] Muhammad Salih, *'Amal-i Salih*, 3 p. 82.

[81] Bernier, *Travels*, pp. 245–7.

[82] Hakim Maharat Khan, 'Bahjat al-'Alam,' fol. 35b.

these huts suffered periodic disaster. In the hot season fires regularly swept through the city, jumping from one tinder dry roof to the next – in 1662 sixty thousand people were killed in three separate fires. During the monsoon rains the mud walls tended to weaken and collapse.[83]

Although the older princes and important amirs did not live in the palace-fortress, they too were considered members of the imperial household. They participated in the court ceremonial, held office in household departments, and performed a number of tasks more filial than official. The imprint of this relationship can be seen in the style of domestic architecture: in Shahjahanabad princes and important nobles constructed mansions after the model of the palace-fortress.

To design and erect palaces great men had to look no further than their own households. Most establishments included architects and builders, and "Bayaz-i Khushbui," the mid-seventeenth-century household manual, contained an entire section on buildings and gardens.[84] These mansions were often quite large. Qamar al-Din Khan's covered an entire block and Safdar Jang's contained room for five thousand soldiers and five hundred horses.[85] Muhammad Salih wrote of the mansions in Shahjah-anabad: "in the courtyard of each one the area of a city is empty."[86]

A high thick wall of stone and in some cases even a moat surrounded the *havili* or *nashiman* (mansion or seat). A lofty gateway (also called the Naqqar Khanah) housed the soldiers of the daily guard and the drummers, trumpeters, and other household musicians (see map 3). A large forecourt surrounded by a row of rooms under an arcade lay immediately inside. Here were places for the soldiers and servants of the household and for the horses, elephants, and attendants of visitors.[87]

To the right and left of the gateway, along the wall fronting the street, were the courtyards that held the men and goods of the great man's establishment. Here were stables for horses, elephants, and camels;

---

[83] Bernier, *Travels*, p. 246.

[84] "Bayaz-i Khushbui," Persian Manuscript Collection, Ethe 2784, India Office Library, fols. 108a–11a. Although the manuscript was transcribed in 1697–8 Habib suggests that it was written during the first twenty years of Shahjahan's reign. *Agrarian System*, p. 421. See also Jagat Rai, "Farhang-i Kardani," Abdus Salam Collection, no. 315, Maulana Azad Library, Aligarh Muslim University, Aligarh, U.P., fols. 15b–16d for a similar section on buildings.

[85] For Safdar Jang's mansion (no. 1 on map 5) see James Forbes, *Oriental Memoirs*, 4 vols. (London: White, Cochrane, and Co., 1813), 4 pp. 63–4. For Qamar al-Din Khan's see no. 16 on map 5.

[86] Muhammad Salih, '*Amal-i Salih*, 3 p. 45.

[87] William Franklin, "An Account of the Present State of Delhi," *Asiatick Researches* 4 (1795) p. 422. "Description of Delhi and Its Environs," *The Asiatic Journal and Monthly Register* 15 (January–June 1823) p. 552; Forbes, *Oriental Memoirs*, 4 pp. 61–2; "Ahwal-i Khan Dauran," Persian Manuscript Collection, Or. 180, British Museum, fol. 179b.

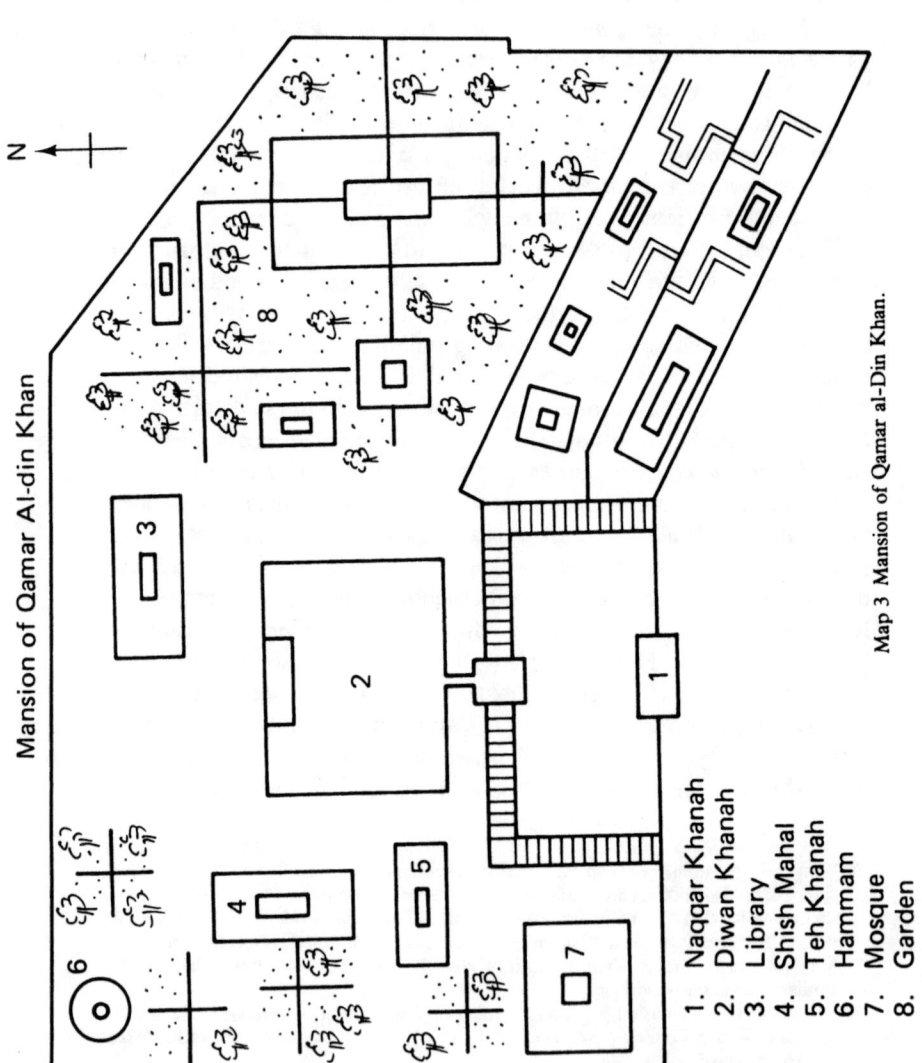

Mansion of Qamar Al-din Khan

Map 3 Mansion of Qamar al-Din Khan.

1. Naqqar Khanah
2. Diwan Khanah
3. Library
4. Shish Mahal
5. Teh Khanah
6. Hammam
7. Mosque
8. Garden

apartments for servants, clerks, artisans, poets, physicians, laborers, religious specialists, astrologers, and soldiers; storerooms for grain, perfume, medicine, furniture, candles, palanquins, tents, swords, bowls, and guns; record offices, treasuries, bakeries, and kitchens; and work-shops for clothing, carpets, goldwork, and fine embroidery – goods enough to sustain the community inside for months.[88]

Opposite the forecourt was the gate to the living quarters of the price or great amir and his family. The area inside was divided into two parts: private-familial and public-official. The *Mahal Sarai* (Women's Area) was off-limits to all but the prince or great amir and the women, children, and servants of his household. These apartments and pavilions were set amidst trees, flowers, pools, and canals. The main structure was the *Shish Mahal* (Glass Room), a room beautifully painted and decorated with tiny pieces of polished glass. In the mansion of Safdar Jang (number 1 on map 5) bits of glittering glass were embedded in the octagonal columns of this room.[89]

The *Teh Khanah* (Underground Chamber) or *Sard Khanah* (Cool Chamber) was usually found in the Mahal Sarai. A set of rooms 30 to 40 feet below ground and arranged around a central pool, this was the place where the great man and his family escaped the searing heat of late afternoon Shahjahanabad. In Safdar Jang's mansion the room was 78 feet long, 27 feet wide, and divided by marble pillars into three galleries. The domed ceiling, painted blue and silver, suggested a midnight sky. Light and air came in through shadowed lattices, positioned so as to avoid the direct glare of the sun. Fountains gushed and gurgled in the central pool.[90]

The public area of the mansion was separated from the Mahal Sarai by a high wall. In the *Diwan Khanah* (Audience Hall) the great man held court and received guests. Mir Abd al-Razaq, an amir of the early eighteenth century, laid brightly colored carpets on the floor of his audience hall, had curtains and vases of flowers on the wall, and a large

[88] "Description of Delhi," p. 552; Anand Ram Mukhlis, "Dastur al-'Amal," Persian Manuscript Collection, Ethe 2125, Indian Office Library, fol. 49b; Forbes, *Oriental Memoirs*, 4 63–4; Franklin, "Account of Delhi," p. 422; "Bayaz-i Khushbui," fols. 5b–108, 126b–137b; "Delhi Newsletters of 1781 AD, "Persian Manuscript Collection, Add. 25020, British Museum, fol. 134a. This last manuscript describes the mansion of Majd al-Daulah, number 5 on map 5.

[89] Franklin, "Account of Delhi," p. 422; "Delhi Newsletters of 1781," fols. 129a–31b; Forbes, *Oriental Memoirs*, 4 pp. 64–5.

[90] For Safdar Jang's Teh Khanah see Franklin, "Account of Delhi," p. 422 and Forbes, *Oriental Memoirs*, 4 pp. 64–5. For the chamber in Sa'adat Khan's mansion (number 10) see Franklin, "Account of Delhi," p. 422.

mirror at one side. Guests were served coffee and offered specially prepared glass *huqqas* (waterpipes).[91]

Near the Diwan Khanah stood the library. Here the prince or great amir drafted state papers and composed the poems and brief pieces that every skilled courtier was expected to produce. The library contained a large selection of books, the household manual listing a core holding of fifty-two Arabic and Persian works. A close acquaintance with these and others, with the ability to slip apt quotations into conversation and writing, was a *sine qua non* for a successful great amir.[92]

Apartments and halls were richly furnished. In summer a fine white cloth masked the cotton mattresses that covered the floors and in winter a carpet of silk. In the audience hall officials and guests sat on carved wooden seats inlaid with gold and silver and cushioned with pillows. In most rooms, however, people sat on mattresses with the aid of cushions covered in brocade, velvet, or flowered satin. The amir's cushions were embroidered in silk and crisscrossed with gold and silver threads. The walls and ceilings were painted with flower and fruit designs and sparkled with gilding and pieces of glass. Vases of flowers hung from niches in the walls. In the mansion of Raushan al-Daulah (number 7 on map 5) golden bedsteads covered with gold-embroidered carpets stood in every room.[93]

A bath was an indispensable part of the noble mansion. Sa'adat Khan's bath (number 10 on map 5), for example, had five rooms and a dome of glazed glass. The household manual contains the dimensions of bath-houses in Sirhind and in the garden of Nur Sarai.[94] The mosques in these mansions were meant for the devotions of the great man, his family, and household. The dimensions of an *'Idgah* (place for solemn feasts) are given in the household manual.[95]

---

[91] For the mansion of 'Abd al-Razaq see Dargah Quli Khan, "Risalah-i Salar Jang," fols. 108a–b. The Diwan Khanah in the mansion of Raushan al-Daulah (number 7) is described briefly in Muhammad Baksh Ashob, "Tarikh-i Shahadat-i Farrukhsiyar-u-Julus-i Muhammad Shah," Persian Manuscript Collection, Or. 1015, British Museum, London, fol. 48b.

[92] "Bayaz-i Khushbui," fols. 137b–9b; "Ahwal-i Khan Dauran," Persian Manuscript Collection, Or. 180, British Museum, London, fols. 161b–2b.

[93] Bernier, *Travels*, pp. 247–8; Major Polier, "Extracts of Letters from Major Polier at Delhi to Col. Ironside at Belgram, May 22, 1776," *Asiatic Annual Register* 2 (1800):2 pp. 29–30; 'Abd al-Baqi, *Ma'asir-i Rahimi*, 2 p. 496; Forbes, *Oriental Memoirs*, p. 64; "Bayaz-i Khushbui," fol. 132a; Bashir al-Din Ahmad, *Waqiat.*, 2 p. 375. The furnishings of Raushan al-Daulah's mansion are described in Ashob, "Tarikh-i Muhammad Shah," fol. 48b.

[94] "Bayaz-i Khush-i Khushbui," fols. 109a–b; "Description of Delhi," p. 552; "Delhi Newsletters of 1781," fol. 134a; Gulshan Ali Jaunpuri, "Surat-i Hal," Persian Manuscript Collection, Add. 16,805, British Museum, fol. 19a; See Franklin, "Account of Delhi," p. 422 for a description of the bath in Sa'adat Khan's mansion.

[95] "Bayaz-i Khushbui," fols. 108b–9a. For mosques in mansions see *List of Monuments*, 1 p. 45, 47 and Bashir al-Din Ahmad, *Waqiat*, 2 p. 151.

The *peice de résistance*, however, of every elite mansion was its *Khanah Bagh* (House Garden). Gardens were divided into rectangles by watercourses that tumbled down several levels before reaching a central pool. In the middle of the pool on a pedestal stood a summer house. Screens of wetted reeds placed in the windows cooled the blistering winds of summer. Trees shaded a multitude of flowers and contributed fruit to the kitchen in season. For the ambitious builder the household manual contained plans of such famous gardens as Sahibabad in Shahjahanabad, Dahra outside Agra, and Nur Sarai. The manual also included instructions on the care and nurture of trees.[96]

In Shahjahanabad princely and great amiri households included boats which were launched from private docks along the river. These brought the great men to the riverfront gate of the Hall of Special Audience and carried them and their families upriver and down to gardens and festivals.[97] On the 11th of Zal-Haj 1671 the emperor Aurangzeb took a boat to Humayun's tomb to offer prayers.[98]

Since the entourage of a prince or great noble often swelled to overflowing proportions, small, straw-thatched, mud huts surrounded most mansions. Here resided the members of the household who had been unable to acquire accommodation within. Outside also stood the shops and stalls catering to the needs of the great household. By virtue of their size and population, these mansions dominated their sectors of the city just as the palace-fortress dominated the urban area as a whole. Contemporary descriptions of them as forts (*qasr*),[99] the statement of an English traveller that they were considerably larger than the palaces of the European nobility,[100] and the description of an eighteenth-century French traveller attest to their size and complexity. The Frenchman wrote:

[96] "Bayaz-i Khushbui" fols. 109–11a, 154a–6a; 'Abd al-Hamid, *Badshah Namah*, 1, pt 1, p. 243; Franklin, "Account of Delhi," p. 422; Dargah Kuli Khan, "Risalah-i Salar Jang," fol. 108a; Gulshan, "Surat-i Hal," fol. 19a; Bernier, *Travels*, pp. 247–8; Thomas Twining, *Travels in India a Hundred Years Ago*, ed. William H.G. Twining (London: James R. Osgood, McIlvaine and Co., 1893), pp. 222, 225.

[97] Anand Ram, "Mirat al-Istilah," fol. 166b; Shah Nawaz Khan, *Ma'asir al-Umara*, 1 pp. 241–7; Anand Ram Mukhlis, "Waqai'i-Sayr-i Ganga," London. India Office Persian Manuscript Collection, Ethe 3724, fols. 1–14.

[98] "Akhbarat-i Darbar-i Mu'allah," London, Royal Asiatic Society, Persian Manuscript Collection, no. 133, reel 3, 11th Haj, 13th year.

[99] Abu al-Fazl, *Akbar Namah*, 2 p. 365; Muhammad Ali Khan Ansari, "Tarikh-i Muzzafari," Persian Manuscript Collection, Or. 466, British Museum, fol. 262b; Muhammad Wali Allah b. Ahmad Ali Farrukhabadi, "Tarikh-i Farrukhabad," Persian Manuscript Collection, Or. 1718, British Museum, fol. 4a.

[100] Forbes, *Oriental Memoirs*, 4 pp. 61–2.

there are many mansions of the nobles, which one can compare to small towns
and in which reside the women, equipment, and bazars (or public markets) of
the nobles...[101]

Emperors and governors regarded the building of such structures as
threats. In Surat during the early seventeenth century the English were
not allowed to build walled structures or to rent houses near the fort or the
central mosque.[102] In Shahjahanabad in 1677 the Emperor Aurangzeb
banned the construction of permanent structures by mansabdars of more
than 400 zat.[103]

These mansions were costly. Although Muhammad Salih gave a range
of one hundred thousand to two million rupees,[104] the latter figure was
probably inflated and the upper limit for a single mansion probably didn't
much exceed the four hundred thousand rupees expended by Dara
Shikoh.[105] Since the structures themselves were expensive and the land
they enclosed one of the few examples of valuable real estate in Mughal
India, emperors were scrupulous about rights to them. If a man had clear
title, his rights were respected and he was able to counter inquiries and
investigations.[106] When Shahjahan settled on the site for the Taj Mahal,
for example, he gave Rajah Jai Singh four mansions in Akbarabad for his
land and buildings.[107]

The mansions of princes and great amirs were grouped in three areas:
along the river near the palace-fortress, about the Jami' Masjid, and on
the periphery of the walled city near the main gates (see map 5). On the
banks of the river upstream and down from the palace-fortress lay the
choice sites. Safdar Jang's mansion (number 1), the largest and finest in
the city, took up a good deal of room. It was the residence of the heir-
apparent up to 1739 and thereafter the home of the *de facto* ruler of the
city under the weak and ineffectual emperors of the late eighteenth and
early nineteenth centuries. The mansions of Dara Shikoh (number 2), Ali
Mardan Khan (number 3), and Sa'adullah Khan/Ghazi al-Din Khan
(number 28) were along the river also. Mansions five, six, and seven were
constructed near the river by prestigious men and are in this group also.

[101] M. Gentile, *Mémoires sur l'Indoustan or Empire Mogol* (Paris: Chex Petit Librarie de
S.A.R. Monsieur et de S.A.S. le Duc de Bourbon, 1822), p. 188.

[102] William Foster, ed., *English Factory Records, 1618–21* (Oxford: Clarendon Press, 1906),
26, pp. 38–40.

[103] Muhammad Saqi, *Maasir-i Alamqiri*, p. 100.

[104] Muhammad Salih, *'Amal-i Salih*, 3 p. 45.

[105] Ibid., 2 p. 458, 3 p. 118.

[106] Manucci, *Storia do Mogor*, 2 p. 15.

[107] *A Descriptive List of Farmans, Manushurs, and Nishans Addressed by the Imperial Mughals
to the Princes of Rajasthan* (Bikaner, Rajasthan: Directorate of Archives, 1962), p. 55.

As the palace-fortress was the center of political life so the Jami' Masjid was the center of religious life. Around it rose smaller mansions of lower-ranking great amirs. Among these were the mansions of Khan Dauran (number 24), the wazir of Muhammad Shah, and Sarbuland Khan (number 25), one-time governor of Gujarat. Numbers 20, 21, 22, 23, 26, and 27 belong to this group also.

The third group included the mansions near the city walls. The palaces of Nawab Sa'adat Khan (number 10), the first Nawab of Oudh, near the Kabul gate, and of Qamar al-Din Khan (number 16), Wazir under Muhammad Shah, near Ajmiri gate, were two of the most magnificent in the city. Mansions 4, 9, 11, 14, 15, 17, 18, and 19 were also located near the walls. The attraction of this location was its access to the suburbs, the disadvantage its distance from the palace-fortress. To overcome the disadvantage nobles stationed agents at court with a supply of pigeons to relay important messages back and forth.[108]

Mosque

In the religious architecture of Mughal India the mosque (*masjid*) predominated. Mosques were more numerous and significant than *dargahs* (tombs), *khangahs* (monasteries), *imambarahs* (places for the celebration of the Muharram festival), and *'idgahs*. Most towns and cities contained both a central congregation mosque, the *Masjid-i Jami'* (Friday Mosque), and a number of other mosques. Because of the public character of Islamic worship, a large, open, four-sided courtyard was the central element of every mosque. A roofed area at the western end of the courtyard served as the prayer hall and, in the center of the western wall, was a recess or alcove (*mihrab*) which indicated the direction of prayer. To the right of the mihrab was a pulpit where the *imam* (leader) read the Quran and conducted prayers and the *khatib* (reader) delivered the sermon. One or more *minarets* (towers), from which the *mu'azzin* (crier) gave the call to prayer, stood in the corners of the courtyard. A portion of the prayer hall was screened off for women. The main entrance to the mosque was on the east, and around the courtyard were apartments for travellers and scholars. A large pool where worshippers washed their hands and faces lay in the middle of the courtyard. Most mosques also contained a *musafir khanah* (hostel) and a *madrassah* (religious school).

To build a mosque was a virtuous act. A verse from the Quran adorned the outside of many mosques in India, though not in other parts of the

[108] Manucci, *Storia do Mogor*, 2 p. 439.

Islamic world:

> Who so buildeth for God a place of worship,
> be it like the nest of a Qata-bird
> God buildeth for him a house in paradise.[109]

The builder of a mosque often provided a source of income for upkeep, repairs, and salaries. The *waqf* or dedication was managed by a *mutawalli* (superintendent of financial affairs). In mosques that were two-storied, rents from rooms in the lower half comprised the waqf income. Builders of other mosques dedicated the income from land, baths, wells, graveyards, and shops.

Early in his reign Shahjahan had ordered the building of mosques in every city that contained Muslims.[110] The command was followed in Shahjahanabad: "in every lane, bazaar, square, and street they have erected mosques."[111] And in the early 1740s Joseph Tieffenthaler, a German Jesuit, observed:

Delhi contains a great number of mosques built at great expense; there are two constructed of red stone transported here from Fatepour, two others whose domes are gilded with gold. The number of small ones is unknowable.[112]

The archeological survey of the city, conducted in the early part of this century, listed 410 structures in the walled city.[113] Of the 378 outside the palace-fortress, 202 (53 percent) were mosques. Two hundred of these were built between 1639 and 1857 and one hundred (see table 2) between 1639 and 1739. These one hundred can be divided into an intraurban central place hierarchy of three levels. Like the hierarchy of towns and cities, levels in this hierarchy are distinguished according to the location and size of the mosques and the kind and frequency of the services they provided.

At the top of the hierarchy was the Jami' Masjid (see table 3). This was the largest mosque in all India and the only structure in the city with the mass and presence to challenge the preeminence of the palace-fortress. The official historian wrote that its foundations were greater than the foundations of heaven[114] and local Muslims organized their descriptions

---

[109] J. Horowitz, "A List of the Published Mohammedan Inscriptions of India," *Epigraphia Indo-Moslemica* (1909–10), p. 32.

[110] Muhammad Salih, *'Amal-i Salih*, 3 p. 51.

[111] Sujan Rai, "Khulasat al-Tawarikh," fol. 25a.

[112] Jean Bernoulli, gen. ed., *Description Historique and Geographie de l'India*, 3 vols. (Berlin: Chreien Sigismund Spener, 1786), 1: *Geographique de l'Indoustan*, by Joseph Tieffenthaler, p. 126.

[113] *List of Monuments*, 1.

[114] Muhammad Salih, *'Amal-i Salih*, 3 p. 51; Muhammad Salih, "Bahar-i Sukhan," fol. 297b.

Table 2   *Mosques constructed in Shahjahanabad, 1639–1857*

	Dated mosques: 56		Total mosques: 200	
	1	2	3	4
	Number (actual)	Percentage	Percentage	Number (est.)
i. 1639–1739	28	50	50	100
ii. 1739–1803	13	21	21	42
iii. 1803–1857	15	29	29	58
	56	100	100	200

Source: List of Muhammadan and Hindu Monuments in Delhi Zail, vols. 1–2

Table 3   *Central place hierarchy of mosques in Shahjahanabad, 1639–1739*

Name	Builder	Date	Location
I. Sovereign			
Jami' Masjid	Shahjahan	1650–6	No. 37
II. Elite			
Fathpuri Masjid	Fathpuri Begum (wife of Shahjahan)	1650	No. 29
Akbarabadi Masjid	Akbarabadi Begum (wife of Shahjahan)	1650	No. 30
Sirhindi Masjid	Sirhindi Begum (wife of Shahjahan)	1650	No. 31
Aurangabadi Masjid	Aurangabadi Begum (wife of Aurangzeb)	1703	No. 32
Zinat al-Masajid	Zinat al-Nisa Begum (daughter of Aurangzeb)	1707	No. 33
Sonari Masjid	Raushan al-Daulah (great amir)	1721	No. 34
Masjid Sharif al-Daulah	Sharif al-Daulah (great amir)	1722	No. 35
Fakr al-Masajid	Fakh al-Nisa Begum (wife of Nawab Shuja'at Khan)	1728	No. 36
III. Neighborhood			
Mosque of—(name of neighborhood)	Amirs, merchants cast/craft groups	1648–1739	City

of the streets and mahallahs of the city around it.[115] Its foundations were laid on 6 October 1650 and, under the supervision of Fazil Khan, *Khan Saman* (head of Shahjahan's household), and Sa'addullah Khan five

---

[115] See Ghulam Muhammad Khan, "Travels in Upper Hindustan," Persian Manuscript Collection, Ethe 2725, India Office Library, London; Sangin Beg, "Sair al-Manazil"; Sayyid Ahmad Khan, *Asar*; and Bashir al-Din Ahmad, *Waqiat*.

thousand workers labored daily for six years. Its cost was one million rupees.

The mosque proper was on the second story, well above the surrounding city. The courtyard was a square, one hundred yards on a side and over the prayer hall at the western end were three large domes. Seven mihrabs had been carved in the western wall, and minarets marked the four corners of the courtyard. In the middle of the open area was a tank with fountains. Like the palace-fortress, the Jami' Masjid was built primarily of red sandstone from Fathpur Sikri. Stairways led from the street to great doors in the eastern, southern, and northern sides of the courtyard and at the foot of each stairway was a chawk. In the early nineteenth century a man could buy kabobs, sweet drinks, and chickens at the southern gate and be entertained by magicians, jugglers, and storytellers at the northern. The eastern gate, connected to Khas Bazaar by stairway of thirty-five steps, was the emperor's entrance. Cloth and pigeons were sold here. There was no gate on the western side but in the chawk below stood a madrassah and a hospital where sick people were treated at the emperor's expense.[116]

The Jami' Masjid was the Friday mosque for the emperor and his household and the mosque princes and great amirs attended on holidays and festivals. For example, in 1666 Aurangzeb often rode to the mosque for prayer before beginning the day's work in the great audience halls.[117] It was, in addition, the public forum for Muslims of the city and, to a certain degree, for Muslims of the empire at large. It was the place where changes in ruler and dynasty were announced and the place where people congregated to register displeasure with religious, political, or social policies.

Level two, the elite level, consisted of a group of eight mosques built by *begums* (women of rank) and great amirs. Outstanding in this group were the Fathpuri and Akbarabadi mosques. Built of red sandstone in the early days of the city and occupying prominent locations in the two main bazaars, these structures were worthy of their builders, wives of Shahjahan. Of the remaining six mosques, four were built by begums – three of whom were members of the imperial family. Great amirs built the other two.

These mosques occupied choice locations on the two major thoroughfares of the city. Though dwarfed in size and significance by the Jami' Masjid, they were nevertheless impressive pieces of architecture. They provided for their sectors of the city some of the services that the Jami'

[116] Muhammad Salih, *'Amal-i Salih*, 3 pp. 51–5; Muhammad Waris, "Padshah Namah," fols. 513b–17b; Sayyid Ahmad Khan, *Asar*, pp. 272–83; Sharma, *Delhi*, pp. 143–4.
[117] "Akhbarat-i Darbar-i Mu'allah," reel 3, 8th year.

Masjid provided for the city as a whole. They served as congregational mosques on Fridays and holidays and as rallying points for the inhabitants of the area.

The neighborhood level of ninety-one mosques occupied the bottom of the hierarchy. These were small and undistinguished, erected by amirs, mansabdars, merchants, and caste/craft groups, and were located in mansions and walled neighborhoods throughout the city. According to Islamic law a building within a mansion had to be available to a public wider than the owner's family for it to qualify as a proper place of worship.[118] Regular attendance of the great man's entourage guaranteed the legitimacy of these mosques. In neighborhood mosques the Muslims of Shahjahanabad performed the ordinary, everyday duties of the religious life.

The materials on mosques suggest, as did the materials on the palace-fortress and the mansion, the dominance of the great men in the life of the city. They were responsible for all nine mosques in levels 1 and 2. These were the largest in the city and held a substantial proportion of the Muslim populace on Fridays and holidays. Although comprising only 9 percent of the mosques erected between 1639–1739, they were responsible for a much larger percentage of the money expended. The Jami' Masjid alone cost one million rupees. At least thirty of the ninety-one mosques at the neighborhood level were the work of great amirs.[119] It is likely, furthermore, that a good many of the remaining sixty-one stood in mansions that cannot be identified or were erected by great amirs in lanes and mahallahs for the benefit of caste/craft groups.

Bazaars

The two major thoroughfares in Shahjahanabad were called bazaars, streets lined on both sides with shops of merchants, artisans, and others. The largest and richest stretched from the Lahori gate of the fort to the Fathpuri mosque. Built in 1650 by Jahanara Begum, this street was 40 yards wide and 1520 yards long and held 1560 shops and porticos. The Paradise Canal flowed through its center, watering a row of trees that provided shade and a place to rest. Although in the earliest sources there was no special name for the street as a whole (it was simply the bazaar in

---

[118] Aurangzeb's mosque in the palace-fortress, the Moti Masjid, is the prime example. For the mosque in Qamar al-Din's mansion see the map. Other examples can be found in *List of Monuments* 1 pp. 44, 89–90. Neil B.E. Baillie, ed. and trans., *A Digest of Muhammadan Law*, 2 vols. (London: Smith, Elder, and Co., 1865–69), 1 p. 605.

[119] There were mosques in all twenty-eight mansions. The Moti Masjid and the mosque in Ghazi al-Din Khan's tomb bring the total to thirty.

the direction of Lahore), each of the sections had been named. The 480-yard section from the Lahori gate of the fort to the *chawk* (square) of the *Kotwali Chabutra* (Magistrate's Platform) was called *Urdu Bazaar* (Camp Market) and served the soldiers, servants, clerks, artisans, and artists of the imperial household.

From the Magistrate's platform to Jahanara Begum's chawk was a bazaar 480 yards long. Called *Ashrafi* (Moneychangers') or *Jauhari* (Jewellers') Bazaar, it seems to have been the financial sector. The chawk was an octagon with sides of one hundred yards and a large pool in its center. To the north, Jahanara built a *caravansarai* (inn) and a garden and, to the south, a bath. On certain nights the moonlight reflected pale and silvery from the central pool and gave to the area the name *Chandni Chawk* (Silver or Moonlight Square). This name slowly displaced all others until the entire bazaar, from the Lahori gate to the Fathpuri masjid, became known as Chandni Chawk. In front of Fathpuri mosque was a platform and below that a pool. A sarai for scholars and travellers stood nearby.[120]

The shops that lined the sides of the bazaar occupied small rooms under arcades. Thin partitions separated the shops, and at the back of each one a door led to a small warehouse where surplus goods were stored. Above the warehouse lived the merchant, his family, and servants.[121] In these shops could be found spicy kabobs, beautifully scented flowers, and astrologers. Rubies, emeralds, and pearls were there; glass *huqqas* (waterpipes) and eyeglasses from China; and a variety of sweets.[122] Scattered here and there were coffeehouses where amirs gathered to listen to poetry, engage in light conversation, and watch the passing scene.[123]

The other major bazaar in Shahjahanabad stretched from the Akbarabadi gate of the fort to the Akbarabadi gate of the city. It was 1050 yards long, 30 yards wide, and had 888 shops. Built in 1650 by Nawab Akbarabadi Begum, it also boasted a branch of the Paradise Canal. At the head of the bazaar, just south of the palace gate, Akbarabadi Begum built a magnificent mosque of black, red, and creamy white called '*Ashat Panahi* (Great Protection). Near the mosque she erected a sarai and across the street a hammam. In the middle of the street she laid out a square 160 yards long and 60 yards wide.[124] In the early eighteenth century Raushan al-Daulah put up strings of lights along the canal.[125] Originally known as

[120] Muhammad Salih, '*Amal-i Salih*, 3 pp. 46–8.
[121] Bernier, *Travels*, pp. 245–6.
[122] Dargah Quli Khan, "Risalah-i Salar Jang," fols. 88a–9a.
[123] Ibid., fols. 89a–b; Anand Ram Mukhlis, "Mir' at al-Istilah," fols. 218a–b.
[124] Muhammad Salih, '*Amal-i Salih*, 3 pp. 48–9.
[125] Ashob, "Ta'rikh-i Muhammad Shah," fols. 51b–2a.

the bazaar in the direction of Akbarabad, it later came to be called Faiz Bazaar (Bazaar of Plenty).[126]

Outside the Akbarabadi gate of the fort Sa'adullah Khan constructed a large square in the middle of *Khas Bazaar* (Special Bazaar), the street which connected the Jami' Masjid and the palace-fortress. Here dancing girls, physicians (who, according to Dargah Quli Khan, passed off bags of dirt as medicine), story-tellers, and astrologers plied their trades; here also were shops that dispensed cloth, medicine, hot food, weapons, birds, fruits, flowers, wild animals, and sugarcane.[127] Although these were the largest and richest markets in the city, they were by no means the only places of commercial activity. Shops and stalls could be found in lanes and byways and on street corners throughout.[128]

Suburbs

The city of Shahjahanabad was not limited to the area enclosed by the great walls. The walled area was only the hub of an urban complex that extended several miles into the countryside on the north, south, and west and along the opposite bank of the river on the east. About half of the population resided in the suburbs, and the ring of gardens, tombs, bazaars, and mahallahs contained a good deal of the economic and social activity of the city.

The precise area and configuration of the suburbs, however, cannot be determined. Bernier wrote: "I cannot undertake to define exactly the circumference, because these suburbs are interspersed with extensive gardens and open spaces."[129] To the north and south the city extended well beyond the Kashmiri and Akbarabadi gates. John Campbell, who visited the city in 1668, said it was seven leagues (three to four miles) from north to south and in the early eighteenth century the author of "Bahjat al-Alam" said it was 6-7 kurohs.[130] In 1747 Joseph Tieffenthaler said the suburbs extended eight miles from the Arab gate in the south (near the Humayun's tomb) to the Salt market in the north.[131] The city also extended beyond the walls on the west to the tomb of Qutb al-Qutab, according to the author of "Bahjat al-Alam," and to Jai Singh

---

[126] Muhammad Salih, *'Amal-i Salih*, 3 p. 48.

[127] Dargah Quli Khan, "Risalah-i Salar Jang." fols. 86b–8a; Anand Ram Mukhlis, "Mir'at al-Istilah," fols. 53b–4a.

[128] Tieffenthaler, *Geographique de l'Indoustan*, 1 p. 127.

[129] Bernier, *Travels*, p. 242.

[130] R.C. Temple, "The Travels of Richard Bell (and John Campbell) in the East Indies, Persia, and Palestine," *The Indian Antiquary* 35 (1906) p. 173. Hakim Mahrat Khan. "Bahjat at-'Alam," fol. 35b.

[131] Tieffenthaler, *Geographique de l'Indoustan*, 1 p. 3.

Pura, according to Tieffenthaler.[132] John Campbell estimated that the
circumference of the city, including suburbs, was about fifteen leagues
(seven to nine miles).[133] Thus, the total area in 1739 was probably
about 3300 acres: 1500 acres for the walled city and about 1800 acres
for the nearby suburbs of Mughalpura, Sabzimandi, Paharganj, Jai Sing
Pura, and the rest. Although the inner city boasted the central bazaars,
the palace-fortress, and the Jami' Masjid and about 75 percent of the
population, it is well to remember that the suburbs contained as many as
fifty-two bazaars and thirty-six mandis,[134] the tombs of holy men and
saints, and the gardens and garden tombs of important men and women.

Probably the largest and most important of the suburban mahallahs
was Paharganj, located just outside Ajmiri gate (see map 4). Tieffenthaler listed this as one of the five major bazaars of the city and the only one
outside the walls.[135] It was the principal grain market, where food grains
from across the river were stored before being distributed to shopkeepers
and peddlers for sale within the city. Linking Paharganj to the
Akbarabadi gate was another wholesale bazaar called Shahganj.

South and to the east, on the opposite bank of the Jamuna, were
Patparganj and Shahdara. In these mahallahs resided wholesale grain
merchants. The grain which they imported from the doab was stored in
large walled enclosures, then ferried across the river and sold in
Paharganj. Both mahallahs were completely destroyed in the disorder of
the mid-eighteenth century.[136]

Jai Singh Pura, another well-known mahallah, was located near
Paharganj. Named after the famous Rajput amir, it probably held Jai
Singh's mansion in the late seventeenth century and the homes of Rajput
amirs and mansabdars in the first half of the eighteenth century.[137] South
of Jai Singh Pura lay Rakabganj. This mahallah was named after its
principal inhabitants, *banjaras* (grain dealers), who were in the household
or stirrup (*rikab*) of the emperor.

[132] Ibid. Hakim Mahrafat Khan, "Bahjat al-'Alam," fol. 35b.
[133] Temple, "Travels of Bell and Campbell," p. 173.
[134] T. Fortescue, "Report on the Revenue System of the Delhi Territory, 1820" in *Records
of the Delhi Residency and Agency, 1807–87* (Lahore: Punjab Government Press, 1911),
p. 169.
[135] Tieffenthaler, *Geographique de l'Indoustan*, 1 p. 127.
[136] Sayyid Nur al-Din Husain Khan Bahadur Fakhri, "Tarikhi-i Najib al-Daulah," Persian
Manuscript Collection, Add. 24,410, London, British Museum, fols. 134–8. James
Grant, "Firhist-i Subahjat-i Hindustan," Persian Manuscript Collection, Ethe 433,
India Office Library, London, fol. 20a; Anand Ram Mukhlis, "Waqa'i-i Sayr-i Ganga,"
fols. 1–14. An 1808 map of Shahjahanabad shows Patparganj. See *A Catalogue of
Manuscripts and Printed Reports, Field Books, Memoirs and Maps of the Indian Surveys
Deposited in the Map Room of the Indian Office* (London, 1878), p. 241.
[137] Jean Law de Lauriston, *Memoires sur quelques Affaires de l'Empire Mogol, 1756–61* (Paris:
Alfred Martineau, 1913), p. 115.

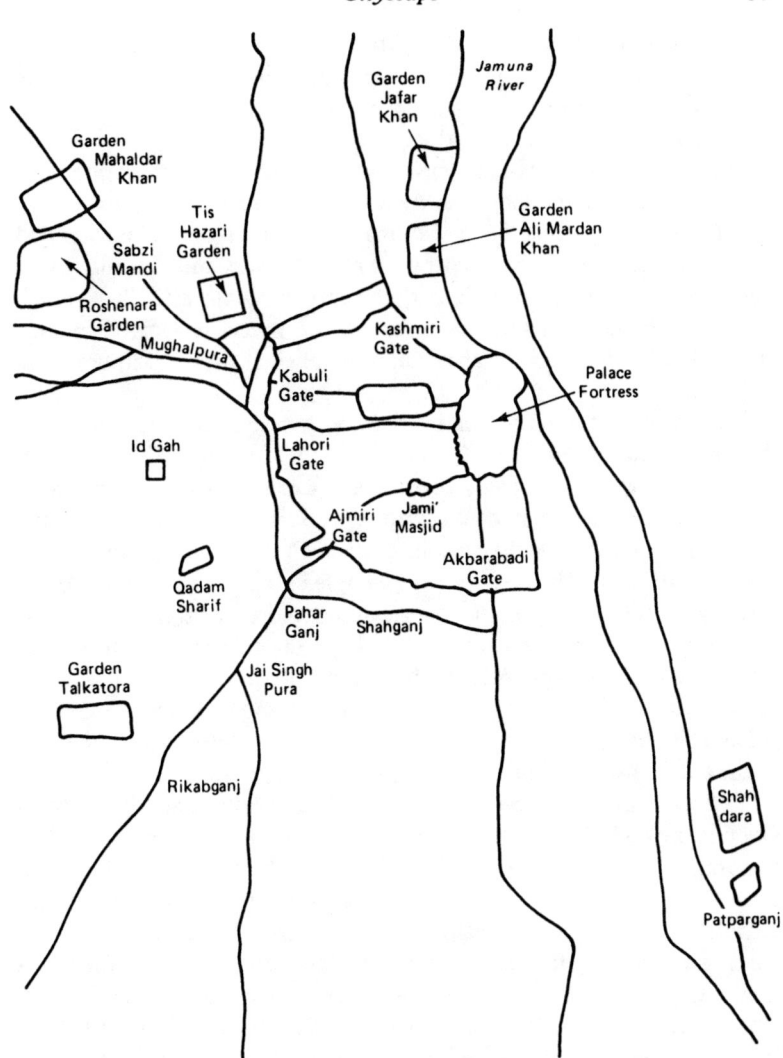

Map 4   Suburbs of Shahjahanabad 1739.

Immediately beyond the Kabul gate of the city was Mughalpura. The Paradise Canal split this suburb, watering gardens and houses on its way into the city. Tradition has it that Mughals (i.e., Central Asian immigrants) had resided in this area since the days of the Khalji Sultans.[138] North of Mughalpura lay Sabzimandi, another populous residential and commercial area. As its name suggests, it may once have been the principal vegetable (*sabzi*) market of the city.[139] The Mori and Kashmiri gates were connected by a row of bazaars and mahallahs that were destroyed in the mid-eighteenth century. Other mahallahs which appear in the sources but which cannot be precisely located include Malkaganj, Sayyidwara, Tarkaganj, Abdullahnagar, Wakilpura, and Najafganj.[140]

Tombs of saints, rulers, and other important men and women dotted the countryside around the city. Sites of celebrations at the *'urs* or death, anniversary of the occupant, these were places of rest and relaxation during the rest of the year. According to Sujan Rai, the tomb of the Emperor Humayun was the most important. Built by the senior widow of the emperor, it was the first mature example in India of the garden tomb. Its *chahar bagh* (four-garden) design influenced other tombs, the most famous of which was the Taj Mahal. In India the area around a tomb was thought to be sacred and many high-ranking men and women chose to be buried nearby. The courtyard of Humayun's tomb contained the graves of Dara Shikoh, Humayun's wives, and the later Mughal rulers Jahandar Shah, Farrukhsiyar, Rafi al-Daulah, and Alamgir II.[141]

The tomb of Shaikh Nizam al-Din Auliya, a Sufi saint who came to Delhi in the mid-thirteenth century, was one of the most auspicious. The two emperors of his day, Ala al-Din Khalji and Muhammad bin Tughluq, were devoted to him, and his original tomb, erected sometime after his death in A.D. 1325, was repaired and decorated by the Emperor Firuz Shah Tughluq in the late fourteenth century. That building has disappeared and the present structure, erected in 1562–3 by Faridun Khan, has been renovated several times. Buried in the courtyard are Jahanara Begum, the Emperor Muhammad Shah, and Amir Khusrao, the famous Persian poet of Sultanate Delhi. Twice each year, on the *'urs*

---

[138] Franklin, "Account of Delhi," p. 420; Jadunath Sarkar, *Fall of the Mughal Empire*, 4 vols. (Calcutta: M.C. Sarkar and Sons, 1932–50; reprint ed., Poona; Orient Longman's Ltd., 1971), 1 p. 296.

[139] Sangin Beg, "Sair al-Manazil", fol. 63; Ghulam Muhammad Khan, "Travels," fol. 41a.

[140] Ghulam Muhammad Khan, "Travels," fol. 40b; Jadunath Sarkar, *Delhi During the Anarchy, 1749–88* (Calcutta: Superintendent of Government Printing, 1921), p. 5; Jadunath Sarkar, trans., *Delhi Affairs (1761·88), Persian Records of Maratha History, 1* (Bombay: Director of Archives, 1953), p. 124.

[141] Sujan Rai, "Khulasat al-Tawarikh," fol. 26a; Sharma, *Delhi*, pp. 107–8.

(death commemoration) of both Nizam al-Din and Amir Khusrao, great celebrations were held. Dargah Quli Khan provides a lively and colorful account of these in the early 1740s.[142]

Nearby stood the tomb of Abd al-Rahim Khan-i Khanan, one of the most accomplished great amirs of the early seventeenth century. Erected long before his death in 1626, the tomb served as a garden and pleasure area during his visits to the city.[143]

A popular place of pilgrimage for the people of Shahjahanabad was the *Qadam Sharif* (the sacred footprint). Located about one and a half miles south of the Lahori gate, this tomb was built by the Emperor Firuz Shah in 1376. Although originally intended for himself, the tomb now contains Fath Khan, Firuz Shah's favorite son, who died unexpectedly. In addition to the tomb proper, the enclosure contained a mosque, school, and dwellings for students and teachers. The marble cast of a footprint was placed over the grave of Fath Khan. The traditional explanation is that Makdum Jahanian Jahan Gash, Firuz Shah's spiritual guide, brought a footprint of the prophet back from Mecca and placed it there. Although the tomb's original occupant had been forgotten by the late seventeenth century, the annual 'urs was one of the high points of the religious year. Raushan al-Daulah cleaned the tomb for the festival and distributed food to the celebrants.[144]

The tomb of Ghazi al-Din Khan, a great amir under Aurangzeb, was located just outside the Ajmiri gate of the city. Built well before his death in 1710, the complex included a mosque and a school in addition to the tomb proper.[145] About a quarter of a mile to the northeast of the Qadam Sharif lay the tomb of Khawaja Baqi Billah, one of the great sufi saints of North India. Born in Kabul, he journeyed to Medina and is said to have introduced the Naqshbandi Sufi order to India. He died in 1603 and his 'urs was a great occasion during the late seventeenth century.[146] Sayyid Husain Rasul Numa was buried in Gulabi Bagh, about one and a half miles west of the Ajmiri gate. He was one of the most popular saints of the city during the seventeenth century, and his tomb was an important place of pilgrimage.[147]

---

[142] Sharma, *Delhi*, pp. 115–17; *List of Monuments*, 2 pp. 117–22; Dargah Quli Khan, "Risalah-i Salar Jang," fols. 81b–2a.

[143] Sharma, *Delhi*, pp. 120–1; *List of Monuments*, 2 pp. 128–9; *Ma'asir-i Rahimi* 2 p. 612.

[144] Sharma, *Delhi*, p. 133, *List of Monuments*, 2 pp. 241–4; Dargah Quli Khan, "Risalah-i Salar Jang," fols. 79a–b; Ashob, "Tarikh-i Muhammad Shah," fols. 47b–56a.

[145] *List of Monuments*, 2 p. 2; Sayyid Ahmad Khan, *Asar*, pp. 300–5.

[146] Sayyid Ahmad Khan, *Asar*, pp. 255–6; *List of Monuments*, 2 pp. 237–9; Dargah Quli Khan, "Risalah-i Salar Jang," fol. 83b.

[147] Sayyid Ahmad Khan, *Asar.*, p. 290; *List of Monuments*, 2 pp. 231–2; Dargah Quli Khan, "Risalah-i Salar Jang," fols. 83b–4a.

In 1650 Raushan Ara Begum, daughter of Shahjahan and supporter of Aurangzeb in the War of Succession, constructed in Sabzimandi the garden tomb in which she was buried.[148] Later, Zinat al-Nisa Begum, daughter of Aurangzeb, laid out a garden tomb in Tis Hazari Garden, just outside the Kabul gate of the city. Her tomb, like that of Raushan Ara, was a place of pleasure and rest before her death in 1706.[149]

Tombs of two other famous saints were found beyond the suburbs of Shahjahanabad to the south. Nestled among the remains of earlier Delhis, these tombs were probably only visited during the 'urs celebrations. Nasir al-Din Muhammad, entitled *Raushan Chiragh-i Dihli* (Illuminated Lamp of Delhi), succeeded Nizam al-Din as head of the Chistiya order. On his death in 1356 a tomb was constructed near the village where he lived. In the early eighteenth century a mosque was erected by the Emperor Farrukhsiyar.[150] Khwaja Qutb al-Din Bakhtiyar Kaki, popularly known as Qutb Sahib, died in 1236. The courtyard surrounding his tomb was considered auspicious and three Mughal rulers were buried there: Bahadur Shah I, Shah Alam II, and Akbar II.[151]

In the Muslim countries of West Asia the garden occupied an important place in the plan and build of cities. The hot, dry climate put a premium on shaded areas filled with running water, trees, and flowers. The Quran promised each Muslim a place in the heavenly paradise, and paradise in Islamic tradition is a garden. The paradise garden of the Quran, enclosed and cut by four swiftly flowing rivers, contained basins, fountains, grass, and fruit trees.

Mughal gardens were rectangular, surrounded by high walls broken by gateways, and topped with towers. The principal design, from which the most intricate and elaborate variations developed, featured a central pool containing a small open structure called a *barahdari* (summer house). Four wide canals led from the pool to the surrounding walls. Smaller canals branched off from the major waterways and subdivided the large rectangles. Colored flowers, cypress trees (symbols of death and eternity), almond, plum, and mango trees (symbols of life and hope), plumed birds, and fish of different sizes and colors filled the fully appointed garden.

Members of imperial and noble families built gardens on the banks of the Jamuna and in tree-shaded groves near the city gates. While the city was being built Shahjahan laid out a garden called Khizrabad on the banks

---

[148] Sharma, *Delhi*, p. 139; *List of Monuments* 2 pp. 266–7.
[149] Sayyid Ahmad Khan, *Asar*, p. 299.
[150] Sharma, *Delhi*, p. 77; Dargah Quli Khan, "Risalah-i Salar Jang," fols. 82a–b.
[151] Sharma, *Delhi*, pp. 62–3; Sayyid Ahmad Khan, *Asar*, p. 110; Dargah Quli Khan, "Risalah-i Salar Jang," fols. 80a–b.

of the Jamuna about five miles south of the Akbarabadi gate of the city. Here, in 1658, Aurangzeb imprisoned his brother Dara Shikoh.[152] Outside the Kabul gate of the city Shahjahan constructed a garden filled with nim trees called *Tis Hazari Bagh* (Garden of Three Thousand). Zinat al-Nisa Begum, daughter of Aurangzeb, and Malka Zamani, wife of Muhammad Shah, were buried there.[153]

In 1650 Raushan Ara Begum constructed a large garden in Sab-zimandi.[154] Somewhat later, Sirhindi Begum, wife of Shahjahan, built a garden and tomb in the same place.[155] Six miles west of the Lahore gate of the city lay a large garden later called Shalimar. The garden was constructed in 1653–4 and in 1658 Aurangzeb was crowned emperor there. Its original name was 'Azzabad Garden and it may have been built by 'Azz al-Nisa Begum, Akbarabadi Mahal, a wife of Shahjahan who constructed a mosque in the city.[156]

Gardens continued to be built after the initial burst of construction in the 1650s. In 1710–11 Mahaldar Khan built a spacious garden beyond Sabzimandi[157] and a garden called Tal Katora was laid out near Rikabganj. Little is known of the builder but it is said that one of the emperors of the late seventeenth or early eighteenth centuries construc-ted it, and it is thought to have been a *shikargah* (hunting lodge) of Muhammad Shah.[158] An eighteenth-century source mentions the garden of Mohsan Khan, which often served as a resting place for the Emperor Farrukhsiyar.[159] Along the river north of Kashmiri gate lay several gardens. The garden of Ali Mardan Khan was nearest the gate, and the garden of Jaffar Khan was immediately beyond. Muhammad Shah spent a good deal of time in the garden of Jaffar Khan during the latter years of his reign.[160]

The supreme example in Shahjahanabad of the garden-builder's art, and the only garden of size within the walls, was the one erected by Jahanara Begum north of Chandni Chawk. Called *Sahibabad* (Abode of the Master) and erected in 1650, this garden enclosed a rectangular area of about fifty acres. The Paradise Canal provided water for canals,

[152] Manucci, *Storia do Mogor*, 1 p. 337.
[153] Franklin, "An Account of Delhi," 4 p. 421.
[154] Sayyid Ahmad Khan, *Asar*, p. 288; *List of Monuments*, 2 pp. 266–7.
[155] Sayyid Ahmad Khan, *Asar*, pp. 288–9
[156] Sharma, *Delhi*, p. 138; Villiers-Stuart, *Gardens*, pp. 103–5; Sayyid Ahmad Khan, *Asar*, pp. 287–8; *List of Monuments*, 4 pp. 33–4.
[157] Sayyid Ahmad Khan, *Asar*, p. 325; *List of Monuments*, 2 pp. 270–1.
[158] *List of Monuments*, 2 p. 228; Irvine, *Later Mughals*, 2 p. 289.
[159] Seid Gholam Hussein Khan, *Seir al-Mutagherin*, 1 p. 69.
[160] Ghulam Muhammad Khan, *Travels*, fol. 40b; Jadunath Sarkar, "A Contemporary Picture of the Mughal Court in 1743", *Journal of the Bihar and Orissa Research Society* 17 (1931) p. 349; Ashob, "Tarikh-i Muhammad Shah," fol. 58b.

waterfalls, fountains, and pools. Flowers and trees surrounded the barahdaris which were barely visible behind the drifting spray of the fountains. Women of the imperial household played with their children here and rested from the midsummer heat.[161]

To ensure a stable supply of water, cities in Mughal India were located on or near rivers. Canals, built by emperors and great amirs, channeled water for drinking, washing, and irrigating to houses, gardens, shops, pools, and baths. In 1615–16 the great amir Abd al-Rahim Khan-i Khanan constructed a canal in Burhanpur which carried water from the Tapti river to *Lal Bagh* (Red Garden).[162] In 1639–40 Ali Mardan Khan proposed the construction of a canal outside Lahore. Shahjahan agreed and in little more than a year the builders of Ali Mardan's establishment completed *Shah Nahr* (King's Canal) a channel that carried water over one hundred miles from the source of the river Ravi in the mountains to the city.[163]

The longest canal and one of the most impressive engineering feats of the Mughal period was the Paradise Canal. This canal carried water from a point on the Jamuna seventy-five miles upstream to the city. The first section is said to have been built by Sultan Firuz Shah Tughluq during the years 1355–8. It brought water seventy miles from the Jamuna to Shah's hunting preserve at Safidun but was a primitive affair and only flowed during the monsoons. During Akbar's reign the governor of Delhi, Shihab al-Din Khan, ordered the original canal cleared and extended to Hansi and Hissar. As a result, the canal became known as *Nahr-i Shihab* (Shihab's Canal).

In 1639 Shahjahan ordered the repair of the canal up to the point reached by Shihab al-Din and, because of his expertise, Ali Mardan Khan was given the responsibility for the work. A channel from Hansi and Hissar to the northwestern suburbs of the city was excavated – a distance of about seventy-eight miles. The men of Ali Mardan Khan's household constructed an acqueduct of five arches (162 feet long and 24 feet wide) to bridge the drain carrying overflow water from the *Najafgarh Jhil* (Najafgarh Reservoir). The canal flowed through the suburbs watering gardens, mansions, and houses and entered Shahjahanabad by the Kabul gate. Bakhtawar Khan, a great amir under Aurangzeb, built a bridge over the canal, and Mir Muhammad Shafiz, an influential sufi saint of the early eighteenth century, lived for forty years on its banks.[164]

[161] Muhammad Salih, *'Amal-i Salih*, 3 p. 47.
[162] 'Abd al-Baqi, *Ma'asir-i Rahimi*, 2 pp. 601–2.
[163] Shah Nawaz Khan, *Ma'asir al-Umara*, 2 pp. 795–807; 'Abd al-Hamid, *Badshah Namah*, 2 pp. 168–9.
[164] Muhammad Salih, *'Amal-i Salih*, 3 p. 29; Muhammad Waris, "Padshah Namah," fols. 401–A; Franklin, "Account of Delhi," p. 420; Hamilton, *Description of Hindostan*, 1

Once inside it split in two. One branch met Chandni Chawk near Fathpuri Masjid and flowed down the middle of the bazar to Faiz Bazar. The other branch entered Sahibabad garden and ran to the northeastern corner of the palace-fortress near Shah Burj. An ingenious device called a *Shutrgulu* (Camel's Neck) is said to have lifted the stream from ground level to the floor of the fort. A marble channel directed water to the buildings and apartments along the eastern wall while smaller canals diverted the flow to gardens and waterways.

Water moved regularly from the Jamuna to the city until the middle of the eighteenth century. The canal proved a boon to cultivators and the taxes they paid the superintending amir (Safdar Jang is said to have received two million five hundred thousand rupees one year) were ample incentive to keep it open.[165] With the collapse of order and government, however, the canal again ran dry.

The Paradise Canal was responsible for much that was fresh, green, and beautiful in Shahjahanabad. Sujan Rai wrote:

[it] confers freshness on the gardens in the suburbs of the capital, lends happiness to the streets and bazaars, and enhances the splendor of the imperial palaces.[166]

A mid-eighteenth-century writer observed:

[the canal] brought greenness to Delhi. It ran in all of the city from lane to lane, and the wells became full from it. Having flowed to the mansions of the princes and amirs it flowed into the city – to Chandni Chawk, to the Chawk of Sa'adullah Khan, to Paharganj, to Ajmiri Gate, to the grazing places, to the other mahallahs, and to all the lanes and bazaars of the city.[167]

In Mughal India *caravansarais* (inns for merchants and travellers) were found at regular intervals along major highways and in cities. Like gardens and mansions, sarais were walled, and travellers entered through one of several large gateways. The walls were serrated with battlements and at each of the four corners were bastions. Rows of identical arched compartments separated by thin partitions lined the sides of the buildings. A pool of water, a well, a mosque, stables, trees, flowers, and a *katra* (walled enclosure) for storing travellers' goods were found in most sarais. Constructed by the great for reasons of charity, religious duty, and fame, they were open to merchants, scholars, religious specialists, and other travellers but not to soldiers. The average sarai had room for eight

p. 414; Polier, "Extracts of Letters," p. 37; Chaturman Rai, "Chahar Gulshan," fol 14b; Bakhtawar Khan, "Mirat al-Alam." Persian Manuscript Collection, Add. 7657, London, British Museum, fols. 252a–3b.
165 Polier, "Extracts of Letters," p. 37.
166 Sujan Rai, "Khulasat al-Tawarikh," fol. 29b.
167 Chaturman Rai, "Chahar Gulshan," fols. 37a–b.

hundred to a thousand travellers and housed barbers, tailors, washerman, blacksmiths, sellers of grass and straw, physicians, dancing girls, and musicians. To establish order and security the Mughals posted an official with a contingent of soldiers to each sarai.[168]

Fathpuri Begum erected an inn for pilgrims near her mosque in Chandni Chawk[169] and Akbarabadi Begum did the same for hers in Faiz Bazar.[170] In 1671–2 Bakhtawar Khan built a sarai called Bakhtawar Nagar outside the city[171] and in the early eighteenth century Ruhallah Khan built a large sarai and mosque beyond Mughalpura.[172] Afrid Khan built a sarai outside the walls in 1608[173] and Dargah Quli Khan described the Arab Sarai near the tomb of Nizam al-Din[174]

The caravansarai erected by Jahanara Begum near the entrance to her garden in Chandni Chawk was the outstanding example of its type. Bernier considered it, next to the Jami' Masjid, the most imposing structure in the city. It was square and two-storied, had towers at each corner, and contained ninety rooms, each beautifully painted and appointed. In the middle of the courtyard was a garden filled with watercourses, pools, trees and flowers. Only the richest and most eminent of Persian and Uzbek merchants were allowed to put up there.[175] Jahanara wrote:

> I will build a sarai, large and fine like no other in Hindustan. The wanderer who enters its courts will be restored in body and soul and my name will never be forgotten.[176]

Population

It is difficult to estimate the population of Shahjahanabad in 1650. Although some Persian sources provide the number of households or mahallahs in a town or city,[177] there are no such data for Shahjahanabad. The only population information of any sort during the pre-British

---

[168] Manucci, *Storia do Mogor*, 1 pp. 67–70, 115.
[169] Muhammad Salih, *'Amal-i Salih*, 3 p. 48.
[170] Ibid., 3 p. 49.
[171] Bakhtawar Khan, "Mir'at al-Alam," fols. 252–3b.
[172] *List of Monuments*, 2 p. 263.
[173] Sayyid Ahmad Khan, *Asar*, p. 256.
[174] Dargah Quli Khan, "Risalah-i Salar Jang," fols. 100b–1b.
[175] Muhammad Salih, *'Amal-i Salih*, 3 p. 47; Bernier, *Travels*, pp. 280–1; Manucci, *Storia do Mogor*, 1 pp. 212–13.
[176] Butenschen, *Jahanara Begum*, p. 30.
[177] See Bhadani, "Population of Marwar," pp. 415–27 for the number of households in seventeenth-century Rajasthani cities. See also Abu al-Fazl, *Akbar-Namah* 3 p. 346 for a census of the empire in the twenty-fifth year of Akbar's reign.

period comes from 1793, when a visiting British officer estimated that the city container thirty-six *muhallahs* (quarters).[178]

In 1650 the great camp contained 300,000–325,000 persons.[179] As in 1600 this collection of noble, princely, and imperial households seems to have constituted about 80 per cent of the population of the capital city.[180] As a result, Shahjahanabad in 1650 probably numbered between 375,000–400,000 persons. Since most of the princes and great amirs lived with their households in large mansions inside the walled area[181], there were probably about 250,000–300,000 persons residing in the 1500 acres within the walls. In the 1800 acres of the nearby suburbs were found the homes of lower-ranking mansabdars and of the soldiers, merchants, servants, laborers, and others who were not part of the households of the great men: a population of about 100,000–150,000 persons.

This estimate is supported by Francois Bernier who lived in the city from 1659 to 1663 and judged it to be about size of Paris which, during the late seventeenth century, had a population of about 500,000 persons.[182] In addition, Jean de Thevenot, a Frenchman who travelled in Western India during 1666, stated that Shahjahanabad had a population of about 400,000.[183] These estimates of knowledgeable contemporaries contrast sharply with the inflated figures of later travellers who reported traditions giving Shahjahanabad a population of about two million in 1700.[184]

During the period 1639–1739 the city experienced great fluctuations in size and activity. Shahjahan and his court didn't move to the new capital until 1648 and the Emperor Aurangzeb left the city for good in 1679. As a result, Shahjahanabad probably sustained its initial population of 400,000 for only about thirty years. The great camp went with Aurangzeb to the Deccan in 1679, and he remained there for almost thirty years, fighting a fruitless, enervating war that only ended with his death in 1707. Dependent on the 20 percent of the population that was not part of the great camp, the city declined dramatically during these years. Bernier wrote:

---

[178] Franklin, "An Account of Delhi," p. 426

[179] See the discussion in Chapter 3 below.

[180] For a discussion of the population of Agra in 1600 see Stephen P. Blake, "The Hierarchy of Central Places in North India During The Mughal Period of Indian History," *South Asia* 6 (1983) pp. 21–5.

[181] Tavernier, *Travels*, 1 pp. 78–9.

[182] Bernier, *Travels*, p. 282; F.L. Carsten, ed., *The Ascendancy of France – 1648–88, The New Cambridge Modern History* 4 (Cambridge: Cambridge University Press, 1961), p. 246.

[183] Sen, ed., *Indian Travels of Thevenot and Careri*, p. 61.

[184] Seid Gholam Hossein Khan, *Seir Mutaqherin*, p. 187, n. 154; Hamilton, *A Description of Hindostan*, 1 pp. 413–14; Leopold Von Orlich, *Travels in India*, trans. H. Evans Lloyd, 2 vols. (London: Longman, Brown, Green, and Longman's 1845) 2 p. 4.

The whole population of Delhi, the capital city, is in fact collected in the camp, because deriving its employment and maintenance from the court and army, it has no alternative but to follow them in their march or to perish from want during their absence.[185]

Another traveller observed of the city "it appears a desert when the Emperor is absent...there hardly remains the sixth part [of its population] in his absence."[186] In 1696 the newly appointed governor of Lahore, a man from Hyderabad in South India, wanted to see the gardens and rooms of the palace-fortress. Aqil Khan, commander of the fort, denied his request because the rooms of the palace were dusty and uncarpeted and because the governor of Lahore was not an important enough person to justify a thorough cleaning.[187] In 1698 Aurangzeb wrote a letter to Asad Khan asking for a map and a detailed description of the condition of the buildings and gardens in the city. He wanted to know the extent of the destruction so that he could allocate money to repair the ruined structures both inside and outside the palace-fortress.[188] Finally, the Jesuit fathers, in their report of 1686, referring to the devastation the transfer of the court to Shahjahanabad in 1648 had had on the Christians of Agra, wrote: "When Aurangzeb left Delhi for the Deccan a similar effect was produced on the Christian community at Delhi."[189]

Bahadur Shah, Aurangzeb's successor, returned to North India in 1707 and the city began to revive. But since he spent the five years of his reign touring, never really living in the palace-fortress, the full rebirth of the city had to await Bahadur Shah's successor in 1712. At that point, with the return of the men, animals, and equipment of the great camp, the city quickly regained its former size and probably maintained a population of about 400,000 until the invasion of Nadir Shah in 1739.

---

[185] Bernier, *Travels*, pp. 280–1.
[186] Sen, ed., *Thevenot and Careri*, p. 61.
[187] Muhammad Saqi, *Ma'asir-i 'Alamqiri*, p. 383.
[188] Inayat Allah, "Ruka'at-i Alamgiri," trans. Jamshid H. Bilimoria in *Ruka'at-i Alamgiri* (Delhi: Idarah-i (Adabiyat-i Delhi, 1972), p. 116.
[189] Edward Maclagan, *The Jesuits and the Great Mughals* (London: Burns Oates and Washbourne Otd., 1932), p. 279. This argument about the decline of the city after 1679 appears, at first glance, to be contradicted by Sujan Rai's description of Shahjahanabad. The "Khulasat al-Tawarikh," written between 1695 and 1699, portrays a city of great size, beauty, and activity. However, there is considerable evidence to suggest that this impression is misleading. In the first place, Sujan Rai's descriptions of towns and cities are, except for those of his native Punjab, taken for the most part directly from the *A'in-i Akbari* (c. 1595). In the second place, there is no evidence in any of the statistics of the expansion of the empire under Aurangzeb. (Jadunath Sarkar, trans., *The India of Auranzeb*, Calcutta: Bose Brothers, 1901), p. xiv). All of this suggests that the description of Shahjahanabad in the "Khulasat al-Tawarikh" reflects the latter part of Shahjahan's reign (1648–58) and the early part of Aurangzeb's reign (1658–79) rather than the late seventeenth century.

Conclusion

In the cities of Mughal India, as in other cities of Islamic West Asia, public buildings were the result of private impulse. Baths, mosques, wells, caravansarais, bridges, canals, and gardens were erected, repaired, and maintained not by the state or municipality but by the urban nobility. In Agra, for example, Shahjahan spent six million rupees on a congregational mosque of marble and on other buildings in the fort, and five million rupees on the Taj Mahal. In Shahjahanabad he lavished six million rupees on the palace-fortress and one million on the Jami' Masjid. In Lahore he spent five million rupees on buildings and gardens; in Kabul one million two hundred thousand on the mosque, fort, and city walls; in Kashmir eight hundred thousand on various structures; in Qandahar eight hundred thousand rupees on the fort; and in Ajmir, Ahmadabad, and other places one million two hundred thousand rupees on assorted buildings.[190] In addition, Aurangzeb built and repaired mosques, erected caravansarais, and established *bulghar khanahs* (free kitchens) in cities across the realm.[191]

Great amirs engaged in similar activities. Abd al-Rahim Khan-i Khanan built a congregational mosque, a bath, a garden, a tank, and a mahallah in Burhanpur, a garden in Ahmadabad, and a sarai and garden in Lahore.[192] Munim Khan erected mansions, sarais, and *katras* (walled markets) in several cities.[193] And Raushan al-Daulah, the great amir who built two mosques and a mansion in Shahjahanabad, erected in Panipat a madrassah and a tomb and in Thaska an assembly hall, a free kitchen, and a sarai for pilgrims.[194]

Construction of public buildings, like the giving of alms, was a religious duty and the great men of Shahjahanabad acquired merit and a kind of immortality.

> He is not dead who leaves behind him on earth
> bridge and mosque, well and sarai.[195]

The Iranian architects who worked on the design and plan of Shahjahanabad were influenced by the cosmological ideas of the *Rasail* of the Ikhwan al-Safa. For them the central symbolic principal was the analogy between the microcosm (man) and the macrocosm (the universe). A similar analogy – between the palace-fortress as microcosm and the city

[190] Muhammad Salih, *'Amal-i Salih*, 2 pp. 556–8; 'Abd al-Hamid, *Badshah Namah*, 2 pp. 711–14.
[191] Muhammad Saqi, *Ma'asir-i 'Alamqiri*, p. 315.
[192] 'Abd al-Baqi, *Ma'asir-i Rahimi*, 2 pp. 595–610.
[193] Shah Nawaz Khan, *Ma'asir al-Umara*, 3 pp. 667–77.
[194] Ibid., 2 pp. 333–6.
[195] Muhammad 'Ali Khan, "Ta'rikh-i Muzzafari," fol. 262b.

as macrocosm – is also helpful in understanding the design and organization of the city.

As microcosm the palace-fortress of the emperor served as the model
for the city at large. According to Arab geographers, a mosque, a market,
and a bath were the basic requirements for a town or city. Shahjahan's
great fortress – the citadel or little city – contained all of these elements
and was, in a certain sense, the city in miniature. The plan of the palace-
fortress guided that of the city. Like the imperial residence, the city was
divided into two parts, special and ordinary. From the perspective of the
city, the palace-fortress was the inner, secluded area where crucial
decisions were made and the ceremonial of the state was enacted. Like the
quarters of the imperial household in the palace-fortress, it was the seat of
power accessible only to those of status and importance. In the city
outside the palace walls, as in the area of the palace-fortress beyond the
imperial living quarters, the public, ordinary business of the state was
conducted. Mansions of princes and amirs (themselves models of the
palace-fortress) organized and directed their sectors of the city in the
same way that the homes of soldiers, administrators, and others centered
the smaller neighborhoods in the outer area of the palace-fortress.

The layout of streets in the palace-fortress guided the street plan in the
city at large. In both places the major east–west street was the central
bazaar and in both the north–south thoroughfare intersected this street at
the principal entrance to the inner sanctum – before the Naqqar Khanah
in the palace-fortress and before the Lahori gate of the fortress in the city.

The analogy between microcosm and macrocosm also holds from the
perspective of the city at large. Just as the palace-fortress suggests the city
in miniature so the city itself symbolizes the mansion of the emperor, the
palace-fortress writ large. Just as princes and great amirs built mansions
or mahallahs for their extended households in Shahjahanabad and other
cities and named them after themselves, so the Mughal emperors built
cities named after themselves dominated by their households and the
households of the great men of their courts. Thus, Shahjahanabad,
Akbarabad (built by the emperor Akbar), and many of the great cities of
the period are best understood as the mansions or palaces of the Mughal
emperors or their great amirs.

Najib al-Daulah, the great amir who ruled Shahjahanabad in the 1760s
and 1770s as deputy of the Afghan Ahmad Shah Durrani, built a large
quarter or mansion near Shampur for his extended household. It included
a mansion, mosque, madrassah, bath, and houses for his various
dependants and was called Najibabad.[196] Likewise, Muhammad Khan

---

[196] Nur al-Din Husain, "Tarikh-i Najib al-Daulah," fols. 134b–8b.

Bangash founded the city of Farrukhabad in 1714 because the Emperor Farrukhsiyar wanted a city named after himself. Muhammad Khan first built a palace-fortress in the middle of the walled area. In the surrounding area he erected large walled mansions (forts) for each of his thirty-two sons. The merchants, artisans, laborers, and artists who were unattached to any of the great households lived in caste/craft quarters in the middle of the area.[197]

Faizabad, the original seat of the Nawabs of Oudh, was founded in the mid-eighteenth century by Sa'adat Khan. He built a wooden bungalow in the middle of a walled area that included accommodations for the cavalry, infantry, artillery, and other establishments of his household. Safdar Jang, his successor, named the place Faizabad and constructed gardens and markets outside the walls. Inside were houses for the officers of the state. After Safdar Jang's death Shujah al-Daulah came to Faizabad and rebuilt Sa'adat Khan's wall. His clients built houses outside and he excavated a moat to protect and contain the whole thing. Eventually he erected two more walls.[198]

Finally, there is the story of Makramat Khan, the great amir who supervised most of the construction of Shahjahanabad. After inspecting his new capital Shahjahan complained that, except for the one in the palace-fortress, the bazaars were not octagonal and covered like those of Baghdad and Isfahan. Makaramat Khan, reflecting the idea of city as mansion, said that if Shahjahan would agree to name the city after him he would pay into the imperial treasury all that had been spent on construction.[199]

Appendix: Mansions and mosques in Shahjahanabad, 1739

Maps were common in Mughal India. Crude maps of the world were available as well as imprecise maps of the empire itself.[200] In addition, there were maps of cities and plans of buildings. Shahjahan had examined plans of covered bazaars and maps of Baghdad and Isfahan.[201] When Nadir Shah left Shahjahanabad he took a map of the city[202] and he was so impressed by its plan and build that he is said to have constructed a city

---

[197] Muhammad Wali, "Tarikh-i Farrukhabad," fols. 3a–4a.
[198] Muhammad Faiz Baksh, "Tarikh-i Farah Bakhsh," Persian Manuscript Collection, Or. 1015, London, British Museum, fols. 150a–3b.
[199] Shah Nawaz Khan, *Ma'asir al-Umara*, 3 pp. 460–77.
[200] Irfan Habib, "Cartography in Mughal India," *Medieval India: A Miscellany* 4 (1977) pp. 122–34.
[201] Shah Nawaz Khan, *Ma'asir al-Umara*, 3 pp. 460–77.
[202] Fraser, *Nadir Shah*, p. 221.

SHAHJAHANABAD: 1739

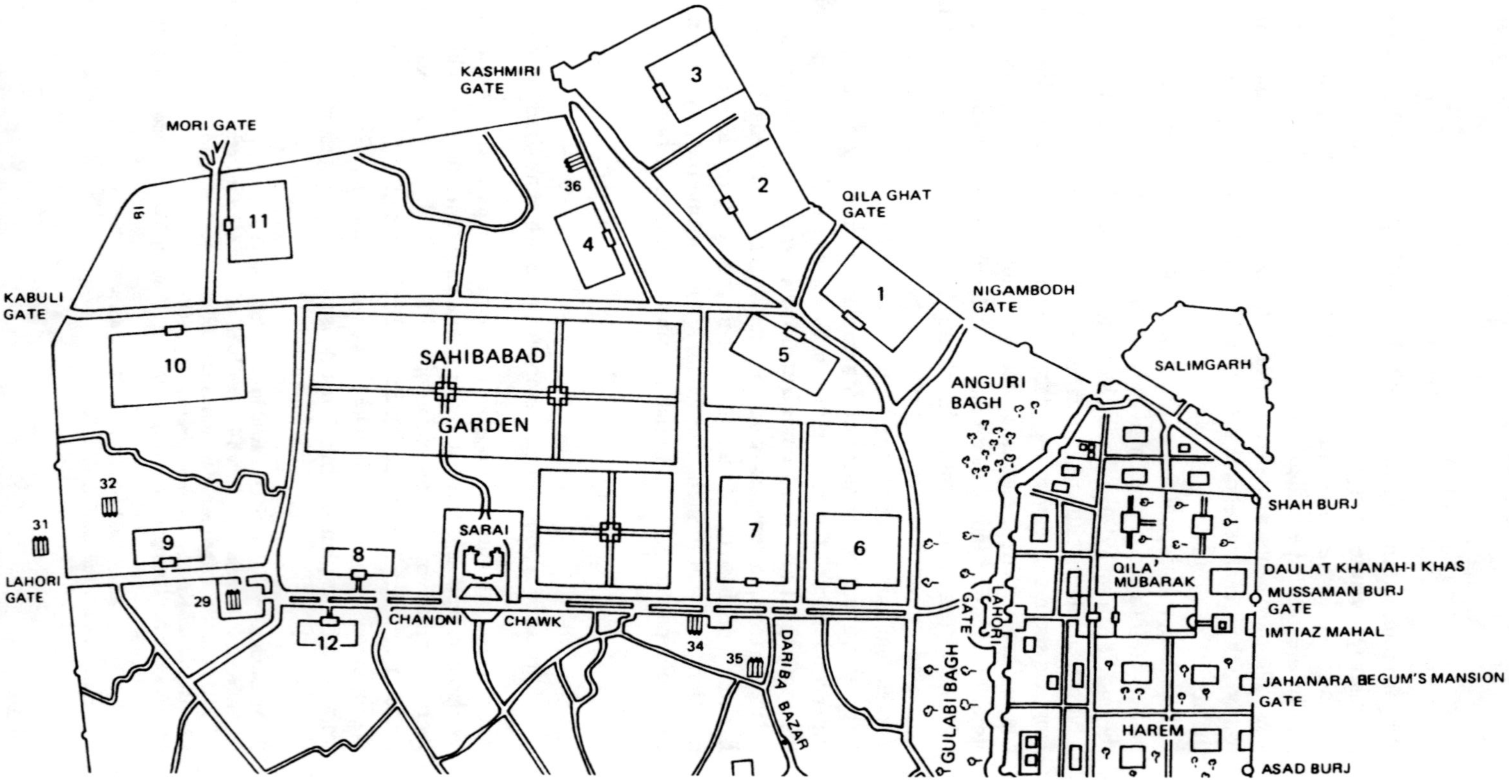

KASHMIRI GATE
MORI GATE
QILA GHAT GATE
NIGAMBODH GATE
KABULI GATE
SALIMGARH
ANGURI BAGH
SAHIBABAD GARDEN
SARAI
CHANDNI CHAWK
DARIBA BAZAR
GULABI BAGH
LAHORI GATE
LAHORI GATE
QILA' MUBARAK
HAREM
SHAH BURJ
DAULAT KHANAH-I KHAS
MUSSAMAN BURJ GATE
IMTIAZ MAHAL
JAHANARA BEGUM'S MANSION
GATE
ASAD BURJ
1
2
3
4
5
6
7
8
9
10
11
12
29
31
32
34
35
36

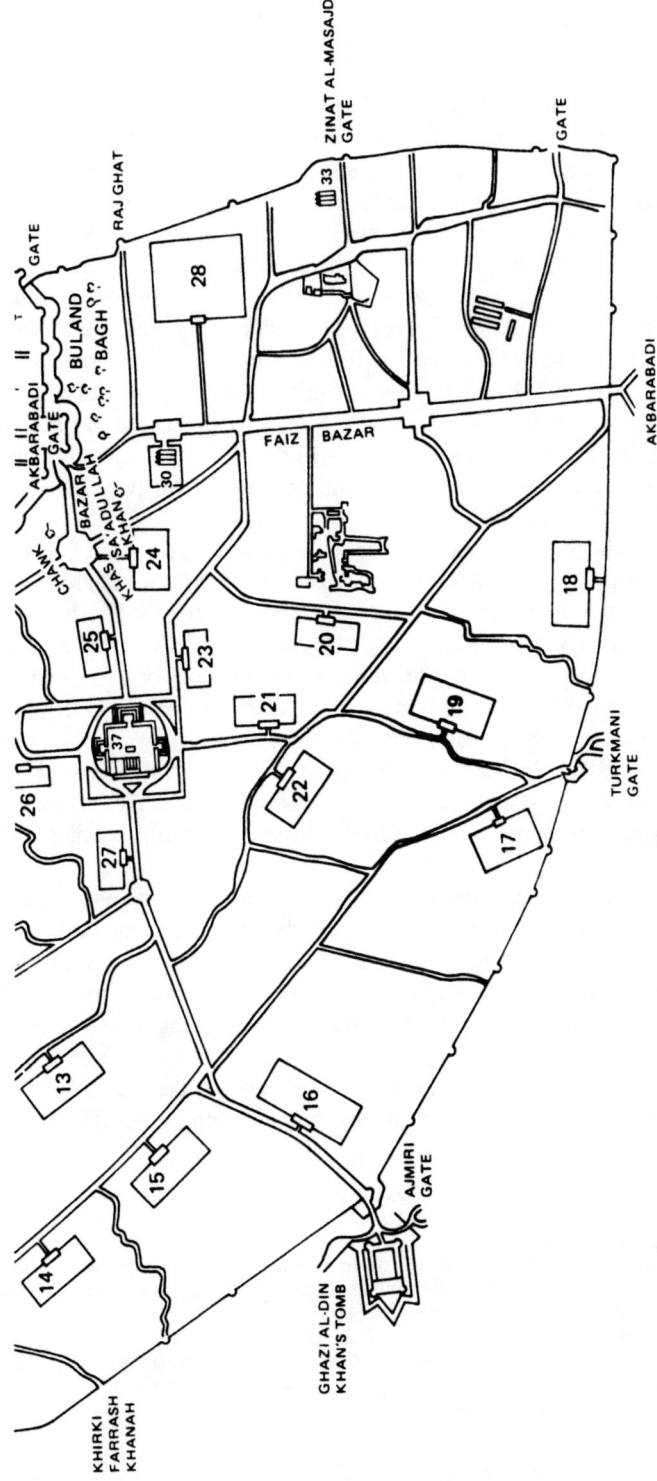

Map 5   Mansions and mosques in Shahjahanabad 1739.

one-quarter the size in Khurasan in 1741.[203] In 1792 the English traveller
Thomas Twining bought a colorful map of Shahjahanabad – red and
black lines on yellow paper – and maps of Agra and the Taj as well.[204]

On this map an attempt is made to locate the major mansions and
mosques constructed in the city between its founding in 1639 and the
invasion of Nadir Shah in 1739. The outline came from a Survey of India
map of the mid-nineteenth century. To determine the locations and
builders of these structures, however, travellers' accounts, early maps,
biographical works, archeological studies, and historical chronicles in
Persian, Urdu, and English were consulted. One of the most useful
sources was a large Urdu-Persian map of the city preserved in the India
Office Library. Although the map itself is not dated it was probably drawn
in the early nineteenth century, sometime between the British takeover of
the city in 1803 and 1842.[205]

The original builder of many of these mansions is not known. For some
structures the history is clear: for example, the mansions of Safdar Jang
(no. 1), Dara Shikoh (no. 2), Ali Mardan Khan (no. 3), Shaista Khan
(no. 6), Muzzafar Khan (no. 17), Bakhtawar Khan (no. 22), and
Sa'adullah Khan (no. 28). But for most of the mansions only the name of
the late seventeenth- or early eighteenth-century occupant is available. It
seems clear, however, that these residences, like those above, were
constructed either during the period 1639–48 (when the palace-fortress
was built) or during the period 1646–56 (when the imperial court took up
residence and structures like the Jami' Masjid and the surrounding walls
were erected).

Because the imperial court moved so often, residing for long periods in
cities other than the capital, many of the princes and great amirs
constructed mansions in several of the large cities of the realm. Thus, Asaf
Khan, a great amir of the early seventeenth century, erected mansions in
Lahore, Delhi, and Agra;[206] Iradat Khan, an early eighteenth-century
amir, maintained palaces in Lahore and Agra;[207] Abd al-Rahim Khan-i
Khanan, the ornament of Jahangir's court, constructed mansions and
gardens in many cities of the realm;[208] and Munim Khan, an early

---

[203] Khwaja Abd al-Karim, "Bayan-i Waqa'i," Persian Manuscript Collection, Add. 8909,
London, British Museum, fols. 43a–b.

[204] Twining, *Travels*, p. 256.

[205] For the map see *A Catalogue of Maps in the India Office*, p. 241. See Sayyid Ahmad Khan,
Asar, pp. 348–51 for the Zafar Mahal built in the Hayat Baksh garden in 1842 and not
shown on the map.

[206] Shah Nawaz Khan, *Ma'asir al-Umara*, 1 pp. 151–60.

[207] *A Translation of the Memoirs of Eradut Khan*, trans. Jonathan Scott (London: John
Stockdale, 1786), p. 94.

[208] *Ma'asir-i Rahimi* 2 pp. 600–12.

eighteenth-century amir, aspired to build mansions in every city of the realm in order to perpetuate his name.[209] As a result, it is likely that most of the major mansions in the city were erected by the great men of Shahjahan's court during the period 1639–56. And, in fact, the official historian states, without mentioning names or structures, that the princes and famous (*namdar*) amirs built mansions according to their tastes and inclinations, ranging in cost from Rs. 100,000 to Rs. 2,000,000, on the banks of the river to the right and left of the palace-fortress.[210]

1. The mansion of Safdar Jang

Dara Shikoh built a magnificent mansion on the banks of the Jamuna next to the palace-fortress. It was the largest and finest in the city and, in its original state in the mid-seventeenth century, comprised two structures, mansions one and two. In the late seventeenth or early eighteenth centuries the original mansion was divided. Safdar Jang, wazir of Ahmad Shah, occupied the structure nearest the fort in the mid-eighteenth century. He was the nephew and son-in-law of Sa'adat Khan, Nawab of Oudh, and succeeded to the Nawabi on his uncle's death in 1739.

Because of its location and size, this palace became the home of the emperor's most powerful subordinate during the seventeenth and eighteenth centuries. Dara Shikoh, Shahjahan's favorite son and chosen successor, constructed the palace in the space of four years (1639–43) at a cost of four hundred thousand rupees. Like his father, Dara exhibited a keen interest in architecture. He built a magnificent mansion in Agra with a large underground room that contained several tall mirrors imported from Aleppo. Shahjahan admired the structure and visited it several times.[211]

In 1662 Prince Mu'azzam, son and eventual successor of Aurangzeb, lived there. The mansion was damaged during the invasion of Nadir Shah and it may have been at this point that it was divided. In any event, Safdar Jang first occupied his half in 1744 and probably lived there until 1752, when his appointment as wazir ended. From 1755–7 the Rohilla chieftain Najib al-Daulah controlled Shahjahanabad as nominee of the Afghan invader Ahmed Shah Abdali and lived in the palace. Najib lost his place in 1757–8 but regained it following Abdali's victory at Panipat in 1761 and ruled the city from his old residence until 1770. In 1782 Najaf Quli Khan, an important amir under Shah Alam, lived in the palace, and in 1785 it

[209] Shah Nawaz Khan, *Ma'asir al-Umara*, 3 p. 676.
[210] Muhammad Salih, *'Amal-i Salih*, 3 p. 45; Shah Nawaz Khan, *Ma'asir al-Umara*, 3 pp. 460–77.
[211] Lahauri, *Badshahnamah*, 2 p. 474.

was said to have been the property of Asaf al-Daulah, Nawab of Oudh. On the British takeover in 1803 the mansion was turned into quarters for garrison officer and later it was converted into a munitions storehouse.[212]

2. The mansion of Dara Shikoh

Much less is known about this part of the original mansion. The Archeological Survey calls it Dara Shikoh's library and though that may have been one of its functions it almost certainly had other uses. The Survey errs in listing 'Ali Mardan Khan as its owner in 1639. In 1803 the mansion became the British Residence.[213]

3. The mansion of 'Ali Mardan Khan

'Ali Mardan Khan came to India in 1637, received the title of Amir al-Umara, and earned the reputation of a skillful builder. On his arrival Shahjahan gave him the mansion of Itiqad Khan in Agra, said to be the most artistic in the city. Shahjahan had admired the structure and Itiqad Khan had given it to him as pishkash. Later 'Ali Mardan built his own mansions in the new capital. In 1667, in anticipation of her arrival in the city, Jahan Ara Begum ordered that this mansion be cleaned and readied. Prince Azam Shah, third son of Aurangzeb, lived here during most of his father's reign. In 1713, on the succession of Farrukhsiyar, Sayyid Abd al-Allah Khan, elder of the two Sayyid brothers of Barha, obtained the title of Qutb al-Mulk and took over the mansion.[214]

4. The mansion of Lutfullah Khan

Lutfullah Khan was an amir of the early eighteenth century. In 1715 Qutb al-Mulk confiscated his mansion.[215]

---

[212] Muhammad Salih, *'Amal-i Salih*, 3 p. 118; 'Abd al-Hamid, *Badshah Namah*, 2 p. 333; Shah Nawaz Khan, *Ma'asir al-Umara*, 1 pp. 365–8; Manucci, *Storia do Mogor*, 2 p. 50; Forbes, *Oriental Memoirs*, 4 p. 260; Bashir al-Din Ahmad, *Waqiat*, 2 p. 292; Lady Maria Nugent, *A Journal From the Year 1811 to the Year 1815*, 2 vols. (London: n.p., 1839), 1 p. 416; Ghulam Muhammad Khan, "Travels in Upper Hindustan," fol. 38b. Sayyid Nur al-Din, "Ta'rikh-i Najib al-Daulah," fol. 15a; Y.M.M. Querbeuf, ed., *Lettres Edifantes and Curieuses Ecrites des Missions Etranqers*, 25 vols. (Paris: n.p, 1780–3), 4 p. 260.

[213] *List of Monuments*, 1 p. 186; Nugent, *Journal*, 2 p. 2.

[214] Shah Nawaz Khan, *Ma'asir al-Umara*, 1 pp. 180–2; 2 pp. 795–807; Ghulam Muhammad, "Travels," fol. 38b; "Dastur al-'Amal," Persian Manuscript Collection, Or. 1690, London, British Museum, fol. 162a; "Akhbarat-i Darbar-i Mu'allah," reel 3, Rabi I, ninth year.

[215] Shah Nawaz Khan, *Ma'asir al-Umara*, 3 pp. 177–8; Ghulam Muhammad, "Travels," fol. 38b.

5. The mansion of Majd al-Daulah

Abdul Majid Khan Majd al-Daulah, an amir under Muhammad Shah and Ahmad Shah, lived in this mansion in the early eighteenth century. His son, Abdul Ahad Majd al-Daulah, inherited the palace and played an important part in the political intrigues of the 1780s.[216]

6. The mansion of Shaista Khan

Shaista Khan, Amir al-Umara, held the post of wazir under Shahjahan and constructed this mansion opposite the Lahori gate of the palace-fortress. Asad Khan Asaf al-Daulah acquired the palace in the reign of Aurangzeb and his son, Zulfiqar Khan Amir al-Umara, inherited it. Zulfiqar Khan was killed in 1713 and Sayyid Hussain Ali Khan Amir al-Umara took over the place. In 1715 the Emperor Farrukhsiyar fiancée resided here before the wedding ceremony. Farrukhsiyar later gave the mansion to Mir Jumla and then to Samsam al-Daulah. In 1757 the Afghans dug it up in search of buried treasure.[217]

7. The mansion of Raushan al-Daulah

Zafar Khan, Raushan al-Daulah Rustam Jang, was an important amir during the reign of Muhammad Shah and one of the most prolific builders in the history of the city. He lived in this mansion during the early part of the eighteenth century and erected two large mosques in the central part of the city. He was also responsible for cleaning and repairing the Qadam Sharif. In 1773 a female relative of Shah Alam lived here.[218]

8. The mansion of Ghazi Ram

Ghazi Ram, one of Shahjahan's astrologers, is said to have built this palace during the early days of the city. The gateway still stands.[219]

---

[216] Ghulam Muhammad, "Travels," fol. 38b; "Delhi Newsletters of 1781," fols. 129a–31b, 34a.

[217] Shah Khan, *Ma'asir al-Umara*, 2 pp. 690–706; Khafi Khan, *Muntakhab al-Lubab*, ed. Maulavi Kabir al-Din Ahmed and Sir Wolseley Haig, 3 vols. (Calcutta: Asiatic Society of Bengal, 1869–1925), 2 p. 770; "Tarikh-i 'Alamgir Sani," Persian Manuscript Collection, Or. 1749, London, British Museum, fol. 100b.

[218] Shah Nawaz Khan, *Ma'asir al-Umara*, 2 pp 333–6; Ghulam Muhammad, "Travels," fol. 38b; Muhammad Baksh, "Tarikh-i . . Muhammad Shah," fols. 47b–56a.

[219] *List of Monuments*, 1 p. 158

9. The mansion of Habshi Khan

Sadi Miftah Habshi Khan, an amir under both Shahjahan and Aurangzeb, constructed this mansion near the Fathpuri mosque. Sidi Faulad Khan, kotwal under Muhammad Shah, repaired the place and lived there during the early eighteenth century.[220]

10. The mansion of Sa'adat Khan

This mansion, near the Kabuli gate, was one of the largest in the city. One source mentions six separate gateways. Sa'adat Khan Burhan al-Mulk, first Nawab of Oudh, resided here during the early part of Muhammad Shah's reign. He died on the eve of Nadir Shah's invasion and his house was looted and ransacked by the Persians.[221]

11. The mansion of Ismail Khan

Nothing is known of the Ismail Khan after whom this mansion was named. In 1772 Najaf Quli Khan barricaded himself here and defied the emperor.[222]

12. The mansion of Haider Quli Khan

Haidar Quli, an amir under Muhammad Shah, was appointed commander of the artillery by Sayyid Hussain Ali of Barha.[223]

13. The mansion of Shir Afghan Khan

The mansion was named after an amir of the early eighteenth century. The poet Gulshan was a member of Shir Afghan Khan's household and described this place in flowery phrases.[224]

14. The mansion of Sipahdar Khan

Sipahdar Khan, son of Aurangzeb's foster brother, achieved a rank of three thousand zat. His palace was on the periphery of the city near the Wardrobe Gate.[225]

---

[220] Ibid., 1 pp. 158, 159.
[221] Shah Nawaz Khan, *Ma'asir al-Umara*, 1 pp. 463–6; Ghulam Muhammad, "Travels," fol. 39a; *List of Monuments*, 1:170–1, 173–5. The archeological survey confuses this Nawab, the first, with his successor Safdar Jang.
[222] Sarkar, *Fall of the Mughal Empire*, 3 p. 53.
[223] List of Monuments, 1 p. 120.
[224] Ibid., 1 pp. 120–1; Gulshan, "Surat-i Hal," fols. 17b–19b.
[225] Ibid., 1 p. 97.

15. The mansion of Adinah Beg Khan

This noble was an amir under Muhammad Shah. His mansion lay on the road from the Lahori Gate to the Turkomani Gate.[226]

16. The mansion of Qamar al-Din Khan

Qamar al-Din Khan, Muhammad Shah's wazir from 1724 to 1748, lived in one of the largest and finest mansions of the city. Entitled Itimad al-Daulah II, Qamar al-Din was an indolent and indifferent administrator and the empire drifted during his tenure. In 1761, early in his second rule of the city, Najib al-Daulah resided here briefly. In 1788 one of the lieutenants of Ghulam Qadir, the Afghan General, occupied the place. After the British conquest it was converted into the customs house.[227]

17. The mansion of Muzzafar Khan

An amir under Jahangir and Shahjahan, Muzzafar Khan built this mansion near the Turkomani gate of the city. Muzzafar Khan was given the title Khan Jahan and the rank of five thousand zat, five thousand suwar by Shahjahan.[228]

18. The mansion of Mir Khan

Although Amir Khan, Umdat al-Mulk, was one of the confidants of Muhammad Shah, he never held an important government post. His father, Amir Khan I, had been governor of Lahore under Aurangzeb for twenty-two years. Mir Khan himself was a fascinating, accomplished man with great power over Muhammad Shah, and he attracted scholars, artists, poets, and musicians to his court.[229]

19. The mansion of Mir Hashim

Nothing is known of this noble beyond the tradition concerning his place of residence.[230]

[226] Ibid.
[227] Shah Nawaz Khan, *Ma'asir al-Umara*, 1 pp. 358–61; Ghulam Muhammad, "Travels," fol. 40a; *List of Monuments*, 1 pp. 81–2, 85; Sayyid Nur al-Din, "Ta'rikh-i Najib al-Daulah," fol. 75b; Nugent, *Journal*, 1 p. 417.
[228] Shah Nawaz Khan, *Ma'asir al-Umara*, 1 p. 758; *List of Monuments*, 1 p. 72; Bashir al-Din Ahmad, *Waqiat*, 2 p. 158; Lahauri, *Badshah Namah*, 1 p. 348.
[229] *List of Monuments*, 1 pp. 40–1, 53; Shah Nawaz Khan, *Ma'asir al-Umara*, 2 pp. 476–7; Dargah Quli Khan, "Risalah-i Salar Jang," fol. 116.
[230] *List of Monuments*, 1 p. 47.

20. *The mansion of Azam Khan*

Nawab Azam Khan, son of Nawab Amir Khan, lived in this mansion near the Jami' Masjid during the reign of Muhammad Shah.[231]

21. *Mitiya Mahal*

Although the builder of this mansion is unknown a number of important amirs lived here. It is said to have been the home of Shahjahan during the construction of the palace-fortress, and at one time it was the residence of Azizabadi Begum, wife of a Mughal prince. Later Bahadur Shah II conferred it on one of his grandsons.[232]

22. *The mansion of Bakhtawar Khan*

In addition to this palace near the Jami' Masjid, Bakhtawar Khan constructed a caravansarai outside the walls of the city. He also wrote *Mir'at al-'Alam*, a history of the first ten years of Aurangzeb's reign.[233]

23. *The mansion of Ahmad 'Ali Khan*

Nothing is known of the original builder beyond his name.[234]

24. *The mansion of Khan Dauran*

Khan Dauran Khan, wazir under Muhammad Shah, lived in this palace near the Jami' Masjid. Persian soldiers resided here during Nadir Shah's occupation of the city in 1739.[235]

25. *The mansion of Sarbuland Khan*

Sarbuland Khan Nawab Mubariz al-Mulk was Governor of both Patna and Gujarat, under Farrukhsiyar and Muhammad Shah respectively. Relieved of the latter post in 1730 and ordered back to Shahjahanabad, he shut himself in his mansion to avoid the hounding of creditors.[236]

---

[231] Ibid., 1 p. 47.
[232] Ibid.
[233] Ibid., 1 p. 47; Bakhtawar Khan, "Mirat al-Alam," fols. 252a–3b.
[234] Ibid., 1 p. 46.
[235] Shah Nawaz Khan, *Ma'asir al-Umara*, 1 pp. 819–25; Bashir al-Din Ahmad, *Waqiat*, 2 p. 142; *List of Monuments*, 1 p. 45; Fraser, *Nadir Shah*, p. 182.
[236] Fraser, *Nadir Shah*, p. 185; Shah Nawaz Khan, *Ma'asir al-Umara*, 3 pp. 801–6.

26. The mansion of Ustad Hamid

Ustad Hamid, one of the master builders of the palace-fortress, constructed this home in a lane near the Jami' Masjid.[237]

27. The mansion of Shahji

Although the original builder of this mansion is unknown, it is said that Shahji, Nawab Shahdi Khan, lived here during the late eighteenth century. A house in such a choice spot, however, must have been constructed in the seventeenth or early eighteenth centuries.[238]

28. The mansion of Sa'adullah Khan/Ghazi al-Din Khan

This palace was one of the finest in the city. Sa'adullah Khan, an experienced builder, supervised construction of the Jami' Masjid and laid out the square before the Akbarabadi Gate of the fort. In 1772 Nizam al-Mulk, son of Ghazi al-Din Khan I, stayed here during a visit to the city. In 1729 Nizam al-Mulk had his mansion ransacked and in 1788 Ghulam Qadir alighted at the mansion of Ghazi al-Din Khan near the palace-fortress. All of this suggests that the mansion passed from Sa'adullah Khan to Nizam al-Mulk and on to his son and grandson, Ghazi al-Din Khan II and III.[239]

29. Fathpuri Masjid

Fathpuri Begum, wife of Shahjahan, built this mosque at the western end of Chandni Chawk in 1650.[240]

30. Akbarabadi Masjid

Akbarabadi Begum, wife of Shahjahan, built this mosque in 1650 in Faiz Bazar.[241]

31. Sirhindi Masjid

Sirhindi Begum, wife of Shahjahan, built this mosque just outside the Lahori gate of the city in 1650.[242]

[237] *List of Monuments*, 1 p. 141; Muhammad Waris, "Padshah Namah," fol. 401.
[238] *List of Monuments*, 1 p. 133.
[239] Ashob, "Tarikh-i Muhammad Shah," fol. 129a; Ghulam Muhammad, "Travels," fol. 38a; Manucci, *Storia do Mogor*, 1 p. 229; Shah Nawaz Khan, *Ma'asir al-Umara*, 2 pp. 141–9, 847–56, 3 pp. 837, 848.
[240] Muhammad Salih, *'Amal-i Salih*, 3 p. 48.
[241] Ibid., 3 pp. 48–9.
[242] Sayyid Ahmad Khan, *Asar*, p. 287.

32. Aurangabadi Masjid

Aurangabadi Begum, wife of Aurangzeb, built this mosque near the Lahori gate of the city in 1703.[243]

33. Zinat al-Masajid

Zinat al-Nisa Begum, daughter of Aurangzeb, built this mosque in 1707. It is located south of the palace-fortress on the bank of the Jamuna.[244]

34. Sonhari Masjid

Raushan al-Daulah Zafar Khan built this mosque near the Kotwali Chabutra in 1721.[245]

35. Masjid of Sharif al-Daulah

Sharif al-Daulah Bahadur built this mosque in Dariba Bazar, just off Chandni Chawk, in 1722.[246]

36. Fakr al-Masajid

Fakr al-Nisa Khanum, wife of Nawab Shuja'at Khan, built this mosque near the Kashmiri Gate of the city in 1728.[247]

37. Jami' Masjid

Shahjahan built this mosque near the middle of the city during the years 1650-56.[248]

---

[243] Ibid., p. 299; *List of Monuments*, 1 p. 170.
[244] Sayyid Ahmad Khan, *Asar*, p. 300; *List of Monuments*, 1 p. 31.
[245] Sayyid Ahmad Khan, *Asar*, p. 309.
[246] Ibid.
[247] Ibid., p. 322–5.
[248] Muhammad Salih, *'Amal-i Salih*, 3 p. 52; Sayyid Ahmad Khan, pp. 272–7; Muhammad Waris, "Padshah Namah," fol. 513b–17b.

3

Society

To understand the structure of society in Shahjahanabad it is necessary to reexamine the metaphors of sovereign city as mansion and patrimonial-bureaucratic empire as household. The emperor tried to organize urban society on the model of the patriarchal household, attempting to establish in the city the personal control and intimacy which he could not manage in the empire at large. The inhabitants of Shahjahanabad interacted with one another like persons in the household of an extended family. Collateral and cadet branches of the main family might live in outbuildings at some remove from the great house, but all inhabitants of the city were thought to be related, however tenuously, to the great patriarch and to be part of the same household. For the city at large the paradigm was the palace-fortress. The structure of society in the imperial residence, replicated on a smaller scale in the mansions of princes and great amirs, set the pattern for the city as a whole.

Elite quarter

The palaces and mansions of the great men were the central institutions of Shahjahanabad. The glue that held the city together, these organizations typified and distinguished the sovereign city. In the ancient Near East the central urban institution was the temple, in classical Greece the market and temple, in medieval Europe the burg or faubourg and, in the countries of Islamic West Asia, the ethnic quarter.[1] In Mughal India the extended households of emperors, princes, and great amirs comprised a special kind of quarter, the elite quarter.

Indian cities had been divided into quarters from earliest times.

---

[1] Jean Comhaire and Werner J. Cahnman, *How Cities Grew: The Historical Sociology of Cities* (Madison, N.J.: Florham Park Press, 1959), pp. 35–8.

According to the *Silpasastras*, Sanskrit texts on architecture and city planning, the cities of ancient Hindu India were composed of residential subdivisions called *gramas* or *padas*. Inhabited by people of the same caste, craft, profession, or tribe, these quarters were arranged in a pattern that depended on the size and function of the city.[2]

In the cities of Mughal India the quarter or *mahallah* was the major form of residental organization. Neighbors were "people of the mahallah" – persons who occupied an adjacent house or who attended the mosque of the mahallah[3] – and one of the first duties of a city magistrate was to see that the urban area was divided into mahallahs.[4] In Mughal cities there were caste/craft and elite mahallahs both.

Caste/craft mahallahs were headed by chiefs (*chaudhuris*) of caste councils (*panchayats*). Chiefs settled intramahallah quarrels, judged disputes over land and other property, and decided questions of ritual status. They negotiated taxes with city authorities, arranged security against both internal and external disturbances, and consulted with other chaudhuris on matters of common interest.[5] Mahallahs were surrounded by high walls and contained houses, shops and stalls where food, clothing, and other supplies were sold, wells and tanks for water, and resthouses for travellers. People gathered in mosques and temples to hear political announcements, celebrate marriages, and exchange gossip.[6]

The palaces and mansions of the great men constituted elite mahallahs. A mid-eighteenth-century historian wrote of Ahmadabad, the capital of the independent kingdom of Gujarat during the pre-Mughal period and a provincial headquarters under the Mughals:

> Since in the beginning the city was not greatly populated, each of the princes and nobles selected a place [*makan*] for his mansion [*hisar*] and the houses of their followers were built alongside. That place was called a quarter [purah] . . . Each purah was like a city . . . in all of them were traders, artisans, craftsmen, laborers, government servants, and soldiers, both Hindu and Muslim.[7]

---

[2] Examples of several patterns are given in Dutt, *Town Planning*, pp. 142–3.
[3] Charles Hamilton, trans., *The Hedaya or Guide: A Commentary on the Mussulman Laws*, 2nd edn (London: W.H. Allen and Co., 1870), p. 689; Baillie, *Digest of Moohummudan Law*, 1 p. 580.
[4] Abu al-Fazl, *A'in*, 1 p. 284; 'Ali Muhammad Khan, *Mir'at-i Ahmadi*, ed. Syed Nawab 'Ali, 2 vols. (Baroda, India: Oriental Institute, 1927–8), 1 p. 168.
[5] Pearson, *Merchants and Rulers*, pp. 123–4 and John F. Richards, *Mughal Administration in Golconda* (Oxford: Oxford University Press, 1975), pp. 185–7 show headmen dealing with the government and one another in Ahmadabad and Hyderabad.
[6] Descriptions of mahallahs erected in Burhanpur and Shahjahanabad can be found in 'Abd al-Baqi, *Ma'asir-i Rahimi*, 2 pp. 606–7 and Dargah Quli Khan, "Risalah-i Salar Jang," fol. 102b.
[7] 'Ali Muhammad Khan, *Mir'at-i Ahmadi Supplement*, pp. 11–12.

Another historian wrote of Shahjahanabad:

in the beginning when Shahjahanabad was first constructed there was no mahallah in which there was not the mansion of an Iranian amir and those mahallahs were known by the names of those amirs.[8]

Palace–fortress

The palace-fortress of the Mughal emperor contained a great many persons. The only one of its kind, this elite mahallah served as the model for princes and great amirs as they organized their households and built their mansions. The largest single group of men in the palace-fortress and the principal component of the imperial household were military men: cavalrymen and footsoldiers. *Ahadis* (single troopers) served as cavalrymen in the emperor's private bodyguard or as officials in the departments of the imperial household. They were paid directly by the emperor and attached to him personally. In 1648 there were about 7,000 ahadis in the imperial household.[9]

Another group of cavalrymen, *walashahis* (belonging to the king) or *mansabdaran-i khassa* (special officeholders), were found in the emperor's bodyguard. In 1719 there were 5,000–6,000 of these men in the imperial household.[10] Thus, in 1650 there were probably about 10,000 cavalrymen in the palace-fortress: 5,000 ahadis (the other 2,000 served as administrators and officials) and 5,000 walashahis. In 1681 the Emperor Aurangzeb had 10,000 cavalrymen in his bodyguard.[11]

Ahsham (attendants) included the military men who were neither mansabdars nor cavalrymen.[12] Like ahadis and walashahis, they were paid directly by the emperor, were members of the imperial household, and lived in the palace-fortress. In 1648 there were about 10,000 of these men (mostly artillerymen and musketeers) in Shahjahan's household.[13]

Cavalrymen did not live alone. Each was the center of a small group of three or four persons that included a wife, a groom, a personal servant,

---

[8] Shah Nawaz Khan, *Ma'asir al-Umara*, 3 p. 690. No one else has written about elite mahallahs in Mughal India. Jadunath Sarkar maintained that the mahallahs of Mughal cities were "self-contained and inhabited mainly by people of one profession or caste." *Mughal Administration*, 4th edn (Calcutta: M.C. Sarkar and Sons, 1952), p. 210. And H.K. Naqvi asserted that Shahjahanabad "seems to have had some craft-wise arrangement. Each set of people had separate wards." *Urban Centres*, p. 88.

[9] Lahauri, *Badshah Namah*, 2 p. 715.

[10] Khafi Khan, *Muntakhab al-Lubab*, 2 pp. 802–5.

[11] Muhammad Saqi, *Ma'asir-i 'Alamgiri*, p. 198.

[12] "Zawabit-i 'Alamgiri," Persian Manuscript Collection, Or. 1641, London, British Museum, fols. 58b–60b.

[13] Lahauri, *Badshah Namah*, 2 p. 715.

and perhaps a camel driver or general laborer.[14] These persons occupied small, mud, straw-thatched huts in the outer area of the palace-fortress or near the walls. Taking three as the size of the average entourage adds on additional 30,000 persons to the emperor's establishment.

The imperial household also included departments responsible for nonmilitary activities. State officials and records were housed in the palace-fortress along with the mints, treasuries, departments of weights and measures, and other central offices and departments. Workshops and storerooms were there and departments that looked after horses, elephants, and hunting leopards. The imperial establishment included carpenters, blacksmiths, leather-workers, diggers, fire-works makers, and axemen. There were musicians, dancing girls, poets, calligraphers, historians, and astrologers. In order to stock and man the covered bazaar that led from the Lahori gate of the fort to the square in front of the Nagar Khanah, the imperial household included merchants. In addition, there were the women and servants of the harem. This segment of the household numbered between 5,000 and 10,000 persons (2,000 of whom were ahadis) and seven thousand is the estimate here.

Thus, in 1650 the palace-fortress contained about 57,000 persons: 10,000 cavalrymen, 30,000 servants and dependants, 10,000 artillerymen and musketeers, and 7,000 family, servants, clerks, officials, and other nonmilitary persons. The percentage of cavalrymen here, about 18 percent, agrees with the statements of travellers that about 20–25 percent of the imperial household were horsemen.[15]

Princely and great amiri mansions

The mansions of the great men centered, organized, and held together their sectors of the city. Princes and great amirs were responsible for maintaining and supplying a certain number of well-armed, well-trained, and well-mounted cavalrymen and, as a result, the military was the largest single category in princely and great amiri households as well.

During the mid to late seventeenth century the title "amir" referred to any mansabdar with a zat rank of 1000 or above. "Great amir" (*amir-i ayan* or *amir-i 'azaam*), a further but less formal division, designated the highest ranking sixty or seventy amirs. None of the administrative manuals mentions a specific rank criterion for great amir, but in 1648 the

[14] See Fraser, *Nadir Shah*, pp. 154–5; Manucci, *Storia do Mogor*, 2 p. 69, fn. 78; Bernier, *Travels*, pp. 353, 380–1.
[15] Bernier, *Travels*, p. 381; Das, *Norris Embassy*, p. 266.

title seems to have been applied to the top sixty-nine amirs, those with zat ranks from 2500 to 7000.[16]

These great men were divided into two groups. The first group, *umara-i hazir-i rikab* (amirs in the presence of the [imperial] stirrup) or *umara-i hazir* (amirs of the [imperial] presence), was stationed at court. *Umara-i ta'inat* (amirs on duty) or *umara-i subahjat* (amirs of the provinces) were assigned elsewhere.[17] Princes and great amirs were divided about equally between the two groups and so in Shahjahanabad in 1650 there were probably about thirty-seven great men: two princes and thirty-five great amirs.[18]

In 1648 the average suwar rank of the four princes was 12,500 and of the sixty-nine great amirs 3100. The administrative manuals state that an official at court had to maintain only about 25 percent of the cavalrymen of his suwar rank.[19] Thus, the two princes included about 3,125 cavalrymen in each of their households and the thirty-five great amirs about 775. These horsemen, like those in the imperial household, had retinues of approximately three persons each. As a result, cavalrymen and their households totalled about 12,500 persons (3,125 horsemen and 9,375 retinue) in princely mansions and about 3,100 persons (775 horsemen and 2,325 retinue) in great amiri mansions.

Like the imperial palace-fortress, these mahallahs contained merchants, traders, moneylenders, grooms, cart-drivers, tent-pitchers, torchbearers, camel-drivers, elephant-men, blacksmiths, ironmongers, and surgeons.[20] Each household contained departments that cared for books, clothing, utensils, and weapons and, like the emperor, princes and great amirs supported poets, calligraphers, musicians, astrologers, and religious specialists. Here also were the women, servants, and guards of the harem.

On the assumption that cavalrymen comprised about 20 percent of these households, the number of persons who provided goods and services was 3,125 for princely mansions and 775 for great amiri mansions. Thus, the princely mansion held about 15,625 persons (3,125

---

[16] Lahauri, *Badshah Namah*, 1 p. 429; 2 pp. 717–25; 'Zawabit-i 'Alamgiri,'' fol. 16a; Sen, ed., *Travels of Thevenot and Careri*, p. 243.

[17] Muhammad Saqi, *Ma'asir-i 'Alamqiri*, pp. 163, 222; "Zawabit-i 'Alamgiri,'' fol. 31a.

[18] Francois Berner remarked that he never saw less than twenty-five of these men at court. *Travels*, p. 213.

[19] Lahauri, *Badshah Namah*, 2 p. 506; "Zawabit-i 'Alamgiri,'' fol. 31a; "Dastur al-'Amal-i 'Alamgiri,'' Persian Manuscript Collection, Add. 6599, British Museum, fols. 133b, 185a.

[20] See the description of Dara Shikoh's entourage in 1658. Manucci, *Storia do Mogor*, 1 p. 254. Norris gives a similar account of the household of Asad Khan, Aurangzeb's wazir, in 1701. Das, *Norris Embassy*, p. 266.

horsemen, 9,375 servants and dependants of horsemen, and 3,125 support persons, retinue, and harem) and the great amiri mansion about 3,875 persons (775 horsemen, 2,325 servants and dependants of horsemen, and 775 support perons, retinue, and harem).

Social structure in elite quarters

The structure of society in the elite mahallahs of Shahjahanabad was like that in the extended family of a patriarchal household. The emperor stood as father to the persons in the palace-fortress, binding them to him and to one another as fellow members of one great family. Princes and great amirs established similar relationships with the persons of their households, replicating on a lesser scale in their mansions the more elaborate structure of the palace-fortress.

This form of interpersonal exchange, called patron-client by most scholars, characterized a good many premodern civilizations. In these societies great men offered peasants and townspeople economic aid and protection in return for respect, loyalty, praise, and support. These were relationships between persons who were socially, politically, or economically superior and their inferiors. The patron-client tie was dyadic, vertical, and many-stranded; it was one-to-one and encompassed a variety of interactions. Since the relationship was informal and personal, without explicitly stated rights and obligations, there were in many societies ceremonies which validated and reinforced it, masking its asymmetrical character and giving clients a kind of ritual compensation.[21]

Although our knowledge of rural society in North India during the Mughal period is sketchy, there is some evidence that patron-client interactions constituted, in addition to caste and kinship, a third kind of social institution. In a document of the late seventeenth century we find, in what was probably a typical village, three groups of taxpayers: a small group of rich persons who were zamindars, moneylenders, or grain merchants (7 percent); a second group of peasants who tilled relatively large amounts of land (19 percent); and a third group of peasants who worked smallish plots (74 percent).[22]

The land-controlling peasants dominated village society and were served by artisans, landless laborers (tanners, scavengers, and other low-caste persons), and servants. Some artisans worked by the job, were paid in cash or in kind, and had no enduring relationships with their

---

[21] Eric Wolfe, *Peasants* (Englewood Cliffs, N.J.: Prentice-Hall, 1966), pp. 52–3, 86–9; Jan Bremen, *Patronage and Exploitation: Changing Agrarian Relations in South Gujarat, India* (Berkeley, Los Angeles, and London: University of California Press, 1974), pp. 18–20.

[22] Habib, *Agrarian System*, p. 120.

employers: weavers, potters, dyers, goldsmiths, and blacksmiths, for example. But other servants and artisans – barbers, watercarriers, carpenters, sweepers, and washermen – seem to have established longer-term, patron-client-like relationships. Clients were members of peasant households and received protection and support at appropriate times.[23]

In addition, patron-client ties were likely forged between the vast majority of poor peasants and the zamindars and headmen who controlled the land in the village and occupied the posts of power. These intravillage alliances supported patrons in their drive for influence and position both within the village and outside. There is also evidence that zamindars and headmen sought patrons in the surrounding society, forming ties with the rulers of the little kingdoms nearby.[24]

In India the patron-client relationship was expressed in the idiom of kinship. According to a recent study, the tendency in Bengal, and probably in all of North India, was to reach out and include as kin all of the people with whom one had solidarity relationships.[25] Thus, in North Indian villages inhabitants tended to address one another, regardless of caste or relationship, in kinship terms. The village was understood to be one great extended family.[26] In Bengal, all of the people attached to a single household were considered part of "one's own group." Not only were members of the master's family included but the cook, barber, washerman, and sweeper as well. These servants called the master and his wife mother and father and were considered part of the household.[27]

In the households of emperors, princes, and great amirs a number of

[23] Ibid., pp. 114–81; Siddiqi, *Land Revenue Administration*, pp. 18–19; Tom G. Kessinger, *Vilayatpur: 1848–1968* (Berkeley, Los Angeles, and London: University of California Press, 1974), pp. 54–90; B.R. Grover, "An Integrated Pattern of Commercial Life in the Rural Society of North India during the 17th–18th Centuries," *Proceedings: Indian Historical Records Commission* 37 (1966) pp. 125, 130. Raychaudhuri characterized these interactions during the Mughal period as patron-client. See Tapan Raychaudhuri and Irfan Habib, ed. *The Cambridge Economic History of India*, 2 vols. (Cambridge: Cambridge University Press, 1982), 1 pp. 279–80. A similar set of relationships appears to have existed between land-controlling peasants and lesser cultivators in Delhi and Awadh in the late eighteenth century. See C.A. Bayly, *Rulers, Townsmen, and Bazars: North Indian Society in the Age of British Expansion, 1780–1870* (Cambridge: Cambridge University Press, 1983), pp. 42–4.

[24] See Eric Miller, "Caste and Territory in Malabar," *American Anthropologist* 56 (1954) pp. 410–20; Bernard S. Cohn, "Political Systems in Eighteenth Century India: The Banaras Region," *Journal of the American Oriental Society* 82 (1962) pp. 312–20.

[25] Ronald B. Inden and Ralph W. Nicohlas, *Kinship in Bengali Culture* (Chicago and London: University of Chicago Press, 1977), p. 93.

[26] Harold A. Gould, "The Hindu Jajmani System: A Case of Economic Particularism," *Southwestern Journal of Anthropology*, 14 (Winter, 1958) pp. 34–5; William L. Rowe, "Changing Rural Class Structure and the Jajmani System," *Human Organization* 22 (1963) p. 42; Stanley A. Freed, "Fictive Kinship in a North Indian Village," *Ethnology* 2 (1963) pp. 86–103.

[27] Inden and Nicholas, *Kinship in Bengali Culture*, pp. 32–4, 87–93.

lower-ranking mansabdars were related. Fathers and sons, uncles and nephews, brothers and cousins, these were men who had chosen to follow a common patron. Their preexisting ties of blood reinforced the vertical patron-client bonds and served to strengthen the sense of family among the members of the great household.[28]

Public ritual

Patron-client ties were often strengthened, renewed, and reaffirmed in public ceremonies. Public rituals reinvigorated these relationships and served to sanctify and validate the social order. Such ceremonies not only reflected and exemplified the structure of society but shaped and ordered it as well.[29] They were active as well as passive agents. Public rituals were solemn spectacles, marked by a sense of dignity and occasion and characterized by a precise observance of rules and regulations.

In Mughal India the ritual that most clearly symbolized the social order and was most efficacious in strengthening the patron-client ties that ran through the social hierarchy was that at the imperial court.[30] Although princes and great amirs held court in their own mansions, it was the daily ritual in the imperial palace-fortress that sustained and validated the structure of society in the city and in the empire at large.

All Mughal mansabdars were required to attend, at regular and specified intervals, the *darbar* (court) of the emperor. A'in 9 of Book 2 of the *A'in-i Akbari* established a schedule for the staffing of the public ritual which brought the entire corps of officeholders to court over a two- to three-year period. In addition, individual mansabdars had to return for changes of assignment, for promotion, and, if possible, for the celebrations on New Year's Day, 'Id, and the emperor's birthday.

[28] John F. Richards, "Norms of Comportment Among Imperial Mughal Officers," in Barbara D. Metcalfe, ed., *Moral Conduct and Authority: The Place of Adab in South Asian Islam* (Berkeley and London: University of California Press, 1984), p. 255–89.

[29] For a discussion of the shaping role of courtly ritual in a premodern Asian state see Clifford Geertz, *Neqara: The Theater State in Bali* (Princeton, N.J.: Princeton University Press, 1980), pp. 13–14, 104–5.

[30] Several scholars have touched on the topic of patron-client relationships during the Mughal period. Peter Hardy has mentioned the use of the extended patrimonial household by Mughal rulers. John Richards has put forward a theory about patron-client-like ties between Mughal emperors and amirs and between amirs and lower-ranking mansabdars; and Norman Ziegler has described patron-client relationships between Rajput rulers and nobles and between Rajput nobles and Mughal emperors. See Peter Hardy, *The Muslims of British India* (Cambridge: Cambridge University Press, 1972), pp. 12–14; Richards, "Norms of Comportment;" and Norman P. Ziegler, "Some Notes on Rajput Loyalties During the Mughal period," in J.F. Richards, ed., *Kingship and Authority in South Asia*, pp. 225–6. Marshall Hodgson has also argued that the mansions of nobles dominated the cities of West Asia during the tenth through the eighteenth centuries. *Venture*, 2 pp. 108–12.

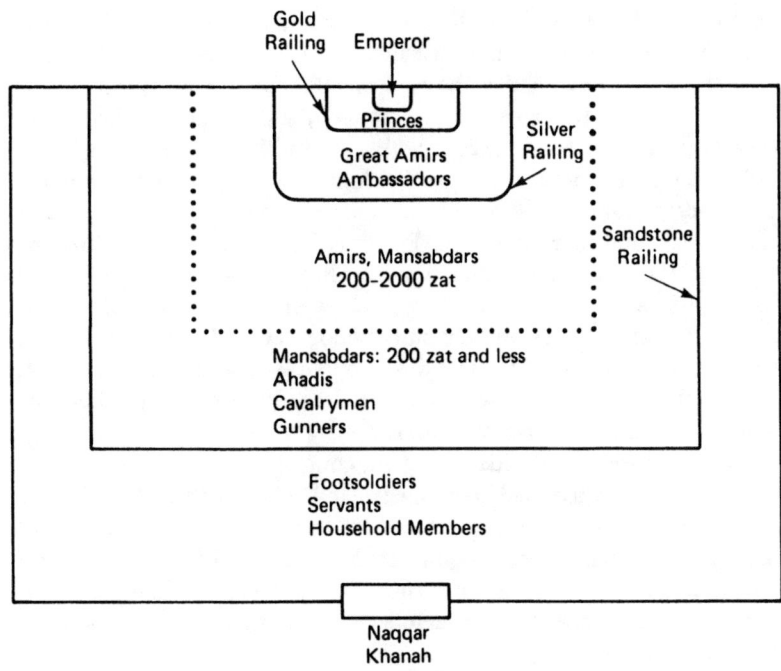

Figure 1 Hall of Ordinary Audience.

The Mughal emperor spent his entire day in a series of public audiences or rituals designed, in part at least, to fashion the disparate parts of the empire into a single harmonious whole. For Shahjahan, as for the other emperors, the day began in the *Jharoka-i Darshan* (Balcony of Audience). In Shahjahanabad this delicately carved structure hung from the eastern wall of the palace-fortress, overlooking a sandy beach at the edge of the river Jamuna. Every morning the emperor showed himself to his subjects (gave darshan), accepted petitions, inspected horses and elephants, and reviewed the contingents of mansabdars. Sitting darshan – bestowing the benefit of his presence – was a Hindu custom that each Mughal emperor followed. Any person, no matter his wealth, status or religion, could participate in this ritual. In this way the Mughal emperors reached out to the meanest and poorest of their subjects, especially the Hindus, enfolding them into the great household that was the empire.[31]

After his stint in the Jharoka-i Darshan the emperor moved to the Hall

[31] Lahori, *Badshahnamah*, 1 pp. 143–4; Muhammad Salih, *'Amal-i Salih*, 1 pp. 242–3; Chandar Bhan, "Chahar Chaman," fols. 9–10.

of Ordinary Audience. In Shahjahanabad and in similar halls in Agra and Lahore, he sat in an elevated balcony five or six feet above the floor. Located at the closed end of the hall, this balcony, called the Seat of the Shadow of God, was covered by a canopy, supported by four marble pillars, and decorated at the back with a beautiful mosaic of colored tiles. Below, a railing of gold about five feet high enclosed a small semicircular area reserved for imperial princes (see figure 1). A chair for the emperor's favorite son and heir-apparent – Prince Salim (later Shahjahan) during Jahangir's reign and Dara Shikoh under Shahjahan – stood here. Fifteen feet beyond a five-foot-high railing of silver encircled a somewhat larger area where great amirs, foreign ambassadors, and other visitors of note stood. The remainder of the hall was restricted to mansabdars with ranks from 200 to 2000 zat. Here also rich merchants from Iraq, Khorasan, Rum, Syria, China, Turkistan, and Europe waited for the opportunity to display their wares. Outside lay a great courtyard surrounded by a high wall in which porticos had been constructed. The courtyard was divided in two by a railing of red sandstone. The area closest to the hall was set aside for ahadis, musketeers, gunners, horsemen of amirs, and mansabdars of 200 zat or less. The outer ring of the courtyard held footsoldiers, servants, retainers, and other members of imperial, princely, and great amiri households.

In the Hall of Ordinary Audience the emperor dealt with the routine details of government. He read reports, received ambassadors, and admitted mansabdars to imperial service. He also conferred titles, granted increases in rank, assigned stipends to deserving men, awarded ceremonial robes (*khil'ats*), and presented gifts of money, horses, elephants, and jewels. The ritual here symbolized the emperor's role as head of state. All officials had a place in this hall and all participated in the ceremony. No one was excluded from the great household.[32]

Having finished the ceremony in the Hall of Ordinary Audience, Shahjahan immediately retired to the Hall of Special Audience. Here the Emperor dealt with the confidential affairs of state. The vakil and wazir presented delicate matters which could not be discussed in public and the diwans gave an overview of the military and administrative personnel and the finances. Here also the princes and great amirs had an opportunity to talk directly with the emperor while he often drafted orders in his own handwriting. In the Hall of Special Audience the emperor inspected the productions of his karkhanahs: jewelry, gold and silver work, fine cloth, diamonds, manuscripts in Arabic and Persian, specimens of calligraphy,

---

[32] Lahauri, *Badshah Namah*, 1 pp. 221–2; Muhammad Salih, *'Amal-i Salih*, 1 p. 244; Chandar Bhan, "Chahar Chaman," fols. 11–23; Manucci, *Storia do Mogor*, 1 pp. 88–9.

swords, guns, and artillery. He examined maps and models of royal buildings. He attended to the debates of philosophers and the works of poets, looked at the works of painters, and interviewed physicians and astronomers. He watched gladiators, boxers, and wrestlers and listened to singers. In the ceremonial in the Hall of Special Audience the emperor forged close and intimate ties with the great men of state. He also brought within the compass of the great household the artistic, cultural, and intellectual specialists of the day.[33]

The *Shah Burj* (King's Tower) or *Khilvat Gah* (Private Place) was the most private audience chamber of all. Here the most delicate and sensitive of state matters were discussed with the emperor's closest confidants. The emperor established a close circle of friends that he could count on for advice and help.[34]

Attending court was an arduous task that required great concentration. A fifteenth-century writer on ethics observed: "The companionship of princes has been compared to entering a conflagration or associating with a tiger."[35] Under the Mughals there were a number of rules about how to behave in court. Called "regulations of the presence" (*zawabit-i huzur*), these emphasized the gravity and dignity of the ritual and the paramount role of the emperor as provider of order, peace, and security. All petitioners were required to signify submission by placing their palms first on the ground and then on their foreheads. During Akbar's time and later some persons prostrated themselves on the floor but this was considered blasphemous because it mimicked the posture of prayer. During the audience itself all persons had to stand in silence before the balcony. Petitions, reports, and gifts were handed to an official, never directly to the emperor.[36]

A great amir who had been away campaigning violated several rules of court at Aurangzeb's camp in the Deccan. The Emperor remarked:

How can it be that servants brought up in the household would unlearn etiquette by reason of their going away from court? Evidently the Khan's eyesight has been affected.[37]

He ordered the man to wear eyeglasses to court for three days.

It was vitally important that a Mughal mansabdar attend the public ritual. To be excluded was to be denied access to riches, position, fame, and, in a certain sense, to have one's very existence put in doubt. Only by

---

[33] Lahori, *Badshah Namah*, 1 pp. 148–9; Chandar Bhan, "Chahar Chaman," fols. 23–32.
[34] Chandar Bhan, "Chahar Chaman," fols. 39–42.
[35] W.F. Thompson, *A Practical Philosophy of the Muhammadan People, A Translation of the Akhlak-i-Jalaly* (London: Oriental Translation Fund, 1839), p. 418.
[36] Abu al-Fazl, *A'in*, 1 pp. 155–7.
[37] Hamid al-Din, *Akham-i 'Alamgiri*, p. 84.

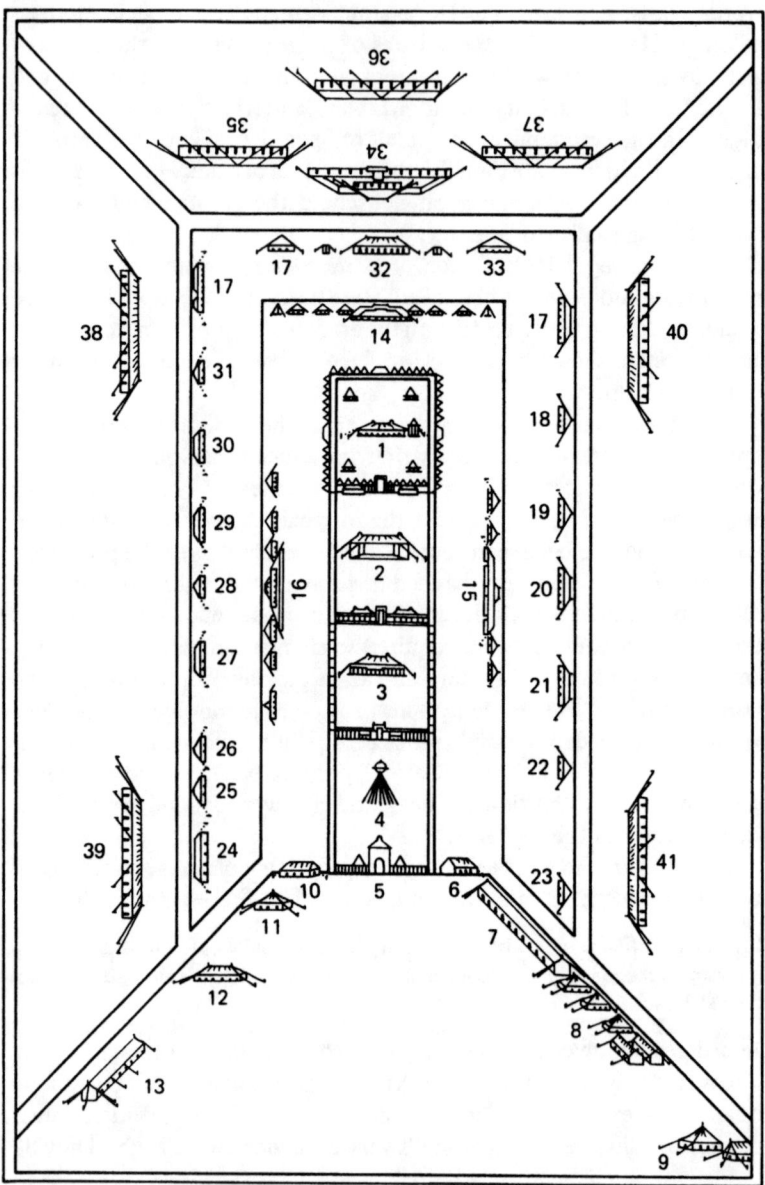

Figure 2   The Emperor's establishment in the imperial camp (source: Abu al-Fazl, *A'in*, 1 p. 336 on facing plate I).

Imperial household on tour

1. The imperial harem (*shabistan-i iqbal*). At the right side is the *do-ashiyana manzil* (two-storied structure).
2. Open space with canopy (*shamyana*) which functioned as the Hall of Special Audience (*Diwan-i 'Khas*).
3. Hall of Ordinary Audience (*Diwan-i 'Am*).
4. The great camp light (*akas diya*).
5. The Naqqar Khanah (*Drum Room*).
6. The house where the saddles were kept (*zin khanah*).
7. The imperial stables (*istabal*).
8. Tents of the superintendents and overseers of the stables.
9. Tents of the clerk of the elephant stables.
10. The imperal office (*daftar*).
11. Tent for palkis and carts.
12. Artillery tent (*top-khanah*).
13. Tent where the hunting leopards were kept (*chila-khanah*).
14. The tents of Maryam Makani (Akbar's mother), Gul Badan Begam (Humayun's sister) and Prince Danyal.
15. The tents of Sultan Salim (Jahangir) to the right of the harem.
16. The tents of Sultan Murad to the left of the harem.
17. Store rooms and workshops (*buyutat*).
18. Tent for keeping basins (*aftabchi khanah*).
19. Tent for perfumes (*khushbui-khanah*).
20. Tent for storing mattress (*toshak khanah*).
21. Tent for the tailors, etc.
22. Wardrobe (*kurkyaraq khanah*).
23. Tent for the lamps, candles, oil (*chiragh-khanah*).
24. Tents for keeping fresh Ganges water (*abdar khanah*).
25. Tent for making sharbat and other drinks.
26. Tent for storing pan leaves.
27. Tent for storing fruit (*mewa khanah*).
28. Tent for the imperial plates (*rikab khanah*).
29. Imperial kitchen (*matbakh*).
30. Imperial bakery (*nanba khanah*).
31. Storeroom for spices (*hawej khanah*).
32. The imperial guard.
33. The arsenal (*qur khanah*).
34. Women's apartments.
35–41. Guard houses.
Source: Abu al-Fazl, *A'in*, ed. Blochmann, 1 pp. 41–3, 45, 50–1, 101.

regularly appearing in the daily audience could a mansabdar reaffirm his loyalty and devotion and have his place in the social hierarchy validated and legitimized. A Muslim historian of the late eighteenth century, writing of the decline of Bengal under the British, noted the importance of the public ritual.

The fifth cause consists in the difference betwixt the manner in which the English in office appear in public and that which it has been at all times customary to hold a durbar in this country. [Indian sovereigns] ... appeared publically in all their pomp, grandeur, and glory. They were surrounded at some distance by their ministers and officers, and they gave a general audience.... the English Gentlemen.... appear seldom in public audiences and whenever they come to appear at all, it is to betray extreme uneasiness, impatience, and anger.... Hence it follows naturally that they must be in the dark with respect to the real state of the country, and the circumstances of the subjects; and hence multitudes of people remain deprived of the sight of their rulers, and never see anything of that benignity and that munificence which might be expected from people that now sit on the throne of kings and figure as representatives of Emperors.[38]

The ceremonial in the audience halls of the imperial palace-fortress served to strengthen, energize, and sustain the structure of Mughal rule, daily reaffirming and validating the ordered arrangement of Mughal society. The care with which categories of persons were distinguished, the effort made to include all groups of people, and the attempts to ensure that everyone spoke and acted correctly suggested that the ritual was much more than a gaudy charade. For important sessions the emperor ordered the household astrologers to cast charts. The emperor was the sun, the great amirs the planets, and the lesser mansabdars the minor heavenly bodies. The whole audience was designed to remind those present that the king was the center not just of the household and the empire but of the universe itself and that any threat to his position would shake the very foundations of the state.

The ritual in the public audience halls of princely and great amiri mansions was a pared-down, simplified version of that in the palace-fortress. For princes and great amirs, as for the emperor, the daily audience was a time to conduct routine household business. Great men read reports, reviewed troops, received petitions, and listened to complaints. They exchanged gifts with members of their households and with others; giving khil'ats, money, horses, and rugs and receiving pishkash. The emperor kept a close watch over these ceremonies and the history of the period is filled with examples of great men adopting practices which infringed imperial prerogatives. No one but the emperor

---

[38] Seid Gholam Hussein Khan, *Seir Mutaqherin*, 3 pp. 199–200.

could hold court sitting in a balcony, organize elephant fights, confer titles, forcibly convert persons to Islam, require salutes, put seals on petitions, or be accompanied by drums.[39] Now that we understand the function of the public ritual these prohibitions seem rational responses to a threat to the integrity of the state rather than the hysterical symptoms of a despot's swollen pride.

Imperial camp

During the period 1556–1739 Mughal emperors spent nearly 40 percent of their time in camp, on tours of one year or more. The camp of the longer, larger expeditions – called *urdu-i humayun* (royal or imperial camp), *urdu-i mu'alla* (exalted or sublime camp), *mu'askar-i iqbal* (camp of good fortune), or *urdu-i zafar-qarin* (victorious camp) – was carefully organized.[40] The Emperor Akbar established the basic structure in the late sixteenth century and it retained that form, virtually unchanged, until the middle of the eighteenth century. Abu al-Fazl wrote:

a great many of the victorious troops became attached to the victorious stirrup in whatever direction an expedition might go. . . . on account of the people and the large number of military men, days might pass before a soldier could find his dwelling; how then could a stranger reach [his dwelling]? The world conqueror by his great wisdom invented a method [of encamping the army] and gave the troops repose and rest.[41]

Although figure 2, taken from the *A'in-i Akbari*, shows the layout of Akbar's establishment in the imperial camp, it is clear from the descriptions of Bernier and Careri that this basic arrangement held for the late seventeenth century as well.[42] A wall of cloth screens, six or seven feet high, surrounded an inner area that, like the private sector of the palace-fortress, was entered through a gate called the Naqqar-Khanah (no. 5). Here were the Halls of Ordinary and Special Audience (nos. 2 and 3) and living quarters for the women and children of the imperial harem

[39] Jahangir, *Tuzuk-i Jahangiri*, 1 p. 205.
[40] The first two phrases appear frequently in the histories of Shahjahan and Aurangzeb. For the third see Abu al-Fazl, *A'in*, ed. Blochmann, 1 p. 27. "Victorious camp" was a phrase found, for the most part, on coins. See Stanley Lane-Poole, *The Coins of the Mughal Emperors in the British Museum* (London: Trustees of the British Museum, 1892), pp. 19, 31; V.P. Roe, *Catalogue of the Coins in the Central Museum, Nagpur: Coins of the Mughal Emperors* (Bombay: Government of Maharashtra, 1969), p. 30; M.K. Husain, *Catalogue of the Coins of the Mughal Emperors* (Bombay: Government of Maharashtra, 1968), p. 2.
[41] Abu al-Fazl, *A'in*, ed. Blochmann, 1 p. 43.
[42] See Bernier, *Travels*, pp. 361–7; Sen, ed., *Thevenot and Careri*, pp. 219–21.

(no. 1). The tents that served as audience halls were furnished with red and gold tapestries and rich rugs.[43] On tour the emperor held court in the Hall of Ordinary Audience, reaffirming the patron-client ties between him and those amirs and mansabdars who had not been able to participate in the ceremonial at the palace-fortress.

The tents of the other members of the imperial family (nos. 14–16) were pitched outside this inner area. A high, bright red wall of screens, used only by the emperor, encircled the private quarters of the imperial household and notified the rest of the camp of the emperor's location.[44] Beyond the red wall were tents for the rest of the establishment. Like the public area of the palace-fortress, this piece of ground held tents for stables, records, treasuries, workshops, wardrobes, arsenals, and kitchens. Here also stood tents for artisans, laborers, servants, for storerooms (nos. 17–34) and for cavalrymen, footsoldiers, and artillerymen (nos. 35–41).

Merchants, traders, shopkeepers, and moneylenders were part of the imperial household on tour. Food, clothing, credit, and equipment were provided in the bazaars that lined the streets of the imperial establishment.[45] Around the entire complex, like the great enclosure of the palace-fortress, ran a final wall of screens. The area enclosed was extensive: one observer of the late eighteenth century estimated that the emperor's household in camp included 120 tents and had a circumference of $1\frac{1}{4}$ miles.[46]

The princes and great amirs at court accompanied the emperor on tour.[47] In the imperial camp princely and great amiri establishments were governed by strict rules. As in Shahjahanabad, a wide area separated their households from that of the emperor. The quarters of the great men faced the Hall of Public Audience, princes and great amirs pitching their tents nearby and to the right while amirs and other mansabdars were to the left and farther back.[48] Princely establishments could not cover more ground than the imperial complex,[49] and great amirs could not put up tents that

[43] For illustrations of the rich interiors see H. Knizova and J. Marek, *The Jenghiz Khan Miniatures* (London: Spring Books, 1963), pp. 17–18, plates 1 and 40.
[44] Abu al-Fazl, *A'in*, ed. Blochmann, 1 pp. 41, 50; Hamid al-Din, *Ahkam-i 'Alamgiri*, p. 22; Sen, ed., *Thevenot and Careri*, p. 217; Anand Ram, "Mir'at al-Istilah," fols. 203a–b.
[45] Manucci, *Storia do Mogor*, 1 p. 254; Bernier, *Travels*, p. 365.
[46] Seid Gholam Hussein Khan, *Seir al-Mutagherin*, 1 p. 25, fn. 32.
[47] "Zawabit-i 'Alamgiri," fol. 309a.
[48] Father Monserrate, *The Commentary of Father Monserrate*, S.J., trans. J.S. Hoyland and annotated S.N. Banerjee (London: Humphrey, Milford), 1922, pp. 75–6.
[49] Aurangzeb had the camp surveyor carefully check the dimensions of his son's establishments. Muhammad Saqi, *Ma'asir-i 'Alamgiri*, p. 373.

were taller than the emperor's.[50] Princes and great amirs had first claim, after the emperor, to the high ground of the site.[51]

The residential complexes of princes and great amirs had an inner area, cut off from the rest of the household by a wall of screens, which held the audience hall and living quarters. Outside was the public area where tents for cavalrymen, artisans, officials, records, and animals were pitched. Each prince or great amir maintained a separate bazaar staffed by client merchants.[52] Around the entire area ran a high wall of screens.[53]

Emperors, princes, and great amirs did not abandon their households when they went on tour. Rather, like patriarchs of extended families, they took their client populations with them, assuming responsibility for their welfare, and providing protection, support, and sustenance during the long absences. Such commitment underlines the strength of the patron-client ties in Shahjahanabad and the loyalty, warmth, and respect that characterized them.

Social structure in Shahjahanabad

To move from a description of social organization in elite households to a statement about social structure in the city at large it is necessary to estimate the number of persons in the palace-fortress and the great mansions. How many people were involved in this web of patron-client relationships? What proportion of the urban population did they represent?

To answer these questions one must look again at the imperial camp. Table 4 presents an estimate of its population in 1650. The figures in lines 1–3 are taken from the earlier discussion while those in line 4 pertain to another group of officeholders. These were the lower-ranking mansabdars who filled subordinate positions at court or in the households of princes and great amirs. In the Hall of Ordinary Audience they stood outside the silver railing but within the pillared enclosure.

The *Badshah Namah* lists 369 mansabdars in this category in 1648, men with zat ranks between 500 and 2000.[54] Like the great amirs, these men were divided about equally between the court and the provinces and had an average suwar rank of about 500. They also were required to muster only about 25 percent of their contingents for duty at court, and thus maintained an average of about 125 cavalrymen each. Each

[50] Manucci, *Storia do Mogor*, 2 p. 68.
[51] At one point the Amir al-Umara under Aurangzeb evicted a lower-ranking amir and took the upper slope for himself. Muhammad Saqi, *Ma'asir-i 'Alamgiri*, p. 475.
[52] Muhammad Saqi, *Ma'asir 'Alamgiri*, p. 332; Sen, ed., *Thevenot and Careri*, p. 218.
[53] Bernier, *Travels*, p. 366; Monserrate, *Commentary*, pp. 75–6.
[54] Lahauri, *Badshah Namah*, 2 pp. 725–52.

Table 4 *Population of the Imperial Camp in 1650*

Officeholder	No.	Cavalry	Others	Total (household)	Total (camp)
Emperor	1	10,000	47,000	57,000	57,000
Princes	2	3,125	12,500	15,625	31,250
Great amirs (2500–700 zat)	35	775	3,100	3,875	135,625
Amirs (500–2000 zat)	150	125	500	625	93,750
Totals	188	62,125	255,500	77,125	317,625

cavalryman had a retinue of about three persons. Laborers, servants, artisans, religious personnel, and the women, children, and servants of the harem filled the households of these mansabdars as well. Assuming that cavalrymen comprised about 20 percent of their establishments, each of these men would have had about 625 persons in this household (125 cavalrymen and 500 non-military persons).

Thus, in 1650, the imperial camp probably contained about 320,000 persons. Although this is a rough estimate, with an error of perhaps 10 to 20 percent on either side, it is buttressed by contemporary evidence. Two European observers reported 50,000–60,000 horsemen in Aurangzeb's camp in the late eighteenth century[55] and Careri estimated its circumference at thirty miles.[56] In addition, Francois Bernier estimated the population of Shahjahan's great camp at 300,000–400,000.[57]

The imperial camp had a substantial impact on Shahjahanabad. In the first place, it incorporated the administration of the city. In Akbar's camp there was a two-storied wooden structure with a jharoka next to the imperial harem. Here, as in the jharoka in the palace-fortress, the emperor dispensed darshan, inspected elephants, and received petitions from dissatisfied litigants.[58] The Hall of Ordinary Audience of the camp (no. 3 of figure 2), a large tent guarded by many men, stood just inside the entry gate to the imperial enclosure.[59] Its location here, as in the palace-fortress, indicated its nature. In both places the emperor dealt with the ordinary, every-day affairs of state. The Hall of Special Audience in Akbar's camp was situated deep within the imperial enclosure, near the imperial living quarters (no. 2 of figure 2). It was constructed of carpets, had an awning to protect it from sun and rain, and had doors and locks.[60]

[55] Manucci, *Storia do Mogor*, 2 p. 397; Sen, ed., *Thevenot and Careri*, p. 218.
[56] Sen, ed., *Thevenot and Careri*, p. 218.
[57] Bernier, *Travels*, pp. 380–1.
[58] Abu al-Fazl, *A'in*, 1 p. 56.
[59] See Bernier, *Travels*, p. 361 for its location under Aurangzeb.
[60] Abu al-Fazl, *A'in*, 1 p. 48.

Here, as in the palace-fortress, the emperor consulted with the important nobility on the confidential military, financial, and administrative affairs of state.

When the emperor was in residence, the capital was governed by household officials – those who remained with the emperor whether he was in camp or city. During the early 1650s, for example, Naubat Khan was both the kotwal of the city and the kotwal of the *urdu* (camp) or *urdu-i mu'allah* (auspicious camp).[61] And Anand Ram described a man from the emperor's household who held the *"kotwali* [city magistrateship] of the auspicious stirrup [of the emperor] and of dar al-khilafat Shahjahanabad."*[62] In addition, the *qazi* (judge) of the camp court was often the chief qazi (*qazi al-quzat*) of the realm.[63]

It appears that the household officials also took over the administration of the capital provinces. Delhi and Agra, for example, seem only to have had regular administrators when the emperor was absent. Thus, in 1637 Shahjahan left Agra for Lahore and appointed officers to the general superintendence (*harasat*) of the city, to the charge (*qila'dari*) of the palace-fortress, to the policing (*faujdari*) of both sides of the Jamuna, and to the magistrateship (*kotwali*) of the city.[64] In 1644 he made the same journey and agin appointed a new set of officials.[65] And, in 1650, before leaving Shahjahanabad he appointed Khaliullah Khan subahdar of the province and Mir Muhammad Sharif Bakshi and Waqi-Nawis.[66]

The imperial camp also disrupted the economic life of any city it touched. In 1630 a Dutch merchant at Burhanpur found it impossible to get his consignment of saltpeter until the imperial camp had taken its share and left.[67] In 1639 an English merchant at Agra complained that the king and his amirs had commandeered all available carts when they left the city, and in 1648 the Dutch agent in Shahjahanabad reported that the emperor had requisitioned so many carts and camels for his journey to Ajmir that there were not enough left for the English merchants.[68]

[61] M. Athar Ali, *The Apparatus of Empire: Awards, Ranks, Offices, and Titles of the Mughal Nobility (1574–1658)* (Delhi: Oxford University Press, 1985), nos. 5446, 5781, and 6191.
[62] Anand Ram, "Mirat al-Istilah," fol. 158b.
[63] Sameeruddin Siddiqi, "The Institution of the Qazi Under the Mughals," *Medieval India* 1 (1969) pp. 240–59.
[64] Lahauri, *Badshah Namah*, 2 p. 110.
[65] Ibid., 2 pp. 407–8.
[66] Athar Ali, *Apparatus*, nos. 5410–5412.
[67] "Orme Manuscripts," India Office Library, O.V. 329.1, fols. 26a–b.
[68] William Foster, *English Factories in India: 1637–41* (Oxford: Clareden Press, 1912), pp. 191–2; Director Joust Diericky to the Governor-General, 2 August 1648, *Transcripts and Translations of Dutch Records at the Hague: Letters from India. 1600–1699*. India Office Library, London, 16, 507, p. 9.

In 1648 Shahjahan moved his household and the princes, great amirs, and other court officials (in effect, the imperial camp) from Agra to Shahjahanabad. The effect was an immediate and drastic decline. The Jats, an unruly peasant group, increased their attacks on Agra soon after the departure of the Emperor.[69] This activity caused Aurangzeb in 1659 to erect the first wall ever to encircle the city.[70] In 1656 the English East India Company abandoned its factory and sometime later the Dutch appear to have followed suit.[71] In the late 1680s, according to a report received by the Raja of Jaipur, the Jats pillaged Akbar's tomb near the city and attacked the villages near the Taj Mahal.[72] Finally, the only contemporary account of the move – concerning its effect on the Agra Christians – suggests that the city suffered a considerable blow:

The bulk of the converts. . . were in the most abject poverty, earning a bare living by such occupations as the making of bangles or lacework, and always on the verge of famine. When the capital was removed from Agra, many of the more prosperous Christians left town, and the converts who remained were faced by a considerable amount of unemployment and a marked fall in the prices obtained for the articles they produced.[73]

By the early eighteenth century Agra had declined to the point where an historian of Aurangzeb's reign omitted its name from a list of the eight most important cities of the realm.[74]

The great camp contained the cavalry, soldiers, and officials of the imperial household and the establishments of princes, great amirs, and

---

[69] Orme Manuscripts, O.V. 329.1, fols. 26a–b.
[70] Muhammad Kazim, *'Alamgir Namah*, 1 pp. 423–5.
[71] William Foster, *The English Factories in India: 1655–60* (Oxford: Clarendon Press, 1921), p. 72. The last Dutch tomb in the city is dated 1679. E.A.H. Blunt, *A List of the Inscription on Christian Tombs and Tablets of Historical Interest in the United Provinces of Agra and Oudh.* (Allahabad: Government Press, U.P., 1911), p. 57.
[72] *A Descriptive List of the Vakil Reports Addressed to The Rulers of Jaipur* 1 (Persian) (Bikaner: Rajasthan State Archives, 1967), p. 20.
[73] Edward Maclagan, *The Jesuits and the Great Mughals* (London: Burns Oates and Washbourne Ltd, 1932), p. 279. The passage draws from the Annual Reports of 1675 and 1686.
[74] Bhimsen Burhanpuri, "Nuskha-i Dilkusha," Persian Manuscript Collection, Or. 23, London, British Museum, fol. 149b. The effect of the imperial court's departure on Agra has been controversial. Several scholars have argued that Agra remained a viable and bustling city after Shahjahan's departure. See Habib, *Agrarian System.* p. 76 and Nakvi, *Urban Centres*, p. 19. A close look at the evidence, however, suggests otherwise. The French travellers Bernier and Tavernier, the two sources cited by Habib, visited Agra in the early 1660s, some twelve to fifteen years after the move. (See Bernier, *Travels*, p. 284 and Tavernier, *Travels*, 1 p. 86.) Both men speak of Agra's superiority in terms of buildings rather than people. Bernier wrote:

But Agra, having been a favourite and more frequent abode of the kings of Hindoustan since the days of Ekbar, by whom it was built and named Akberabad, it surpasses Delhi in other mansabdars, and it had a major impact on the capital city. The relationship between the two settlements tends to support the population estimates (320,000 for the imperial camp and 400,000 for Shahjahanabad) and suggests that a substantial proportion of the city (probably about 75 percent) belonged to imperial, princely, and great amiri households.

For the people of Shahjahanabad social interaction took place in a hierarchy of households. The household of the Mughal emperor in the palace-fortress was the largest, and the structure of society there set the pattern for the rest of the city. The households of princes and great amirs in walled mansions around the city held a good many persons and served as neighborhood foci. Amirs and lower-ranking mansabdars maintained reduced establishments in smaller houses near the palace-fortress or the mansions of their patrons. These elite quarters contained the bulk of the urban population during the seventeenth and early eighteenth centuries, and the patron-client relationships between the great men and the persons of their households were an important aspect of the social organization of the city.

The structure of society in the city at large, however, was more than the sum of that in the individual great households. There was a sense in which the city itself was an extended family. This is best seen in the dual function of the ceremonies in the palace-fortress. The imperial rituals, to be sure, were intended to strengthen the patron-client ties between the emperor and those who lived in the palace-fortress but they had a larger purpose as well. They also served to mold the princes, great amirs, and other mansabdars into a great extended family whose members were the urban population and whose mansions was the city itself. Individual mansions and houses were to the city as rooms for the households of adult sons were to the patriarchal compound. The patron-client relationships between the emperor and the great men and between them and the members of their households bound the entire city together in a kind of vast extended family.

extent, in the multitude of residences belonging to Omrahs and Rajas, and of the good stone or brick houses inhabited by private individuals, and in the number and conveniency of its Karvan-serrahs."

It may well be that Agra contained more buildings and could quite comfortably house the emperor and the court when they chose to visit. But to suggest that a premodern state could support the continued existence of two cities, three to four hundred thousand persons apiece separated by scarcely ninety miles, oversteps the bounds of credibility.

4

Economy

The patrimonial-bureaucratic emperor intended the economy of the sovereign city to be an extension of his own household. Resources were to be managed and distributed as if the city were a great estate; there was to be no place for markets or independent economic agents. Goods were to be produced in household workshops and exchange was to take place between fellow clients within the precincts of the extended family. While this ideal was finally unattainable, the households of emperors, princes, great amirs, and other high-ranking mansabdars did dominate the economy of Shahjahanabad. They produced the bulk of the goods and services, controlled the process of exchange, and constituted the principal units of utilization or consumption.

Given the agrarian nature of the Mughal economy it is not surprising that little attention should have been devoted to economic activity in towns and cities.[1] It is equally unsurprising, in view of the source of most of the evidence, that the available studies should concentrate on the coastal cities.[2] While. these works are extremely useful, it is well to remember that they deal with atypical situations. The coastal centers were a distinct minority in the urban hierarchy of Mughal India. The towns and cities of the interior provided the great bulk of the urban population.

---

[1] For a general introduction to the economy of Mughal India see Habib and Raychaudhuri, ed., *The Cambridge Economic History of India*, vol. 1. See also Stephen P. Blake, "The Urban Economy in Premodern Muslim India: Shahjahanabad, 1639–1739," *Modern Asian Studies* 21: (1987) pp. 447–71 for a discussion of various approaches to premodern economic organization.

[2] See Pearson, *Merchants and Rulers*; Ashin Das Gupta, *Indian Merchants and the Decline of Surat: 1700–1750* (Wiesbaden: Franz SteinerVerlag, 1979); Balkrishna Govind Gokhale, *Surat in the Seventeenth Century: A Study in the Urban History of Premodern India*, Scandinavian Institute of Asian Monograph Series, no. 29 (London: Curzon Press, 1979).

Production

"A city may be defined as a place where artisans (*pisha-var*) of various kinds dwell."[3] This statement by Abu al-Fazl sums up the state of manufacturing in the cities of Mughal India. Nonagricultural production was, for the most part, handicraft production and the artisans, craftsmen, and workmen of Shahjahanabad turned out a wide variety of goods.

Urban artisans and craftsmen were divided into two groups. The first group consisted of those persons who maintained control over their product until it was sold in the market and included relatively well-to-do artisans who owned their equipment and produced luxury goods for a limited market as well as poorer artisans who produced ordinary goods for the larger market. The second group included those artisans who had no control over their goods. For these persons, the materials, in some cases the tools, and the final product remained the property of someone else.[4]

Although we have no way of ascertaining precisely how many artisans fell into one group or the other, the evidence seems to suggest, both for Shahjahanabad and the coastal cities, that there were very few independent artisans producing for the market. Most urban artisans seem to have worked with the materials and, in many cases, the equipment of someone else.

Artisans who worked under the putting-out system, for example, were not independent. The textile industry, the largest in the subcontinent, seems to have been organized largely on this basis. Merchants and brokers advanced cloth to weavers, specifying quality, quantity, and design. The finished product was collected, paid for, and shipped to the consumer and, in many cases, never reached the Indian marketplace.

In Shahjahanabad artisans, craftsmen, and service workers were organized in four ways. Goods and services were produced in karkhanahs of emperors, karkhanahs of princes and great amirs, merchant karkhanahs, and houses of independent craftsmen.

Imperial karkhanahs

Rulers and nobles maintained karkhanahs in seventeenth-century Iran, Fatimid Egypt (ninth and tenth centuries), and thirteenth- and

---

[3] Abu al-Fazl, *A'in*, ed. Blochmann, 2 p. 240.
[4] Irfan Habib, "Potentialities of Capitalistic Development in the Economy of Mughal India," *The Journal of Economic History* 29 (1969) p. 66; Ishwar Prakash, "Organization of Industrial Production in Urban Centres in India During the 17th Century with Special Reference to Textiles," in *Reading in Economic History*, ed. B.N. Ganguli (New Delhi: Asia Publishing House, 1964). p. 48.

fourteenth-century Delhi as well as in Mughal India.[5] Karkhanah
workers had very little control over their labor. Equipment and materials
were provided and designs and standards of workmanship were set.
Workmen, however, were highly valued and in Mughal India at least they
were relatively well paid.[6] The households of Mughal emperors contained many karkhanahs. Abu al-Fazl wrote that Akbar maintained over
one hundred and that each one "resembled a city or rather a small state."[7]
While this statement is exaggerated – a count of those actually described
in the *A'in* reveals the traditional thirty-six – it does suggest the scale and
importance of such workshops in the imperial household.[8]

Karkhanahs were places where work was done, and those in the
imperial household can be divided into three groups. The first consisted
of the workshops dedicated to the needs of the imperial family. Here were
stables for horses, elephants, cows, camels, and mules; storerooms for
sedan chairs, candle-sticks, utensils, and jewels; libraries; workshops that
produced carpets, goldwork, and jewelry; departments that cared for
widows and the harem; and, finally, kitchens and storerooms for grain,
fruit, pots and utensils.[9]

The second group turned out goods and services for a public beyond
the household. Here were departments for records, construction, and
laborers. Here also was the household mint which, along with the other
imperial mints, produced the specie for the empire. Karkhanahs for
swords, matchlocks, cannons, and ammunition contained weapons
manufactured in the household, bought in the bazaars, and received as
gifts.[10]

The third group of karkhanahs contained the gifts which the emperor
presented in the Hall of Ordinary Audience. Although cash, horses,
and precious jewels were sometimes given, Mughal emperors typically
presented ceremonial robes (*khil'ats*) to the participants in the public
ritual. The custom can be traced to the early Mongols, who gave robes to

---

[5] For Safavid Iran see Chapter 7 below. For Fatimid Egypt see *Encyclopaedia of Islam*, 2nd
edn., "Egypt," pp. 17–18; and for Delhi in the thirteenth and fourteenth centuries see
Shams Siraj Afif, *Ta'rikh-i Firuz Shahi*, ed. Maulavi Vilayat Husain (Calcutta: Asiatic
Society of Bengal, 1891), pp. 337–43.
[6] Tapan Raychaudhuri, "The State and The Economy: Mughal Empire," *Cambridge
Economic History of India*, 1 p. 178.
[7] Abu al-Fazl, *A'in*, ed. Blochmann, 1 p. 9.
[8] For a listing of the thirty-six karkhanahs see "Dastur al-'Amal-i 'Alamgiri," fol. 53b.
[9] Abu al-Fazl, *A'in*, ed. Blochmann, 1 pp. 43–5, 48–58, 67–72, 101–11, 127–53, 167–74;
"Dastur al-'Amal-i 'Alamgiri," fols. 54a–5b; "Zawabit-i 'Alamgiri," fols. 113b–4a;
Jagat Rai, "Farhang-i Kardani," fol. 25b; Bernier, *Travels*, p. 259; "Khilaq al-Siyaq,"
Persian Manuscript Collection, no. 314, National Archives of India, p. 96.
[10] Abu al-Fazl, *A'in*, 1 pp. 12–39, 118–27; Rai, "Farhang-i Kardani," fol. 25b; "Zawabit-i
'Alamgiri," fol. 134a; "Dastur al-'Amal-i 'Alamgiri," fols. 54a–5a.

their dependants, and probably came to the Mughals through the Timurids.[11] In 1576 Akbar gave the *amir-i haj* (noble in charge of the pilgrimage to Mecca) twelve thousand khil'ats to distribute in the holy city.[12]

Khil'ats were divided into three ranks. The lowest, given to ordinary mansabdars, were stored in the *khil'at khanah* (robe storehouse) and consisted of a turban, an overcoat, and a cummerbund.[13] Khil'ats of the second rank included an ornament for the turban and a belt in addition to the three basic pieces and were stored in the *toshak-khanah* (wardrobe). During the eighteenth century they were presented to great amirs with ranks from five thousand to seven thousand zat.[14] The highest-ranking khil'ats consisted of a half-sleeved coat in addition to the five previous pieces, were stored in the *toshak khanah-i khas* (special wardrobe), and were given to great amirs with ranks of seven thousand zat and above.[15] Highest of all, and reserved for intimate friends, were the robes which the emperor himself had worn.[16]

Princely and great amiri karkhanahs

In the households of princes and great amirs, as in the imperial household, mir samans or diwans exercised overall control, treasurers kept the cash, accountants watched collections and disbursements, supervisors maintained horsemen, and darogahs managed karkhanahs.[17]

Princely and great amiri karkhanahs can be divided into two groups. The first group included those workshops which provided for the immediate needs of the household. Here were stables for horses, elephants, and camels; rooms where books, perfumes, medicines, candles, and palanquins were repaired, classified, and stored; workshops for carpets, clothing, and goldwork; the accounting and record offices and

---

[11] William Rubruck, *The Journey of William of Rubruck to the Eastern Parts of the World: 1253–55*, trans. William Woodville Rockhill (London: Hakluyt Society, 1900), p. 207.
[12] Abu al-Fazl, *Akbar Namah*, 3 p. 192.
[13] Anand Ram, "Mir-at al-Istilah," fol. 124a; "Zawabit-i 'Alamgiri," fol. 134a.
[14] Anand Ram, "Mir'at al-Istilah," fol. 124a; "Zawabit-i, 'Alamgiri," fol. 134a; "Dastur al-'Amal-i 'Alamgiri," fol. 54a.
[15] Anand Ram, "Mur'at al-Istilah," fol. 124a.
[16] Ibid., fol. 124b; Manucci, *Storia do Mogor*, 2 p. 436.
[17] For karkhanahs in the households of Abu al-Fazl, Khwaja Abu al-Husan, Maqarrab Khan, Amir al-Umara Samsam al-Daulah, and Raushan al-Daulah see Shah Nawaz Khan, *Ma'asir al-Umara*, 2 p. 620, 3 p. 381; Lahauri, *Amal-i Salih*, 1 p. 455; "Ahwal-i Khan Dauran," fols. 156a–87a; and Ashob, "Tarikh-i Muhammad Shah," fols. 48a–b. See also Anand Ram, "Mir'at al-Istilah," fol. 117b; and Pelsaert, *Jahangir's India*, p. 55.

ιhe treasuries; storehouses for swords, matchlocks, cannons, and ammunition; and, finally, the kitchens and stores of water, food, and grain.[18]

The second group of karkhanahs produced, stored, and cared for the gifts which princes and great amirs presented in the Hall of Ordinary Audience and in the audience halls of their own mansions. During the public ritual in the palace-fortress, princes and great amirs offered the emperor pishkash – horses, jewels, guns, and carpets. In their own audience halls they presented their clients with khil'ats.[19] The giving of khil'ats and pishkash symbolized the intermediate position of the great men. They were both clients to emperors and patrons to the men of their households.

The karkhanahs of princes and great amirs were famous. A visitor to Shahjahanabad in the early part of the eighteenth century, overawed by the spectacle of Chandni Chawk, wrote: "the [shops] were of such fineness and goodness that they were not equalled by the karkhanahs of the amirs."[20] In 1648 the two princes, thirty-five great amirs, and high-ranking mansabdars controlled about 29 percent of state revenues while the emperor controlled about 14 percent.[21] Thus, the karkhanahs of princes, great amirs, and other mansabdars probably produced about twice as much as the imperial karkhanahs.

Merchant karkhanahs

In Mughal India there was a clear distinction between merchants and traders, on the one hand, and bankers (*sarrafs*) and moneylenders (*sahukars*) on the other. Moneylenders put out small sums to peasants, soliders, and traders while bankers accepted deposits, issued bills of exchange, and loaned large sums to officials and nobles. Bankers advanced money to merchants but did not, for the most part, engage in trading activities themselves. On the other hand, the great wholesale merchants, the most wealthy and powerful of the class, occasionally lent money to one another. In the usual course of business, however, they

---

[18] Ashob, "Tarikh-i Muhammad Shah," fol. 48b; "Ahwal-i Khan Dauran," fols. 161a–86b; "Bayaz-i Khushbui," fols. 5b–103b, 126b–39b.

[19] Shaikh Farid gave khil'ats to members of his household each year. Shah Nawaz Khan, *Ma'asir al-Umara*, 2 p. 639. Samsam al-Daulah Khan Dauran maintained a karkhanah for gift khil'ats (*dad-khil'ats*). "Ahwal-i Khan Dauran," fol. 164b. The Rajah of Jaipur also gave khil'ats to his clients. "Delhi Newslatter – 1779–82," fol. 206b.

[20] Nawab Dargah Quli Khan, "Risalah-i Salar Jang," fol. 89b.

[21] A. Jan Qaisar, "Distribution of the Revenue Resources of the Mughal Empire Among the Nobility," India History Congress, *Proceedings of the Twenty-Seventh Session* (Aligarh, Uttar Pradesh: n.p., 1967), pp. 237–43.

deposited their funds with bankers and stayed out of the moneylending business altogether.[22]

In addition to wealthy wholesale merchants, there seem to have been two other categories of traders in Mughal India. A group of smaller wholesale merchants, centered in revenue circle headquarters and city suburbs, supplied cloth and grain to periodic markets in villages and neighborhood markets in cities. The largest group, however, were the small retail merchants who worked directly from shops or stalls in towns and cities or carried goods from periodic market to periodic market in the countryside.

Merchants in Mughal India were organized on the basis of family and caste. The wholesale merchant houses maintained branches in several towns and cities. Junior traders ran these branches and lived together in establishments maintained by the firm, leaving wives and families at home. In towns and cities retail merchants of a particular good – grain, salt, cloth, or indigo – typically belonged to a single caste. And it was the caste council that handled social, ritual, political, and economic disputes. Merchants in Mughal India, unlike those in medieval Europe, did not form guilds that incorporated, established prices and conditions of trade, and negotiated with princes and kings for property rights and protection. The only organizations that were at all similar were the merchant councils of Ahmadabad in the sixteenth and seventeenth centuries and those of Benares in the late eighteenth and early nineteenth centuries. Although these included all urban merchants and settled some commercial disputes, they had nothing of the significance and power of medieval European guilds. Moreover, such associations do not seem to have spread to other parts of the subcontinent during the Mughal period. They were not, for example, found in Shahjahanabad or Surat during the late seventeenth and early eighteenth centuries.[23]

During the Mughal period the premier merchant group in North India seems to have been the Khattris, a Hindu caste of traders and administrators from the Punjab. This caste dominated commerce in Agra

---

[22] Irfan Habib, "Banking in Mughal India," in *Contributions to Indian Economic History* (Calcutta: F.K.L. Mukhopadhyay and Company, 1960), 1 pp. 18–19; Irfan Habib, "Usury in Medieval India," *Comparative Studies in Society and History* 6 (1963–4) p. 406.

[23] Pearson, *Merchants and Rulers*, pp. 123–4; Das Gupta, *Indian Merchants and the Decline of Surat*, p. 14; Ashin Das Gupta, "Indian Merchants and the Trade in the Indian Ocean, 1500–1700," in *Cambridge Economic History of India*, 1 pp. 407–33; Timberg, *Marwaris*, p. 5; C.A. Bayly, "Indian Merchants in a 'Traditional' Setting: Benares, 1780–1830," in Clive Dewey and A.G. Hopkins, ed., *The Imperial Impact: Studies in The Economic History of Africa and India* (University of London: Institute of Commonwealth Studies – Commonwealth Papers, no. 21, 1978), pp. 171–93.

and Lahore during the seventeenth century[24] and, along with certain Gujerati and Rajasthani merchants, controlled trade in Shahjahanabad as well. Although they worked mainly as household merchants and administrators for the emperors, princes, and great amirs, many of the Khattris managed to achieve a certain wealth and status. The most successful maintained substantial households in large mansions containing one or two camels or elephants, horses of different breeds, karkhanahs and servants. Anand Ram Mukhils, who served as *vakil* (agent) from 1720 to 1748 for Muhammad Shah's Wazir, Qamar al-Din Khan, is an example. Born in Shahjahanabad in 1697, he lived in a fine mansion in the suburb of Vakilpura with a number of other Khattri traders and administrators.[25]

The Khattris had a great deal of pride in their close association with the Mughals, taking on the externals of the Indo-Islamic lifestyle. They spoke Persian at court and Punjabi at home; wore Indo-Islamic jewelry and dress at court and a dhoti and Khattri jewelry at home. In 1710, in the midst of a war against the Sikhs, the Emperor Farrukhsiyar ordered all Hindus at court to shave their beards. Because of their positions at court as merchants, revenue-farmers, and administrators, and because they needed peace in order to profit, the Khattris decided to support the Mughals and complied with the order.[26]

Still, in all, the Khattri merchants of Shahjahanabad, like traders and merchants in other parts of seventeenth- and eighteenth-century India, appear to have had little direct influence on Mughal policy. Unlike their Muslim counterparts in Damascus and Aleppo during the Mamluk period (fourteenth–sixteenth centuries), they secured few if any posts in the military/administrative system. In Mughal India merchants were not protected by the Mughal government. They were subject to illegal tolls and taxes, robberies were common, and arbitrary payments were often demanded. In fact, many of traders expected to be plundered by rulers. Forced loans were common (the price of protection), and the Hindu law books sanctioned seizure of 25 percent of a merchant's goods in times of danger.[27]

Between 1648 and 1857, ninety-six temples were erected in Shahjah-

[24] Manrique, *Travels*, 2 p. 156; Pelsaert, *Jahangir's India*, p. 30.
[25] For Anand Ram see "Waqa'i-i Sayri-i Ganga," fols. 1–14 and "Ahwal-i Nuskah-i Sawanih," Persian Manuscript Collection, Ethe 410, London, India Office Library, fols. 15–98.
[26] C.A. Bayly, "Patrons and Politics in Northern India," in *Locality, Province, and Nation: Essays on Indian Politics, 1870–1940*, ed. John Gallagher, Gordon Johnson, and Anil Seal (Cambridge: Cambridge University Press, 1973), pp. 35, 42; Bayly, *Rulers, Townsmen, and Bazars*, pp. 155, 387–8; Khafi Khan, *Muntakhab al-Lubab*, 2 p. 674.
[27] Bayly, *Rulers, Townsmen, and Bazars*, p. 391.

anabad, twelve of which had inscriptions and could be dated. Of the twelve, ten were constructed during the British period (1803–57), two during the period of destruction and decline in the eighteenth century (1739–1803), and none at all during the period of Shahjahanabad's glory (1639–1739). Since Hindu merchants were the major patrons of religious activity in Shahjahanabad and since most of the temples stood in the central bazaars near the homes of merchants, the lack of building in the seventeenth and early eighteenth centuries suggests the economic and political impotence of Khattri merchants.[28]

Why was this? Why were the merchants of Mughal India and Shahjahanabad so lacking in power and influence? During the Mughal period India was a land of great abundance; it was richly watered and yielded two crops a year. Compared to the countries of Western Asia and Western Europe, India had an economy that was highly productive and relatively self-sufficient, independent for the most part of imports. As a result, the Mughal government derived almost all of its revenues from taxes on agricultural production. Up to 1700, customs revenues were probably less than one percent of land revenues.[29] Other trade-related taxes, like the *rahdari* (inland transit tax) and market taxes, either generated insignificant sums or flowed into the coffers of local authorities. In Mughal India trade seems to have been both underassessed and undertaxed. In Gujarat, for example, imported goods were taxed at a rate of only about 5 percent while a levy of 30–50 percent was imposed on the surplus product of the peasant.[30] In the early seventeenth century Pietro Della Valle, the Italian merchant, pointed out that seizing Mughal ships did not affect imperial policy because the emperor was very wealthy and did not value trade.[31] In 1689 John Child, governor of Bombay, wrote to the East India Company that their dispute with the Emperor was inconclusive because of his lack of interest in trade.[32]

The Mughal attitude toward commerce and merchants was, at least in part, an economic decision. To have guaranteed the safety of merchants on highways, to have abolished the tolls levied by local chieftains and officials, to have lowered urban transaction costs – all of this would have

[28] For the twelve dated temples see *List of Monuments* 1 pp. 65, 101, 107, 109, 116, 132, 139, 140, 141, 152, and 165. For a similar argument about the role of merchants in Mughal India see John F. Richards, "Mughal State Finance and the Premodern World Economy," *Comparative Studies in Society and History* 23 (1981) pp. 285–308.
[29] Sarkar, *Studies in Aurangzeb's Reign*, p. 273.
[30] Pearson, *Merchants and Rulers*, pp. 23–4, 88–91.
[31] *Travels of Pietro Della Valle*, ed. E. Gray, 2 vols. (London: Hakluyt Society, 1892), 2 pp. 417–19.
[32] K.N. Chaudhuri, *The Trading World of Asia and the English East India Company: 1660–1760*, (Cambridge: Cambridge University Press, 1978), p. 111.

been extremely expensive. The Mughal emperors, like the French and
Spanish rulers of the same period, could see no economic benefit in
establishing merchant rights and encouraging market efficiencies.[33] For
the emperors it made more sense, on purely economic grounds, to sell
monopolies, to wink at or join in the collection of illegal tolls, and to
pocket whatever presents or bribes could be extracted.

This is not, however, to deny the existence of certain conditions
favorable to merchants. Loans could be secured at reasonable rates of
interest, idle balances could be deposited for the short or medium term,
and bills of exchange were issued. Insurance was available on goods
shipped overland by caravan or overseas. Nevertheless, the expansion of
commerce was impeded by the Mughal emperor's judgment that the costs
of protecting and insuring merchant rights far exceeded the benefits. It
was not until the English East India Company began to extend its control
over the subcontinent in the late eighteenth and early nineteenth
centuries and introduced the principles of private property, sanctity of
contract, and rule of law that a true market economy hospitable to
merchants began to develop.

There is no doubt that in some parts of Mughal India merchants
recruited artisans and organized workshops, providing materials and
tools, specifying design and quality, and paying daily wages. Most of this
acitivity, however, seems to have taken place in or near the commercial
cities of the coast.[34] Merchants founded karkhanahs for the same reasons
that they established the putting-out system, i.e., to overcome the
deficiencies of the market.

Given the example of imperial, princely, and great amiri households, it
is likely that merchants in Shahjahanabad also established karkhanahs.
This does not seem to have been a popular practice, however. Neither
Bernier, Manucci, nor any of the other seventeenth- and eighteenth-
century visitors mentioned such establishments, and the first report
seems to be Bishop's Heber's description in 1824 of a merchant karkhanah
where Kashmiri weavers produced wool shawls.[35]

Independent workshops

How were the independent artisans in the cities of Mughal India
organized? Several scholars, citing evidence from the *A'in-i Akbari* and

---

[33] Douglas C. North and Robert Paul Thomas, *The Rise of the Western World: A New
Economic History* (Cambridge: Cambridge University Press, 1973), pp. 120–32.
[34] See Prakash, "Organization of Industrial Production," pp. 48–9; Naqvi, *Urban Centres*,
p. 155, Foster, *English Factories: 1618–21*, p. 198.
[35] Heber, *Narrative*, 1 p. 555.

the cities of Gujarat, have hypothesized the existence of professional organizations or guilds.[36] Although what these writers understand by guilds is not entirely clear, the reference seems to be to medieval Europe Mughal Indian guilds, it is implied, were economic associations formed, like those of medieval Italy, Germany, and France, to regulate the number of craftsmen, set prices and output, and establish standards of quality.

To conceive of the independent artisans of Mughal India in this way seems to me a mistake. In the first place, the passage from the *A'in Akbari* refers to a structure imposed by the government rather than to an independent economic organization. Although the standard English translation says of the city magistrate "of every guild of artificers, he should name one as guildmaster,"[37] the original Persian words suggest a more general meaning. The two words *jauq* and *sar-guroh* ("guild" and "guildmaster") mean respectively a troop, body, or company of men and a chief, leader, or head.[38] The word *sinf* (guild), moreover, had been used for centuries to describe the craft associations of West Asia and was available to Abu al-Fazl. As a result, the most accurate translation of the phrase would seem to be "of every group of artisans, he should name one as head." The purpose of the appointment, the sources make clear, was to help the government control and tax urban artisans.[39]

The evidence from the cities of Gujarat does not stand up to scrutiny either. The artisan groups in Ahmadabad and Surat, for example, seem to have been social and religious rather than economic organizations, and, like caste councils in villages, existed primarily to settle questions of marriage, ritual status, and religious observance. They did not handle the economic issues that were the *raison d'être* of medieval European guilds.[40]

In Shahjahanabad, as in other cities, independent artisans probably had caste councils to deal with social, ritual, and religious issues. And, as the *A'in* suggests, such councils were probably utilized by government

---

[36] See Naqvi, *Urbanisation and Urban Centers*, p. 6; Prakash, "Organization of Industrial Production," p. 51; and A.I. Chicherov, *India: Economic Development in the 16th–18th Centuries*, trans. Don Danemanis (Moscow: "nauka" Publishing House, 1971), pp. 84–5. For Gujarat see V.S. Bendrey, *A Study of Muslim Inscriptions* (Bombay: Karnatak Publishing House, 1944), pp. 124–5.

[37] Abu al-Fazl, *A'in*, trans. Blochmann, 2 p. 44.

[38] Ibid., ed. Blochmann, 1 p. 284.

[39] Richards, *Mughal Administration*, pp. 185–7.

[40] Pearson, *Merchants and Rulers*, pp. 123–4. For similar arguments about artisan organizations in West Asia see G. Baer, "The Administrative, Economic, and Social Functions of the Turkish Guilds," *International Journal of Middle East Studies* 1 (1970) pp. 28–50 and G. Baer, "Guilds in Middle Eastern History," in *Studies in the Economic History of the Middle East*, ed. M.A. Cook (London: Oxford University Press, 1970), pp. 11–13.

officials for purposes of taxation and regulation. It does not appear, however, that independent artisans accounted for a large percentage of urban production. In fact, contemporary accounts point to the difficult conditions in which these men had to work and to their limited numbers. Bernier wrote:

> Nothing but sheer necessity or blows from a cudgel keeps him employed; he never can become rich, and he feels it no trifling matter if he can have the means of satisfying the cravings of hunger and of covering his body with the coarsest raiment.[41]

> Workshops, occupied by skillful artisans, will be vainly sought for in Delhi.[42]

Although there is no way of determining precisely the contribution of each mode of production to the total output of goods and services, there is enough evidence to come to a general conclusion. Karkhanahs of emperors, princes, and great amirs were dominant and accounted for the lion's share of production. As a result, the productive process in Shahjahanabad was oriented toward the great households not the marketplace and the bulk of production did not reach the open market.

Both the Dutch and English merchants found the selection of manufactured goods in Shahjahanabad (and earlier in Agra) extremely limited. In the first half of the seventeenth century, the companies found carpets so difficult to obtain in Agra that they turned to Iran and Isfahan.[43] The English grew disenchanted with the prospects for other articles as well: in 1618 one merchant wrote "the report sent to England that quantities of rare stuffs may be had in Agra is not true."[44] And in 1631 another observed of that city that it "affords little to satisfy so many buyers, especially the Dutch and the English."[45]

Following the shift of the imperial court to Shahjahanabad in 1648 identical complaints began to surface. Bernier, for example, character-ized the markets of the city as "ill-supplied" and Manucci observed "Although it is the seat of the principal court, there are not many manufactures."[46] During the years 1617–34, furthermore, North Indian goods comprised only 7 percent of the total volume of cotton materials

[41] Bernier, *Travels*, p. 229.
[42] Ibid., p. 254.
[43] Foster, *English Factories: 1618–21*, p. 168; Director Joust Diericky to the Governor-General, 19 September, 1948, *Transcripts and Translations of Dutch Records at the Hague: Letters from India: 1600–1699*, India Office Library, London, 16, 507, p. 1.
[44] Foster, *English Factories: 1618–21*, pp. 46–7.
[45] William Foster, *The English Factories in India: 1630–33* (Oxford: Clarendon Press, 1910), p. 129.
[46] Bernier, *Travels*, p. 254; Manucci, *Storia do Mogor*, 2 p. 396.

annually exported by the Dutch and English.[47] And, during the period 1618–67, the English East India Company included cotton goods from Northern India in their shipments from Surat – the major port of Western India – in only twenty of the fifty years covered.[48]

Exchange

Of the five kinds of exchange listed by Scott Cook in his work on premodern economic organization[49] three seem to have figured in the economy of Shahjahanabad. Goods and services were distributed from one person to many, were given as gifts in the courts of great men, and were exchanged in markets.

Clients in the great households were probably not compensated according to marketplace standards – on the number of services rendered or goods produced. Rather, like members of extended peasant households, these persons were given periodic payments in cash and in kind. Like a patriarch, the great patron periodically redistributed the wealth and resources of his household. Ceremonial gift-giving took place in the audience halls of the emperors and great men and, as we have seen, these exchanges were symbolic acts whose primary function was to strengthen a relationship rather than to accomplish a distribution of wealth.

Marketplace exchange was also characteristic of Shahjahanabad. In premodern peasant societies markets coexisted with other forms of exchange and many goods and services changed hands in nonmarket transactions. In premodern markets economic and noneconomic functions were combined. Peasants came to market not only to sell their products and to buy goods and services but to take care of political, legal, and administrative matters as well, to attend meetings, visit religious centers, see friends and relatives, and have ritual services performed.[50]

In Mughal India markets were small and isolated. Gluts or scarcities sent prices plummeting or soaring in one market while another a few

---

[47] Naqvi, *Urban Centres*, p. 226. Her figure of 4.5 percent is wrong; the correct percentage is 7.

[48] Ibid., p. 222.

[49] See Scott Cook, "Production, Ecology, and Economic Anthropology: Notes Toward an Integrated Frame of Reference," *Social Science Information* 12 (1973) pp. 25–52; and Scott Cook, "Economic Anthropology: Problems in Theory, Method, and Analysis," in ed. John J. Honigman, *Handbook of Social and Cultural Anthropology* (Chicago: Rand McNally, 1973), pp. 795–860. For a criticism of other approaches to premodern economics see Scott Cook, "The Obsolete 'Anti-Market' Mentality: A Critique of the Substantive Approach to Economic Anthropology," *American Anthropologist* 68 (1966) pp. 323–45; and Scott Cook, "Structural Substantivism: A Critical Review of Marshall Sahlins' Stone Age Economics," *Comparative Studies in Society and History* 16 (1974) pp. 355–79.

[50] Cook, "Economic Anthropology," pp. 829–30.

miles away would be unaffected. High transportation costs prevented the regular, organized movement of bulk commodities overland (the banjara trade was irregular and spasmodic) and riverine trade was miniscule compared to the size of the sector. Only high-value, low-bulk commodities moved regularly in interregional trade. In the coastal towns and cities and along caravan routes markets were also erratic and unreliable. Prices fluctuated from day to day and from season to season, the number of buyers and sellers rose and fell irregularly, and the quantity and quality of goods was unpredictable. In Surat during the early eighteenth century, for example, markets were small, easily glutted, and erratic, and merchants were insecure, finding it impossible to make rational calculations.[51]

In such markets, according to one scholar, premodern traders and merchants followed four rules. Traders tried to establish personal positions in the marketplace – they wanted to develop long-term relationships with wealthy buyers and often this meant granting concessions on price, credit, or quality. Merchants preferred small-profit, high-turnover deals in order to keep their capital occupied. Traders aspired to sell wholesale, thereby insulating themselves against the uncertainties of retail trade. And, finally, merchants and traders wanted to deal in smaller, lighter goods of greater value; they wanted to buy dear and sell dear.[52] It is apparent from the career of Banarsidas, a Jain merchant of the mid-seventeenth century who lived in Agra and dealt with the imperial court, that Mughal traders followed most of these rules.[53]

Markets

Urban geographers have found that the theory of central place applies to marketplaces within cities as well as to market towns in regions. Urban markets can be distinguished and ranked according to number of customers, size of marketing area, and variety of goods and services. In some cities three levels have been distinguished and in others four.[54] In

[51] Das Gupta, *Indian Merchants*, p. 22.
[52] Manning Nash, *Primitive and Peasant Economic Systems* (San Francisco: Chandler Publishing Co., 1966), pp. 87–8.
[53] Ramesh Chandra Sharma, "The Ardha-Kathanak, A Neglected Source of Mughal History," *Indica* 7 (1970) pp. 49–73, 105–20. See also Das Gupta, *Indian Merchants*, pp. 11–18.
[54] Hans Carol, "Hierarchy of Central Place Functions Within the City," *Annals of the Association of American Geographers* 50 (1960) pp. 419–38; A.K. Dutt, "Intra-City Hierarchy of Central Places: Calcutta As a Case Study," *Professional Geographer* 2 (1969) p. 18–20.

Shahjahanabad there seems to have been a three-fold hierarchy: neighborhood markets, regional markets, and central markets.

In neighborhood markets grain, cloth, salt, fruit, and vegetables were
sold. The most numerous variety in the city, these markets served the
smallest area, had the fewest customers, and offered a limited selection of
goods. For the most part, they served that portion of the population who
were not clients of great men and members of elite households.

The petty shopkeepers in neighborhood markets obtained their
supplies from the large wholesale marts of the suburbs. The most
important of these was Paharganj, the grain market. Located just outside
the Ajmiri gate, Paharganj held a customs house where the emperor's
men collected taxes and checked prices. According to an early nineteenth
century report, the city also contained wholesale markets for leather
goods, metal utensils, horned cattle, sheep and goats, wood, soap, gold-
leaf design, fireworks, fish, cheese, and building materials.[55] The
enormous supply of manure and the ready market made the cultivation of
fruits and vegetables in gardens near the wall extremely profitable.

In the cities of Mughal India, as in other contemporaneous West Asian
cities, urban officials controlled trade by specifying the places where
goods could be bought and sold. Merchants were not allowed to sell their
goods without going through the designated markets.[56] To each market
the kotwal appointed a darogah who set prices (appraisers were available)
and collected taxes.[57] Urban markets were divided into mahals. Over
each mahal the kotwal set an official who supervised the darogahs and
collected their revenue. In 1720 Shahjahanabad was divided into four
mahals.[58]

Regional markets stood within or nearby the imperial palace-fortress
and the great mansions. Like neighborhood markets, regional markets
sold grain, fruit, vegetables, and cloth but they differed in serving more
people spread over a larger area and in providing a wider selection of
goods. The merchants who staffed these markets, many of whom were
Khattris, should be seen as clients, members of elite households, and
not as independent businessmen. Bernier described the great men as

[55] T. Fortescue, "Report on the Revenue System of the Delhi Territory, 1820,"
pp. 131–76.
[56] Ibid.; Abd al-Qadir bin Maluk Shah urf al-Badaoni, *Muntakhab-ut-Tawarikh*, 3 vols.,
trans. G.S.A. Ranking and W.H. Lowe (Calcutta; Asiatic Society of Bengal, 1884–98), 2
p. 404.
[57] *Selected Waqai of Deccan*, ed. Dr. Yusuf Husain (Hyderabad: Central Records Office,
1953), p. 23; "Revenue Tables of Subahs and Parganahs in Reigns of Shahjahan and
Aurangzeb," Persian Manuscript Collection, Or. 1779, British Museum,
fols. 224b–226a; Sarkar, *Fall of the Mughal Empire*, 2 pp. 175–6.
[58] "Chahar Gulshan," fols. 41b. For a list of mahals in the city in the late eighteenth and
early nineteenth centuries see James Grant, "Firhist-i Subajat-i Hindustan," Persian
Manuscript Collection, Ethe 433, India Office Library, fols. 20a–1a.

"patrons" in their relationship to merchants,[59] and the household merchants of Amir Khan Sindhi, a great amir under Aurangzeb, procured goods at one half to one third the market price.[60] Banarsidas, the Jain merchant, wrote of his grandfather:

He studied Hindi and Persian and became the merchant (*modi*) of a Mughal nobleman...He was a favorite of the nobleman and dealt in giving things on credit.[61]

Client merchants worked with household officials to obtain grain, vegetables, fruit, iron, weapons, leather goods, and other equipment.[62] Grain dealers, the most important merchants, supplied the household bazaar from the wholesale markets outside the city and, in some cases, served as moneylenders, giving advances to the great man and his retinue in the last few months before harvest when household treasuries were low.[63] They also advanced money to *banjaras* (caravan traders), ensuring a steady supply of grain for their patrons on tour.[64]

In Shahjahanabad household bazaars stood inside or nearby the great residences. The imperial palace-fortress featured bazaars in both places. The Urdu (*Army*) Bazaar ran from the Lahore gate of the fort to the food of Chandni Chawk and the *Chatta* (covered) Bazaar connected the Lahore gate and the Naqqar Khanah. The Urdu Bazaar probably performed the functions of a neighbourhood market, selling staples to household members, while the covered bazaar supplied the finer goods of limited demand.

The bazaars in princely and great amiri households were located either inside or outside the mansion walls. Gentile, in the passage quoted above, characterized amiri mansions as small towns and mentioned the "bazaars (or public markets)" they contained,[65] and the household bazaar of Safdar Jang was just outside the gateway to his mansion.[66]

The great central bazaars of Chandni Chawk, Faiz Bazar, and Chawk Sa'adullah Khan catered to the entire city. At the apex of the urban hierarchy, central markets performed the functions of markets at the two

[59] Bernier, *Travels*, pp. 228–30.
[60] Shah Nawaz Khan, *Ma'asir al-Umara*, 1 pp. 303–10.
[61] Sharma, "The Ardha-Kathanak," pp. 52, 108.
[62] For the merchants in Samsam al-Daulah's household see "Ahwal-i Khan Dauran," fols. 169a, 181b–2a. Manucci describes a merchant who had the responsibility for providing a great amir's household with vegetables during a trip to Kashmir. *Storia do Mogor*, 2 p. 416.
[63] Habib, "Usury," pp. 6–16.
[64] *Calendar of Persian Correspondence*, 9, 1790–1 (New Delhi: National Archives of India, 1949), p. 48.
[65] Gentile, *Memoires*, p. 188.
[66] "Tarikh-i Ahmad Shahi," fols. 17a–b.

lower levels plus a special set all their own. In these bazaars customers could buy the grain, vegetables, fruit, and rough cloth of the neighborhood markets, the fine cloth, leather goods, weapons, ironwork, and riding equipment of the regional markets, and, in addition, goods and services of a rarity, quality, and richness unavailable elsewhere.

Shahjahanabad was also at the apex of the hierarchy of towns and cities in North India. It encapsulated the entire central-place hierarchy, performing the economic, administrative, police, and religious functions of all the places below it as well as a set uniquely its own.[67] The economic functions unique to the city were located in the central bazaars, which drew customers from the entire empire as well as from the city at large.

Merchants from other provinces of the empire and from other countries brought their goods to the central bazaars of Shahjahanabad. A contemporary account mentions traders from Turkey, Zanzibar, Syria, Yemen, Arabia, Iraq, Khorasan, China, and Tibet in addition to Europeans from England and Holland. These men brought rubies from Badakshan, pearls from Oman, and fresh fruits from Kashmir and Central Asia. They supplied weapons, fine cloth, perfumes, elephants, horses, camels, birds, water pipes, and delicate sweetmeats.[68] The East India Company merchants sold tapestries, wool, and broadcloth.[69] Here could be found dancing girls and boys, storytellers who talked about fasting during the month of Ramadan and the month of the haj (Journey to Mecca), and the death of Husain in the month of Muharram. Physicians sold remedies for coughs, syphilis, gonorrhea, and impotence. The wine shops were so enticing that 100-year-old ascetics were tempted.[70] The profusion of rich goods stunned travellers. One man wrote that from these bazaars an amir could outfit one thousand soldiers in an hour.[71] Another calculated that all of the goods for a royal festival or the household of a wazir could be purchased in a single day.[72] And a third told the story of a great amir's young son who spent 100,000 rupees in an idle walk through Chandni Chawk without affecting the supply of goods.[73]

[67] For a discussion of the central-place hierarchy in Mughal North India see Blake, "Hierarchy of Central Places," *South Asia* 6 (1983) pp. 1–32.

[68] Sujan Rai, "Khulasat al-Tawarikh," fol. 18a.

[69] William Foster, *The English Factories in India: 1637–41* (Oxford: Clarendon Press, 1912), p. 228; William Foster, *The English Factories in India: 1646–50*, p. 305; William Jesson to Surat, 7 May 1656, *English Factory Records: 1655–60*, India Office Library, London, 103 pp. 120–1.

[70] Dargah Quli Khan, "Risalah," fols. 86–9a.

[71] Sujan Rai, "Khulasat al-Tawarikh," fol. 18a.

[72] Kurtaza Husain, *Hadiqat-ul-Aqalim*, (Lucknow: n.p., 1879–81) p. 41

[73] Dargah Quli Khan, "Risalah," fol. 89b. For other descriptions see Chandar Bhan, "Chahar Chaman," fols. 142–3; Shah Nawaz Khan, *Ma'asir al-Umara*, 3 p. 473; and Bernier, *Travels*, pp. 248–51.

The foreign and domestic merchants who supplied Chandni Chawk, Faiz Bazaar, and Chawk Sa'adullah Khan were not members of elite households. Unlike client merchants, these men arranged their own schedules, controlled their own goods, and sold to many customers. This does not mean, however, that they operated in a free market, where contact was fleeting, exchanges faceless, and prices set. To the contrary, these merchants probably tried to find personal niches in the market-place. They wanted to establish closer relationships with several of the great men. Merchants developed manners and a pleasant address in order to attach themselves to the great households. Goods were described in Persian couplets and sherberts were offered to the nobles and princes and their wives. For those who sold jewels, perfumes, horses, goldwork, and precious cloth such connections would have been especially important. There would not have been more than fifty households that could have afforded such items and a successful merchant would have required access to three or four at least.

Utilization

Utilization encompasses activities which (1) lead to the production of more goods, the employment of resources as capital and (2) involve the immediate consumption of goods, the employment of resources for direct-want satisfaction. Capital may be empolyed as a productive asset, as a fund for investment, or as control over purchasing power. Direct consumption, on the other hand, is the end of the economic cycle. The resource drops out of circulation or is embodied in a person.[74]

The major unit of utilization in Mughal India was not the firm – the characteristic form of economic organization in modern Western societies – but the household. This was, of course, true of village India where 90–95 percent of the population lived but it was also true of towns and cities. In Shahjahanabad the great households constituted the major units of utilization or consumption.

These households contained about 75 percent of the urban population and by virtue of their size alone would have played a major role in the process of utilization. But it is important, if we are to understand the economic organization of Shahjahanabad and its role in the hierarchy of central places, to stress the enormous wealth of the great men. It's not just that they controlled the resources of the city but also that they held a significant percentage of the wealth of the empire at large.

---

[74] Cook, "Economic Anthropology," pp. 838–9.

In 1650 there were about 8,000 mansabdars in the Mughal Empire. Most of these held low ranks, filled positions of little responsibility, and were paid trifling sums. In the Mughal system it was the highest-ranking officials, those at the very top of the hierarchy, who held the major posts and controlled the resources. In 1650 the top 445 mansabdars received 61 percent of total revenues, the four princes and sixty-nine great amirs alone receiving almost 38 percent.[75]

As a result, a substantial share of the wealth of the empire – over 40 percent in fact – was concentrated in Shahjahanabad. The two princes and thirty-five great amirs controlled about 19 percent of annual revenues, the one hundred and fifty mansabdars another 10 percent, and the emperor himself about 14 percent. Over 75 percent of this money was devoted to the clients of the great men – it was not all disposable income.[76] Nevertheless, elite households, by virtue of their wealth and status, completely dominated the economic process in Shahjahanabad.

The imperial household shaped and ordered the urban economy. In patrimonial-bureaucratic empires the extended household (*oikos*) of the master was the dominant unit. Satisfaction of his needs and wants, not capitalistic acquisition or rationalized production was the primary motive. The ideal was to be entirely self-sufficient; the land of the ruler providing food and raw materials, and the household workshops, manned by unfree laborers, producing goods and services. Although self-sufficiency was in practice unattainable and although the master was often forced to turn to the marketplace, patrimonial-bureaucratic rulers were uncomfortable with independent economic agents. They discouraged the development of enterprises based on division of labor and specialization and would not uphold or create property rights. In patrimonial-bureaucratic empires cities contained both households and markets, mixed economies that were dominated by the great men.[77]

In Mughal India the emperor considered the economic resources of both city and empire his personal preserve. He might assign a portion of the revenues from one realm or the other but he did not consider either to be free or independent. Just as technological and organizational deficiencies might require a compromise of the patrimonial ideal in administration so also in the case of the economy. But the ideal of running both city and empire as one big household workshop remained and was never abandoned.

[75] Qaisar, "Distribution of Revenue Resources," pp. 237–43.
[76] Ibid.
[77] Weber, *Economy and Society*, 1 pp. 381–3.

5

Courtly and popular culture

The culture of Shahjahanabad exhibited both courtly and popular aspects. To understand urban culture one must examine the entertainments of the common folk as well as the artistic activities of the great men. The dancing of young boys in the square in front of the palace-fortress and the religious celebrations at the tombs of sufi saints were just as important a part of the cultural life of the city as was the display of talent by poets, dancers, and singers in the audience halls of the imperial palace and the great amiri mansions.

Courtly culture

The high culture of the sovereign city focused, for the most part, on the courts of the emperors, princes, and great amirs. In Shahjahanabad the households of the great men constituted the salons of urban society, the places where the greatest poets, painters, musicians, calligraphers, and dancers displayed their talents. The great men themselves devoted a good deal of time and energy to the artistic aspects of their lives, perfecting a highly refined cultural idiom that included mastery of the arts both of peace and of war. They collected paintings, carpets, and manuscripts, built and decorated palaces, gardens, mosques, and tombs, and wrote poetry. They also displayed their skill at shooting and riding during hunts and tours, and they understood wrestling and hand-to-hand combat. For the Mughal nobility the arts of both peace and war were a necessary and integral part of everyday life. Their practice of these arts made them much more than dilettantes; they were sophisticated patrons and collectors able to tell at a glance the difference between the well made and the extraordinary. Talent was rewarded and their households contained the most able and productive artists and warriors of the time.

Focusing cultural activity on the court had not been traditional in the lands between the Nile and Oxus rivers. During the early years of the pre-Islamic period, the temple served as cultural center and, later, with the development of commerce and industry, merchants emerged as major supporters of cultural and artistic activity. By the sixteenth century, however, with the shift of power and prestige away from the Nile-to-Oxus region, the commercial classes began to lose influence. Two of the three major Islamic states of the day, the Ottomans and Mughals (the Safavids were the third), were found outside the arid lands of the central region and depended heavily on agricultural production. In both the Ottoman and Mughal states cultivation of the high arts of civilization came to be the province of the emperor and his court.[1]

Although the culture of the Mughal court, practiced by the 70–100 high-ranking amirs and the artists and militarymen they patronized, was not in complete conformity with the *sharia* (Islamic law code); it strayed no further from the religious ideal than had the courtly styles of earlier Islamic states. In fact, from about A.D. 750, when the capital of the Abbasid state shifted from Damascus to Baghdad and Persians began to fill positions of governmental responsibility, Muslim divines had criticized rulers and their courts for departing from the path of true discipline. Rulers of the Seljuk, Mongol, Safavid, and Ottoman states, for example, had all been censured for impurity and apostasy.

Akbar's attempts to broaden his base of support and to create an ethic that would appeal to the indigenous elite was similar to the efforts of the Abbasid ruler al-Mansur to include Persians in his Arab-dominated state, and to the policies of the Seljuks and Il-Khanids, Turkish and Mongol rulers respectively, to fashion a system that would gain local support. For the Seljuks and Il-Khanids in Iran it was the rulers rather than the conquered who were "Persianized and Islamicized"; nevertheless, it is clear that Akbar's creation of a state system broad enough to include the non-Muslim elite was not unknown in Islamic history.

High culture in Mughal India then, if not strictly orthodox, was certainly in accordance with accommodations made by other Muslim dynasties to the demands of ruling successfully. In the arts both of peace and of war the basic style was a blending of Hindu and Muslim elements into an Indo-Muslim or Indo-Persian composite. By the Mughal period the basic elements of this style had been established and the syncretistic nature of the arts had become accepted.

The high culture of the imperial court was paradigmatic for mansabdars, administrators, and cavalrymen. Emperors, princes, and great amirs displayed their skills at court and on the battlefield, manifesting the

---

[1] For a discussion see Hodgson, *Venture of Islam*, 3 pp. 81–2.

ideal of the fully cultured man. This ideal combined the two professional types of the Islamic world: *ahl-i qalam* (men of the pen) and *ahl-i saif* (men of the sword). Men of the pen were clerks, accountants, supervisors, treasurers, and revenue collectors. Men of the sword were commanders, cavalrymen, and troopers. By their wit and polish, their eloquence and style, their stamina, courage, and strength, and their skills with horses, guns, and swords, the great men set standards for both groups of men and, combining them in a graceful and commanding way, embodied the ideal against which they must measure themselves and toward which they must aspire.

In the Islamic world "men of the sword" and "men of the pen" had been recognized as distinct classes for a long time. In the mid-eleventh century Ibn Miskawaih distinguished the two groups in an Arabic work entitled *Tahdhib al-Akhlaq*. But it was *Akhlaq-i Nasiri*, a work on ethics by Nasir al-Din Tusi that was the most influential. Composed in A.D. 1235 in Persian, it soon became required reading for educated Muslims in West Asia and India. In the section "On the Government of the Realm and the Manners of Kings," Tusi stated that an emperor's first duty was to maintain harmony among the four classes of mankind: (1) men of the pen, masters of the sciences and branches of knowledge – canon-lawyers, judges, secretaries, accountants, geometers, astronomers, physicians, and poets; (2) men of the sword, supporters of the realm and guardians of the state – fighters, warriors, volunteers, skirmishers, frontier-guards, sentries, and valiant men; (3) men of negotiation – merchants, tradesmen, craftsmen, and tax-collectors; and (4) men of husbandry – sowers, farmers, ploughmen, and agriculturists.[2]

Soon after, manuals outlining the duties of the "men of the pen" and the "men of the sword" begin to appear. Books by Ibn al-Wardi (d. 1349) and Ibn Nubatta (d. 1366) in the fourteenth century were followed by a number of similar works in the first half of the fifteenth century.[3] In the early fifteenth century al-Qalqashandi completed an encyclopedia for "men of the pen" giving sample letters and documents and including a great deal of information on religion, history, and society.[4]

Ibn Khaldun analyzed the role of the two groups in the evolution of states. In his monumental history, finished in the first years of the fifteenth century, he stated that "men of th sword" are dominant at the founding and the collapse of dynasties. In the beginning, soldiers are crucial in establishing power and securing peace and order and are

---

[2] Nasir al-Din Tusi, *The Nasirean Ethics*, trans. G.M. Wickens (London: George Allen and Unwin, Ltd., 1964), p. 230.
[3] See *Encyclopaedia of Islam*, 2nd edn s.v. "kalam."
[4] Hodgson, *Venture of Islam*, 2 p. 467.

favored over administrators and secretaries. At the end, when group feeling has weakened and the state is tottering, the military again becomes ascendant. It is during the middle years, when rulers are established, that "men of the pen" gain the upper hand. They collect taxes and administer the law, rising to positions of power and authority and eclipsing the "men of the sword."[5]

Such concepts were widespread in Mughal India. In his preface to the *A'in*, Abu al-Fazl listed "men of the sword" and "men of the pen" among the four groups of mankind, taking his definitions and descriptions directly from Tusi. And *Akhlaq-i Nasiri* was one of the books most often read to the emperor Akbar.[6] Abu al-Fazl also used the terms when describing Ghazi Khan Badakshi, an amir who came to India from Iran in the nineteenth year of Akbar's reign. He had studied the traditional and rational sciences under Mulla Isami and had a thorough knowledge of Sufism. He had great ability and was distinguished in battle. Abu al-Fazl wrote that his courage made his wisdom illustrious and that his sword (*saif*) exalted the dignity of his pen (*qalam*).[7]

During Shahjahan's reign Islam Khan was said to combine the ability of a wazir and the dignity of an amir. He was a good writer and poet and accompanied the emperor on tour. His military capacity and sound learning had earned him the distinction of lord of the sword and the pen (*sahib-i saif-o-qalam*).[8] And Chandra Bhan Brahman, in describing the great men in the audience hall of the Hall of Ordinary Audience, referred to a group of them as lords of the sword and the pen (*sahiban-i saif-o-qalam*).[9]

Who were the men who embodied the Mughal ideal of courtly culture? What were their ranks? Where were they born? What were their religious and ethnic background?

In 1648 the title "great amir" was given to the sixty-nine amirs with zat ranks of 2500 and above. Since the average zat rank increased steadily over the last half of the seventeenth and the first half of the eighteenth centuries, the qualifying rank for great amir probably rose also. Whatever the exact cutoff, it is probably safe to assume that the highest-ranking 70–100 amirs were designated "great amir" during the period 1639–1739.

In his book on the Mughal nobility Athar Ali divided the amirs of Aurangzeb's reign into two groups: those who had achieved their highest

[5] Ibn Khaldun, *The Muqaddimah*, 3 vols., trans. Franz Rosenthal (Princeton: Princeton University Press, 1958), 2 pp. 46–7.
[6] *Ain*, 1 pp. 3, 115.
[7] *Ma'asir al-Umara* 2 pp. 857–62; *Akbar-Namah* 3 p. 436.
[8] *Ma'asir al-Umara* 1 pp. 162–6.
[9] Chandar Bhan Brahman, "Chandar Chaman," fol. 12.

Table 5   *Great amirs (2500–7000 zat): 1658–1678*

1 Country of birth		2 Group		3 Subgroup		4 Relative in mansab-dari system	
India	137	Indian	73	Indian		Father	94
Iran	16	Irani	64			Brother	5
Turan	6	Turani	33	Rajput	24	Grandfather	4
Turkey	2	Unknown	9	Shaikhzada	18	Uncle	2
Balkh	2			Afghan	14	None	74
Badakshan	1			Maratha	13		
Bukhara	1			Other Hindu	13		
Unknown	14						
				Zamindar	22		
				Deccani	16		
Totals	179		179				179

Source: Athar Ali, *Mughal Nobility*, pp. 175–214

ranks during the periods 1658–78 and 1679–1707. In the first group there were 179 noblemen with zat ranks of 2500 or more. Since a certain percentage of these either died or retired, there were probably no more than about 100 great amirs active at any one time.[10]

To an overwhelming degree these men native-born: 76 percent, 137 out of 179, had been born in the subcontinent and only 28 (16 percent) had come from abroad (see table 5). Given the central role of the Persian language in Mughal culture and government it is not strange to discover that Iran supplied more immigrant great amirs than all other countries combined. Men from Turan, Balk, Badakshan, and Bukhara all spoke Turkish and were, for the most part, of Turko-Mongol descent. The ratio between immigrants and Indian-born in the mid seventeenth century was in sharp contrast to the situation 100 years earlier. At the beginning of Akbar's reign, nearly 70 percent of the amirs were foreign, men who had come to India with Akbar's father or who had arrived after his accession in 1556. Over the years the flow of immigrants slowed and the percentage of nobility with Indian roots increased.

The Mughals were acutely aware of cultural differences, and high-ranking mansabdars were seen to belong to loosely defined racial, religious, and tribal groups. Of the three major groups of the period 1658–78, the largest, seventy-three persons (41 percent of the total), was the Indian, an omnibus category that included a number of subgroups. The second largest group was the Irani (sixty-four persons, 36 percent of the total) while the Turani (thirty-three persons, 18 percent) was the smallest.

[10] Athar Ali, *Mughal Nobility*, pp. 7–37, Appendix, pp. 175–214.

It is not easy to list the defining characteristics of an Irani great amir. Columns 1 and 2 of table 5 show that Iranian birth was not the sole criterion. Indeed, only one-quarter (sixteen out of sixty-four) of the Iranis were immigrants.[11] Fluent command of Persian was not the principal characteristic either. All great amirs spoke and wrote an easy, stylish Persian but, except for the recently immigrated, it would not have been their mother tongue, the one used at home.[12] The Irani group seems to have included not only those who were born abroad but the recently immigrated and their descendants as well. Color was an important factor. Then, as now, persons living in India were acutely conscious of skin color, and Iranian great amirs had complexions several shades lighter than those of the Indian group.[13] Also, most Iranis were Shi'is – either overtly or covertly.

Membership in the Turani group was not limited to those who had been born abroad either. Of the thirty-three Turani great amirs less than one-third (twelve out of thirty-three) had come from Central Asia. The immigrants, to be sure, were Turkish-speakers and of Turko-Mongol descent but the rest of the group were Indian-born and, like the Iranis, spoke Persian at court and Urdu at home. The bulk of Turani great amirs were probably descendants of recent immigrants or of earlier immigrants who had intermarried.[14] Turanis were Sunnis but, like the Iranis, had to be light-complected. Turanis enjoyed a certain prestige in India because they were of the same heritage as the ruling dynasty. Under Humayun and Akbar, they had outnumbered Iranis and had held positions of great responsibility. But, under Jahangir and Shahjahan, they suffered a decline in numbers and importance and by the early years of Aurangzeb's reign had been substantially eclipsed by the Iranis. Contemporaries lumped Iranis and Turanis together as "Mughals" because they looked alike, were foreigners or descendants of foreigners, and shared many of the same attitudes and characteristics.

The Indian group was the largest of the three and membership here, as in the other two, was not determined by place of birth. To be sure, all

---

[11] Aurangzeb talks about Iranis, "whether born in *vilayat* [Iran] or Hindustan," Hamid al-Din Khan, *Akham-i 'Alamgiri*, p. 39.

[12] Most scholars, however, define this group in terms of birthplace and mother tongue. See Athar Ali, *Mughal Nobility*, pp. 18–19; Muhammad Yasin, *A Social History of Islamic India: 1605–1748* (New Delhi: Munshiram Manoharlal Publishers Pvt. Ltd., 1971), pp. 6–8; Zahiruddin Malik, *The Reign of Muhammad Shah: 1719–48* (New York: Asia Publishing House, 1977), p. 22.

[13] To be considered a Mughal (that is, an Irani or a Turani), according to Bernier, a foreigner had to profess Islam and have a white skin. *Travels*, p. 3.

[14] For the standard definition of "Turani" in terms of birthplace and mother tongue see Malik, *Muhammad Shah*, p. 22; Yasin, *Social History*, p. 9; and Athar Ali, *Mughal Nobility*, p. 8.

members of the Indian group had been born in the sub-continent but not all Indian-born great amirs were "Indian"; nearly half of them were members of the Irani or Turani groups. Rajputs, Hindu warrior clans from north India who had been drawn into the Mughal system by Akbar, comprised just over one-third (twenty-four out of seventy-three) of the Indian group. These men had much the same warrior ethic as the Muslim great amirs, adopted the trappings of courtly high culture, and were, for the most part, zamindars.[15]

In this context, zamindar does not refer to the local landcontrollers (village headmen mostly) who served as intermediate revenue collectors between the village and the revenue circle headquarters. For the most part, Rajput zamindars were important chieftains who controlled large amounts of land. To integrate these men into the empire the Mughals awarded them titles and high ranks in the mansabdari system. They let Rajput great amirs keep their ancestral estates, redefining them as the lands which mansabdars were assigned as part of their pay. The term "zamindar" overlapped the other Indian subcategories and applied to a few of the Maratha great amirs as well.

Shaikhzadas were the second largest of the Indian subgroups. This term refers to Hindu converts or to descendants of those who had long ago immigrated and intermarried with Hindu converts. The shaikhzadi great amirs in Athar Ali's list, however, were members of long-established clans of Indian Muslims, the most numerous and prominent being the Sayyids of Barha.

Afghans, the third largest of the groups, were men who had been born in and around present-day Afghanistan. Afghan great amirs retained their tribal ties and were not highly regarded at court. They were seen as turbulent, untrustworthy, and uncultured.

Marathas were Hindu warriors from Western India who began fighting the extension of Mughal rule to peninsular India under Shiva-ji, their first and greatest leader. During the late seventeenth and early eighteenth centuries, Maratha leaders alternately supported and opposed the Mughals. Like the Afghans, the Marathas were not fully incorporated into the Mughal system, and these great amirs were probably not as skilled and as practiced in the arts of courtly culture as the others. 'Other Hindus' comprised those Hindu great amirs who were neither Rajput nor Maratha. It included members of the writer and accountant castes mostly, Kayasthas and Khattris who had managed to achieve high rank.

The "Deccani" subcategory, like the "zamindari," overlapped the others. "Deccani", a geographical term, referred to those great amirs

---

[15] For a discussion see Ziegler, "Some Notes on Rajput Loyalties," pp. 215–51.

who had been in the service of the two independent South Indian Muslim states (Bijapur and Golkunda) before Mughal conquest. It also included the Rajput and Maratha great amirs who had come from South India to join the Mughals.

Column 4 demonstrates the extent to which great amirs were themselves close relatives of mansabdars. Athar Ali has shown that under the Mughals the status of *khanazad* (literally, house-born or direct descendant) was the single most important factor in achieving high rank. During the period 1658–78, 44 percent of the 486 mansabdars with a rank of 1000 zat or more were khanazads.[16] For the 179 who were great amirs the figure was 57 percent: 94 had fathers in Mughal service; 5, brothers; 4, grandfathers; and 2, uncles. Nevertheless, with nearly half (43 percent) of the highest ranking amirs having no hereditary connections, the Mughal system was relatively open. Even those whose initial appointment had been the result of family had to start at a much lower rank than their predecessors and their ascent up the Mughal ladder of success depended entirely on their own talent and ability.

The 70–100 great amirs who were the principal actors in the courtly culture of Mughal India had been, for the most part, born in India of fathers who were part of the Mughal system. They belonged to one of three large, loosely defined groups that were too diverse and fragmented to have a sense of common identity or purpose. For North Indian Muslims the relevant solidarities seem to have been birth-defined groups called "biradaris" and "qaums". Biradaris were the lineage groups within which an individual Muslim must marry, and qaums were the Muslim equivalent of the jati or subcaste. For Muslims, though, the qaum bond was weaker; considerations of ritual purity were less important and Muslims could marry outside the qaum.[17]

Mughal rulers wanted to prevent lineage groups from forming alliances. They were careful about the composition of amiri contingents, decreeing that cavalrymen should come from different religious and ethnic groups. In the public ritual of the palace-fortress the Mughal emperor elaborated a web of patron-client ties with representatives of these groups. During the later Mughal period the substitution of territorial identities for those of race and religion began to develop. As the number of immigrants declined and the connection to India grew stronger, amirs began to think of themselves as Deccanis, Bengalis,

---

[16] Athar Ali, *Mughal Nobility*, p. 11.
[17] For a discussion of Muslim social structure in the nineteenth century see David Lelyveld, *Aligarh's First Generation: Muslim Solidarity in British India* (Princeton: Princeton University Press, 1978), pp. 20–6. See also Zafar Iman, ed., *Muslims in India* (New Delhi: Orient Longman's, 1975).

Awadhis, and Gujaratis, irrespective of their religious or ethnic back-grounds. Irani, Turani, Afghani, and Shaikhzadi identities began to merge and in some cases even to be submerged in the increasing attachment to place.

Men of the pen

The great amir who embodied the the culture of the Mughal court had mastered the arts both of peace and of war. He combined the skills and talents of the men of the sword and the pen. In Mughal India, as in other parts of the Islamic world, there arose a class of writers, accountants, and administrators who performed the every-day functions of the state. These men, who developed their own culture and came to be called "men of the pen", had deep roots in Islamic history and can probably be traced back to the Iranian scribes and administrators of the early Abbasid state.

The ancestors of the "men of the pen" were probably the *adibs* (possessors of *adab*). As developed in the high Abbasid period (ninth and tenth centuries A.D.), adab denoted the pattern of civilized living that had grown up around the imperial court in Baghdad. The court established standards for cultivated, civilized life and boasted the most elegant practitioners of the arts. At the beginning of Abbasid rule adab meant the civility, courtesy, and refinement of the cities in contrast to the rough and unsophisticated manners of the desert. Adab implied the sum of knowledge that makes a man courteous and urbane and included profane as well as religious learning. From the early Abbasid period onward the content of adab expanded to include elements from the many non-Arabic cultures (especially the Iranian) to which Muslims were exposed. As a result, by about the ninth century there had come into existence a body of adab literature centered on man, his qualities, passions, and environment; a literature whose mastery was indispensable for the cultured, civilized Muslim of West Asia.[18]

Adab culture was the province, for the most part, of the scribes, clerks, and managers who administered the Abbasid state. Unrelated to the great landed aristocratic families of Iran, these men traced their origins to low-ranking Arab families, newly risen Iranian converts, and aspiring merchant families. The members of this class were urbane and cosmo-politan but, other than dedication to an administrative career, had little in common with one another.

For the adib, control of a language and its literature was of paramount

---

[18] *Encyclopedia of Islam*, 2nd edn, "adab"; Ira M. Lapidus, "Knowledge, Virtue, and Action: The Classical Muslim Conception of *Adab* and the Nature of Religious Fulfillment in Islam," in Metcalf, ed., *Moral Conduct and Authority*, pp. 38–61.

importance. During the eighth through the tenth centuries mastery of spoken and written Arabic distinguished the cultured man at the caliphal court. Elegant speech, studied with historical allusions and fragments of poetry, was universally admired. An intimate knowledge of Arabic literature and a lucid, flowing prose style commanded praise. Highly prized among courtiers was the ability to compose orders, diplomatic correspondence, and proclamations in a highly ornamented style. The purpose of the prose was to divert and entertain through sheer verbal virtuosity and to impart information about the world. Poetry, however, was king of the verbal arts. It was composed according to strict formal standards governing rhythm, rhyme, form, subject matter, and verbal usage and was chanted or sung in public. A faultless grip on the mechanics of Arabic was indispensable, and a detailed study of Arabic grammer, syntax, and vocabulary was the bedrock of every adib's education.

Other art forms also found a place in the courtly culture of West Asia. Rulers, nobles, and merchants patronized architects and lavished money on palaces, mansions, gardens, baths, tombs, and mosques. Painting didn't develop a following until the later centuries, when the Persian influence had become quite strong. Following the Mongol conquest, painters in West and Central Asia were encouraged and patronized in courtly circles. Calligraphy emerged during this period as well. Several styles of handwriting were created and used to decorate books, mosques, and tombs. Finally, men of taste and refinement patronized wood-workers, metalworkers, weavers, rug-makers, potters, porcelain-makers, embroiders, and other skilled artisans.[19]

Although the word "adab" was sometimes used in Mughal India, the term that seems to have been most current was "mirzai"; i.e., gentility or gentlemanliness, the behavior or manners of a prince or gentleman. Dargah Quli Khan, in describing one of the most sophisticated female singers of Shahjahanabad, remarked that she possessed adab to such a degree that many well-bred persons wanted to acquire instruction from her.[20] Mostly, however, "mirzai" was the term used for men of refinement and culture. Thus, Mirza Jan-i Janan, the famous poet and sufi of early eighteenth-century Shahjahanabad, had "acquired all of the arts of mirzai",[21] and Jafar Khan, a great amir under Aurangzeb, had excellent manners – no one could equal him in mirzai etiquette (*mirzai munshi*).[22] Finally, the Mirza Namah, an early seventeenth-century

---

[19] For a discussion of adab culture see Hodgson, *Venture*, 1 pp. 445–71.
[20] "Risalah-i Salar Jang," fols. 123a–4.
[21] Ibid., fols. 103a–5.
[22] Khafi Khan, *Muntakhab al-Lubab*, 2 p. 235.

manual on manners and culture, laid down the rules of mirzai (*qanun-i mirzai*).[23]

In Mughal India "men of the pen" were clerks, secretaries, accountants, revenue officials, and superintendents. They often held low ranks in the mansabdari system – 20–200 zat – and filled administrative positions in the towns and cities that served as revenue circle, district, and provincial headquarters. In the imperial household they managed mints, arsenals, workshops, libraries, and storerooms. Other men held similar positions in the households of high-ranking amirs but because they were not in the imperial system they did not hold mansabdari ranks.

Low-ranking mansabdars of the imperial household and unranked men of amiri establishments did not command high salaries. Revenue circle officials received 10–17 rupees a month (about the same as cavalrymen), sarkar and provincial officials were paid perhaps 50–100 rupees per month, and managers in the imperial household earned no more than 500 rupees per month. Nevertheless, these men seem to have had unofficial sources of income and to have been able to support cultured and refined life-styles. They faked revenue records, remitting less than they collected; took in valuable coins and passed on damaged ones; deposited tax receipts with moneylenders, keeping the interest for themselves; and demanded bribes for fulfilling their duties.[24]

Some of these men were Muslim, immigrant administrators or Hindu converts, but most of the Mughal "men of the pen" seem to have come from the traditional Hindu writer and clerical castes. In North India these were the Kayasths and Khattris and in South India the Brahmans. Kayasths are thought to have been the first Hindu caste to learn Persian (in the early fifteenth century under Sikander Lodi) and, by the time of Akbar, had taken up positions throughout the empire. Khattris too learned Persian and soon became important managers and administrators in North India. Hindus had held a monopoly on all lower ranks in the revenue department from before the time of Akbar, and most of the munshis in the imperial departments from 1650 onwards were Hindus. For the most part, the nobles and princes of the late seventeenth and early eighteenth centuries had Hindu munshis to write their letters also. Persian-born were too costly and Indian Muslims were not especially interested.[25]

[23] Maulawi M. Hidayat Husain, ed. and trans., "The Mirza-Namah (The Book of the Perfect Gentleman) of Mirza Kamran with an English Translation," *Journal of the Asiatic Society of Bengal*, n.s. 9 (1913) p. 9.

[24] I.A. Khan, "The Middle Classes in the Mughal Empire," *Proceedings: Indian History Congress* (1975) pp. 113–41.

[25] Aziz Ahmad, *Studies in Islamic Culture in the Indian Environment* (Oxford: Clarendon Press, 1964), pp. 105–7. For the Kayasths see Karen Isaksen Leonard, *Social History of*

"Men of the pen" mastered Persian, the language of the court, and during the seventeenth and eighteenth centuries produced works of history, poetry, and literature. Chandra Bhan Brahman, Anand Ram Mukhlis, and Sujan Rai are good examples of Hindu "men of the pen" as writers of Persian. These men adopted Muslim dress and learned the etiquette of the court ceremonial. In their domestic arrangements they followed the pattern of the Mughal amirs. They were less observant of ritual than other Hindus and somewhat less conscious of caste. They had the resources to build beautiful homes and to patronize talented artists and skilled artisans.

One of these men was Raja Raghunath who, in the twenty-third year of Shahjahan's reign, was given the title of Rai, the gift of a gold pen-case, and promoted to recordkeeper of the household lands (*khalisa*).[26] And another was Banarsidas, a Jain merchant from Jaunpur, who had learned Hindi and Persian in addition to arithmetic accounting and the assaying of coins.[27]

"Men of the pen," however, were not the principal practitioners of high culture during the Mughal period. The 70–100 great amirs of the imperial court undertook a rigorous program of study and training that enabled them not only to master the basic skills of the "men of the pen" but also to extend and refine their abilities and talents and to express them in a new, beautiful, and striking way.

Unlike the largely Hindu "men of the pen," the great amirs were predominately Muslim. Over three-quarters (77 percent) of the 179 great amirs of the period 1658–78 fell into this category, and so the education and training of the typical great amir had a substantial Islamic element. Every adult Muslim male had to be able to recite the basic creed, perform the five prayers, and read, if not understand, the Quran. Some of amirs had tutors for this early training while others studied in *maktabs* (grammer schools) or *madrasahs* (secondary schools). The syllabus, developed in the late fifteenth century and revised and expanded in *c.* 1600, was that of Sikander Lodi, and it directed Muslim education in India until about 1750.[28]

For the typical great amir schooling began at age four with the memorization of verses from the Quran. In order to understand the sacred book and the classical works of law and theology, the study of

an Indian Caste: The Kayasths of Hyderabad (Berkeley: University of California Press, 1978).

26 *Ma'asir al-Umara* 2 p. 282.
27 "Ardha-Katanak," *Indica* 7 (1970) p. 52.
28 M. Mujeeb, *The Indian Muslims* (London: George Allen and Unwin, Ltd., 1967), pp. 404–8.

Arabic grammar, diction, and syntax followed. Then came Islamic law (*fiqh*) and the principles of jurisprudence. After this *tafsir* (exegesis of the Quran), *hadith* (traditions of the prophet), *kalam* (scholastic philosophy), and *mantiq* (logic) were begun.[29]

Persian was the language of court and administration and had to be mastered. Except for those newly arrived from Iran, Persian was familiar but foreign – a language of culture with a status somewhat similar to that of French among the nineteenth-century Russian nobility. It was probably not often spoken in the home. Khan Dauran, for example, thought it pretentious to use Persian in everyday conversation; it left one open to ridicule and criticism.[30] And the Mirza Namah stated that a knowledge of Arabic, Persian, and Turkish was necessary in addition to the native Hindustani.[31]

Every educated man knew the *Gulistan* and *Bustan* of Sa'adi, the poems of Hafiz, and the *Shah-Namah* of Firdausi. In addition, great amirs learned to express themselves forcefully and eloquently, both in speech and in writing. The syllabus included *ma'ani* (rhetoric, the theory of literary style), *bayan* (clearness of speech), *badi* (beauty), *uruz* (prosody), *quwafi* (syllables), and *adab* (literature and learning).[32] Great men also studied mathematics, learned a bit about medicine, and practiced calligraphy. A refined and elegant hand was a valued accomplishment.

In Mughal India great amirs amassed libraries. The household manual listed fifty-two core works[33] but most men boasted far greater collections. Abd al-Rahim Khan-i Khanan, for example, had a magnificent library (we don't know exactly how many volumes) that required a staff of ninety-five calligraphers, guilders, book-binders, painters, cutters, collators, and illuminators.[34]

While the imperial court was the primary stage on which these men exhibited their taste and style, there were other venues as well. Great amirs arranged *musha'iras* (literary evenings) in their mansions. Poets came to read their works and to gain recognition. The audience was sophisticated and responded with stylized praise and criticism, and success here meant patronage and reputation. Sometimes there was controversy. Girami Kashmiri, a poet from Kashmir, came to Shahjahanabad in the 1730s with his poems under his arm. He recited them in

---

[29] "Mirza-Namah," p. 9.
[30] Zahiruddin Malik, *A Mughal Statesman of the Eighteenth Century: Khan-i Dauran, Mir Bakshi of Muhammad Shah* (Delhi: Asia Publishing House, 1973), pp. 108–9.
[31] "Mirza Namah," p. 9.
[32] M. Zaki, "Organization of Islamic Learning Under the Sayyids and Lodis," *Medieval India* 4 (1977) pp. 1–9; "Mirza Namah," pp. 9–10.
[33] "Bayaz-i Khushbui," fols. 137b–9b.
[34] Abd al-Baqi, *Ma'asir-i Rahimi*, 3 pp. 1681–8.

the style of his home province and caused a great deal of argument at one musha'ira.[35] At the coffeehouses in Chandni Chawk great men gathered daily to sip the dark, bitter brew and discuss literary and cultural matters.[36].

Babur, the founder of the Mughal dynasty, was one of the masters of early Turkish prose and poetry. The *Babur-Namah*, his autobiography, is one of the masterpieces of Turkish prose, and he produced a body of poetry in Chaghatai Turkish second only to that of Mir Ali Shir. Garden design interested him also, and he built a number of gardens in the Central Asian style, taking great pains over the layout of fountains and waterways and the placement of trees and flowers. Babut was fluent in Persian and an accomplished poet in that language, superior to most of the other amirs and the equal of the average court poet. He was a skilled calligraphist as well.[37]

Humayun, Babur's son, marked the transition from Turkish to Persian among the Mughal elite. During his reign a few men continued to speak Turkish and Humayun himself used it in private conversations but Persian was the language of his verse and prose and it became the standard at court. Humayun spent the middle years of his reign (1540–55) in exile at the Safavid court of Iran. During this period, he became acquainted with the leading Persian men of letters and his presence gave impetus to a movement already underway, the emigration of poets and writers from Iran to India. Under the Safavids, Shi'ism became the dominant sect of Islam in Iran. Those who wouldn't accept Shi'ism were persecuted, and during the following 100–50 years many poets, writers, painters, and calligraphers emigrated to India.

The Emperor Akbar has been called "illiterate," and it is probably true that his abilities to read and write were limited. Nevertheless, he had a great library, said to contain over 26,000 books, and works of poetry, literature, and history were read to him regularly. He had a strong memory and learned significant portions of the poetry of Hafiz and Rumi. He was curious, intelligent, and spoke a stylish Persian, reciting both Hindi and Persian poetry at court and composing verses extemporaneously in both languages. He exhibited a strong interest in music, calligraphy, and painting and patronized a distinguished collection of poets, historians, calligraphers, philosophers, theologians, physicians, painters, and musicians. Akbar may not have been able to read or write but he was certainly educated and highly cultured.

---

[35] "Risalah-i Salar Jang," fols 108a–9.
[36] Ibid., fols. 88–9a.
[37] Zahir al-Din Muhammad Babur, *Babur-Namah*, trans. Annette Susan Beveridge (reprint edn; New Delhi: Oriental Books Reprint Corporation, 1970), pp. 531–3.

The Emperor Jahangir was a poet and prose writer of distinction. He composed a good deal of Persian poetry but it is on his memoirs, *Tuzuk-i Jahangiri*, that his reputation rests. The style is simple and powerful, and the language and content portray a man of sensitivity and intelligence. In addition to poetry and literature, Jahangir was interested in history, geography, botany, biology, zoology, alchemy, calligraphy, and music. He was a connoisseur of painting and had a keen eye; when confronted by a picture painted by several men, he could specify which artist had painted which part.[38]

The Emperor Shahjahan was more interested in the visual and monumental arts than in the verbal. Although he is said to have composed verse in Persian, we have no examples and the *firmans* (orders) ascribed to him are almost certainly not from his hand. Nevertheless, Chandar Bhan testifies to the exquisite character of his handwriting, his knowledge of mathematics, and his acute eye for jewels.[39] Shahjahan patronized men of letters and impressive works of history and poetry were produced during his reign. Architecture, however, was the art form in which he felt most at home. It catered to the great wealth at the disposal of him and his courtiers and satisfied their desires for fame and immortality.

Aurangzeb was the least cultured of the great emperors. His appears to have been a narrow personality, that of a man geared to numbers and details, and he did not possess the imagination or curiosity of a man of culture. Nevertheless, Aurangzeb was well-educated and had mastered the basic skills of the "men of the pen." Proficient in Arabic and Persian, he was a skilled calligrapher. He had committed much of the Quran to memory and spent many hours studying hadiths, legal cases, and works of jurisprudence. He disliked painting, music, poetry, and architecture on the grounds, he said, that they were unIslamic but more likely for reasons of temperament and training. He abolished the post of *malik al-shuara* (master of poetry) and discontinued the stipends of many poets. He abolished the earlier practice of commissioning works of painting, music, and architecture (except for mosques).[40] An historian of his reign wrote: "he possessed great skill in prose composition and letters and was well-versed in prose and poetry but holding to the precept of holy verse – 'it is the erring who follow the poets' – he did not incline to the hearing of useless poetry."[41]

Not only were the Mughal emperors practitioners of the arts but they played a major role in Shahjahanabad and the other capitals as patrons of

[38] Jahangir, *Tuzuki-i Jahangiri*, p. 235.
[39] Chandar Bhan Braham, "Chahar Chaman," fol. 48.
[40] Khafi Khan, *Muntakhab al-Lubab*, 2 pp. 214–15.
[41] Musta'idd Khan, *Ma'asir-i 'Alamgiri*, p. 318.

cultural activity. Departments devoted to painting, jewels, goldworking, gold lace-making, satin and woolen weaving, carpets, building, dancing, and music were found in the imperial household.[42] And, during their daily audiences the emperors examined the products of these departments. For example, during his stint in the Hall of Special Audience Shahjahan inspected the work of diamond-cutters, inlayers, enamellers, jewellers, and gold and silver workers; examined rare and exquisite cloths; glanced through Arabic and Persian books from the royal library; admired works of painting and calligraphy; and praised and rewarded the verses of the household poets.[43] The court poet, Abu Talib Kalim, an immigrant from Hamadan in Iran, died in 1652 after composing many poems on the glories of the new capital.[44] Shahjahan joined the arguments of scholars and theologians; listened to Greek and Indian physicians report cures for various diseases; attended to the discussions of astronomers, astrologers, and calculators on the theory and practice of their art; and examined the drawings of designers and architects. Singers and musicians (*kalavant* and *tawaif*) provided relaxation and enjoyment in the harem at the end of the day. Shahjahan's favorites were Kavindra, Chitra Khan, Lal Khan, and Srimen.[45]

Muhammad Shah was also very fond of music, and Dargah Quli wrote of Shuja'at Khan, one of the principal *kalavants* (singers) of the high presence,[46] Boli Khan, a kalavant and member of the imperial household,[47] and Jattah, the *qawwal* (singer), the ornament of sufi assemblies and the beloved of the imperial establishment.[48] Two female singers were also patronized by the emperor: Chamani, one of the famous persons of the city, was honored and revered and given large sums of money[49], and Kamal Bai, a kalavant and dancer, adorned the society of the imperial presence. After Nadir Shah's invasion the emperor grew despondent and was less interested in song and dance and Kamal Bai was able to play for other persons.[50]

Taqi, an actor, was the head of a group of beautiful young boys in Muhammad Shah's household and was so important that even the great amirs of the *khilvat-gah* (the inner sanctum) spoke respectfully to him.[51] Chak Mak and Mani were young male dancers who had seduced the emperor with their beauty and skill.[52]

[42] "Dastur al-Amal-i 'Alamgiri," fols. 53b–105a.
[43] Chandar Bhan Brahman, "Chahar Chaman," fols. 26–32.
[44] Abu Talib Khan Kalim, "Diwan-i Kalim," Persian Manuscript Collection, Add. 24,002, British Museum, London, fols. 53b–4b.
[45] Chandar Bhan Brahman, "Chahar Chaman," fols. 26–32; Waris, Padshah Namah," fols. 71, 80, 100b.
[46] "Risalah-i Salar Jang," fols. 116–a.   [47] Ibid., fol. 116a.
[48] Ibid., fols. 120–a.   [49] Ibid., fols. 124–a.   [50] Ibid., fols. 127–a.
[51] Ibid., fols. 118–a.   [52] Ibid., fols. 125–a.

Like the emperors, the princes and great amirs of the Mughal court were an accomplished group. For the great men, as for the "men of the pen," command of the language and knowledge of literature were the primary virtues. The author of the Mirza Namah wrote:

In society he (Mirza) should try to guard against the shame of commiting any mistake in conversation, for such incorrectness in speech is considered a great fault in a Mirza.[53]

Men of culture must have committed a good deal of Arabic and Persian verse to memory and be able to interject it into conversation and state documents at will. Khan Dauran, for example, spoke an elegant Urdu, ornamented with Persian phrases, that won him praise and fame at the court of Muhammad Shah.[54] Regardless of talent, all great amirs were expected to compose correct examples of the various genres of Persian poetry. The Mirza Namah pointed out that all cultured men should know the *Gulistan* and *Bustan* of Sa'adi and be quick at composition. It was acceptable to chant or recite a verse or two in public, if one possessed a good voice, but the careful mirza should not do so regularly or he would be taken for a professional poet or singer.[55] Abd al-Rahim Khan-i Khanan had mastered Persian, Arabic, Turkish, Sanskrit, and Hindi and could compose poetry in each, though he was particularly skilled in Persian and Hindi. Famed for his facility at translation, he rendered the *Babur-Namah* into Persian and translated court documents from Persian to Hindi at sight. He was unsurpassed in *insha* (diplomatic correspondence) and once drafted a letter of introduction for Akbar's ambassador to the court of Abdullah Khan Uzbeg, ruler of Khurasan, that drew raves from the Uzbeg court.[56]

The cultured prince or great amir was expected to display distinction in household appointments and dress as well as in speech and manner. He smoked scented tobacco blended with hashish in his *huqqa* (water pipe) and crushed precious gems such as emeralds and pearls in his wine. Brightly colored coats, shirts, and trousers were tailored to a tight fit; an elaborately decorated scarf encircled his waist and held a dagger; and in his hand he carried a carved stick. But the turban – a long piece (as much as twenty feet) of fine linen, laced with gold thread and ornamented with jewels – was the capstone of the great amiri outfit. It was decorated with jewelled pendants or aigrettes and tied into astonishing shapes that took two or three hours to complete.[57] Mirza Abu Said, a great amir under Shahjahan known for his mirzai, was so fastidious that the imperial darbar

---

[53] "Mirza Namah," p. 9.   [54] Malik, *Khan Dauran*, pp. 108–9.
[55] "Mirza Namah," pp. 9–10.   [56] Abd al-Baqi, *Ma'asir-i Rahimi*, 2 pp. 535–6.
[57] Anand Ram Mukhlis, *Chamanistan*, (Lucknow: n.p. 1877), p. 88.

had usually ended by the time he had finished tying his turban – and, because the wind disturbed it, he refused to go riding.[58]

Among the great amirs of Shahjahanabad in the late 1730s there was Azam Khan, a talented singer who had command of all of the famous songs of Hindustan.[59] Mirza Manu, the son of a great amir, was a skilled magician who attracted many persons to the gatherings at his mansion.[60] Latif Khan, whose assembly set the standard for the young amirs of his day, was a singer who captivated the great amirs (*umdah*). He also presented the foremost singers and musicians of the city – Niamat Khan and Nur Bai, for example – at his mansion.[61] Javid Khan, the son of Latif Ali Khan Diwan, was famed for his skill at reciting *marsiyas* (elegies on the death of Husain) and performed at many of the *ashura khanahs* (places where the death of Husain was commemorated) of the city.[62] Mir Abdul Razzaq was preeminent in interior design. The great hall of his palace was furnished with colored carpets, curtains, and glass vases and in the middle stood a large mirror on which he had inscribed a poem. He served coffee and jellies to his guests, offered them perfumes and huqqas, and had books of the ancient poets for them to read.[63]

Like the emperors, the great amirs collected and patronized talent. The typical household, like that of Khan Dauran, had a library where calligraphers worked, karkhanahs where artisans made carpets and goldwork, and a storeroom for perfumes.[64] All great men maintained poets in their households. Abdur Rahim Khan-i Khanan, for example, supported many poets, giving his favorites their weight in gold as a reward.[65] Khan Dauran sponsored musha'iras that drew poets from his own household and beyond,[66] and Sharif Khan Alamgiri numbered Ibrahim Ali Khan, one of the famous poets of Shahjahanabad, among his dependants.[67] In addition, many of the great amirs of the city regularly attended musha'iras at the houses of poets like Siraj al-Din Ali Khan Arzu.[68]

Many of the great amirs of Shahjahanabad were also interested in music and singing. Shah Nawaz Khan Safavi, a great amir under Shahjahan, had more singers and musicians in his household than any other amir;[69] Azam Shah, an amir under Muhammad Shah, included Shah Bazu, the best sahuramchi player in the city, in his household[70]; and Amir Khan, one of the most cultured and accomplished great amirs of his time,

[58] Ma'asir al-Umara 3 pp. 513–16.   [59] "Risalah-i Salar Jang," fols. 95a–6.
[60] Ibid., fol. 96.   [61] Ibid., fol. 96–7.   [62] Ibid., fols. 109a–10a.
[63] Ibid., fols. 107a–8a.   [64] "Ahwal-i Khan Dauran," fols. 156a–87a.
[65] Ma'asir al-Umara 1 pp. 693–713.   [66] "Ahwal-i Khan Davran," fols. 161a–2.
[67] "Risalah-i Salar Jang," fol. 107a.   [68] Ibid., fols. 106–a.
[69] Ma'asir al-Umara 2 pp. 670–6.   [70] "Risalah-i Salar Jang," fol. 117a.

supported two of the most famous singers of the city: Burhani Amir Khani, famed for his pronunciation, and Rahim Khan Jhan, an expert khiyal singer.[71] Finally, in the early eighteenth century, the great amirs of the city clamored to see Nur Bai, a popular female singer. Their elephants clogged the lanes outside her house, and they gained admittance to her gatherings only by offering large sums of money.[72]

Itimad al-Daulah, another of Muhammad Shah's amirs, included in his entourage the dancer Bhania, an elephant driver by caste. He had a great reputation among the amirs, and at one point during a performance he was given drinking glasses worth 70,000 rupees each.[73] Khush Hali, a Hindu dancing girl and favorite of the great men of the city, was also part of Itimad al-Daulah's establishment.[74]

The great men also supported religious celebrations of various kinds. Vazir al-Mulk staged the celebration of the 'urs of Abdul Qadir Jilani, the famous Sufi saint of Baghdad, at his mansion. There was music, dancing, beautiful boys, and a great deal of wine and food.[75] On the 12th of Rabi I, the 'urs of the prophet Muhammad was held at the Arab Serai outside of the walled city. Khan Zaman, one of the great amirs of the time, decorated the entire area[76]

Gusal Singh, one of the imperial pillars of a thousand under Muhammad Shah, constructed a quarter named Gusalpurah outside the walls of the city. The atmosphere was redolent of sensuality and lust. It was a place of forbidden pleasure, offering wine, prostitutes, singing, and dancing. The power of *ihtisab* (moral censorship) did not reach there.[77]

The great men of the Mughal Empire – emperors, princes, and great amirs – refined the skills of the "men of the pen," raising them to a pitch of perfection never before seen. Secretaries, superintendents, and administrators had neither the talent, the training, nor the wealth to attain the cultural ideal while emperors, princes, and great amirs had the education, leisure, and resources to express what was beautiful, graceful, and valued. The courts of the great men were the final arbiters of taste, the places where the most talented poets, historians, calligraphers, musicians, dancers, painters, and singers performed. At court competition was great and critical acumen keen, and the artist who captured the praise of these audiences had scaled the pinnacle of success. Such artists were taken into imperial and great amiri households and lavishly rewarded.

---

[71] Ibid., fol. 116. [72] Ibid., fols. 123a–4. [73] Ibid., fol. 125. [74] Ibid.
[75] Ibid., fols. 98–100a. [76] Ibid., fols. 100a–2a. [77] Ibid., fols. 102a–3.

Men of the sword

Emperors, princes, and great amirs were not effete, overcultured courtiers, skilled at reciting poetry, composing state documents, judging the dancing and singing of courtesans, and nothing more. They were accomplished soldiers as well, trained in horseback riding, archery, sword fighting, and firearms, able to command the respect of their troops and to lead them in battle. Mughal great men combined the skills and talents of the "men of the pen" with those of the "men of the sword."

The ancestors of the "men of the sword" were probably the Seljuk Turks, a group of nomadic warriors who overran much of West Asia in the early part of the tenth century A.D. They adopted Islam and were converted to settled rule by the Persian administrators of the area. Under their tutelage, the Seljuk rulers adopted the trappings of kings and gave up irregular raiding and plunder for the rewards of routinized tax-collection. Other nomadic warriors (the Mongols and Timurid Turks, for example) invaded West Asia during the following centuries and were domesticated and absorbed as well. From that time forward a split developed between the military elite who ruled and protected the state and the clerks and managers who ran the administrative apparatus, a split that was reflected in the categories "men of the sword" and "men of the pen."

Mughal "men of the sword" were commanders and cavalrymen. Like the "men of the pen," these men were specialists, devoting their lives to the arts of war. Commanders or low-ranking mansabdars were the most important of the Mughal "men of the sword." Holding ranks from 20–400 zat, these men filled minor posts in imperial, princely, or great amiri contingents. They were, however, disbarred from higher positions by their educational and cultural deficiencies.

Ahadis or single cavalrymen served in the emperor's private bodyguard and cavalrymen served in princely and amiri households. Cavalrymen, who made up the bulk of the "men of the sword," received a good salary. They were paid 200 rupees a year, out of which they had to provide horses, armor, weapons, and servants. "Men of the sword" followed an honorable profession in Mughal India and both ahadis and cavalrymen were respectable men in Muslim society. Many of them, in fact, rose from the ranks to fill posts in the lower reaches of the mansabdari system.

To enter Mughal service "men of the sword" required patrons: blood relatives or fellow members of tribes, castes, or ethnic groups. A commander who wanted mansabdari rank was introduced to the mir bakshi by his patron and, if found properly armed and supplied, was

presented to the emperor. Ahadis also needed the personal approval of
the emperor but individual cavalrymen were checked less carefully.
Recruited by their amirs, they were examined by the bakshi's office and
then entered on the rolls.

"Men of the sword" wore heavy, cumbersome body armor. The
central piece, for those who could afford it, was a cuirass with a quilted
jacket beneath. Most cavalrymen, however, put on long, heavy, quilted
coats which stopped arrows and deadened sword blows. Cotton trousers
fastened with a shawl covered the lower body. Mansabdars wore steel
helmets while cavalrymen protected their heads with folds of quilted
cloth. Mailed gloves and leggings were worn by the well-to-do. Strong,
well-trained horses were indispensable to "men of the sword" and
mansabdars put armor on the chests and hindquarters of their mounts.
For most cavalrymen, however, heavy quilts provided the only
protection.

"Men of the sword" handled their weapons with skill. Since Mughal
cavalrymen did most of their fighting at close quarters, swords, lances,
and daggers were important. Scimitars, short swords with curved blades,
and long straight swords with broad blades hung from belts or were slung
over the shoulder. On his left arm or over his shoulder a cavalrymen
carried a shield of steel or hide. Some men used battle axes while others
wielded bayonets and javelins; many carried long, heavy lances of iron.
Daggers came into play in hand-to-hand fighting.

Although firearms had been available in Mughal India from the late
sixteenth century, they were cumbersome and difficult to use and the bow
and arrow remained the major long-distance weapon of the Mughal
cavalry until at least the middle of the eighteenth century. Bows were four
feet long and double-curved, made of horn, wood, bamboo, ivory, or
steel, and strung with catgut. Bowmen carried arrows of wood or steel in
quivers slung over their shoulders, leather guards protected their arms,
and rings of steel guarded their thumbs and fingers. Manuscripts of the
eighteenth century were devoted entirely to archery, and Bernier
observed that a Mughal archer could loose six arrows before a musketeer
could fire twice. The Mughals rated the sword better than the dagger, the
spear better than the sword, and the bow and arrow superior to them
both.[78]

No regular drill or exercise was required of "men of the sword." Great
amirs did not schedule maneuvers or mount war games, and so
cavalrymen in amiri contingents and low-ranking mansabdars kept
themselves in fighting trim by individual drilling and exercise. To build

[78] Bernier, *Travels*, p. 48.

strength and stamina they exercised with dumb-bells, heavy sticks of wood, clubs, and chainbows. Daily rehearsal of a coordinated sequence of movements called *kasarat* developed agility and quickness. "Men of the sword" wrestled and engaged in mock fights with heavy sticks and shields, they jousted at tent-pegs with lances, shot arrows at small targets while galloping full speed, they trained their horses to stand on their hind legs and jump forward in a maneuver designed to attack elephants.[79]

"Men of the sword," however, had no monopoly on the arts of war in Mughal India. Emperors, princes, and great amirs were skilled in horseback riding, archery, sword-fighting, and firearms and did not defer to cavalrymen and low-ranking mansabdars in their mastery of the soldier's art. These men developed the skills, stamina, and strength to prevail in individual combat and to lead by example in battle. With greater resources and better training, they raised the art of war to a new level.

For the great man training began early. At about age nine he learned the use of matchlocks and pistols, the fundamentals of archery and horsemanship, and was introduced to wrestling. In succeeding years he followed a regime of exercise, training, and competition that developed his endurance and ability and whetted his appetite for battle. Wrestling, a national pastime in Iran, was a favorite activity in Mughal India. Young men learned a variety of holds and techniques – Lucknow wrestling masters taught special tricks designed to overcome deficiencies in weight or height[80] – which they tried out in local competitions. In Shahjahanabad in the 1730s Mahabat Khan, one of the great amirs under Muhammad Shah, had wrestling exhibitions in the sandy area in front of his mansion. Both soldiers and other young men of his household participated; spectators walked by and sweets were served.[81] Sword-fighting skills were perfected in stick-fighting, the Indian techniques having been originally developed in Arabia and Iran. Training in hand-to-hand combat – for example, how to defend against dagger attacks was included also. Hunts, races, and games of polo developed horsemanship, and practice at the range and in the saddle sharpened skills in archery and firearms. Aurangzeb advised his sons:

If you are on a journey, but it is a day of halt . . spend 48 minutes of the morning in archery and musket practice.

Gradually make yourself perfect in the habit of wearing arms. Let your sweat dry before you take off your coat and lie down, lest you should fall ill.[82]

---

[79] Irvine, *Army*, pp. 182–9.
[80] Abdul Halim Sharar, *Lucknow: The last Phase of An Oriental Culture*, trans. and ed. E.S. Harcourt and Fakhir Hussain (Boulder, Col.: Westview Press, 1976), p. 113.
[81] "Risalah-i Salar Jang," fol. 103a.   [82] *Adab-i 'Alamgiri*, 1 p. 374.

And this same commitment to life in camp on horseback is admired in the description of Shaikh Farid Murtaza Khan Bukhari, a great amir under Jahangir. He is said to have never entered a dwelling of his own but to have always stayed in the advance camp.[83]

Horses were an important element in imperial and great amiri households. The horse represented his master on parade and in battle, and for great amirs and emperors that meant elaborately decorated and accoutered mounts. On the horse's head was an aigrette like the one in his master's turban, around his neck was a golden necklace, and encircling his fetlocks were heavy anklets. Raushan al-Daulah, a great amir under Muhammad Shah, imported breeds from Arabia and Turkey unmatched even in imperial stables, and his equipment was of gold and silver.[84]

Armor and weapons were highly prized in Mughal India, and emperors, princes, and great amirs maintained a number of departments devoted to the materials and arts of war. The emperor Aurangzeb, for example, had departments dealing with stirrups and riding equipment, swords, guns, elephants, horses, camels, bows, rifles, artillery, tents, and drums.[85] In Shahjahan's daily audience in the Hall of Special Audience he inspected inlaid and bejeweled swords from India and Yemen, armor like David's, and matchlocks. Swordsmen and boxers danced, cut, and sparred before him.[86] In Khan Dauran's household there were departments for swords, guns, cannon, camels, elephants, Iraqi and Arabian horses, ammunition, and artillery.[87]

From the late seventeenth century onward, emperors, princes, and great amirs do not seem to have made much use of the bow and arrow in battle. They left these weapons, by and large, to the "men of the sword" under their command and used firearms instead. Matchlocks had long carved barrels (some of Akbar's were 66 inches) and a tripod was often needed for firing. They required powder flasks, bullet pouches, priming horns, matchcords, flints, and steels, and it is no wonder that an extra servant was needed to carry and service them. Flintlocks were not common until the late eighteenth century, having been introduced by the Europeans, and percussion weapons were not available at all. Pistols are not mentioned in the *A'in*, and they don't seem to have been employed in India until the early eighteenth century. They were weapons of the wealthy and required a servant for carrying, loading, and servicing.[88]

---

[83] *Ma'asir al-Umara* 2, pp. 633–41.
[84] Ashob, "Tarikh-i Muhammad Shah," fol. 48b.
[85] "Dastur al-Amal 'Alamgiri," fols. 53b–5b.
[86] Chandar Bhan Braham, "Chahar Chaman," fols. 32–3.
[87] "Ahwal-i Khan Dauran," fols. 156a–87a.
[88] For some examples see, *The Indian Heritage: Court Life and Arts Under Mughal Rule* (London: Victoria and Albert Museum, 1982), pp. 134–8.

Cannons were found in the imperial household from Akbar's time but the Mughals never really learned to deploy them to advantage. The bigger the better was the Mughal principal, and they manufactured heavy, immobile cannons which were decorated and named but which could not be fired rapidly and were easily captured. Light artillery consisted of small field pieces of brass which were mounted on carriages and could be wheeled from place to place and fired rapidly. Here, as well, the Mughals had no sense of tactics, and they were never able to use these pieces very effectively.

Emperors, princes, and great amirs mastered the skills of individual combat but they do not seem to have devoted much thought to strategy and maneuvers. How then did Mughal commanders develop battle plans? How did they train their troops in the tactics of mass warfare? One answer is that they did not develop plans and that their troops were relatively untrained. The emperor Aurangzeb, for example, complained that he had not been taught how to besiege towns, take fortresses, and fight pitched battles.[89] This is not the whole answer, however. Emperors, princes, and great amirs did engage in maneuvers of a sort, giving cavalrymen and their commanders some experience in large-scale, set-piece combat.

During the Mughal period the imperial court spent a great deal of time on tour. In camp the great men were better able to practice the arts of war. A good part of each day was spent on horseback, refining skills in archery, swordsmanship, and firearms. Some of this was actual combat: many expeditions were intended to quell minor disturbances, pacify rebellious zamindars, and show the flag in fractious parts of the Empire.

Nevertheless, the principal method of developing the soldier's art on tour was hunting. In many parts of Northern and Central India imperial hunting preserves had been established, and emperors, princes, and great amirs spent significant portions of many expeditions finding, riding down, shooting, and killing wild animals. Hunting tigers and lions was a royal prerogative, and only a few great amirs were allowed to participate. Ordinarily, the great cats were shot by musket or bow and arrow from the backs of elephants but sometimes they were approached on horseback. Great men hunted elephants from the backs of other elephants. Deer, rhinoceri, blue bulls, wild asses, and cheetah were chased on horseback and shot with bow and arrow or matchlock. The Mughals trained cheetah to kill deer and blue bulls, employed packs of hunting dogs, and took up falconry, a sport that had a long history in Arabia and Iran.[90]

---

[89] Bernier, *Travels*, p. 161; Manucci, *Storia*, 2 pp. 29–33.
[90] For typical hunts of the period see Abu al-Fazal, *Akbar-Namah*, 2 pp. 281–2 and Jahangir, *Tuzuk*, pp. 39–40, 57, 59–60.

Hunts were of two kinds, either small informal, spur of the moment, and with only a few men or large and well-organized, involving the mansabdars and cavalrymen of the camp. The first was a common occurrence on tour. Emperors, princes, and great amirs would halt for several days in order to hunt nearby and would often go for a brief shoot at the end of a day's march.

The other variety of hunt, however, involved a great number of men, was staged in one of the imperial preserves, and was carefully organized and coordinated. Called a *qamargah* (moon-shaped) hunt or a *shikar-i jarga* (circular hunt), this was a large-scale maneuver. A great many cavalrymen (as many as 50,000 sometimes) were deployed in a huge circle. At a signal they began to move forward, contracting the circle, beating the underbrush, and trapping the game within. When the circle had closed and the animals had become closely confined, the great men entered the ring and began a general slaughter. The encircling cavalry-men shot and killed those animals which tried to escape and those which remained after the great men had left.[91] The Mughals, descendants through Babur of Timur and Chinghiz Khan, organized their hunt after the Mongol pattern. The Persian historian Juvaini reveals the Mongol hunt, like the Mughal, to be kind of wargame, an exercise for developing the coordination, discipline, courage, and individual skills of large-scale battle.

[Chinghiz Khan] has given careful attention to the matter of the hunt and has said that the hunting of wild animals is a proper occupation for amirs and that instruction and training [in it] is necessary for warriors and men at arms; not only for the game, but also to become... familiarized with handling the bow and enduring hardships... any time the khan undertakes a great hunt [*shikar-i buzurg*]... he orders the soldiers... to prepare to hunt... For one, two, or three months they maintain a hunting ring [*halqa-i shikar*]... and if unexpectedly an animal should escape, an exhaustive inquiry as to the cause is made and amirs of 1,000, 100, and 10 are beaten and often even put to death because of it. And if, for example, a man does not keep to the lines, but takes a step backwards or forwards, he is severely punished and never excused... when the ring has contracted such that the wild animals cannot move, first the khan rides in with his retinue... then... the princes, the noya, the commanders, and the soldiers... now war – with its killing, counting of the dead, and sparing of survivors – is quite similar and analogous in every detail.[92]

Emperors, princes, and great amirs were the embodiment of high culture in Mughal India. They mastered the basic skills of the men both of

[91] For the qamargah hunt see Anand Ram, "Mir'at al-Istilah," fol. 183b.
[92] Ala al-din Ata Malik-i Juwayni, *Tarikh-i Jahan Gusha*, ed. Mirza Muhammad, 3 vols. (London: Luzac and Co., 1912–37), 1 pp. 19–21.

the pen and of the sword, refining and developing these two aspects of courtly culture and expressing in a more elegant, elaborate, and practiced form all that was valued at the Mughal court. Mughal "men of the pen" did not have the education or resources to cultivate the full range of the fine arts. Their expertise was confined, by and large, to fluency in Persian and mastery of the prose of state documents, chronicles, memoranda, and diplomatic correspondence. Their knowledge of Persian, furthermore, was limited to the standard authors, and their poetical compositions were perfunctory. Painting, music, dance, and architecture were beyond them.

The great men, on the other hand, had interests that were catholic, deep, and abiding, their abilities frequently rose above the ordinary and, because of their training, they were able to recognize talent. A grounding in Islamic theology and Arabic poetry and prose enabled the great men to remain in touch with their heritage. Their knowledge of Persian was fluent and profound, and they composed acceptable, often praiseworthy, specimens of poetry. Their prose was refined and elegant. In addition, individual emperors, princes, and great amirs exhibited skill in calligraphy, painting, architecture, music, and dance. But it was their appreciation of these other art forms, their ability to recognize and reward genius, that was crucial. At the courts of the emperors and great amirs the greatest artists of the day displayed their talents and received the praise and reward they were due.

The great men mastered the arts of war as well. Becoming expert in the basic military skills, they soon surpassed the "men of the sword" who had neither the resources, the training, nor the opportunities to match them. Their horses were inferior, their equipment rudimentary, and their roles subordinate. Their military skills were confined, by and large, to the sword, dagger, and lance in close combat and the bow and arrow at longer range. Although discipline was lax and coordination minimal in Mughal armies, "men of the sword" found themselves circumscribed, their roles limited, and they were not able to fully express themselves.

The great men, on the other hand, developed expertise across the full range of the military arts. They were given extensive training in wrestling, in the use of the lance, and in hand-to-hand combat with sword and dagger. Archery masters drilled them in the use of the bow and arrow. Their horses were well-bred and carefully trained, strong and able to endure and, since the great men did not have to worry about replacements, they could ride and fight with verve and abandon. Their armor was well-made and ornate; it provided more protection and was less cumbersome than that of the "men of the sword," and it enabled them to move more easily in battle. These men became expert marksmen as well, having the resources and leisure to master the cumbersome and expensive weapons.

Of the exponents of the arts of war in Mughal India, emperors and great amirs were the only ones who gave any thought to tactics and strategy. They were the ones who deployed soldiers in the qamargah hunt and made an effort, however limited and feeble, to develop the co-ordination and planning necessary for success in large-scale warfare. In the arts of war as in the arts of peace, the great men patronized the able and talented. They recognized achievement in battle, rewarding and recommending for promotion those of their clients (cavalrymen and low-ranking mansabdars) who displayed skill and courage. They also provided a market for new developments in technology and strategy. European innovations in firearms were taken up by the emperors and eventually, European tactics, especially in the use of infantry, were adopted.

Emperors, princes, and great amirs perfected the skills of the men both of the pen and the sword, becoming more expert in each set of activities than either of the specialists. By refining their skills and mastering the arts both of peace and of war, they carried the courtly culture of Mughal India to new heights. Emperors, princes, and great amirs combined the abilities and attributes of the two cultural styles, summing up and expressing in a new, elegant, and unique way the courtly culture of Mughal India.

The men who attained this ideal are described in several ways. Abu al-Fazl wrote of one of Akbar's great amirs:

Khwaja Abd al-Majid, because of his ability, had been distinguished by the title of Asaf Khan, and had been raised from the pen [*qalam*] to the sword [*saif*] and had joined those who wear both the sword and the pen and are masters both of war and of peace.[93]

Shaikh Farid Murtaza Khan Bukhari, a great amir of the early seventeenth century, received the title lord of the sword and the pen (*sahib-i saif-o-qalam*) at the accession of the emperor Jahangir.[94]

Chandar Bhan Brahman described Shahjahan's great amirs as "men of learning and perfection, wielding both the sword and the pen with mastery."[95] And Rajah Bikramit Rai Rayan, a Brahman whose name was Sundar Das and who had been an administrator under Prince Shahjahan, was promoted to Mir Saman and, because of his spirit and lofty nature, was raised from the pen to the sword.[96] Finally, it was said of one of

---

[93] Abu al-Fazal, *Akbar Namah*, 2 p. 182.
[94] *Ma'asir al-Umara*, 2 pp. 633–41.
[95] Chandar Bhan Brahman, "Chahar Chaman," fols. 9b–10a.
[96] Ma'asir al-Umara 2 pp. 183–95.

Aurangzeb's great amirs on his death in 1697:

> In his assemblies the topics of conversation were mostly verse, prose, sword, jewel, horse, elephant, and aphrodisiacs.[97]

The ideal types – "men of the sword" and "men of the pen" – are also found in the other two Islamic empires of the period: the Ottoman in Turkey and the Safavid in Iran. In Ottoman Turkey the *askeri* or ruling class was divided into three groups: "men of the sword" (military specialists and administrators); men of learning (legal experts who were judges and teachers); and "men of the pen" (administrators). Although the great men of the Ottoman state had to combine, to some degree at least, the skills and abilities of both types in order to advance, the Ottomans don't seem to have had the same expectation of balance and fusion that the Mughals had.[98]

The ruling class in Safavid Iran was divided into Turkish horsemen and soldiers ("men of the sword") and Persian administrators ("men of the pen"). Throughout the Safavid period these two groups were in conflict. The Iranians thought the Turks coarse and uncouth, lacking any appreciation for poetry and the other fine arts. The Turks, on the other hand, looked down on the Persians as effete and unable to pacify and protect their own country. This conflict is said by one recent commentator to have been a major cause for the collapse of the regime. The Safavid emperors were never able to integrate the two types into a coherent, unified governing system.[99]

According to Cornell Fleischer, the major post-Mongol states of the Islamic world – the Ottoman, Safavid, and Mughal – fashioned different syntheses in their attempts to integrate, on the one hand, the steppe, nomadic, Chinghiz-Khanid tradition with, on the other hand, the Iranian, settled, sedentary Islamic tradition. In this light, the sword–pen fusion of the Mughals is best understood as the Indian way of achieving a synthesis. What the Mughals did was to fashion a composite ideal that valued the contributions, skills, and talents of both traditions – the nomadic Chinghiz-Khanid tradition ("the men of the sword") and the settled, Iranian, Islamic tradition ("the men of the pen") – and that integrated them into a system offering places both for the low-ranking specialists and the high-ranking generalists. Thus, the Mughals found a

---

[97] Musta'idd Khan, *Ma'asir-i 'Alamgiri*, p. 390.

[98] Cornell H. Fleischer, *Bureaucrat and Intellectual in the Ottoman Empire: The Historian Mustafa Ali (1541–1600)* (Princeton: Princeton University Press, 1986), pp. 5–7.

[99] Roger M. Savory, *Iran Under the Safavids*, (Cambridge: Cambridge University Press, 1980), pp. 32–3; Roger M. Savory, "The Safavid Administrative System," in Jackson and Lockhart, ed., *The Cambridge History of Iran*, p. 371.

way to include in a single unified system the writer, administrative castes of the Hindus (the Kayasthas, Khattris, and Brahmins), the warrior castes of the Hindus (the Rajputs and, in the earlier period, the Marathas), the Muslim military groups (the Afghans and Turanis), and the Muslim administrative groups (the Iranis). The Mughal system molded a religiously and ethnically diverse group of men into a synthetic, composite, functioning whole.[100]

In fact, the sedentary–peripatetic style of government of the Mughal rulers is another example of the Indian synthesis. Although the emperors of the period 1556–1739 spent nearly 40 percent of their time away from their capitals on trips of one year or more, they still managed to build large and impressive cities and to display a considerable amount of interest and skill in the sedentary arts of civilization.[101] Just as the sword–pen composite reflected the synthesis of the traditions at the individual level so the camp–city dichotomy reflected the same synthesis at the level of the empire itself.

Popular culture

This description of popular culture in Shahjahanabad is based largely on *Risalah Salar Jang* (Treatise of Salar Jang), an account by Nawab Dargah Quli Khan Salar Jang of his three-year residence in the capital (1737–40). Dargah Quli Khan was born in Aurangabad in Central India in 1710. In

---

[100] Fleischer, *Bureaucrat and Intellectual*, pp. 286–7. J.F. Richards has recently written about courtly culture. "Norms of Comportment," in Metcalf, ed., *Moral Conduct and Authority*. He looks at two groups of men – the nobles (amirs and great amirs) and what he calls the technical officers (my "men of the pen"). He argues that a common code for conduct, summed up in the word *khanazadi* (which he translates as devoted, familial, hereditary service to the emperor), defines the attitudes and activities of both groups. The nobles and technical officers who were *khanazads* (i.e., who had fathers or other close relatives in Mughal service) shared a corporate identity and common cultural ethic, he maintains. Richards' article is interesting and illuminates several important issues. It is useful to be reminded that among both the amirs and the "men of the pen" there was a stable group of men whose families had long served the emperor. And his detailed account of one of the Hindu "men of the pen," the historian Bhimsen, is absorbing.

Nevertheless, it seems to me that Richards' analysis of courtly culture is incomplete and that his understanding of Mughal ideology is flawed. Khanazads never constituted more than 50 percent of Mughal amirs, and there is no evidence that these men felt a corporate identity that cut across the ties of caste, race, and tribe. Secondly, there does not seem to be any evidence in the sources of the use of "khanazadi" in Richards' sense. In the example he cites (p. 262, fn. 45), the noun refers to belonging to a long-time mansabdari family but it does not imply any of Richards' meanings about code for conduct or ideology. Thirdly, Richards has failed to take account of the arts of war. In Mughal India great amirs were expected to master both sets of activities, not just those of the "men of the pen."

[101] For a discussion see Blake, "Patrimonial-Bureaucratic Empire," pp. 90–3.

1724, at the age of fourteen, he entered the service of Nawab Nizam al-Mulk Asaf Jah, the governor of the Mughal province of the Deccan. At the age of 20, six years later, he was included among the close personal attendants of Nizam al-Mulk, and by 1737 he had risen to the post of historian in the household of his patron.

The story of Dargah Quli's family and its connection to India is a familiar one. His great-great grandfather came to India from Qandahar in 1638. He was admitted to Mughal service and rose to a responsible post in the household of Prince Aurangzeb. His grandfather remained a Mughal officeholder, and his father, on the basis of the family's loyalty and service, was posted to Aurangabad, where Dargah Quli was born.[102]

Dargah Quli's account of his three-year stay in Shahjahanabad is lively, detailed, frank, and often disapproving. Almost nothing emerges of the political and military events of the period. The battle against the Mahrattas (the reason for Nizam al-Mulk coming north in the first place) and the defense of Shahjahanabad against the Persian ruler Nadir Shah are not mentioned at all, and the aftermath of the Mughal defeat – Nadir Shah's entry into the city and the fierce fighting and destruction that ensued – is only touched on once. Perhaps this is because, as official historian, Dargah Quli described these events in a traditional but no longer available account of his patron's activities. In any event, *Risalah-i Salar Jang* contains the details of daily life in the city, a description that would never have been included in any official chronicle.

Religious celebrations

Probably the most important aspects of popular culture in Shahjahanabad during this period were the celebrations at the tombs of Sufi saints. According to J.S. Trimingham, Sufism has passed through three stages. The first, the *khanqah* stage, lasted from the eighth to the twelfth centuries and was characterized by a loose and unstructured organization with no formal bond between master and student. The master was not an intermediary between God and man, and the khanqah was primarily a place where wandering Sufis pursued the devotional life under the direction of a master.

The second or *tariqa* stage began in the thirteenth century and was distinguished by the formation of mystical schools around masters. In wsocial structure this phase featured the *pir-murid* (master-disciple)

---

[102] See Charles Rieu, *Catalogue of the Persian Manuscripts in the British Museum*, 3 vols. (Oxford: Trustees of the British Museum, 1881; reprint edn, 1966) 2 p. 858; Muhammad Umar, "Glimpses of a Dying Culture From a Personal Dairy," *Journal of Indian History* 43 (1965) p. 468.

relationship and a greater degree of systematization, differentiation, and specialization. The third or *ta'ifa* stage began in the fifteenth century and was characterized by membership in a cult association (*ta'ifa*) and the veneration and worship of a pir who was the spiritual intermediary between the disciple and God. Pirs became saints and orders became saint-cults centered on the spiritual power or *barakat* of the saint. Leadership of the cults became hereditary and the spiritual power of the saint was thought to pass to his descendants and to the tomb itself.[103]

In the third stage (that exemplified in Shahjahanabad) Sufism became more devotional than mystical. Women as well as men became important participants in the celebrations, and the devotees offered flowers, coins, and food in the belief that the pir would answer prayers for wealth, peace, and children. The devotional practices at the shrines of Sufi saints were similar to those of Hindu pilgrims at Hindu shrines: circumambulation, touching clothes, turbans, or other relics, lighting candles, offering gifts (*nazr*) of flowers or coins to the saint's successors, praying, talking with fellow devotees, and singing devotional songs.

The most important religious celebration in Shahjahanabad in the early eighteenth century, and probably the most popular festival of any kind, was that held at the *Qadam Sharif* (sacred footprint). This marks a difference between Shahjahanabad of this period and Delhi of the thirteenth and fourteenth centuries, when the 'urs at the tombs of Bakhtiyar Kaki and Nizam al-Din were the most popular.[104] The Qadam Sharif was an enclosed tomb, originally built by Firuz Shah Tughlugh (1351–88) for himself, but used instead for his favorite son, Fath Khan, who died unexpectedly before him. According to tradition, Firuz Shah's spiritual guide, Makhdum Jahanian Jahan Gasht brought from Mecca at the emperor's request a stone bearing the prophet's footprint and it was placed on Fath Khan's tomb. On Thursday in the month of Rabi I, a great throng gathered at the tomb and, according to Dargah Quli, people were healed by drinking water from the tank in the courtyard. At the time of the 'urs of the prophet Muhammad people circumambulated the tomb and presented offerings. Miraculous healings took place and the prayers of the faithful were answered. On the 12th of Muharram there was a great pilgrimage to commemorate the deaths of Hussain and Abbas, the sons of Ali, and women wanting sons came for blessings.[105]

In the eighteenth century, as in the thirteenth and fourteenth centuries, the celebrations at the tombs of Bakhtiyar Kaki and Nizam al-

---

[103] See J.S. Trimingham, *The Sufi Orders in Islam* (Oxford: Oxford University Press, 1971).
[104] Simon Digby, "Tabarrukat and Succession Among the Great Chishti Shaikhs of the Delhi Sultanate," in Frykenberg, ed., *Delhi Through The Ages*, pp. 63–103.
[105] "Risalah-i Salar Jang," fols. 78a–9a.

Din Auliya were very popular. The tomb of Khwaja Qutb al-Din
Bakhtiyar Kaki was located near Lal Kot about fourteen miles from
Shahjahanabad. Popularly known as Qutb Sahib, Bakhtiyar Kaki came to
India with the early Muslim conquerors and became a disciple of Khwaja
Mu'in al-Din Chishti of Ajmir. He lived and worked during the reign of
the emperor Iltutmish (1211–36) and died in 1236. Several emperors
were buried in the environs of his tomb: Bahadur Shah (1707–12), Shah
Alam II (1759–1806), and Akbar II (1806–37). In Dargah Quli's time the
people made pilgrimages to the tomb throughout the year (but especially
on Thursdays) and circumambulated it, chanting their desires and
wishes. Storytellers abounded in the grounds.[106]

The other popular place of pilgrimage in the area was the tomb of
Nizam al-Din Auliya (1236–1325). Nizam al-Din came to Delhi with his
mother in the mid thirteenth century, became the disciple of Shaikh Farid
Shakarganj of the Chishti order, and was appointed his successor. He was
very popular and influential during his day – the emperors Ala al-Din
Khalji and Muhammad Tughluq were both devoted to him. Many
important persons were buried in the vicinity of the tomb: Amir Khusrao,
Nizam al-Din's disciple and a famous poet; Jahanara Begum, Shahjahan's
faithful daughter; and the emperor Muhammad Shah (1719–48). A great
crowd, entertained by storytellers, actors, and dancers, celebrated the
'urs of Nizam al-Din on the 14th of Rabi II. The 'urs of Amir Khusrao
was a special event also. The singers, poets, and dancers at his tomb
created a magnificent spectacle.[107]

The tomb of Hasrat Nasir al-Din Chiragh-i Delhi, Nizam al-Din's
successor as head of the Chishti order, was about six miles south of
Shahjahanabad. The day of pilgrimage was Sunday, and a great crowd of
both Muslims and Hindus gathered, especially during the month of
Diwali. Pilgrims pitched their tents, bathed in the nearby fountains and,
according to Dargah Quli, were healed. Music of the tabor and jew's harp
floated over the grounds and there were miracles for all. He was a lamp
(*chiragh*) for all of Hindustan, not just for Shahjahanabad.[108]

The spring festival of the Hindu year, Basant, was celebrated in
Shahjahanabad with a round of pilgrimages to the most popular tombs of
the area. In each of the spring months there was a seven-day festival. On
the first day a great crowd gathered at the Qadam Sharif. Merchants,
storytellers, singers, dancers, and musicians were everywhere. On the
second day the entire group moved to the tomb of Qutb Sahib,
circumambulated the tomb, and lighted candles. On the third day they
journeyed to the tomb of Nizam al-Din for circumambulation and a time

---

[106] Ibid., fols. 79a–80a.   [107] Ibid., fols. 80–2.   [108] Ibid., fols. 82–3.

of listening to mystical poetry and song. On the fourth day the pilgrims gathered at the tomb of Hasrat Shah Hasan Rasul Numah where they circumambulated and listened to songs and stories. On the fifth day they trooped to the tomb of Shah Turkoman inside the city walls where the chief qawwals of the city came to sing and pay their respects. On the sixth day they returned to the houses of the emperors and great amirs (their patrons), and began again the worldly round. On the seventh day the singers gathered at the great tomb in Ahadipurah, drank wine, and danced.[109]

There were also celebrations at the tombs of several other less popular saints: Hasrat Shah Turkoman Biabani,[110] Hasrat Baqi Billah,[111] and Hasrat Shah Hasan Rasul Numah.[112] During the 'urs at the tomb of Mirza Bidil (1685–1720), the famous poet of the city, his works were chanted by his disciples for the benefit of his soul.[113] The 'urs at Humayun's tomb was brilliantly lighted and drew great crowds. However, according to Dargah Quli, it was highly immoral: drunkenness, male and female prostitutes, and no intervention by the *muhtashib* (censor).[114]

The commemoration of the death of Husain, Ali's son, on the 10th of Muharram (the day of Ashura) was a special time for the Shi'is of the city. It was held at the tomb of Shah Aziz Ullah outside the walls of the city and many marsiyas wer sung.[115] Probably because he was Shi'i himself, and because there were a number of Shi'is in the city, Dargah Quli devoted a good deal of space to the various aspects of Muharram.

Javid Khan, the son of one of Muhammad Shah's great amirs, was quite skilled in the art of marsiya-reciting and he and his three brothers were sought-after in the ashura-houses of the city. His marsiyas were a mine of grief and a quarry of anguish.[116] Mir Abdullah carried the *ta'ziya* (representation of the tomb of Husain) and his marsiyas captured the ear of heaven. During Muharram many people flocked to the ta'aziya houses to hear him, and many young men wanted to learn the art of marsiya-reciting at his feet.[117] Shaikh Sultan was orginally from Eastern India (*purab*) but he learned the correct pronunciation of north India (Hindustan). His singing was exceptional and he caused the people in every ashura house that he entered to grieve greatly.[118] Mirza Abu Turab had genius and brought anguish to the ta'aziah attenders. His chanting was a necessity in all the sacred places.[119] The shriek of distress and the chants and cries of Mirza Ibrahim caused similar outbreaks in his listeners.[120] Mirza Darvish Husain, who ranked just behind Mir Abdullah

[109] Ibid., fols. 97–9.   [110] Ibid., fol. 83.   [111] Ibid., fol. 83a.
[112] Ibid., fols. 83a–4.   [113] Ibid., fols. 84–4a.   [114] Ibid., fols. 84a–5.
[115] Ibid., fols.93–3a.   [116] Ibid., fols. 109a–10a.   [117] Ibid., fols. 110a–1.
[118] Ibid., fol. 111.   [119] Ibid., fol. 111a.   [120] Ibid.

was a favorite of the great amirs and their sons and was once given Rs. 100,000.[121] Muhammad Nadim chanted in Urdu (*rekhta*), brought forth sorrow and lamentation, and silenced the Persian-speakers.[122]

In addition to the commemorations at the Qadam Sharif the Prophet Muhammad was also venerated at the Arab Sarai. On the day of his 'urs – 12 of Rabi I – nearly 2000 Arabs gathered in the mosque in the middle of the sarai and chanted qasidas in Arabic in praise of the prophet. They chanted all night, became ecstatic, and in the morning read from the Quran. Because of the proverbial hospitality of the Arabs, many people attended the 'urs and were served dates and coffee by beautiful Arab boys. After the evening prayers qawwals sang Sufi poems that sent the onlookers into ecstasy.[123]

In addition to the celebrations at the tombs of famous saints, a great many people in Shahjahanabad during the early eighteenth century attended gatherings at the houses of living Sufi saints. Here pilgrims received guidance, advice, and a measure of peace and contentment, a rest from the cares and pressures of every-day life. Here also the pious poor of the city gathered to rest, pray, and eat. Shah Hafiz Shah Sa'adullah, of the Naqshbandi order, had fame and followers but he allowed no poetry or singing at his house.[124] Shah Ghulam Muhammad Dawalpura struck fear and trembling into the hearts of the rich and happy. He gave food which he had obtained from the households of the emperors and nobles to the weak and poor on Fridays. However, he accepted no offerings from the women of the harem.[125] Shah Muhammad Amin was also a member of the Naqshbandi order. He fasted and rose before daylight. People came to his house to pray and meditate and found a holiday from worldly affairs. He was a place of refuge for the great amirs and for the Turani and the Kashmiri clients of Itimad al-Daulah.[126]

Hasrat Nawab Sahib Maham Barha was descended from five hundred years of Turanis. Turani amirs provided the cooked food which he distributed to the poor, and the sultans and other great amirs provided money and gifts. He played the sitar and the nobles forgot their troubles in his music. His conversation was witty and elegant and many people followed him[127]

Some of Nawab Sahib's followers also followed Majnun Nanak Shah. He was very emaciated and poor and practiced strict austerities. He had an abode on the bank of the river and gave audiences to both Hindu and Muslim pilgrims. His followers gave him flowers, sweets, and fruit which he distributed to the poor people in his audiences. Wealthy Hindus

---

[121] Ibid.   [122] Ibid., fol. 112a.   [123] Ibid., fols. 100a–2a.   [124] Ibid., fols. 89a–b.
[125] Ibid., fols. 89b–90a.   [126] Ibid., fols. 90a – 91.   [127] Ibid., fols. 91–2.

contributed large sums of money and a great crowd of poor people depended on him for their daily food. Everyone kept silent in his presence, finding the peace and tranquility they were searching for. Women came to him because they thought that, like Majnun in the famous story of Majnun and Laila, he would fulfill their desires. During the rainy season there was drunken hilarity in the area around his abode.[128]

Shah Kamal had no equal as a prince of asceticism. In mystical dancing he had advanced far beyond the other Sufis. Spectators at his gatherings derived great pleasure from readings by the princes of Persian and Urdu poetry.[129] Every Tuesday there was a gathering at the house of Shah Ghulam Muhammad and the most famous singers of the city (including Taj Khan) congregated. His society was a great prize and a model for the other shaikhs of the city. His assemblies were always crowded and many people wanted to become part of his order.[130]

Poets

The citizens of Shahjahanabad had a deep love for poetry. Poets were appreciated for their wit and talent and many people gathered at their homes to pay homage, to listen to their recitations, and, in the case of the poor, to receive food and gifts.

After Mirza Bidil, the most famous poet of early eighteenth-century Shahjahanabad was Mirza Mazhar Jan-i Janan (1702–81). He was a man of many parts, skilled in the arts of both the pen and the sword. A scholar and a gentleman, he had acquired knowledge in all of the religious sciences. He was accomplished with the sword and dagger, a courageous fighter, and the great amirs considered him an equal. However, the allure of divine love had caused him to abandon the world and become a darvish. Reciting his poetry helped free people from desire and, although he gave some attention to the rich, he was devoted primarily to the poor.[131]

Mani Yab Khan, one of the favorites of the emperor (*chidehay-i padshahi*), was an expert at reciting ghazals. He had an elegant voice and perfect understanding. On the 3rd of Safar, on the 'urs of Mirza Bidil, a group of Shahjahanabadi poets gathered at the tomb and, placing Bidil's diwan in the middle, began to recite.[132] Muhammad Ali Hazin, the most distinguished of the poets who had emigrated from Iran, was acknowledged as the best of the group who gathered to honor Mirza Bidil. His verse was like a nail driven into a woman's heart, and many people came to his

---

[128] Ibid., fols. 92–3.   [129] Ibid., fols. 94–4a.   [130] Ibid., fols. 94a–5a.
[131] Ibid., fols. 103a–5.   [132] Ibid., fol. 105.

house to offer homage and gifts. Musicians chanted in the forecourt of his mansion. He was humble, wore ragged clothes, and gave all of his gifts to the poor.[133] Siraj al-Din Ali Khan Arzu had the wittiest and most eloquent poets in his assembly. "Congratulations" "Bless you, make yourself at home" were heard at all times. He read his poetry at the 'urs of Mirza Bidil.[134]

Mir Muhammad Afzal Sabit was a Sufi poet who had given himself to God in complete poverty. Except for writing poetry and publishing Sufi books, his attention was directed entirely toward being a disciple.[135] Mir Shamsuddin Khan Majnun (Insane) wrote in the style of the early masters.[136] Mir Abdul Razzaq Warasta combined the wealth and position of an amir with the simplicity of a *darvish* (monk). His guests recited the poetry of the early masters from the books which he had collected.[137] Mirza Abu al-Hasan Agah, one of the companions of Azim-allah Khan, read from the diwan of Mirza Bidil on the day of the 'urs.[138] Halima Arab played music and recited poetry at her gatherings.[139]

Singers and musicians

In addition to the musicians and singers who were clients of the great men, there were a number of independent artists who played an important role in the cultural life of the city.

Niamat Khan, the bin player, was the equal of the early masters and one of the blessings of Hindustan. He was an author and singer of *khiyal* (a kind of song) and the head of the singers of the city. In wealth and rank he was equal to anyone except the emperor. He sang and played at all of the major 'urs, and every month on the 11th the great amirs of the city gathered at his mansion. He could completely alter his voice and he played and sang with skill until the early hours of the morning.[140] Qasim Ali, one of Niamat Khan's disciples, was honored by the amirs because of his beauty.[141] Panna Bai, another of his disciples, had a voice like a nightingale and cast amorous glances toward her listeners.[142]

Taj Khan Qawwal had a voice fresher than a rose petal and superior to that of the nightingale. On the seventh of every month there was a gathering at his house attended by the faqirs and sheikhs who were connoisseurs of *qawwal* (a special kind of singing).[143] Jani and Ghulam Rasul, sons and successors of Taj Khan, were masters on the tambur and tamburchi and played songs in the style of David (i.e., like the Psalms).[144]

---

[133] Ibid., fols. 105–6. [134] Ibid., fols. 106–6a. [135] Ibid., fols. 106a–7.
[136] Ibid., fol. 107a. [137] Ibid., fols. 107a–8a. [138] Ibid., fol. 109.
[139] Ibid., fol. 109a. [140] Ibid., fols. 112a–13a. [141] Ibid., fol. 115.
[142] Ibid., fols. 126a–7. [143] Ibid., fols. 113a–14. [144] Ibid., fols. 114–a.

Hasan Khan, "lord of the rubab," was the best of the Delhi players and, unlike the others, an orthodox Muslim.[145] Ghulam Muhammad, the sarangi player, captivated his listeners with the first sound of his instrument. They immediately perceived his excellence.[146] Jimsen and Tansen were the equal of their famous ancestor, Tansen Akbarshahi. Once these two played together with Hasan Khan, the rubab player, Ghasi Ram, a pakhvaj player with nimble fingers and perfect mastery, and Husain Khan, the wonder of the age as a dhulak player. A great crowd gathered and it was a memorable evening.[147]

Muin al-Din had a unique talent for qawwali and was not at all interested in wealth.[148] The qawwal singer Burhani was part of the entourage of Shah Kamal, a Sufi saint famed for his dancing. The power of his voice made the hair on the bodies of his listeners stand up and brought them ecstasy.[149] Ibrahim Khan was a famous Hindustani *kalavant* (singer) to whom everyone listened.[150] Darwish, the sabuchah player, was so skilled that beads of shame dripped from the foreheads of the pakhwaj and dhulak players. He invented a combined instrument that produced the sounds of the dhulak, the pakhawaj, and the tambur.[151] An unnamed blind man played his stomach like the dhulak and the pakhawaj. His music was excellent and many people danced to it but his stomach became black and blue.[152]

When Jattah the qawwali sang the Sufis danced about like headless chickens. He knew the words of the sheikhs who had established the order and he had a notebook full of Sufi poems. There was a gathering at his house every week on Sunday.[153] Rahim Khan, Daulat Khan, Kiyan Khan, and Haddu were four brothers who had black skin and were unequalled in the art of khiyal. On the 25th of every month a group of singers and rich people gathered at their home. Daulat Khan, the most famous, sang so quickly that it was nearly impossible to distinguish his words. Rahim Khan was famed for the clearness and simplicity of his speech. Many amirs tried to convince the brothers to join their households.[154] The black-complected Rajji was an extraordinary singer. His throat throbbed like a string when he sang, and he was very selective and performed only the very best of the popular khiyals.[155]

The house of Nur Bai, the popular female singer, was debauched by drink. Her singing was approved by the lords of music, and she played popular tunes for a group of high-ranking women (*begums* and *khanums*) of the court.[156] The singer Chamani was one of the famous persons of

---

[145] Ibid., fol. 114a.   [146] Ibid.   [147] Ibid., fols. 114a, 116a, 117.
[148] Ibid., fol. 115a.   [149] Ibid., fol. 116.   [150] Ibid., fol. 116a.
[151] Ibid., fol. 117a.   [152] Ibid., fol. 118.   [153] Ibid., fols. 120–a.
[154] Ibid., fols. 120a–1.   [155] Ibid., fol. 121a.   [156] Ibid., fols. 123a–4.

Delhi. She was honored in every mansion and given money by the emperors and amirs. Her contemporaries acknowledged her perfection and her assembly ran from evening until morning.[157]

Dancers

Shahjahanabad in the early eighteenth century boasted a number of talented dancers. The mistress of Abu al-Hasan Khan chanted prose and poetry and danced with perfect grace. She was well known but she would not repeat one of her performances no matter how much money she was offered.[158] A crowd gathered every day to watch the dark-complected eunuch Miyan Haiga dance in the square of the Urdu Bazaar in front of the palace-fortress. The respectable people strolled around the bazaar just to look at him. They gathered around him, lost in wonder. A large sum of money was collected from the onlookers and taken to his house.[159] Sultana, the dark-skinned eunuch dancer, was twelve years old. His dancing and singing captivated the city and he was in great demand. Many people purchased an audience with a purse of gold.[160] Dargahi, Sultana's companion, was an older dancer and a zangula player. At the climax of his dance a bell sounded and the cheers drowned out the sound of his playing. It was impossible to tell the difference between his playing and the song of the nightingale.[161]

Saras Rup was a wonderful singer and dancer. He dazzled the Sufis with his beauty and he was so popular that it was impossible to arrange a meeting with him without bringing gifts.[162] The dancer Ad Begum was one of the famous people of the city. Her lower body was painted in a flowered pattern. When she danced at the mansions of the great amirs it was impossible to distinguish between the real and the painted clothing.[163] Asa Pura was a Hindu dancing girl (*ram-jani*) who was honored in all of the gatherings. Her singing followed the rules of the great masters and her style was that of the early kalavants.[164] Chak Mak and Mani were famous dancers popular throughout the city. As a singer Chak Mak was so exciting that everyone who saw him was moved to bring gifts. The road outside his house was closed because of the crowd of people bringing gifts.[165]

Kaki Kanka was a dark-skinned dancer of great beauty with a wonderful voice.[166] Zinat and Bahaq were beautiful dancers who roused desire in their audience. Their house was jammed and many people were

---

157 Ibid., fols. 124–a. 158 Ibid., fol. 120. 159 Ibid., fols. 121a–2.
160 Ibid., fol. 122a. 161 Ibid., fols. 122a–3. 162 Ibid., fols. 123–a.
163 Ibid., fol. 124a. 164 Ibid., fol. 125. 165 Ibid., fols. 125–a.
166 Ibid., fol. 125a.

turned away.[167] Ramzani was a dancer and singer whose khiyal on the last day of Ramadan brought gladness to the heart. She ate voraciously and without manners.[168] The dark-skinned Rahman Bai was the daughter of a caste of dancers. Wherever she danced her movements incited lust.[169] Rupan Bai danced as freely as the breeze of spring. She had beautiful form and her improvisations were like fine wine. She performed mostly in the palaces of the great men and collected many honors.[170] Pannu and Tannu were a pair of dancers. Because of his beauty and dignity Pannu was the leader. His form and his singing of khiyals and ragas were admired in the imperial courtyard. Tannu captured souls with his amorous glances.[171]

Actors or mimics

Taqi, the head of the actors of the imperial household, had a great collection of props and costumes. His troupe included beautiful young boys and hermaphrodites.[172] Shah Daniyal Surkhi was an accomplished mimic, a talking parrot. His storytelling was excellent and he sang the ancient Sufi songs. In every assembly he was a guide for the young amirs of the city. He had a great desire for food and the huqqa.[173] Khwasi and Anusha were skillful actors from the imperial household. They performed colorful stories which they had created.[174] Bari, the mimic, was so young and beautiful that it was difficult to look at him directly. Because of his lovely face and excellent voice pious men found it impossible to concentrate.[175]

[167] Ibid., fols. 125a–6.
[168] Ibid., fols. 126–a.
[169] Ibid., fol. 126a.
[170] Ibid., fols. 127a–8.
[171] Ibid., fols. 128–a.
[172] Ibid., fols. 118–a.
[173] Ibid., fols. 118a–19.
[174] Ibid., fol. 118a.
[175] Ibid., fols. 119a–20.

6

Aftermath of imperium, 1739–1857

Nadir Shah's departure in 1739 inaugurated a period of turmoil in the life of Shahjahanabad. The first part of the period, from 1739 to 1803, was a dismal and dispiriting time. The decline of the city was a direct result of the collapse of the Empire, and the story of Shahjahan's capital during the late eighteenth century is one of destruction, misery, and heartache. The second part of the period, from 1803 to 1857, was an interval of peace and healing. Without the clash and blood of the eighteenth century, this story is duller but it does introduce the themes of growth and prosperity. British rule in the city began in 1803 and the fifty-odd years preceding the mutiny witnessed a profound transformation. No longer an imperial capital, hostage to the fortunes of the emperor and his court, Shahjahanabad developed into an upcountry commercial and cultural center, depending on the British army and the new cash crops for its prosperity and on the remnants of the Mughal nobility, newly risen Hindu merchants and professionals, and British administrators for its cultural and intellectual vitality.

Politics

Following the death of the Emperor Aurangzeb in 1707, the Mughal army returned to north India. Although Bahadur Shah, Aurangzeb's successor, spent his entire reign touring and fighting, the presence of the imperial camp helped to reinvigorate Shahjahanabad. To be sure, the emperors of the early eighteenth century were no match for the great Mughals: controlling subordinates and administering the land revenue system were, for the most part, beyond them. These defects, however, were not immediately apparent and Shahjahanabad flourished in the years before 1739.

Disasters, both natural and man-made erupted periodically: in 1716 heavy rains collapsed mud huts in the city, killing 2300 persons;[1] in 1719 an earthquake rumbled and shook for forty days, damaging the palace-fortress and the Jami' Masjid and bringing down many houses and shops;[2] in 1730 a plague swept through north India, taking away many people in the city;[3] and in 1735 heavy rains hit again, lifting the Paradise Canal to five feet and washing away many houses and shops.[4] Nevertheless, these were good years and the comment of Murtaza Husain, who visited the city in 1731, is typical:

[Shahjahanabad] was perfectly brilliant and heavily populated ... in the evening one could not move one gaz [yard] in Chandni Chawk and the Chawk of Sa'adullah Khan because of the great crowds of people.[5]

Anand Ram Mukhlis, a mid-eighteenth-century resident, observed that the city had been free from serious disruption since Timur's invasion of 1398–9 and that in 1739 Shahjahanabad was like a "cage of tumultuous nightingales."[6]

In late 1738 the Persian general Nadir Shah marched without significant opposition to the plains northwest of the city. There at Karnal, facing an army led by feuding noblemen and an inexperienced emperor, he swept to the decisive victory that exposed the dry rot at the heart of the Empire. On entering Shahjahanabad in early 1739 Nadir took up quarters in the palace-fortress. His men were billeted throughout the area and, when a disturbance arose over grain prices, it was difficult for them to regroup and make a stand. In the violence that swept the city several hundred of Nadir's men were slain.

The response was swift and brutal. Persian soldiers ravaged the rich areas of the central city, concentrating their destruction in Chandni Chawk, Faiz Bazar, and the bazaar that ran from the gate of the fort to Kashmiri gate. Houses and shops were put to the torch: according to the French Jesuits the fires lasted for eight days and destroyed two of their churches.[7] About 20,000 persons are thought to have lost their lives. After extorting 150 million rupees in cash and amassing jewelry, clothing, and furniture worth another five million rupees, Nadir Shah took the

---

[1] C.R. Wilson, "The Surman Embassy," in *The Early Annals of the English in Bengal*, 2 vols. (Calcutta: Bengal Secretariat Book Depot, 1910), 2 p. 124.

[2] Seid Gholam Hussein Khan, *Sier Mutaqherin*, 1 pp. 164–5.

[3] Ibid., 1 p. 265.

[4] Ibid., 1 p. 268.

[5] Murtaza Husain, *Hadiqat-ul-Aqalim*, p. 41.

[6] Anand Ram Mukhlis, "Bada'i-i Waqai," Persian Manuscript Collection, no. 409, Maulana Azad Library, Aligarh, Uttar Pradesh, Aligarh Muslim University, fol. 121b.

[7] *Lettres Edifants and Curieuses*, 4 pp. 256–60.

magnificent Peacock Throne and marched out of the city.[8] Anand Ram wrote:

The ruin . . . of its beautiful streets and buildings was such that the labor of years could alone restore the city to its former state of grandeur. . . . The city was reduced to ashes and had the appearance of a plain consumed by fire.[9]

By desecrating the capital, the symbol of the state, Nadir Shah exposed the empire for the wasted skeleton it had become. And while it is useful to stress the attack as the unmistakable sign of the decline that had taken place during the previous thirty years, it is important to remember that the city suffered little permanent damage. Dargah Quli Khan, who visited Shahjahanabad in 1737–40 and lived through the attack, mentioned the events only once.[10] Tieffenthaler passed through in 1747 and remarked on the population, the number of large mosques, the magnificent castle of the emperor, and the general beauty and prosperity of the area.[11] And the author of *Ma'asir al-Umara* wrote:

Nadir Shah's occupation resulted in a setback to the prosperity of the city, but in a short while it returned to normal, and in fact everything is now better and shows progress.[12]

Nadir Shah, murdered in 1747, was succeeded by Ahmad Khan Abdali, an Afghan from Herat. Looking to India for plunder, Ahmad Khan attacked the Punjab in 1748 and was defeated in a brief skirmish by the much larger Mughal army. Muhammad Shah died that same year and was followed to the throne by his son, Ahmad Shah (1748–54), who had been locked away in the harem and had acquired no training in the arts of leadership and administration. Effective control of the Empire passed into the hands of Javid Khan, a eunuch who had been superintendent of the harem, and Udham Bai, the Queen Mother. Under their aegis, the weakened system of revenue administration collapsed entirely; zamindars pocketed the taxes they had collected and nobles squeezed what they could from their jagirs. Because Javid Khan refused to forward revenue from the household lands, even the emperor experienced financial difficulties.

---

[8] Sheikh Muhammad Ali Hazin, *Tarikh-i Ahwal be Tazkirah-i Hal*. ed. F.C. Belfour (London: Oriental Translation Fund, 1831), p. 277–84; Khwaja Abd al-Karim, "Biyan-i Waqai," London, British Museum, Persian Manuscript Collection, Add. 8909, fol. 83a; Jonas Hanway, *An Historical Account of the British Trade Over the Caspian Sea*, 4 vols. (London: Jonas Hanway, 1753), 4 p. 176.

[9] Anand Ram Mukhlis, "Bada' i-i Waqai," fols. 121b–2a.

[10] Dargah Quli Khan, "Risalah-i Salar Jang," fols. 127–a.

[11] Tieffenthaler, *Description Historique*, 1 pp. 124–32.

[12] Samsam al-Daulah, *Ma'asir al-Umara*, 3 p. 473.

In 1752 Ahmad Khan once again entered the Punjab and this time Lahore fell. The emperor summoned Safdar Jang, the virtually independent subahdar of Oudh, to come to his aid. Arriving with a contingent of Mahratta horsemen, Safdar Jang was outraged to find that the Punjab had been ceded to the Persians. Unable to pay his Mahratta mercenaries (he had planned to use the Punjab revenues), Safdar Jang stood aside as they plundered the markets and houses of the suburbs. Civil war broke out when the subahdar refused to call off his troops and leave the capital. With the aid of Afghans from nearby Rohilkhand, Ahmad Shah finally achieved victory but Safdar Jang, in a rage following his defeat, urged the Jats to attack the suburbs. The ferocity of their onslaught drove those inhabitants who had survived the earlier attacks to leave the area entirely or to move inside. This period (1752–3) marked the end of the suburbs. Until the 1830s and 40s when the city began to grow under the British stimulus, Shahjahanabad comprised, for the most part, the area within the walls.

The closing years of Ahmad Shah's reign witnessed the dismemberment of the Empire as well: the Punjab answered to Abdali and the Persians, the Mahrattas had seized Gujarat and Malwa, and the subahdars of Bengal, Oudh, and the Deccan were independent in all but name. The Mughal Empire – that is, the area under the direct control of the emperor – had shrunk to a small island consisting of the capital and a few miles of surrounding territory. Although the walls had not been breached, the city was far from tranquil. Soldiers of the imperial household clamored for pay, breaking into the inner area of the palace-fortress at one point and forcing the emperor to receive them in the Hall of Public Audience,[13] and the populace at large lived in periodic deprivation and constant fear. In 1754 the Mahrattas, still unpaid, fought their way inside the gates. Under terrific pressure, Ahmad Shah was persuaded to leave the palace-fortress and retire to a garden outside the city. He was captured by the Mahrattas but somehow managed to escape and make his way back to Shahjahanabad. He lost his jewelry and artillery, however, and soon after died, as much of shock and disappointment as of anything else.

Ahmad Shah was succeeded by Alamgir II (1754–9). An old man of fifty-four when he assumed the throne, Alamgir was without experience in warfare or government, preferring to spend his time in study and meditation. Responsibility for the state rested with Ghazi al-Din Khan Imad al-Mulk, the wazir. Early in 1754 Imad harassed the inhabitants of the capital in an effort to raise money for the Mahrattas and later both his and the emperor's unpaid soldiers plundered houses and shops.

---

[13] Sarkar, *Delhi During the Anarchy, 1749–99*, p. 4.

In October of 1756 Ahmad Khan Abdali overran Lahore and in January of 1757 he entered Shahjahanabad. Settling into the palace-fortress, he had the *khutba* (Friday sermon) read in his name. Afghan and Persian soldiers were stationed in each mahallah and extorted money from the inhabitants. Leaving the city, Abdali and his men marched south and defeated the Mahrattas and Jats in a brief engagement. On their way back the Afghans plundered the helpless capital once again. Later in the same year the Mahrattas ransacked the houses and shops of the central bazaars. The end to this sorry interlude came in 1759 when Imad al-Mulk murdered his ineffectual master, Alamgir II.[14]

The devastation was complete. In 1758 Jean Law remarked that Shahjahanabad was a desert compared to what it had been before and that the destruction since the time of Nadir Shah had left it in a pitiful state.[15] Murtaza Khan, who visited soon after the departure of the Afghans and Persians, wrote that the city was desolate and destroyed. Ahmad Khan and his men had dug up houses and shops and had driven Alamgir II to the suburbs where he lived in the *Qudsia Bagh* (Qudsia Garden) in tents floored with wooden planks. On the door of the palace-fortress a bin filled with trash replaced the holders which had once overflowed with flowers, cows rather than people strolled the suburbs, and the horses of Najib Khan, tethered in the courtyard of the Hall of Ordinary Audience, littered the area with dung and straw.[16]

The degradation of the city in the 1750s elicited some of the finest poetry of the language from two of the greatest Urdu poets. Mirza Muhammad Rafi (1730–80), pen name Sauda, was the son of a prosperous merchant who had migrated from Kabul to Shahjahanabad. Born in the city, Sauda remained there until 1757, when he left for Farrukhabad. Muhammad Taqi Mir (1722–1810), pen name Mir, was born in Agra and came to Shahjahanabad the year before Nadir Shah's invasion. Returning to Agra for several years, he came back to Shahjahanabad and resided there from 1740 to 1760 and from 1772 to 1782. Both witnessed the fall of the city to Nadir Shah and the devastation that followed and for both it was the fall of a whole civilization.[17]

This experience inspired a new genre of Urdu poetry. The *shahr ashob* (ruined city) genre was a lamentation over the fate of a city. Pessimistic and backward-looking, it asserted the decadence and corrup-

---

[14] Tahmas Khan, "Tazkirah-i Tahmas Khan," Persian Manuscript Collection, Or. 1918, London, British Museum, fols. 64–6.

[15] Jean Law de Lauristan, *Memoires*, pp. 354, 509.

[16] Murtaza Khan, *Hadiqat-ul-Aqalim*, p. 44.

[17] Ralph Russell and Khurshidul Islam, *Three Mughal Poets*, (London: George Allen and Unwin, 1969). p. 82–91, 94–101.

tion of the present day. Although these poets may have been somewhat influenced by the lamentations of the Persian poets over the destruction of the Mongol invasions in the thirteenth century – Sa'adi, for example, had written an elegy on the fall of Baghdad – the genre reached its height in India.

Sauda, the greatest name in the Urdu qasida, wrote "Qasida-i Shahr Ashob" and "Mukhammas-i Shahr Ashob." Both mourned the decline of Shahjahanabad in the 1740s and 50s, describing in painful detail the deprivation, insecurity, and unemployment in the city. He also composed a satire about Shidi Faulad Khan, Kotwal of Shahjahanabad during this period. Instead of protecting the populace, Shidi joined forces with the thieves and murderers and shared the profits of their activities.[18] In the account of his life from 1748–88 (entitled *Zikr-i Mir*) and in his poetry Mir portrayed the decline of the city. His poignant ghazals rendered the despair and sense of loss that he felt at the destruction of all that was beautiful and extraordinary about the city.[19]

Sauda wrote:

How can I describe the desolation of Delhi? There is no house from where the jackal's cry cannot be heard. The mosques at evening are unlit and deserted, and only in one house in a hundred will you see a light burning. Its citizens do not possess even the essential cooking pots, and vermin crawl in the place where in former days men used to welcome the coming of spring with music and rejoicing. The lovely buildings which once made the famished man forget his hunger are in ruins now. In the once-beautiful gardens where the nightingale sang his love songs to the rose, the grass grows waist high around the fallen pillars and the ruined arches.[20]

The Mahrattas under Sadashiv Rao Bhau captured the city in late 1759. As successor to Alamgir II, they crowned Shah Jahan II, a forgotten ruler who lasted only nine months and is usually left out of the dynastic list in favor of the man who succeeded him, Shah Alam (1760–1806). The city had been so devastated in the preceding decade that it had little to offer. Desperate for booty, Sadashiv Bhau pried the silver inlay from the ceiling of the Hall of Private Audience. In 1761 Ahmad Shah Abdali met the Mahrattas on the plains of Panipat. The Afghans possessed superior

[18] See Sauda, Mirza Muhammad Rafi, "Masnavi Dar Shidi Faulad Khan, Kotwal, Shahjahanabad" *Kulliyat-i Sauda*, 2 vols. introduction by Imrat Ashrat, (Allahabad: Ram Narain Lal Bini Madhu, 1971) 1 pp. 279–82, "Mukhammas-i Shahr Ashob," *Kulliyat* 2 pp. 261–6; "Qasida Shahr Ashob," *Kulliyat* 1 pp. 226–30.

[19] Mir Taqi Mir, *Kulliyat-i Mir*, introduction by S. Ihtesham Husain, 2 vols. (Allahabad: Ram Narain Lal Bini Madhu, 1972); *Zikr-i Mir*, edited by Abdul Haq. (Aurangabad: Anjuman-i Taraqqi-i Urdu, 1928).

[20] Sauda, *Kulliyat* 2 pp. 265–6.

artillery and skilled reinforcements from Iran and were better disciplined and led. The Mahrattas were crushed and their hopes for a north Indian empire extinguished. Najib Khan and the Rohilla Afghans, allies of Ahmad Shah at Panipat, were left in charge of the city.

In comparison to the turbulent 1750s, the 1760s under Najib Khan were relatively uneventful. The Mahrattas had been subdued, the emperor had taken refuge in Oudh, and Abdali's Afghans were not to return. The only disturbance of note was the attack of the Jats under Jawahir Singh in 1764. Although Najib managed to keep them outside the walls, a great deal of destruction occurred in the suburbs. The grain market at Shahdara was destroyed and the supply of food was cut off for a long time.

Shah Alam had escaped from Shahjahanabad in 1759 and he spent most of the following decade in the kingdom of Oudh. For the first five years he was under the protection of Shuja al-Daulah, nawab of Oudh, and for the last five he resided in Allahabad as a pensioner of the East India Company. But he never abandoned hope of returning and much of his time was spent planning and scheming, trying to find an ally who would help him regain his throne.

In 1770 Najib al-Daulah died. Shah Alam seized the opportunity and, with the help of the Mahrattas, marched back into Shahjahanabad. The Empire which he returned to head was virtually nonexistent; it consisted of little more than the city and the lands immediately surrounding and it yielded no revenue to speak of. Najaf Khan, the emperor's chief minister, raised an army and was moderately successful in asserting the claims of the emperor, carving out a small kingdom in the vicinity of the capital.

The city, however, failed to respond. In 1772 the Maharatta agent at court reported that Shah Alam had not paid his soldiers for six months and that his stable and karkhanah workers had been forced to fast for three and four days at a time.[21] In 1775 de Modave estimated that a third of the city lay in ruins,[22] and in 1776 Polier reported that the city was "no more than a heap of ruin and rubbish."[23] The mansions of princes and great amirs were delapidated, the woodwork having been used for fuel by the Mahrattas and Rohillas, and the canals in Chandni Chawk and Faiz Bazar were clogged. The suburbs were a pile of rubble. Polier assigned much of the blame to Najib al-Daulah's Afghans:

[they] committed every kind of outrage in the unfortunate city... the devastations and plunders of Nadir Shah and Ahmad Shah Abdali were like violent

---

[21] *Delhi Affairs*, trans. Jadunath Sarkar, p. 55.
[22] Jadunath Sarkar, "The Delhi Empire a Century After Bernier," *Islamic Culture* 11 (1937) p. 385.
[23] Polier, "Extracts of Letters," p. 36.

tempests which. . . carried everything before them but soon subsided; whereas the waste and havoc made by the Rohillas resembled pestilential gales which keep up a continual agitation and finally destroy a country."[24]

In 1780–1 the Russian traveller Yefremov reported that the suburbs were devastated and the city destroyed.[25] In 1782 the failure of the monsoon rains brought famine, disease, and death.[26] In that same year Najaf Khan's cannons demolished houses and shops as he battled his rivals in the city streets. In 1784 thieves stormed the houses of the rich and held merchants and traders ransom.[27] Sikhs and Mewatis prowled suburbs and the affairs of the city were in total confusion.

In 1784 Mahadji Sindhia, the Mahratta general, defeated the struggling imperial forces and took the emperor under his protection. In 1785 the English traveller James Forbes reported that the old city of Delhi (i.e., the area beyond the walls) was a scene of desolation, not a human being in sight. Inside, the houses were low and mean, the streets "despicably poor and thinly inhabited."[28]

In 1787 the Rohilla Afghans under Ghulam Qadir defeated the Mahrattas. Although they occupied Shahjahanabad no more than two months, the Afghans were responsible for the final spasm in the death throes of the city. They robbed the suburbs, breached the walls, and bombarded the palace-fortress. Once inside, they tortured members of the royal family and dug up mansions and gardens looking for treasure. In a fury at finding so little booty, Ghulam Qadir committed the final outrage: he plunged his knife deep into Shah Alam's eyes, forever blinding the anguished emperor. The Afghan general stripped the palace bare, taking money, cloth, and furniture and leaving the nobles, according to the Mahratta correspondent, little more than their noses and ears.[29]

Mahadji Sindhia recaptured the city later in 1788 but the damage had been done. Under the Mahrattas the fifteen years preceding the British takeover were a time of relative tranquillity. Although Ahmad Shah Abdali entered the subcontinent several times during the period 1794–8, he never penetrated far enough to threaten the capital.

In 1792 the English gentleman Thomas Twining was appalled by the

[24] Ibid., p. 41.
[25] *Russian Travellers of India and Persia: 1624–1798*, trans. and ed. P.M. Kemp (Delhi: Jiwan Prakashan, 1959), pp. 85–6.
[26] *Indian Record Series: Browne Correspondence*, ed. Krishna Dayal Bhargave (New Delhi, India: National Archives of India, 1960), pp. 5–6.
[27] *Delhi Affairs*, pp. 108, 124, 129–30, 146.
[28] Forbes, *Oriental Memoirs*, pp. 65–6.
[29] *Delhi Affairs*, p. 198.

ruins beyond the walls and by the houses that had been built in the middle of Chandni Chawk.[30] In 1793 William Franklin found the population small, the commerce trifling, and the canals of Faiz Bazar and Chandni Chawk dried up.[31] In the mid-1790s Mirza Mughal Beg reported that all of the buildings in the suburbs were destroyed and about half of those in the city. The ground inside the walls was strewn with stones and clods of dirt and dotted with mounds of rubble.[32]

In 1803 the British, fresh from impressive victories in southern and eastern India, pushed upcountry. Under General Lake, they defeated the Mahrattas at Aligarh and looked to the capital. Shah Alam asked for protection and, at the battle of Patparganj, Lake defeated Bourquien, the French commander, and his Mahratta cavalry and established British ascendancy in North India.

The British brought peace and security to Shahjahanabad, and a slow, gradual return to health distinguished the half-century before the mutiny. The relationship between them and the emperor was strained and never really resolved until 1858 when Bahadur Shah II was deposed and exiled. Shah Alam had asked Lord Lake for protection but a formal treaty was never drawn up. By an order of 1805 the British set the terms of their protectorate:

(1) Revenue from lands near the city would be set aside for the emperor,
(2) Shah Alam, however, was to have no authority over these lands, collection of revenue and administration of justice being the responsibility of the British.
(3) Two courts of justice under British jurisdiction were established, one for the city and the other for the territory surrounding, and the emperor's only right was to confirm a sentence of death.
(4) Within the palace-fortress itself Shah Alam would administer criminal and civil law.[33]

The terms of the Mahratta and British protectorates did not differ all that much. Both gave the emperor a pension, took over revenue administration, established an agent at court, and retained a monopoly over the use of force. But the Mahrattas acknowledged Shah Alam's status as emperor and accepted the position of minister in his paper government; the British, on the other hand, saw nothing but a powerless pensioner, a blind old man in a shabby court. Although Shah Alam

---

[30] Twining, *Travels*, pp. 219, 241.
[31] Franklin, "Account of Delhi," p. 426.
[32] Mirza Mughal Beg. b. Muhammad Beg, "Sair al-Bilad," Persian Manuscript Collection, Ethe 3731, Indian Office Library, fols. 19b–21b.
[33] Sarkar, *Fall of the Mughal Empire*, 4 pp. 334–7.

complained about the size of his subsidy, the basic disagreement between the two parties stemmed from their divergent conceptions of the role the Mughal emperor should play in the political system of North India. The first three residents felt a deep sympathy for the emperor and treated him with respect and deference. But under the reforming impulse of utilitarianism and evangelical Christianity, the residents who were appointed after 1830 came to regard the throne as a useless vestige of the past and smarted under the demands of court etiquette.

The British takeover in 1803 found the city exhausted. Charles Metcalfe wrote:

Robbing in the city of Dihlee was organized in a systematic manner... The city was shared in Districts among the villagers of the Environs, and the plunder of particular districts was the property of particular villages.[34]

Walter Hamilton, who compiled an account of India in the early nineteenth century, stated that in the late eighteenth century under the Mahrattas land in Shahjahanabad was sold for a trifle or even given away to escape taxation and extortion. The arrival of Lord Lake in 1803 caused land values to double immediately and they increased steadily from then on.[35] Major Throne, a member of Lake's army, was impressed by the great mansions. Even though most of them were in an advanced state of disrepair, their remains testified to the magnificent structures the city had once contained.[36]

The British army occupied the land north and south of the palace-fortress. One battalion laid out a bazaar, set up a hospital, and built accommodations for guns and stables near Kashmiri Gate. Dara Shikoh's mansion became the headquarters of the resident and other palaces to the north were renovated and turned to official use. Two battalions were quartered in the Darya Ganj area east of Faiz Bazar. A magazine was built, a bazaar constructed, and stables for camels, bullocks, and horses established.[37] Qamar al-Din Khan's mansion near Ajmiri Gate became the Customs House.[38]

Soon after their arrival the British began the work of reconstruction. In 1803 they repaired the broken, open sections of the city wall and in 1811 the enclosure was enlarged so as to include the tomb of Ghazi al-Din Khan. In 1817 the minaret of the Jami' Masjid was renovated.[39]

---

[34] C.T. Metcalfe, "Delhi, 1815," *Home Miscellaneous Series*, vol. 776, Indian Office Library, London, p. 1587.

[35] Hamilton, *Description of Hindustan*, 1 p. 421.

[36] Major William Thorne, *Memoir of the War in India* (London: T. Egerton, 1818), p. 159.

[37] Anthony D. King, *Colonial Urban Development: Culture, Social Power, and Environment* (London: Routledge and Kegan Paul, 1976), pp. 189–92.

[38] Nugent, *Journal*, 1 p. 417.   [39] Khan, *Asar*, p. 132.

The city seemed to revive. In 1811 Lady Maria Nugent remarked that Shahjahanabad appeared populous and bustling. The streets were wide, the houses more comfortable, and the people more prosperous than in many of the other places she had visited and there were not as many beggars as in Lucknow.[40] Walter Hamilton, who visited sometime between 1815–1820, was impressed by the brick houses and the remains of the great mansions.[41] And an 1820 report on customs duties revealed a good deal of commercial activity.[42]

During the 1820s middle-class houses were constructed between the Jami' Masjid and the palace-fortress. The sarai of Jahanara Begum in Chandni Chawk held shops and the houses of cultivators and artisans. Moneychangers had congregated near the mosque of Raushan al-Daulah, and in Darya Ganj lumber merchants resided alongside British soldiers. The Paradise Canal had been opened by the British in 1821, allowing water to flow through the parched city, but it soon became clogged again. In the evening people gathered near the steps of the Jami' Masjid to hear storytellers and to shop in the nearby bazaars.[43]

In 1823 an English traveller saw sturdy houses of brick and stone set amid a landscape of ruined mansions. There were not many trees but he did count forty large mosques.[44] Bishop Heber, who spent the winter months of 1824–5 in the city, wrote of houses that were large and high, fine-looking mosques with minarets and domes, streets that were wide and handsome, and rich bazaars. Outside the walls, however – from the Akbarabadi Gate to Humayun's tomb – the eye was assaulted by the ruins of mansions, mosques, gardens, and tombs.[45] The expansion of the city during the 1820s was confined almost exclusively to the area within the walls. All attempts to live outside had been abandoned during the late eighteenth century and people rarely ventured beyond the gates except to visit the tombs and shrines of nearby saints.[46]

In 1828 this began to change. The British shifted their cantonment to a ridge two miles north of Kashmiri Gate. On the fifteen-hundred-acre site they constructed barracks, offices, storerooms, and parade grounds. The move emboldened other inhabitants, and soon the triangle formed by the ridge, the river, and the north wall of the city began to fill with the houses

[40] Nugent, *Journal*, 1 pp. 412–13.
[41] Hamilton, *Description of Hindustan*, 1 pp. 413–14.
[42] T. Fortescue, "Report on the Revenue System of the Delhi Territory, 1820", pp. 131–214.
[43] "Sair al-Manazil," fols. 23–4, 31, 51, 57.
[44] "Description of Delhi and its Environs," p. 552.
[45] Heber, *Narrative of A Journey*, 1 pp. 548, 552, 563.
[46] C.F. Andrew, *Zaka Ullah of Delhi* (Cambridge: W.H. Heffer and Sons, Ltd., 1929), pp. 3–4.

and gardens of agents, merchants, and lower-ranking officials. Thomas Metcalfe, the resident, threw up a great house on the ridge, and it soon became the seat of many official activities.[47]

During the period 1830–57 the British laid out a cemetery, built a church near Kashmiri Gate, established a college in the old residency, constructed a club, and founded a bank, post office, printing press, and photographic studio.[48] In 1852 they opened the Calcutta Gate in the southeastern wall of the city. At the same time the city magistrate ordered the bazaars cleaned, the platforms in front of the shops restored, and the drains repaired and rebuilt. As a result, Chandni Chawk and Faiz Bazar began to look as they had in the palmy days of the mid-seventeenth century.[49] With the shift of the cantonment to the ridge and the resettlement of a section of the European enclave in the triangle (which came to be called the civil station), Muslims and Hindus began to move outside the walls and the repopulation of the suburbs to the south and west began.

The mutiny of 1857 brought a halt to all this. Bahadur Shah II joined or was forced to join the uprising and, while his exact role in the events of that year is unclear, his fate was sealed after the British recaptured the city. The army confiscated the houses and goods of many Muslims, expelled them from the city, and wouldn't allow them to return without a pass. A debate broke out among the civil and military authorities: should Shahjahanabad be destroyed? Cooler heads prevailed and, while whole-sale and systematic destruction was avoided, a good number of buildings were razed in the aftermath.[50] Badahur Shah II was imprisoned, quickly convicted, and exiled to Rangoon. The Mughal Empire was abolished and Shahjahanabad was without an emperor for the first time in over two centuries.

The army occupied the palace-fortress. Soldiers were quartered in the Lahore Gate, the Naqqar Khanah, the Delhi Gate, the Asad Burj, and the Shah Burj and no attention was given to preserving the palaces and gardens in the imperial living quarters.[51] In order to defend the walls a strip of land 450 yards wide was cleared. Shops, gardens, mansions, and stables were swept away and the Akbarabadi mosque, one of the finest in the city, was reduced to rubble. Other mosques were desecrated as well. Fathpuri Masjid was sold to Lala Chunna Mal (a Hindu merchant), the Zinat al-Masajid was turned into a bakery, and the Jami' Masjid was used

[47] King, *Colonial Urban Development*, pp. 193–4.
[48] Ibid., pp. 195–202; Khan, *Asar*, p. 344.
[49] Khan, *Asar*, pp. 133, 135.
[50] Naraini Gupta, *Delhi Between Two Empires: 1803–1931* (Delhi: Oxford University Press, 1981), pp. 25–6.
[51] Ahmad, *Waqiat*, 2 p. 89.

to house British troops. The great Friday mosque, the central sanctuary in the city and a symbolic center for Muslims all over India, was not reopened until 1862.[52]

Between 1857 and 1861 Shahjahanabad was an occupied city. In 1863 Ghalib said it was deserted, its inhabitants impoverished and demoralized.[53] Beginning in the mid-1860s, however, the city began to recover. It was slowly rebuilt and repopulated and it increased in size and activity during the rest of the century.

Population

It is only slightly easier to estimate the population of Shahjahanabad during the period 1739–1857. The figures given by travellers for the late eighteenth and early nineteenth centuries, like those for the seventeenth century, are wildly exaggerated, and reliable census data is not available until 1845–6. Changes in population during this period, however, can be roughly correlated with changes in the fortunes of the Empire. It is obvious, for example, that the number of persons must have declined drastically during the late eighteenth century and that the arrival of the British must have ushered in a period of growth and expansion. While the broad outlines are clear, the details are murky. At this point, estimates of the size of the city over the 200-year period are little more than educated guesses.

The data for the period of the "English peace" (1803–57) are much richer than for the previous period (1739–1803). Table 6 contains estimates and census data for Shahjahanabad during the latter two-thirds of the nineteenth century. The 1833 figure is for the walled city only and does not include the palace-fortress (which was under the jurisdiction of the emperor) or the suburbs (which were largely uninhabited at this point). The 1842 figure reveals a 9 percent increase in the population of the walled city in the intervening decade. This total does not include the palace-fortress either but the omission of the suburbs in 1842 probably made a difference. The cantonment was shifted to the ridge in 1828 and, during the early 1839s, people had only begun to move to the suburbs. By the beginning of the 1840s, however, a significant migration had taken place. That the 1845–6 census showed a suburban population of 22,000 persons suggests there was already an appreciable settlement by 1842.

The British census of 1845–6, while cursory and superficial by modern standards, provided a good deal of information. The walled area,

[52] Gupta, *Delhi Between Two Empires*, pp. 20–76.
[53] Ibid., p. 39.

Table 6   *Population of Shahjahanabad: 1833–1901*

	Walled city	Suburbs	Total (Hindus, Muslims)
1. 1833[a]	120,000	not known	not known
2. 1842[b]	131,000	not known	not known
3. 1845–46[c]	138,000	22,000	160,000 (54% H, 45% M)
4. 1853–54[d]	152,000	not known	not known
5. 1864[e]	not known	not known	142,000 (60% H, 39% M)
6. 1881[f]	not known	not known	173,000 (57% H, 42% M)
7. 1901[g]	not known	not known	208,000 (55% H, 42% M)

[a]Leela Visaria and Pravin Visaria, "Population," in *Cambridge Economic History of India*, 2 p:471.
[b]Gupta, *Delhi Between Two Empires*, p. 4.
[c]Roberts, "Population of Delhi and Its Suburbs," *Selections From the Public Correspondence, Northwest Provinces* (Agra: Government of Northwest Provinces, 1849–51), 1:pp. 182–9.
[d]G.J. Christian, *Report on the Census of the Northwest Provinces of the Bengal Presidency–1853* (Calcutta, India: Government of Northwest Provinces, 1854), p. 51.
[e]*Delhi District Gazetteer, 1883–4*, p. 207.
[f]Ibid.
[g]*Census of 1901*.

excluding the palace-fortress, had increased by about five percent in the preceding three-four years. The suburbs were counted for the first time and, for the first time also, the percentages of Muslims and Hindus were given. In 1853 a second census revealed a 10 percent increase in the population of the walled city. The figures for 1864 and 1881 are for the entire city and include percentages of Muslims and Hindus also.

The startling thing about the 1864 figure is the substantial decline. That the British drove out or scared away a good number of residents after the mutiny is well known but the extent of depopulation is surprising. Assuming that the suburbs had also increased by about ten percent, the total population of the city in 1853 would have been about 176,000. Thus, in the six years between 1858 and 1864 34,000 persons left the city, a decline of about 9 percent. The substantial shift from Muslim to Hindu in the relative weighting of the two groups reflects the fact that a high percentage of the emigrants were Muslim.

By 1881 Shahjahanabad had returned to its premutiny size, increasing by about 22 percent from 1864. One indication of the terrible damage wrought by the mutiny is the twenty-three years it took for the city to recover. The ratio of Muslims to Hindus also increased, indicating that a good number of the emigrants had returned. The 1901 census showed a 20 per cent increase in population, and the ratio of Muslims to Hindus remained about the same.[54]

[54] Almost without exception the population estimates of travellers and other observors are greatly inflated. Hamilton wrote that Shahjahanabad contained between 150,000 and

If the population data for the early years of British rule are scarce, for the latter years of the eighteenth century they are virtually nonexistent. In 1739, just before Nadir Shah's attack, Shahjahanabad probably contained 400,000 persons, divided about equally between the walled city and the suburbs. In 1803, at the time of British takeover, the Mughal capital had probably shrunk to no more than 70,000 persons. From 1833 to 1853 the city grew from 120,000 to 176,000 persons, a total increase of about 47 percent. Assuming the same rate of increase over the previous thirty years and extrapolating backwards yields the 1803 estimate.

The devastation of the eighteenth century reduced the suburbs to rubble, an uninhabited wasteland that contained nothing but jackals and roving marauders by the 1760s. Inside, civil wars raged, unpaid soldiers rioted, and invaders looted, burned, and killed. It is no wonder that on the eve of British takeover the once-mighty capital had been reduced to a shrivelled, wasted husk of itself. The suburbs had long since vanished and the 200,000 persons of the walled area had declined by about two-thirds.[55]

Economy

The period 1739–1857 was a time of economic change also. By the latter part of the eighteenth century the economic system that had character-ized Shahjahanabad during its heyday had collapsed. In the ruins lay the great household karkhanahs and the elaborate hierarchy of markets. In their place new systems of exchange and production began to emerge.

A more rational, market-oriented mode of economic activity geared to demands that extended beyond the city to the subcontinent and the world at large was introduced by the British during the first half of the nineteenth century. During the period 1790–1830 a number of north Indian towns grew and prospered. The Bengal army, stationed in north India during the this time, created a great demand for grain and other services. Satisfying these requirements was quite profitable for merch-ants, artisans, and traders. Markets for cotton, sugar, and opium

---

200,000 persons during the period 1815–20 (Hamilton, *Description of Hindustan*, 4 pp. 421–2); an anonymous traveller put the population at 300,000 persons in 1823 ("Description of Delhi," *Asiatic Journal*, 15 p. 552); and Von Orlich in 1843 estimated the size of the city at about 250,000 (*Travels*, 2 p. 4).

55 Travellers' estimates for period 1739–1803 are also exaggerated. The Jesuit fathers and Jean Law both gave Shahjahanabad a population of one million persons in 1750 (*Seir Mutaqherin*, trans. Haji Mustafa, p. 187, fn. 154; Jean Law, *Memoires*, p. 354). And Von Orlich in 1843 reported a tradition giving Shahjahanabad a population of 500,000 persons in 1750 (*Travels*, 2 p. 4).

increased during these years as well and new groups of merchants began to specialize in these commodities. Under such stimuli urban economies expanded, enriching merchants, artisans, and others. But small-town economies, dependent on national and international demand, were precarious and booms were all too often followed by busts. The new merchants in such towns often challenged the old for leadership and, in a number of places, battle was joined over duties, taxes, and political influence.[56]

Shahjahanabad seems to have undergone a similar transformation. The population growth of the early nineteenth century included not only lower-caste laborers, servants, and artisans but merchants, brokers, traders, and administrators also. Khattri merchants and traders from the Punjab joined impoverished laborers from Rajasthan in moving to the city.[57] These Khattris, however, were new men, drawn by the opportunities of the new order, and were not descendants of the merchants who had served in noble and imperial households. Jain merchants also flocked to the city during this period and the oldest Marwari firm dates to c. 1820.[58] All of these men linked their fortunes to the new government. In 1806, for example, a Hindu merchant loaned the British a large sum at 12 percent and, later, the salt merchants of the city advanced two large loans.[59] In the mid to late nineteenth century Khattri and Jain merchants, like their counterparts in other north Indian towns, developed a fierce rivalry and fought vigorously for influence and position.[60]

The British began to rationalize the economy of the city, establishing property rights and the rule of law, and encouraging a freer, more competitive market system. An old office which had registered transfers of real property was revived. In former times the registration tax had been so high – as much as 13 percent on the sale of houses and land – that it had been routinely evaded. The result had been chronic controversy and litigation. The British lowered the tax to 5 percent, introduced courts of law, and sparked an increase in real-estate activity. Confidence in the peace and security of the new order touched off the upsurge.[61]

In the pre-British period the system of customs duties was unbelievably complex. In 1820 a British official wrote:

The city had eight principal gates, besides smaller outlets and posterns. Besides the gates there are a similar number of out-tolls, exclusive of double the number

[56] Bayly, "Town Building in North India – 1790–1830," pp. 483–504; Bayly, *Rulers, Townsmen, and Bazaars* pp. 238–62.
[57] Gupta, *Delhi Between Two Empires*, p. 5; Bayly, *Rulers*, p. 306.
[58] Timberg, *Marwaris*, p. 117.
[59] Bayly, *Rulers, Townsmen, and Bazars*, p. 213.
[60] Gupta, *Delhi Between Two Empires*, p. 71.
[61] T. Fortescue, "Report on the Revenue System of Delhi Territory, 1820," pp. 134–5.

of irregularly extended posts. Every gate has a different duty and rate; every out-toll a duty and rate differing and separate from the duty taken at the gate; and every distant outpost had once again its own distinct duty, different from the duty which had been taken at the gate and toll; but this was not all. People of different tribes and castes paid different rates. The ultimate destination changed the rate, and last of all the nature of the carriage changed the rate. Now, calculate the gates 8, the tolls 8, the outposts 20; multiply this by the number of known sects and tribes, the number of modes of carriage, and the number of directions, destinations, and multiply this product by the number of articles paying duties (say 900), and find out the result. This result will give the number of rates which did exist at Dehlee.[62]

The British abolished all these tolls and established a single set of rates collected at a single place. This loosened many of the constraints on commercial activity and served to promote the growth and development of urban trade.

Society and culture

The period 1739–1857 witnessed the demise of the patron–client system centered on the palace-fortress and the mansions of princes and great amirs. In the turbulence that swept through the city in the late eighteenth century many of the great men fled or were killed. Although Shah Alam recovered his throne in the early 1770s, he could not resuscitate the empire. His household lands yielded scarcely enough to support his immediate family, and the lands which earlier emperors had administered and been able to assign and which had supported the establishments of princes, great amirs, and other mansabdars had long since passed from imperial control.

Under the British a new system of society founded on different principles and staffed by different men began to emerge. Military triumphs in Bengal, Southern, Central, and Northern India in the late eighteenth and early nineteenth centuries gave the British a monopoly over the use of force. The large armies of regional rulers were defeated and disbanded, thousands of soldiers were thrown out of work, and a way of life for an entire class of Muslims came to an end. The military-administrative system on which the Mughal Empire had been based was destroyed, and the socioeconomic structures of many towns and cities, intertwined and dependent on that system, were rendered obsolete.

In Shahjahanabad the growth of population and the expansion of the economy threw up a new group of merchants. While the descendants of

[62] Ibid., p. 171.

Muslim military and administrative families continued to play a significant though diminished role, these new men, especially those involved with the new cash crops, had the resources to support cultural, religious, and intellectual activities. Other leaders also came forward as new forms of association developed. Centered on schools, courts, religious institutions, and political organizations, these new associations replaced the old patron–client structures and spawned a new middle class of lawyers, teachers, brokers, merchants, bankers, religious specialists, and administrators. While the wealthiest of these new men may have supported large households – loosely organized and considerably reduced imitations of princely and great amiri establishments – most of the population in the rapidly growing city resided in mahallahs formed on caste/craft rather than on patron–client principles.[63]

These sociocultural changes affected residential patterns. During the period 1639–1739 most of the city lived in the palace-fortress or in the great mansions as clients of emperors, princes, and great amirs. During the period 1739–1803 this pattern began to disintegrate as the foundation on which it was based, control by the emperor of large amounts of land, proved increasingly shaky. Many high-ranking amirs left the city at this time and many of those who remained lost control of their lands. The soldiers, merchants, craftsmen, servants, laborers, and artists of the great households either departed also or began to recombine, forming caste, craft, or ethnic mahallahs. Depopulation left mansions and gardens unoccupied, and many of these groups moved inside, coverting the great piles into residential quarters. During Ahmad Shah's reign, for example, refugees from the suburbs took over the garden of Sahibabad in Chandni Chawk, putting up huts and settling in.[64] Another group converted Muzzafar Khan's mansion into a mahallah[65] and, in 1781, caste/craft groups had to be driven from the mansions of Dara Shikoh and Ghazi al-Din Khan in order to free them for imperial use.[66]

As the city grew, the process of conversion accelerated. During the early nineteenth century the house of Fath al-Nisa Begum within the mansion of her father, Qamar al-Din Khan, became the site of a mahallah.[67] Mitiya Mahal, near the Jami' Masjid, was filled with the huts of laborers.[68] The oilmakers converted a large mansion into a quarter, and part of the sprawling residence of Nawab Sa'adat Khan became the

---

[63] For a general discussion see Bayly, *Rulers, Townsmen, and Bazars.*
[64] "Tarikh-i Ahmad Shahi," Persian Manuscript Collection, Or. 2005, London, British Museum, fol. 54b.
[65] *List of Monuments,* 1 p. 72.
[66] "Delhi Newsletters of 1781," fol. 97b.
[67] *List of Monuments,* 1 p. 82.
[68] Khan, *Asar,* p. 702.

mahallah of the oil-sellers.[69] The British themselves, in order to insure peace and tranquility, began to erect permanent barriers and gates at the ends of streets and alleys, marking mahallah boundaries more clearly.[70] As a result, the caste/craft pattern of residential organization pretty much dominated the city by mid-century. The 1845–6 census listed 576 mahallahs within the walled area.[71]

The pattern of extortion reflected these changes also, each invader or emperor organizing his fleecing of the city according to the predominate mode of residential organization. In 1739 Nadir Shah gave five Mughal great amirs the responsibility for collecting tribute from the five parts into which he had divided the city. Anand Ram described how Nizam al-Mulk and Qamar al-Din Khan took seriously their roles as patrons and contributed a good part of the assessments themselves. The other three great amirs, however, made no attempt to pay more than their share.[72] In 1757 Ahmad Shah Abdali sent soldiers to the mansions of individual amirs and to the houses of craft, bazaar, and mahallah headmen.[73] In 1857 Bahadur Shah II collected contributions in cash from individual bankers and merchants and in kind from headmen of trades, bazaars, and crafts.[74]

The structure of cultural activity in Shahjahanabad also changed during the late eighteenth and early nineteenth centuries. During the heyday of the city, artistic endeavor had centered on the households of the great patrons and most of the poets, singers, dancers, painters, musicians, and calligraphers had lived as clients of these men. During the 1739–1803 period, however, cultural activity declined drastically. The disintegration of the Empire, the destruction of the city, and the general exodus of much of the populace culminated in the virtual extinction of artistic activity by the time of British takeover.

The first half of the nineteenth century, on the other hand, was a time of revival. Under Bahadur Shah II the Mughal court reclaimed its role as the school of manners for North India. The emperor, whose pen name was "Zafar," was a skillful but uninspired poet whose tastes ran to philosophy and literature. He patronized poets and men of letters – having a testy, on-again, off-again relationship with Mirza

[69] Sangin Beg, "Sair al-Manazil," fol. 46a; Ahmad, *Waqiat*, 1 p. 158; *List of Monuments*, 1 pp. 170–1.
[70] Spear, *Twilight of the Mughuls* p. 92.
[71] Roberts, "Population of Delhi," p. 182.
[72] Anand Ram, "Bada'i-i Waqai," fols. 124a–b.
[73] "Tarikh-i Alamgir Sani," fols. 9b–10a.
[74] *Press List of Mutiny Papers, 1857* (Calcutta, India: Imperial Record Department, 1921). For collection in cash from shopkeepers, bankers, and merchants see bundle 61, no. 382, p. 85; bundle 61, no. 528, p. 92; bundle 63, no. 11, p. 100; bundle 63, no. 44, p. 102. For collections in kind from chaudhuris of trades, crafts, and bazars see bundle 61, no. 463, p. 88, bundle 61, no. 61–2, p. 74; bundle 61, no. 258, p. 80

Ghalib, the great Urdu poet – and displayed a strong interest in painting.[75] Although the decline of the empire had reduced Shahjahanabad's political influence, its role as a center of culture and an arbiter of grace and style persisted. It was the people of Shahjahanabad, not those of Calcutta, Jaipur, or Lucknow, who exemplified *adamiyat* (polished urbanity).[76]

While the medium of culture in the capital during the first half of the nineteenth century remained Urdu, the style that developed was more secular, stripped of many of its distinctively Islamic elements, and the patrons and practitioners were more diverse, Hindu and British as well as Muslim. The principal difference between the seventeenth and nineteenth centuries lay in the increasing importance of Hindus in the cultural life of the city. Although we have no information about the ratio of Muslims to Hindus in the earlier period, there is reason to believe that Hindu merchants, traders, bankers, artisans, landowners, lawyers, teachers, laborers, and administrators accounted for a substantial portion of the increase in population between 1803 and 1845–6. Thus, it is likely that in 1845–6 the number of Hindus able to patronize the arts was at an all-time high. British administrators, soldiers, merchants, and educators also patronized the arts, especially painting, during the early nineteenth century.[77]

C.F. Andrews called the flowering of cultural, artistic, and intellectual activity in Shahjahanabad during the 1830s and 40s the Delhi Renaissance.[78] It was similar to the Bengal Renaissance in its diffusion of patronage among a middle-class of new men but it differed in its use of Urdu rather than English. To translate works of European philosophy and science into Urdu, first the Vernacular Society and later the Society for the Promotion of Knowledge through the Vernacular were founded. Spurred by the establishment of the first Urdu/Persian printing press in India, Western learning spread rapidly. The center of the Delhi Renaissance was Delhi College, a place of intellectual ferment and excitement that included Hindu, Muslim, and British teachers and administrators. The Archeological Society, dedicated to the preservation of the city's great past, contained a composite membership also.[79]

[75] *Ghalib, 1797–1867, vol. 1: Life and Letters*, ed. and trans. Ralph Russell and Khurshidul Islam (London: George Allen and Unwin Ltd., 1969), chapt. 4.

[76] Gupta, *Delhi Between Empires*, p. 5.

[77] See Mildred Archer, "Artists and Patrons in 'Residency' Delhi," in Frykenberg, ed., *Delhi Through The Ages*, pp. 270–7.

[78] Andrews, *Zaka Ullah*, indroduction; and Gail Minault, "Sayyid Ahmad Dehlavi and the 'Delhi Renaissance'," in Frykenberg, ed., *Delhi Through The Ages*, pp. 287–98.

[79] Gupta, *Delhi Between Empires*, pp. 5–8.

Table 7   *Mosques and temples in Shahjahanabad: 1637–1857*

	Mosques			Temples		
	Dated	Percentage	Total	Dated	Percentage	Total
1. 1639–1857	56		200	12		96
2. 1639–1739	28	(50)	100	0	(0)	0
3. 1739–1803	13	(21)	42	2	(16)	15
4. 1803–1857	15	(29)	58	10	(84)	81

Source: List of Monuments, vols. 1–2.

Table 7, which lists the mosques and temples built in the city over the 218-year period, illustrates these changes. Mosques appear to have been distributed fairly regularly over the three periods: about half in the first hundred years and about a quarter in each of the other two fifty-odd-year periods. Temples, on the other hand, were unevenly distributed. During the first hundred years not many temples appear to have been constructed. In fact, none of the twelve dated temples comes from the first period and only two of the twelve were built during the middle period. The great bulk of the temples, both dated and undated, was built during the British period. This pattern of religious patronage illustrates the shift from the old patron–client, Muslim-dominated system of the seventeenth and early eighteenth centuries to the new secular style of the early nineteenth century in which Hindus, having acquired wealth and position, began to participate on an equal footing with Muslims.

Conclusion

The period from the invasion of Nadir Shah in 1739 to the mutiny and the exile of Bahadur Shah in 1857–8 was a time of great change for Shahjahanabad. In the mid-eighteenth century the iron grid of peace and security which the emperor had imposed upon the city disintegrated. As the mansabdari system collapsed, the imperial army disbanded and the city fell prey to a succession of undisciplined armies and unruly marauders. The population ebbed from the suburbs and walled city and the great households shrivelled up and blew away.

Lord Lake's defeat of the Mahrattas in 1803 inaugurated a new area. The British brought a measure of peace and security and established a stable, consistent framework of government with courts and the rule of law. The city grew steadily through the first half of the nineteenth century, increasing by a total of about 150 percent. The urban area, which had shrunk to the undamaged mahallahs of the walled city, expanded:

first the inner city filled, then a movement beyond the walls began and, by the time of mutiny, the entire area had become settled.

Under the British, market-oriented firms replaced the great households as the central economic institutions. Hindu merchants came to play a much greater role and the demands of the national and international markets interceded to a greater extent. The sociocultural system became less dependent on the emperor and the old nobility and turned more and more to Hindu and Muslim merchants, bankers, lawyers, teachers, and administrators. The caste/craft mahallah spread across the city as bonds of caste, ethnicity, and craft continued to replace those between patron and client.

The cultural life of the city revolved around the imperial court still. Bahadur Shah II patronized the arts and the Mughal court, shorn of all power and accorded less and less respect by the British, remained for many persons the center of style. However, middle-class Hindus and Muslims became more and more involved in artistic activity. Rich Hindu merchants patronized poets, painters, and musicians, and Hindus, Muslims, and Europeans worked together to foster the growth of the new educational and cultural institutions.

7

Comparison and conclusion

The sovereign city is a model which was not limited to Shahjahanabad. As the capital of the patrimonial-bureaucratic empire, the sovereign city was found not only in earlier periods of Mughal Indian history but in other premodern Asian states as well. The city was in a sense an urban deduction from patrimonial-bureaucratic premises and can only be understood as the capital of such a state. The fundamental characteristic of the empire was its personal, familial nature, and the overwhelming ambition of patrimonial-bureaucratic emperors was to absorb state into household and to rule the empire as one great patriarchal domain.

Although the size of their states and the inadequacy of their tools made the achievement of this ambition impossible, these rulers were, nevertheless, able to realize a version of their dream in their capital cities. Where the scale was limited, they were better able to impose household rule. While the dominance of the emperors, the great nobles, and their extended households in the state at large was substantial, in the restricted scale of the sovereign city it was overwhelming. Thwarted in their ambition in the larger arena the rulers were able in the microcosm of the sovereign city to create a personal, familial kind of order. By turning the city into an imperial mansion they achieved, in part at least, their ambition to absorb state into household.

Such an analysis applies not only to Shahjahanabad but also to Agra or Akbarabad, the capital of the Mughal Empire from 1565–1648. It holds for the capitals of the other roughly contemporaneous Asian states as well: for Istanbul, capital of the Ottoman Empire; for Isfahan, capital of the Safavid Empire; for Peking, capital of the Ming Empire; and for Edo, capital of the Tokugawa Shogunate. All of these states exhibit aspects of the patrimonial-bureaucratic empire and all of these cities, great capitals all, reveal their kinship to the household-dominated sovereign city.

Agra

Agra or *Akbarabad* (home of Akbar) was the first capital of the Mughal Empire and it remained the chief center of rule until 1648, when the Emperor Shahjahan finally shifted his headquarters to Shahjahanabad. Having defeated the Lodi Afghans at Panipat near Delhi in 1526, Babur, the founder of the Mughal dynasty, immediately marched on Agra and captured the Afghan treasure. In the four years before his death in 1530 Babur is thought to have constructed several garden complexes in the area, though most seem to have been located on the bank opposite Akbar's city. Although Humayun, Babur's son and successor, founded a city in the Delhi area he also spent a good deal of time at Agra in the ten years before he was driven from India. From 1540 to 1555 the Afghans of Sher Shah ruled North India from Delhi and when Humayun returned he spent the last two years of his life in the Delhi area.[1]

In 1556 Akbar, Humayun's fourteen-year-old son, ascended the throne. The first eight years of his reign were spent extending and consolidating his rule and when Akbar decided to settle down he chose Agra as the site of his new capital. In 1565 construction was begun on a new palace-fortress, situated on the site of an old fort called Badalgarh, and in 1573 it was completed. Mosques, gardens, shops, and the palaces of princes and important amirs began to rise along the banks of the river. Akbar, however, did not limit his building activities to Agra. In 1570 he began building another residence at Fathpur Sikri, some thirty miles west of Agra. In addition, Akbar moved to Lahore in 1585 and spent the next thirteen years putting down the Uzbeg threat from the Northwest.

As a result, it was the reign of Akbar's son and successor, Jahangir, that witnessed the full development of the city. Jahangir erected and renovated a number of structures within the palace-fortress while the great men of his court threw up magnificent structures throughout the area. The mosque of Mu'tamid Khan in the Kashmiri Bazaar was probably the most spectacular of the public buildings. And it is during Jahangir's

---

[1] For information on the city see Abu al-Fazl, *Akbar Namah*, ed. Blochmann, 2 pp. 246–7; Badauni, *Muntakhab al-Tawarikh*, 2 pp. 74–5; Lahauri, *Badshah Namah*, 1, pt. 2 p. 252; Shah Nawaz Khan, *Ma'asir al-Umara*, 1 p. 182; Muhammad Arif Qandahari, *Tarikh-i-Akbari*, ed. Haji Mu'umid-Din Nadwi, Dr. Azhar Ali Dihlawi, Imtiyaz Ali Arshi (Rampur: Hindustan Printing Works, 1962), p. 146; *Encyclopaedia of Islam*, 2nd edn, s.v. "Agra;" Pelsaert, *Jahangir's India*, pp. 1–4; Manucci, *Storia Do Mogor*, 1 p. 130; Bernier, *Travels*, pp. 284–5; Tavernier, *Travels*, 1 p. 86; Foster, ed., *Early Travels*, pp. 226–7; Mundy, *Travels*, 2 pp. 207–8, 214–16; Manrique, *Travels*, 2 pp. 152, 156; Lala Sil Chand, "Tafrih al-Imarat," Persian Manuscript Collection, Or. 6371, London, British Museum; Manik Chand, "Ahwal-i Shahar-i Akbarabad," Persian Manuscript Collection, Or. 2030, London, British Museum; and Sadid al-Din, "Ahwal-i Agra," Persian Manuscript Collection, Or. 1763, London, British Museum.

reign that we first hear of the magnificent mansions that lined the Jamuna on both sides of the river upstream and down from the palace-fortress.

In addition to building a new capital city in the Delhi area, Shahjahan was also responsible for a good deal of the architectural magnificence of Agra and the surrounding area. Soon after his accession, he began work on the palace-fortress. He built a Hall of Special Audience, a bath, a small mosque for the women of his household, the larger Moti Mosque, and the roof and forty pillars of the Hall of Ordinary Audience. He also redecorated the imperial balcony in the public hall. The Jami' Mosque just outside the fort to the northwest was begun by Shahjahan and finished by his daughter Jahanara.

Shahjahan's major project in Agra, however, and the wonder of the age, was the Taj Mahal. Built as a tomb for his beloved wife Mumtaz Mahal, and begun in 1631, the structure was finally finished in 1643. A garden on the opposite bank of the river, now called Mahtab Khan's garden, is said to have been the site for Shahjahan's own tomb, which he never got around to building. The two tombs were to have been linked by a bridge over the river.

Although the Emperor Aurangzeb lived primarily in Shahjahanabad, the new capital, from his accession in 1658 until 1679, when he left North India for the Deccan, he was responsible for the construction of several mosques in Agra. After Aurangzeb's departure, however, the city fell on hard times. The Jats, no longer kept at bay by the imperial troops, attacked the suburbs several times during the late seventeenth century, and the depredations of the later eighteenth century were just as hard on Agra as on Shahjahanabad.

The structure of the Mughal state was set by the end of Akbar's reign and so for Agra as for Shahjahanabad the patrimonial-bureaucratic nature of Mughal rule was the major determinant in the style and function of the city. It is clear that in Agra as in Shahjahanabad the palace-fortress and the mansions of the princes and great amirs were the major structures. Akbar's palace, as renovated and rebuilt by Jahangir and Shahjahan, dominated the city. It occupied the central position on the western bank of the river and was enclosed by a wall nearly four miles in circumference and further separated from the city by a deep moat. The palace enclosed an enormous area which the early seventeenth-century Dutch merchant, Francisco Pelsaert compared to a city, with streets, houses, bazaars, and shops.

The city itself was not surrounded by a wall and, according to the Frenchman Bernier, was not as well planned as Shahjahanabad. There were four or five major streets, running parallel and perpendicular to the river, and at the end of each one was a gate. The principal feature of the cityscape beyond the palace-fortress were the palaces of princes and great amirs strung along both sides of the river upstream and down. As a result, the city was not concentrated in a walled compact area but was stretched in a long thin line along the river-bank. In general the mansions of the highest-ranking princes and great amirs were found nearer the palace and Pelsaert mentions, among others, those of Itiqad Khan, Mahabat Khan, Asad Khan (whose mansion was said to be the most magnificent), and Sultan Khurram (later Shahjahan). Watercourses, flowers, trees, and pools graced the interiors of these great places and the straw-thatched mud huts of soldiers, servants, and other household clients stood both within and without. John Jourdain, an English merchant who spent about six months in Agra during the year 1610, wrote:

There are within the city many fair buildings, but they stand so scattered one from another as though they were afraid one of another; and the reason is that every great man must have his house by himself, because round about his house lie all his servants, everyone in his own house with their horses.[2]

The contrast between the great walled mansions, isolated in shady, garden preserves along the water, and the mean, dusty streets and bazaars in the area outside the palace-fortress was extreme. There stood, for the most part, the straw-thatched mud huts of the servants, artisans, and shop-keepers who were not part of the great households. A middle-class between the inhabitants of the mud huts and the great houses was not to be found in any size, and several times a year fires raged through the city sweeping away the homes of the poor. Travellers likened the city to a royal park or a country town because of all of the trees and gardens.

The economic structure of Agra during the period 1565–1648 was quite similar to that of Shahjahanabad from 1648 to 1739. In Agra, also, the emperor and the great men collected a substantial percentage of the revenues of the Empire at large and, as a result, dominated the processes of production, exchange, and consumption. The imperial palace-fortress in Agra, like its counterpart in Shahajahanabad, contained a good many workshops of various kinds and was a major center of urban production. Within the palace-fortress was an elaborate bazaar that featured goods for the imperial household (especially for the women of the imperial harem) while outside the major gateway was a large market similar to the Urdu Bazaar in front of Shahjahan's fortress. The mansions of princes and great amirs also contained workshops and markets and served as centers of production and exchange.

The central wholesale market for Agra, as for Shahjahanabad, was on

[2] Jourdain, *Journal*, pp. 162–3.

the east or opposite bank of the river from the city proper. In a suburb called Sikandara were the warehouses and homes of the great grain merchants. According to the author of the *Tabaqat-i Akbari*, the river below Agra teemed with boats bringing food and goods of all sorts from the doab. The imperial customs houses were located in Sikandara and goods were taxed before crossing the river.

Like Shahjahanabad Agra had rich central markets catering to the taste and income of the rich men of court. Immediately outside the palace-fortress was a large horse market where hardy, handsome animals from Central Asia were available. White cloth, silk, gold and silver work, carpets, and indigo were sold in the bazaars that lined the sides of the major thoroughfares. Shops of artisans, moneylenders, and astrologers were there also. According to an early seventeenth-century traveller, merchants had their choice of over eighty caravansarais in which to put up.

Despite all of this, however, Agra, like Shahjahanabad, struck European merchants as not having a great number of markets or a wide selection of goods for its size. Pelsaert observed that unlike Lahore, Burhanpur, and Ahmadabad Agra had no remarkable markets. His explanation turned on the spread-out nature of the city and the lack of interest of the emperor but it seems clear, following our analysis of Shahjahanabad, that the lack of markets was due more to the domination of the great households. A large proportion of the goods produced in the city were exchanged in the palace-fortress and great mansions and did not reach the open market.

What all of this suggests is that Agra, like Shahjahanabad, was organized around the mansions of the great men. As in Shahjahanabad the bulk of the population seems to have lived in or around the great households and to have been dependent on the great men for their economic and social well-being. Agra like Shahjahanabad is an example of the sovereign city and the name it was given during the early seventeenth-century, *Akbarabad* (home of Akbar), suggests that it too should be understood as the mansion of the patrimonial-bureaucratic emperor.

Istanbul

The inhabitants of the Ottoman Empire (1389–1923) were divided into two basic classes: the *askeri* or military class, those who represented the ruler's authority (administrators, soldiers, and men of religion) and did not pay taxes; and the ordinary tax-payers who supported the state – farmers, merchants, herdsmen, and artisans. Like the palace-fortress of the Mughal Emperor, the palace of the Ottoman sultan was the center of government. In Istanbul the imperial palace was divided into two parts. In the inner, secluded section lived the sultan with his harem and immediate family.[3]

In the outer section resided the six services or departments that controlled and administered the state. The first service included the religious scholars, judges, physicians, and surgeons. In the second were the commissioners in charge of the palaces, the mint, and the kitchen. The third was made up of the nobles of the imperial stirrup, the largest and most important group of officers in the imperial household. These men commanded the household cavalry and the Janissaries, the Christian slave soldiers of the sultan. The grand vazier was the most important of the nobles. He conducted the court sessions in the imperial palace and was the sultan's chief executive. In the fourth service were the sons of nobles and other special members of the household. The fifth and sixth services, the remainder of the outside services, were made up of the artisans and other specialists of the palace. These included artists, scholars, craftsmen, architects, and poets.

The household of the Ottoman sultan was manned almost entirely by slaves. Many of these men (especially the Janissaries) were educated in the palace and came to occupy high posts in the state. For the Ottoman ruler, as for the other patrimonial-bureaucratic rulers, the aim was to render the imperial officers utterly dependent, like sons in a patriarchal household. The household slaves were loyal to an individual not to the state, and they helped the sultan consolidate his power and authority against the nobility. The other members of the military class adopted the slave system also, and the sultan's palace provided a model for the mansions of vaziers and nobles in the capital and for the palaces of governors in the provinces.

The Ottoman Empire, like the other patrimonial-bureaucratic empires, was agrarian-based. The lands of the central empire were directly administered by the nobles of the sultan's household. In the typical Ottoman province the sultan's cavalrymen were stationed in individual

---

[3] For a discussion of the foundation and organization of the Ottoman state see Halil Inalcik, "The Rise of the Ottoman Empire," and "The Heyday and Decline of the Ottoman Empire," in P.M. Holt, Ann K.S. Lambton, and Bernard Lewis, ed., *The Cambridge History of Islam* (Cambridge: Cambridge University Press, 1970), 1 pp. 295–353; Halil Inalcik, *The Ottoman Empire: The Classical Age 1300–1600*, trans. Norman Itzkowitz and Colin Imber (London: Weidenfeld and Nicolson, 1973); and Fleischer, *Bureaucrat and Intellectual*. For economic organization see Halil Inalcik, "Capital Formation in the Ottoman Empire," *Journal of Economic History* 29 (1969) pp. 97–140. For a discussion of Istanbul see *Encyclopaedia of Islam*, 2nd edn, s.v. "Istanbul"; and Bernard Lewis, *Istanbul and The Civilization of The Ottoman Empire* (Norman: University of Oklahoma Press, 1963).

villages and collected the tax, paid in kind rather than in cash, from the peasants. In return, the cavalrymen rallied in support of the sultan in times of war. In each district the sultan appointed two authorities: a noble from the military class, the sultan's executive authority; and a judge from among the religious scholars, a representative of the sultan's legal authority.

The outlying provinces of the state, like Egypt and Baghdad, were governed more loosely. In such areas the Ottomans stationed a Janissary garrison, a governor, a recordkeeper, and a judge. Taxes from these provinces paid the local military and administrative expenses; of the remainder, a fixed annual sum was sent to the capital. Hereditary provinces belonged to the tribal chieftains of Eastern Anatolia. Hereditary nobles retained the revenues they collected but contributed a fixed number of troops to the sultan.

Istanbul was the capital of the Ottoman state from 1453 until 1923. From about A.D. 330 the official name of the city had been Constantinople and it had flourished as the capital of the Eastern Roman Empire. By about the early thirteenth century, however, the city had fallen on hard times. When Mehemmed II gained entry in 1453 the once mighty capital was no more than a collection of villages, a city in ruins. Mehemmed intended from the very first that Istanbul should be his new capital and he moved quickly to build up its population and trade.

The fundamental principle in the development of Ottoman Istanbul was that it should be an Islamic city, a place where Muslims could live in accordance with their religion. The Islamic character of the city is reflected in its topographical development. The city was created around places of worship, and the first *nahiye* or district was that of Aya Sofya (Great Mosque). The other districts grew up around jami' or congregational mosques erected by sultans and nobles. All of these districts were composed of mahallahs or neighborhoods which were centered on local mosques (*masjids*).

The two basic features of Ottoman Istanbul were the great mosque and the central market district (*bedestan*). The nahiyes and their mahallahs, built by the sultans and the men of the military class, were scattered all around the city. However, the harbor area of the Golden Horn and the main thoroughfare along which armies and caravans passed tended to enforce a kind of unity on the city as a whole.

The sultan's palace in Istanbul was constructed on a promontory overlooking the Bosphorus and the Sea of Marmara and covered 163 acres. The inner and outer sections of the palace contained three courts. The first court, situated between the imperial and middle gates, held a variety of buildings and miscellaneous collection of household personnel.

The second court, between the middle gate and the Gate of Felicity, was open only to those with definite business and contained the audience halls and administrative departments of the household. Beyond the Gate of Felicity lay the private apartments of the sultan's family where the harem, eunuchs, and personal servants lived. The sultan's household included an enormous number of people. In 1609 there were 13,000 palace personnel, 78,000 slave troops (most of them Janissaries), and 3,000 navy men. Most of these lived inside or close by the palace and constituted a significant percentage of the total urban population of about 600,000 (divided about equally between the walled area and the suburbs).

The mansions of nobles and rich merchants were large and walled. Like the sultan's palace, they were divided into inner and outer areas. In the inner area stood pavilions and apartments for the great man's family and servants and a garden. In the courtyards of the outer area were kitchens, bakeries, baths, shops, stables, workshops for craftsmen, and schools for household slaves. In 1650 the city contained about one hundred mansions of important ministers and members of the sultan's family and about one thousand of lesser nobles and merchants. Sultans and great ministers also built villas and gardens outside the walls. These served as hunting lodges, summer residences, and places of retreat.

In 1459, in accordance with the orders of Mehemed II, the great nobles constructed nahiyes (districts) or residential complexes in various parts of the city. Eventually, thirteen districts were established, each containing an average of seventeen mahallahs. A district contained a jami' mosque, an Islamic school, an inn, and the tomb of its founder. The public buildings were supported and sustained by waqfs (dedications), usually rents from the shops, inns, baths, and wells which the founder constructed.

Mahallahs developed around this central core. The mahallah was an organic community with its own identity. The jami' mosque or, in the case of other religions, the church or synagogue, was the central institution. Repair of this structure along with the school and fountains, was the responsibility of the inhabitants. The authorities gave the mahallah the responsibility for maintaining order and paying taxes. The imam of the mosque represented the inhabitants and answered to the government for the muhallah's meeting its obligations. Nearly 90 percent of mahallahs were named after the founder of the local mosque and, according to the waqf registers of 1546, 65 percent of the founders were palace officials, army officers, ulama, or bureaucrats. As members of the military class these men were richer than merchants or craftsmen and were able to establish waqfs to support the public structures.

Like Shahjahanabad, Istanbul was administered by the officers of the imperial household rather than by the provincial bureaucracy. The commandant of the household regiment policed the shores of the Golden Horn, the admiral of the fleet was responsible for the ports, the commanders of the gunners and armorers looked after their areas, and the captain of the Janissaries maintained the overall level of peace and security.

In the Ottoman state, as in the other patrimonial-bureaucratic empires, the imperial household dominated the economy. The primary responsibility of society at large was to preserve and promote the power of the ruler, and the Ottoman economy was organized and directed with this in mind. In the Ottoman state the bulk of government revenues came from taxes on the produce of the land, although customs duties and levies on merchants and mines contributed small but significant amounts. Like the other patrimonial-bureaucratic emperors, the Ottoman sultan controlled a substantial percentage of state revenues. In 1528 50 percent of the total tax of 9.65 million gold ducats flowed into the household treasury of the sultan in Istanbul.

It was Ottoman policy to encourage trade. Merchants were organized into trade guilds, both the wealthy international and interregional traders and the smaller local merchants. Unlike the craft guilds, however, merchant guilds were not subject to the detailed regulations of the religious law. Under the Ottomans merchants were free to accumulate capital and were not greatly circumscribed, a situation quite different from that in Mughal India or Ming China. In the administrative manuals merchants were portrayed favorably. They fulfilled important functions for the state – making loans, acting as intermediaries in the collection of taxes, paying customs duties, serving as agents and ambassadors, and supplying nobles with luxury goods.

In Istanbul there was a thriving class of merchants. Trading activities of all kinds were concentrated in the central market (bedestan) so as to be easily taxed and regulated. The Bayuk Bedestan was an enormous structure with fifteen domes, as strong and sturdy as a fortress. This was the financial and economic center of the city and contained shops for craftsmen and traders and inns for travellers. In Istanbul the sultan banned free trade in cereals and licensed a few privileged merchants to trade in certain essential commodities such as foodstuffs and the raw materials needed by guilds. If one of these merchants was caught smuggling or profiteering his privileges were withdrawn. Prices were fixed but a certain amount of speculation was allowed. The members of the palace establishment often imported grain and made large profits in times of scarcity. Several families of Jewish merchants, who had been encouraged and supported by the sultans, resided in Istanbul.

In Ottoman cities the craft guilds were the mainspring of economic life. They fixed prices, regulated quality, and helped the sultan's household collect taxes. Like the Mughal emperor, the Ottoman sultan established palace workshops employing hundreds of laborers to produce firearms, powder, and various other goods. The craft guilds were subject to the religious law and were allowed no more than a 10–15 percent profit.

Waqfs, which supported charitable objects or religious activities, were registered with religious officials and were of two kinds: (1) monies set aside to construct such pious buildings as mosques, colleges, and hospitals, and (2) the investments which supported these buildings. In Istanbul most of the investments were in baths, bazaars, shops, depots, workshops, and bakeries, establishments which could provide steady rents. In 1475 the sultan confiscated all private waqf properties and brought them under state control and management.

Like the other patrimonial-bureaucratic emperors the Ottoman sultan dominated the economy of the capital city. Yet in Istanbul the sultan seemed to control more by the sheer size of his purse than by the establishment of household workshops or production facilities. Also, merchants in Istanbul, unlike those in Shahjahanabad and Peking, were more independent. They performed many important financial and administrative services for the Ottoman state and, as a result, enjoyed greater prestige and endured less supervision.

In both Istanbul and Shahjahanabad it was the palace of the emperor and the mansions of the nobles that served as the social, economic, and political foci of urban life. In Ottoman Turkey as in Mughal India the whole palace establishment accompanied the sultan on campaign, and in Istanbul as in Shahjahanabad the city was devastated when the ruler departed. There was a substantial drop in population and in the urban markets prices rose, commodities were cornered, and shortages appeared. The similarities are even more apparent when the epithets used for the two cities are compared. For Istanbul the Ottomans used *paytakht-i saltanat* (throne of the sultanate), *dar al-saltana* (seat or home of sovereignty), and *dar al-khilafa* (seat or home of deputyship). The last two were used by the Mughals for Shahjahanabad and in both empires they reflected the conception of the city as the mansion of the emperor.

Mughal historians of the seventeenth century assumed a basic similarity between the two capitals and often used Istanbul as a standard of comparison. Muhammad Salih, the official historian, wrote that Istanbul was not as big as Shahjahanabad;[4] Chandar Bhan Brahman

---

[4] Muhammad Salih, *'Amal-i Salih*, 3 p. 50.

described the Mughal capital as bigger than Istanbul;[5] and Sujan Rai wrote: "the city of Stamboul, the capital of the sultan of Rum, which is famous for its largeness and extent, is not a tenth part of a tenth part of this city."[6]

Isfahan

The Safavids first appeared in northwestern Iran in the fourteenth century and for the next 150 years led an uneventful existence as leaders of the small Sufi sect which bore their name. From the mid-fifteenth century onward, however, the sect became intensely messianic and Shi'i until, attracting more and more followers, it cast off its provincial moorings and set sail for the centers of population and power in the southeast. In 1501 Shah Ismail entered Tabriz at the head of a large army, proclaimed Safavid rule, and declared Shi'ism the state religion. By 1510 the entire country had come under the sway of the new dynasty.[7]

At the apex of the Safavid state was the Shah whose rule, like that of the other patrimonial-bureaucratic emperors, was both personal and absolute. There were three aspects to the legitimacy of Safavid rulers: (1) the old Iranian tradition of the divine right of kings; (2) the claim of the Safavid Shahs to be representatives of the *Mahdi* (the hidden leader of all Shi'is); and (3) the Shah's position as *murshid-i kamil* (perfect leader) of the

---

[5] Chandar Bhan Brahman, "Chahar Chaman," p. 141.

[6] Sujan Rai, "Khulasat al-Tawarikh," fol. 26a.

[7] The best single source on Safavid Iran is Jackson and Lockhart, ed., *The Cambridge History of Iran, Vol. 6: The Timurid and Safavid Periods.* An account of the beginnings of Safavid rule is found in Michel M. Massaoui, *The Origins of the Safavid* (Wiesbaden: Franz Steiner and Verlag GMBH, 1972). The organization of the mature state is described in a book and a series of articles by Savory, *Iran Under the Safavids*; "Safavid Persia," in *The Cambridge History of Islam,* 1 pp. 394–430; "The Safavid State and Polity," *Iranian Studies,* 7, no. 1–2 (Wtr-Spring), 1974, pp. 179–212; "The Principal Offices of the Safavid State During the Reign of Ismail I," *Bulletin of the School of Oriental and African Studies,* 23 (1960) pp. 91–105; "The Principal Offices of the Safavid State During the Reign of Tahmasp I," *Bulletin of the School of Oriental and African Studies,* 24 (1961) pp. 65–85; "The Consolidation of Safavid Power in Persia," *Der Islam,* 41 (1965) pp. 71–94; "Some Notes on the Provincial Administration of the Early Safavid Empire," *Bulletin of the School of Oriental and African Studies,* 27 (1964) pp. 114–28. For the translation of a Savafid administrative manual see *Tadkhirat al-Muluk: A Manual of Safavid Administration (c. 1725),* trans. and explained by V. Minorsky (London: Luzac and Company, 1943). See also Hodgson, *Venture of Islam,* 3 pp. 29–60. A detailed description of Isfahan can be found in John Chardin, *Voyages en Perse et Autres Lieux de l'Orient,* 10 vols. (Paris: Le Ormant, 1811), 7 pp. 273–492; 8 pp. 1–142. The architecture of the city and the palace complex are discussed in Arthur U. Pope, ed., *A Survey of Persian Art,* 6 vols. (London and New York: Oxford University Press, 1939), 2 pp. 1191–9, 1406–7. See also *Encyclopaedia of Islam,* 2nd edn, s.v. "Isfahan"; Eugenio Galdieri, "Les Palais d'Isfahan," *Iranian Studies,* 7 (Wtr-Spring, 1974), pp. 380–5; and Donald Wilbur, "Aspects of the Safavid Ensemble at Isfahan," Ibid., pp. 406–15. The other articles in volume 7 of Iranian Studies are also interesting.

Safaviyya Sufi order. The Shah was thought to have been directly appointed by God and to be the shadow of God on earth. All Safavid officials were considered slaves of the Shah, their lives and property at his disposal.

Under Shah Ismail and the later rulers a conflict developed between the Turkish cavalrymen (*qizilbash* or redhats) who served as officers, soldiers, and governors and the Persian administrators (*tajiks* or non-Turks) who worked as accountants, clerks, judges, and tax collectors. The Persians thought the qizilbash coarse and uncultured and the Turks considered the Persians effete and unmanly. After consolidating his rule, Shah Ismail met the Ottomans at Chaldiran in 1514 and was decisively defeated. This shattered the belief of many in the Shah's invincibility and caused him to lose his supernatural aura. After the death of Ismail in 1524, the qizilbash officers achieved a good deal of independence under the rule of Shah Tahmasp (1524–76).

Shah Abbas (1588–1629), the greatest of Safavid rulers, was the epitome of the patrimonial-bureaucratic ruler. He completely re-organized the governmental apparatus and founded Isfahan. The power of the throne had declined drastically in the twelve years following the death of Tahmasp and Abbas had come to power with the help of the qizilbash chiefs. In order to become independent of these cavalrymen and to establish himself, Abbas recruited a force of military slaves loyal to him alone. Circassians, Georgians, and Armenians, these household troops were quite similar in function and organization to the Janissaries of the Ottoman Sultan. In time this force grew into a standing household army of about 40,000: 10,000–15,000 cavalrymen with muskets; 12,000 musketeers who eventually became cavalry; 12,000 artillerymen; and 3,000 bodyguards. In Iran, as in the other patrimonial-bureaucratic empires, the function of these troops was to cow the nobles and to increase the personal strength and control of the sultan. In order to prevent the great men from establishing independent footholds in the countryside, Abbas, like the other emperors, transferred them from their native areas to other parts of the empire. After Abbas there was a period of decline in the late seventeenth century and the Safavid dynasty finally fell to the Afghans in 1722.

Under the Safavids the nobles maintained large retinues of soldiers, artisans, merchants, and artists and organized them into complex households like that of the Shah. The nobility included both the Turkish and Persian officials. Under Abbas, however, the slaves of the Shah's household began to enter the administration and, by the end of his reign, about 20 percent of the high positions in government were held by these men.

Shah Abbas did not build his new capital on a virgin site. Isfahan had been a town, a provincial center, and a capital at various times before the Safavids. It had been captured by Muhammad's bedouin warriors in the initial expansion in the early seventh century A.D. Under the early Caliphs and the Ummayads Isfahan came within the jurisdiction of the governors of Basra and Iraq. The Buyids captured the city in 927 and it was the Seljuk capital during the eleventh and twelfth centuries.

The Safavid connection with the city began in 1502–3, when Shah Ismail stormed the walls. For some years before the accession of Abbas in 1587 there was a good deal of internal unrest and disorder. Isfahan, however, was the natural political, administrative, and commercial center of the Safavid empire, and it was understandable that Abbas should have chosen it as the site for his new capital.

Although there were later additions by Shah Abbas II and Shah Sultan Husain, the basic city was built by Abbas. Not since Baghdad had the Islamic world seen a city laid out according to an integrated plan that included avenues, palaces, public offices, mosques, madrassahs, bazaars, forts, and gardens. Abbas laid out irrigation systems and founded a market center called Najafabad, fifteen miles west of town, but the core of the new city was the great square or piazza known as the *maidan-i shah* (king's square). It was 507 meters long, 158 meters wide, and was encircled by a water channel 3½ meters by 2. Four gates opened onto the square. One led to the *Ali Qapu* (Sublime Gate) palace of the Shah, another to the vast Qaysariyya or royal bazaar, and the third and fourth to two great mosques – the *Masjid-i Shah* (Shah's mosque) and the Mosque of Shaykh Luft Allah, both built during Abbas's reign. By day the square contained the shops of merchants, artisans, and others and by night it was illuminated by the antics of jugglers, acrobats, and storytellers. It was the site for the New Year's festival and other state occasions and at times served as a royal polo ground.

The Ali Qapu palace was an audience chamber and a gateway to the royal gardens and palaces rather than the main residence of the Shah. The royal bazaar which lay at the north end of the square linked the new city with the old. Abbas had not destroyed the original city and the great bazaar covered an enormous area of 11½ square miles. Nearby were the royal mint and another audience hall, the Chihil Sutun palace. In the gardens which encircled the square were the mansions of the Shah and his nobles.

To the south of the square a broad, tree-lined avenue known as the *Chahar Bagh* (four gardens) bisected an area of gardens and trees where the nobles had their mansions. The avenue crossed the Zayanda-Rud river by the Allahvardi Khan bridge and became the main commercial and residential thoroughfare of the city. It was 2½ miles long and 48 meters wide.

The "royal city" or palace of the Safavid Shahs lay between the Maydan-i Shah and the Chahar Bagh. Within this rectangular area, which had a circumference about 3¼ miles, was a residential complex containing gardens, pavilions, and mansions. Inside or nearby lived the 70,000–75,000 persons of the royal household: 6,000 menials, 20,000 attendants and servants, 40,000 musketeers, cavalrymen, artillerymen, and bodyguards, and 5,000–10,000 artisans, merchants, religious specialists, painters, musicians, and writers.

The Frenchman John Chardin, who visited the city during the latter years of the seventeenth century, said that the beauty of the city was due in large part to the great number of magnificent palaces set in spacious walled gardens around the city. The Shah himself owned some 300 palaces and the slave officials, Turkish officers, and Persian administrators had constructed large mansions along both sides of the river that bisected the city.

According to Chardin the city walls were about eight miles around and the circuit of the entire area, suburbs and all, was twenty-five miles. Each day two thousand sheep were slaughtered. The city contained 162 mosques, 48 colleges, 1802 sarais, 273 baths, and 12 cemeteries. Chardin estimated its population at 600,000 persons, about the size of late-seventeenth-century London.

Like Shahjahan and the other patrimonial-bureaucratic emperors, Shah Abbas imposed his own vision on the new capital. One scholar, in fact, has argued that Abbas wanted to outstrip the imperial achievements of the Mughals and the Ottomans and had designed Isfahan to be a rival of Agra and Istanbul.[8] In addition, because of the close and frequent interaction between Iran and India during the Mughal period, it is not inconceivable that Abbas' achievement in Isfahan should have stimulated and influenced Shahjahan in the planning of his new capital forty years later. In any event, in Isfahan, as in Shahjahanabad, the cityscape centered on the structures of the ruler and his nobles.

Under Abbas the "royal city" and the noble mansions became the centers of cultural and artistic life. The Safavids, like the Mughals, were heirs to the artistic traditions of the Timurid court of fifteenth-century Herat. In Safavid Iran, as in Mughal India, high culture developed around the court, and the Safavid Shahs and their nobles became generous and sophisticated patrons of the arts. The art of the book, for example, was highly developed – calligraphy, binding, and illustration all reaching new

---

[8] Robert Hillenbrand, "Safavid Architecture," in *Cambridge History of Iran* 6 p. 821.

heights. Abbas, however, was more interested in architecture and city planning, and in the arts of economic utility such as ceramics, textiles, and carpets. Carpet-weaving was elevated into a fine art during this period and Abbas probably started the first carpet workshop in Iran in his own household. Textiles were an ancient craft in Iran and, while Persian pottery was not quite up to the quality of the Chinese, the ceramic tiles produced by the Safavids were unsurpassed.

Under Abbas also Isfahan became an important religious center. By the middle of the seventeenth century Shi'i religious festivals were common and Abbas had organized and gained control of the religious classes. Like the other sovereign cities, Isfahan was administered from the imperial household, not by the local provincial officials.

The Safavid state, like the other patrimonial-bureaucratic empires, was agrarian-based and the bulk of government revenues came from taxes on the produce of the land. Under the Safavids, as under the other states, there was a distinction between the state and household spheres of government. Under the early Shahs most of the provinces were in the state sphere, administered by Turkish governors appointed for life. These men resided on their lands and collected taxes, but they did not transmit a great deal of cash, grain, or other goods to the Shah. The provincial governors and officials were supervised by men from the Shah's household but they enjoyed a large amount of independence and freedom.

In the household sphere of government were the provinces under the personal administration of the Shah. The cash and grains from these lands flowed directly to the household treasury and supported the troops and other retainers of the Shah. Abbas strengthened his hold on the state by engineering a large transfer of lands from the state to the household sphere of government. This provided the fiscal basis for the standing army of slave soldiers which he had recruited. In the early seventeenth century, imperial household lands yielded about 22 percent of total state revenues.

Credit facilities were relatively primitive in Safavid Iran and trade was not highly developed. Merchants dealt mostly in cash and the most important item of trade was silk. Nevertheless, Abbas tried to promote international commerce, and he established an overland trading network with Europe that bypassed the Ottoman Empire and was largely in the hands of Armenian merchants. The Armenians were especially important because they handled the silk trade, which was a royal monopoly and was enormously profitable for Abbas. He settled them in the large suburb, called New Julfa, on the south bank of the Zayanda-rud. The internal trade was handled by Persian and Jewish merchants and was tightly controlled.

The Safavid Shahs, like the other patrimonial-bureaucratic rulers, maintained a variety of household workshops. The traditional number was thirty-two or thirty-three and, like the workshops in the households of the Mughal emperors, these included domestic departments (kitchen, stables, and kennels) as well as places of manufacture. The artisans, artists, and craftsmen in the royal workshops – about 5000 under Abbas – were a privileged group and were extremely well-treated. They were paid both in cash and in kind, were given presents for good work, and accompanied the Shah on his travels. The great nobles also maintained workshops in their mansions and produced goods and services for their households. The artisans in Isfahan who did not work either for the Shah or his nobles were organized into guilds. Instead of paying taxes in cash, however, the guilds often met their fiscal obligations by sending articles and goods to the imperial household.

Shah Abbas controlled a substantial percentage of the revenues of the state and derived a steady but significant income from the silk monopoly. Thus, by the end of his reign, Abbas, like the other patrimonial-bureaucratic emperors, had turned the royal household into the dominant economic force not only in the city but in the state as well.

The Safavid Shah, with his semi-divine status, his position as a religious leader, and his household army of slaves, was able to impose the personal, quasi-familial kind of rule characteristic of patrimonial-bureaucratic emperors. In Isfahan as in the other capitals the result was a sovereign city heavily dependent on the initiatives and resources of the ruler and his court. The "royal city" of the Safavid Shahs and the mansions of their nobles were at the very center of the political, economic, and social lives of the city. It is, therefore, quite appropriate to conceive of Isfahan as the mansion of its founder Shah Abbas.

The Mughals recognized the glory of Isfahan and its similarity to their new capital. In the *Mirza Namah* the Mughal amir is counselled to consider Isfahan the best city in the Iran.[9] And Sujan Rai, in describing Shahjahanabad, wrote: "The city... of Isfahan, the capital of the Shah of Persia, which is famous for excellence and beauty, does not come up to even a single quarter of this city."[10]

Even Nadir Shah, who brought such destruction and bloodshed to Shahjahanabad in 1739, was impressed by its plan and build. He carried away with him 300 masons, 200 carpenters, and 100 stonecutters and constructed a city named Nadirabad, modelled after the Mughal capital but one-fourth the size.[11]

[9] "Mirza Namah," p. 5.
[10] Sujan Rai, "Khulasat al-Tawarikh," fol. 26a.
[11] Hanway, *Travels*, 4 pp. 196–7; Khwaja Abd al-Karim, "Biyan-i Waqai," fol. 43a; Sheikh Ali Hazin, *Tarikh-i Ahwal*, pp. 265–72.

Edo

The sixteenth and early seventeenth centuries were an unsettled period in premodern Japan, and it was during these years that the *daimyo* (military noble), the true territorial lord, emerged. The Tokugawa Shogunate (1603–1868) was dominated by these great landed nobles. In 1600, after the battle of Sekigahara, Tokugawa Ieyasu (1542–1616), the founder of the dynasty, became the dominant daimyo or *Shogun* (general or commander). He controlled about 25 percent of state revenues at this time, and by the end of the century the Tokugawa house and its closest retainers had increased their share to about 60 percent.[12]

The Tokugawa shogun was a kind of super-daiymo and ruled the state in a quasi-personal, familial kind of way similar to that of the other patrimonial-bureaucratic rulers. The military nobles whom Ieyasu and succeeding shoguns conquered were divided into three groups: collateral Tokugawa families who were related to Ieyasu and his descendants; "inside" or "house" daimyo, men who had been retainers of Ieyasu before his accession and who were made nobles afterward; and "outside" daimyo, descendants of the ancient landed families who only became retainers and supporters of the Tokugawa house after 1600. In order to control the great daimyo and to strengthen the patron–client ties between him and them, the shogun required that they reside in Edo in alternative years, serve at his court, and leave hostages behind when they departed.

The Tokugawa *bakufu* (government or house) developed out of the great daimyo's rule over his feudal domain and was the archetype of the patrimonial-bureaucratic empire. The government included the shogun, the chief ministers (mostly inside daimyo), and the other officials (primarily liege vassals or personal retainers of the shogun), and the Tokugawa house included all of the people in the government. The house or government was clearly distinguished from the court and the outside daimyo. The collateral or related daimyo were on the borderline. They

---

12 For a discussion of the Tokugawa state see Conrad D. Totman, *Politics in the Tokugawa Bakufu: 1600–1843* (Cambridge: Harvard University Press, 1967); George B. Sansom, *A History of Japan: 1615–1867* (Stanford: Stanford University Press, 1963); John W. Hall, *Government and Local Power in Japan: 500–1700* (Princeton: Princeton University Press, 1966); and John W. Hall and Maurius B. Jansen, ed., *Studies in the Institutional History of Early Modern Japan* (Princeton: Princeton University Press, 1968); John W. Hall, "The Castle Town and Japan's Modern Urbanization," *Far Eastern Quarterly*, 15 (1955) pp. 37–56; and Takukazu Takenaka, "Endogenous Formation and Development of Capitalism in Japan," *Journal of Economic History*, 29 (1969) pp. 141–62. For Edo see Rozman, *Urban Networks*, pp. 46–7, 80–5, 96–103, 294–302; A.L. Sadler, *A Short History of Japanese Architecture* (London and Sydney: Angus and Robertson, Ltd, 1941), pp. 69–83; and Kiyoshi Hirai, *Feudal Architecture of Japan*, trans. Hiroaki Satu and Jeannine Ciliotta (New York and Tokyo; Weatherhill – Heibonsha, 1973), pp. 14, 44.

saw themselves as Tokugawa house members but were viewed by the shogun and other members of the government as a distinct group.

The bulk of officials were liege vassals, called bannerman or housemen, who filled all but the top sixty positions in the government. Most of these men lived in Edo and were supported by the shogun's household. They had four areas of responsibility: the household affairs of the shogun, military matters, administrative affairs, and ceremonial functions.

Tokugawa Ieyasu decided to make Edo (present-day Tokyo) the capital of his new state. He finished his great palace-fortress in 1606 and Edo took its place as the chief *jokamachi* (castle town) of the realm just as Ieyasu was the chief daimyo. In the pacification and unification of Japan in the sixteenth and seventeenth centuries, castle towns played a central role. They became centers of administration and military power, the bases from which the daimyo extended their sway over the surrounding countryside. As the daimyo grew more successful, stamping out their lesser competitors, castle towns grew larger and more complex. Merchants and artisans were attracted to the new centers, not only by the liberal terms offered by the daimyo but also by the opportunities of breaking away from the old guild system. Throughout the sixteenth and seventeenth centuries the castle towns remained military and administrative centers. A high percentage of the population was dependent on the daimyo, and the military nobles controlled all aspects of the city. Edo, a great city, was in most important ways a castle town still.

Edo measured 6000 yards east to west and 4100 north to south and, by 1700, it had a population of about one million persons. At its center was the great palace-fortress and around it, overlooking the bay, were the mansions of the great daimyo and the liege vassals. The palace-fortress was surrounded by stone walls, although most of the interior structures were of wood. It was divided into four areas and cut off from the rest of the city by a ten-mile moat.

The first area was the largest and was located just inside the western moat. Originally, it had held the mansions of several of the important daimyo. After a great fire in 1657, however, it was turned into a combination garden–fire barrier. The second area contained shrines to former shoguns and the quarters of retired shoguns and heirs. Here the Tokugawas worshipped their ancestors. The third area, to the east, held the offices of government officials. The inside daimyo resided here while in office.

The fourth area was cut off from the rest of the palace-fortress by an interior moat of one mile. This innermost enclosure, covering about nine acres, contained the shogun's household quarters. This sector, like the inner apartments in the palaces of the other patrimonial-bureaucratic emperors, housed not only the women, children, and servants of the shogun's family but the records, offices, and officials of state as well. It was divided into three parts. In the great interior (*honmaru*) were rooms for the shogun's wife and family and the other women and servants of his household. The middle interior (*ninomaru*) was the shogun's private realm where he dealt with the business of state, and the third interior (*sannomaru*) held audience halls, council rooms, and government offices.

The palace complex covered an area of about 1728 acres and contained about 100,000 persons. As in the palaces of the other patrimonial-bureaucratic emperors, military men comprised the largest group. The shogun probably maintained about 35,000 soldiers in his household, and another 45,000 were retainers of the inside daimyo and lived here as well. The rest of the populace consisted of merchants, artisans, servants, and other members of the shogunate and daimyo households.

The great daimyo maintained at least three residences in Edo. The upper mansion was either inside the palace-fortress or near one of the gates and was where the noble stayed when the visited the shogun. The middle mansion was larger and farther away from the palace-fortress and had room for gardens. The lower mansion was located in the suburbs. It was smaller and didn't have many buildings or rooms.

The mansions of the nobles in Edo, like the mansions of the great amirs in Shahjahanabad, were modelled after the imperial palace-fortress. In Edo these palaces contained a honmaru where the daimyo's family lived, a ninomaru where the lord had his private quarters and conducted his business and where some of the food and weapons were stored, and a sannomaru which held the administrative offices and quarters for the senior household officials. The largest of these mansions covered between 90–150 acres and held 7000–8000 persons.

The Tokugawa Shogun, like the Mughal Emperor, established regulations regarding the location and size of the daimyo mansions. As a rule the great outside daimyo had large plots inside the palace walls or near the gates but those men with high positions in government were often given ground in the far interior near the inner moat. The mansions of the inside daimyo were spread among those of the great outside lords and they often changed residences as their appointments changed. The related daimyo had mansions near the palace-fortress but beyond the outer moat.

Along the streets in front of the mansions ran the "long house" barracks for the clients of the daimyo who could not find room within the walls. The foot-soldiers and other militarymen of the shogun's house who could not be accommodated within the palace-fortress lived in a set of streets just outside the moat.

The palace-fortress of the shogun, the mansions of the daimyo, and the residences of the shogun's officers and household troops occupied the higher and better parts of the city. The rest of the city contained the homes and business establishments of the merchants, artisans, and others. The Nihonbashi section between the palace-fortress and the bay was the place where many of the merchants and artisans lived. The administrative unit in Edo was called the cho; in the 1630s there were 300 cho and by 1800 there were 1700.

In Tokugawa Japan the four classes of society in descending order of status and importance were: warrior/administrator (*samurai*), farmer, artisan, and trader. In the castle towns, of which Edo was the chief, the ruling class was divided into daimyo, upper-class warriors with their own estates who were vassals to the daimyo, middle-class warriors who were ranking subordinates of the upper class, and lower-class warriors.

The primary fact of social structure in Edo was the large concentration of militarymen. These included both the soldiers under the direct command of the shogun as well as the clients of the daimyo. Out of a population of about one million in 1700, about 50 percent were soldiers and their families; about 200,000–300,000 under the command of the shogun (both household troops and others) and another 300,000–400,000 under the various daimyo. About 40 percent of the rest of the population were merchants and artisans, 5 percent were servants and laborers, and 5 percent were priests, artists, and others. The residences of the daimyo and the military were grouped in a great semi-circle around the palace-fortress and occupied two-thirds of the area of the city.

People came to Edo for three reasons: the requirement that all who received government stipends had to live in Edo, the system of alternative residence among the daimyo and the warriors, and the desire of merchants and artisans to be near the great wealth of the ruling class.

The Tokugawa shogunate, like the other patrimonial-bureaucratic empires, was agrarian-based. The bulk of state revenues came from taxes on rice cultivation. In 1700 the shogun controlled 16 percent of these lands, the liege vassals 10 percent, the inside daimyo 35 percent, and the outside daimyo 37 percent. Thus, the shogun and the close members of his government and household controlled over 60 per cent of the revenues of the state. As in the other patrimonial-bureaucratic empires, much of this revenue, along with that of a good number of the outside daimyo, was concentrated in the capital city.

The land tax was collected in kind from the domains of the shogun and the daimyo. These great men lived in Edo and the other cities, however, and required a group of client merchants ("honorable service merchants") who were responsible for turning rice into cash. They resided in

Osaka, the principal commercial center of Tokugawa Japan, and labored in the offices and storehouses of their great patrons. Receipts from rice sales were sent to Edo by draft and daimyo in financial difficulty often borrowed against future rice shipments. The Osaka merchants were also heavily involved in supplying consumer goods to Edo.

In Edo and the other castle towns, merchants were closely supervised. As in the other patrimonial-bureaucratic states, monopolies were established and the shoguns collected fees from favored merchants. Although merchants were tightly controlled, they were nevertheless attracted to the castle towns by the new opportunities. In this environment the household merchants of the daimyo and shogun were especially favored. They enjoyed freedom from the more onerous restrictions, were exempt from certain taxes, and followed their noble patrons from place to place. Both the household and unaffiliated merchants helped to link the household economy of the countryside to the cash markets of the city. As time passed many of these merchants prospered and, by the end of the seventeenth and the early part of the eighteenth centuries, many warriors were in their debt.

In Edo and the other castle towns artisans were tightly regulated also. The shogun and daimyo organized the craftsmen into cooperative guilds and fraternal associations and appointed leaders. The system was fixed and hereditary and artisans couldn't change crafts easily. Household officials monitored prices, wages, and the quality of goods. In the palace-fortress at Edo a select group of artisans supplied the shogun's household with goods and services. Their wages and the quality of their goods set the standard for the other urban artisans. Guilds were required to work for a certain period each year for the shogun and daimyo households. The Tokugawa economic system, like that of the Ming, represented a step backward. It depended almost entirely on agricultural taxes whereas in earlier periods the rulers and nobles had gotten a good deal of income from commerce and international trade.

The Tokugawa shogunate is a particularly pure example of the patrimonial-bureaucratic empire. The personal, familial element in early modern Japan appears relatively undiluted. The Tokugawa shogun organized his government (*bakufu*) of the state at large as an extension of his rule over his private household lands. It is, in many ways, a textbook example of the attempt by patrimonial rulers to expand their sway from their household lands to the larger empire.

Edo is also an excellent example of the sovereign city. As in the other patrimonial-bureaucratic capitals, the ruler and the great nobles dominated the economic, social, and political life of the city. Their mansions covered almost two-thirds of the city and they held a substantial percentage of state revenues. Their residences served as the centers of local life and dominated the patterns of production, consumption, and exchange in the city.

In Edo, more than in any other of the sovereign cities, the character of the capital as mansion of the patrimonial-bureaucratic ruler stands out. The palace-fortress of the shogun in Edo represents, to a greater degree than in any other of the sovereign cities, a microcosm of the city. Not only were the homes of the shogun's household clients in the great enclosure but the mansions, retainers, and paraphernalia of the great nobles were there also. In no other city did the great nobles actually maintain mansions within the precincts of the imperial palace and nowhere else is the imperial residence so complete a replica of the city at large. The city itself is the palace-fortress writ large: the secluded sector behind the inner moat fulfilling the same function for the palace-fortress as the palace-fortress does for the city at large.

Peking

The Ming Empire (1368–1644) in China was the most highly organized of the four Asian patrimonial-bureaucratic empires. The Chinese civil service was, without a doubt, the closest of the premodern administrations to a modern bureaucracy. Nevertheless, the Ming state exhibited enough patrimonial features to fall within the patrimonial-bureaucratic type and Peking (1421–1644), its capital, seems to follow the sovereign city model.[13]

There were three branches of administration in the Ming state. The civil service manned the administrative posts in the provinces, districts, and subdistricts of the empire. Its members were chosen by examination and were closely regulated and supervised. The army was controlled by the imperial household and was responsible for the peace and security of

---

[13] For a discussion of the Ming state see Charles O. Hucker, *The Traditional Chinese State in Ming Times (1368–1644)* (Tucson: University of Arizona Press, 1961); Farmer, *Early Ming Government*, pp. 58–63, 81, 137; Ray Huang, "Fiscal Administration During the Ming Dynasty," in Charles O. Hucker, ed., *Chinese Government in Ming Times* (New York: Columbia University Press, 1969), pp. 73–129; Ray Huang, *Taxation and Governmental Finance in Sixteenth-Century Ming China* (London: Cambridge University Press, 1974). For Peking see Keith Pratt, *Peking in the Early Seventeenth Century*, (Oxford: Oxford University Press, 1971); Joanne Wakeland, "Local Administration in Sixteenth-Century Peking," unpublished paper; Rozman, *Urban Networks*, passim; Nelson I. Wu, *Chinese and Indian Architecture* (New York: George Braziller, 1963); Lin Yutang, *Imperial Peking: Seven Centuries of China* (New York: Crown Publishers, 1961); Andrew Boyd, *Chinese Architecture and Town Planning: 1500–1901* (Chicago: University of Chicago Press, 1962); and L.C. Arlington and William Lewisohn, *In Search of Old Peking* (Peking: Henri Vetch, 1935).

the realm. The censorate was staffed by degree-holders, men who had come up through the examination system, and it was designed to purge the government of incompetence and dishonesty.

During the Ming Dynasty the government of China was composed of the following elements: the emperor, his clansmen, sons, wives, and servants; the eunuchs, workmen, artisans, administrators, artists, and writers of the imperial household; the nobility, military commanders who had been honored for success in battle and were paid in cash; the army, the largest single component, the result of a tax in kind on a group of military families who substituted sons for grain; and, finally, the scholar-officials who had gained their positions in the civil administration through competitive examination and who received cash stipends and the right to collect fees.

The Ming emperor, like the other patrimonial-bureaucratic rulers, was the ultimate source of power in the state. As the "Son of Heaven," the emperor was responsible for the welfare of the empire. If the emperor treated his people fairly, heaven would see that the state prospered; if he didn't, disaster would come – famine, war, pestilence. The abolition of the prime minister and the secretariat in the late fourteenth century was a momentous change in Chinese institutional history. Because the inner court with its hereditary ruler was no longer balanced by the outer court, where the prime minister acted as a spokesman for the scholar-officials, the authority of the emperor and his household increased enormously.

Imperial princes held important administrative positions. They maintained large households in great palaces and had personal bodyguards and courts of civil and military officials. Because of their power and importance, they were, like the Mughal princes, carefully controlled. The number of their retainers, the size of their palaces, and their incomes were regulated. Their visits to the capital were carefully planned so as to avoid overburdening the treasury.

During the Ming period the traditional Confucian bureaucracy of scholar–officials, that aspect of Chinese government which seems so modern, was overshadowed by the imperial household and the military nobility. As a result, the emperor's influence and authority increased and the patrimonial aspect of Chinese rule expanded at the expense of the bureaucratic.

The capital of the Ming Empire was transferred from Nanking to Peking during the period 1402–21. Construction of the city was completed during the latter part of the period and in 1420 Peking was formally inaugurated. The city had been the site of administrative centers before the Ming period, serving as a secondary capital under the Liao and Chin dynasties before becoming the great Yuan capital of Ta-tu. Great care was given to the orientation and layout of the city but except for the stone walls the materials of construction were dirt and wood.

Peking was surrounded by a wall and a moat and enclosed an area of about twenty-five square miles. It was composed of four separate walled areas: the Forbidden, Imperial, Inner, and Outer cities. There were sixteen gates in the outermost wall and the Forbidden and Imperial cities had four gates each. By 1600 the population probably totalled about 750,000.

In its plan and build, Peking, like the other sovereign cities, reflected the dominance of the imperial household. At its very heart, a fortress within a fortress within a fortress, lay the Forbidden City, a 385-acre enclosure that contained audience halls, private apartments, religious shrines, and about 15,000 persons – the imperial family, personal servants, privileged retainers, and eunuchs. At the center of the Forbidden City stood the Hall of Supreme Harmony. In the middle of this hall on a great throne the Ming emperor exercised absolute power. The buildings in the Forbidden City were of three kinds: temples for religious ceremonies, audience halls, and private apartments for the imperial household.

Completely surrounding the Forbidden City was the Imperial City, a square of about 1900 acres that held a total of perhaps 85,000 persons. Here were the officers and men of the imperial bodyguard and the offices of the six government ministries. Here also were kitchens, granaries, wardrobes, attendants, servants, and workshops. The imperial temple, the ancestral temple of the Chinese emperors, was found in the southeastern sector. Built in 1420 in the style of the ancestoral temple in Nanking, this sacred structure was the site for the rites and sacrifices which the Ming emperors performed five times a year. The Imperial City contained examination halls, elephant stables, and three lakes, around which the emperors built summer palaces. The highest-ranking members of the government lived in the Imperial City among the parks, lakes, pagodas, pavilions, and halls. The greatest gate in the city, the Noon Gate, guarded the entrance to the Forbidden City. Virtually a fortress itself, the Noon Gate was the place where the emperor received ambassadors and merchants.

The Inner City had a perimeter of 12.5 miles and contained a great number of persons. The main roads were wide and held the mansions of army officers along with the homes of architects, goldsmiths, silver-smiths, and other craftsmen who worked in the Imperial City.

The wall around the Chinese or Outer City, which measured five by two miles, was not completed until 1553. In the Outer City lived the poorer inhabitants; common soldiers, laborers, servants, and others. The

Temple of Heaven, however, one of the most sacred spots in all China, had been constructed here in 1420, and nearby stood another project of the early Ming emperors, the Temple of Agriculture.

In China, as in the other patrimonial-bureaucratic empires, the emperor organized and ordered the state from his palace in the capital city. The nature of his rule was reflected in the layout of the city. In Chinese the character for "city" and "wall" was the same. Not only was the entire urban area walled but so were the principal internal parts. At the innermost recesses of the capital city, protected by the concentric walls, was the imperial household, the center of both empire and city.

In Ming China, as in the other patrimonial-bureaucratic empires, the capital was distinguished from the other great cities by the presence of the emperor and the paraphernalia of government. In Peking this meant a massive concentration of imperial relatives, retainers, courtiers, officials, scribes, and soldiers. The emperor maintained a large corps of imperial bodyguards to protect himself and enough other troops to guarantee the security of the city. About 300,000 soldiers, controlled by the nobles and eunuchs of the imperial household, resided in Peking. As in the other cities, these men and their families made up the largest single component of the population. A large part of the rest of the urban populace depended on the imperial household also. Artisans, eunuchs, and officials served the emperor. Hereditary nobles had to live in the capital and attend court regularly while tribal chieftains and men of wealth were often required to stay at court as quasi-hostages. Princes were precluded from residing in the capital and only visited irregularly.

In Peking the imperial household dominated city government. Like Shahjahanabad and the other sovereign cities, Peking was administered by members of the imperial household rather than by the regular provincial and city staff. The urban population was divided into three parts, each of which was governed differently. The group of persons associated with the palace and living in the Forbidden City were controlled by the eunuchs. The eunuchs, nobility, and high officials in the Imperial City were under the supervision of the palace-guard and both of these groups were exempt from local taxes. The merchants, artisans, laborers, and soldiers in the rest of the city were governed by local officials who were themselves regulated by the palace. The county administration looked after certain aspects of urban life but the city was also divided into five wards, each of which was further subdivided into precincts, sub-precincts, and neighborhoods. Precincts had about 20,000 people and neighborhoods about 7,000. Precinct captains often drafted people to work in the palace.

In Peking, as in the other cities, the emperor and the members of the imperial court supplied the amenities of urban life. The palace maintained roads, bridges, watercourses, and fire patrols. The state supplied the urban markets with grain from the taxes it received. Private schools, academies, libraries, and poorhouses were run by the local degree-holders who worked in the Imperial City.

During the Ming period the imperial household's control over the economy increased. Under the Ming, to an extent uncommon in earlier dynasties, both foreign and domestic trade declined and, as a result, land taxes constituted an even greater proportion of government revenues. Under the Ming there was no central financial authority but the emperor, no prime minister or finance minister. The Ming system, like those of the other patrimonial-bureaucratic states, made no clear-cut distinction between state and household income, between governmental and private imperial expenditures.

In the Imperial City there were treasuries, depots, bakeries, confectionaries, dispensaries, distilleries, leatherworkers, silversmiths, and arsenals. The total number of such agencies or workshops, which supplied the imperial household, was about fifty. The artisans performing statute or obligatory labor and their assistants comprised a substantial proportion of the palace populace. Paid mostly in grain rather than in cash, these persons produced for the immediate needs of the imperial household and for the warehouses where the emperors stored the gifts intended for foreign dignitaries and nobles. In the Imperial City also were storehouses for the goods produced elsewhere and shipped to the city.

The Ming emperor derived the predominant proportion of his income from taxes on the produce of the land. The basic unit of reckoning was the picul (1 picul = 107 liters) of rice or wheat. In 1578, 9.5 million piculs (4 million in grain and 4.5 million in cash) were delivered to the Imperial City in Peking, much of it by way of the Grand Canal which was finished during the period 1411–15. This was about 36 percent of the total tax collected and illustrates the dominance of the imperial household in the empire at large. In addition to land taxes families had to provide service levies of raw materials, soldiers, or labor.

Although there was a movement for tax reform in the fifteenth century, and although some taxes were commuted into cash, the imperial household demanded a good part of its revenues in kind. Most administrative expenses were met by service levies and the regular land taxes (both in cash and in kind) were allocated for the army, the imperial princes and clansmen, and the scholar–officials. At one point in the late fifteenth century the imperial household distributed 3.7 million piculs of grain to about 300,000 men. The artisans in the Imperial City were fulfilling service obligations and were not paid by the emperor.

Revenue from the salt monopoly was the second largest item of state income. Salt was produced by the state and sold to merchants who in turn sold it to the public. For most of the Ming period foreign trade was outlawed and the Ming emperor, like the Mughal emperor, got very little income from imports or exports. Inland customs duties and sales taxes were significant sources of revenue however.

In Ming China trade and manufacturing were considered disreputable occupations and were closely regulated. Guilds established standards for merchants and artisans who were regularly inspected by imperial officials. The imperial household also monopolized the production and distribution of such commodities as salt, iron, and rice. In addition, most of the goods consumed by the imperial establishment were manufactured in the workshops of the Imperial City or in workshops elsewhere, like the weaving and dyeing establishments of Nanking.

Like the other sovereign cities, Peking was not a major manufacturing center. Most of the productive capacity of the city was in the imperial household, whose output never reached the open market. Peking, with its great concentration of nobles, officials, and soldiers, was primarily a market. The imperial household consumed enormous amounts of porcelain, jade, rice, tea, silk, cotton, sugar, paper, and books. To handle this trade, most of which came by way of the Grand Canal, the emperor had, in the late sixteenth century, thousands of boats crewed by some 120,000 men.

In the Ming Empire, as in the other patrimonial-bureaucratic empires, the imperial household held the center of state. The Chinese emperor, like the other emperors, appears to have harbored the ambition of governing his empire like a great extended household. Peking offers the example of a ruler trying to satisfy this ambition on a smaller scale, attempting to transform the capital city into a mansion. One scholar writes of an early Ming emperor that he "embodies in his person the political center of the empire"[14] while another notes that the Ming state "followed the familial principal so closely that palace and government were one and indivisable."[15] Furthermore, an early Chinese scholar–official described Changan, the capital of Sui-Tang China (A.D. 583–904), as the mansion of the emperor.[16]

In Shahjahanabad the Mughal emperor was the symbolic center of both city and empire, the man who encompassed within himself and his

[14] Farmer, *Early Ming Government*, p. 137.
[15] Huang, *Taxation and Governmental Finance*, p. 9.
[16] Arthur, F. Wright, "Symbolism and Function: Reflections on Changan and Other Great Cities," *Journal of Asian Studies* 24 (1965) p. 673.

household both capital and state. The emperor was the pivot of a hierarchical, nested series of realms; center of household, city, and Empire. Each individual realm encompassed and embodied those beyond it: the emperor – household, city, and Empire; the household – city and Empire; and the city, the Empire. Descending from his balcony and processing through the crowd of nobles in the Hall of Ordinary Audience down Chandni Chawk to the Lahori Gate the emperor took symbolic control of both city and Empire.

In the Sufi understanding of the world inner or hidden (*batin*) and outer or manifest (*zahir*) were important contrasts. Not only the relationship between man and the universe (the microcosm and the macrocosm) but also the relationships among the parts of the Mughal state could be understood in this way. In man the contrast was between the soul and the body and in the universe between man and the heavens. In the palace-fortress the imperial living quarters were the batin and the rectangle facing the city the zahir; in the city the palace-fortress was the inner and the rest of the area within the walls the outer; and, for the empire at large, the city was the hidden and the rest of the state the manifest. In each pair it was the inner, hidden, batin aspect that was the essence or the soul. Thus, in the structured hierarchy of elements – emperor, household, city, and empire – it was the first which directed, ordered, and controlled, which was higher, more valuable, and sacred.

The movements of body, soul, and spirit within both the microcosm (man) and the macrocosm (universe) were parallelled in the city. In the city, viewed as a microcosm, the centripetal movement was from the walls (the body) through the city proper (the soul) to the Hall of Ordinary Audience (the inner spirit). The prime example of this movement was the gathering of the great men in the palace-fortress on court days and holidays. From the macrocosmic point of view, the centrifugal movement was from the Hall of Ordinary Audience (the earth or body) through the city (the soul) to the walls (the heavens, the home of the spirit). The procession of the imperial court through the city at the beginning of a tour was the paradigm here.

The imperial household was the microcosm whose structure and plan were paradigmatic for the city and the empire as well as for the other great households. In Islam every man was the patriarch or caliph of his own family. Like man, the family was a unity, a society within a society. The structure of society in the imperial household set the standard for both city and empire. As the imperial household ordered the palace-fortress so the palace-fortress ordered the city as a whole. In addition, the mansions of princes, great amirs, and other high-ranking mansabdars (themselves replicas of the palace-fortress) structured the areas around them. The household also ordered the Empire, the relationship between the emperor and the nobles in the Hall of Ordinary Audience standing for that between the imperial administration and the officials in revenue circles, districts, and provinces. Thus, the sovereign city seems best understood as the mansion of the patrimonial-bureaucratic ruler, standing midway between the imperial household and the Empire at large. The city was a microcosm of the Empire, and the household of the emperor in the palace-fortress was a microcosm of the city.

SELECT GLOSSARY

I have used a simplified form of transliteration for the Persian and Urdu words in the text. Here I give the full markings as found in F. Steingass, *A Comprehensive Persian–English Dictionary*.

ahadi (aḥadī) single trooper
'ashura khanah ('ashūra-khāna) place where the death of the Imam Husain is commemorated
barahdari (bārahdarī) summer house
bazaar (bāzār) market
begum (begam) woman of rank
caravansarai (kārwānsarāy) inn for travellers
chawk (chok) square
darbar (darbār) audience
darogah (dārogha) supervisor
darshan (darshan) showing, going into the presence of
diwan (dīwān) financial officer
faujdar (faujdār) army captain
harem (ḥaram) women's quarters
huqqa (ḥuqqa) waterpipe
jami' masjid (jam'i masjid) friday or congregational mosque
khanazad (khāna-zād) house-born
karkhanah (kārkhāna) workshop
khil'at (khil'at) ceremonial robe
khiyal (khiyāl) a kind of song
kotwal (kutwal) city magistrate
madrassah (madrasa) Islamic institution of higher learning
mahallah (maḥalla) quarter
marsiya (marṣiya) Shi'i elegy on the death of the Imam Husain
mansabdar (mansabdār) officeholder
mir bakshi (mīr bakhshī) paymaster general
mir saman (mīr sāmān) head steward of imperial or great amiri household
mirzai (mīrzāī) gentility or gentlemanliness
muhandis (muhandis) architect-planner
musha'ira (mash'ara) literary evening devoted to poetry
pishkash (peshkash) ceremonial offering
qawwal (qauwāl) a kind of song
qila'dar (qal'a-dār) fort commander
sipah salar (sipāh sālār) army commander
subahdar (ṣūbadār) commander of a province
ta'ziya (ta'ziyat) representation of the shrine of the Imam Husain
'urs ('urs) death anniversary commemoration of Sufi saint

SELECT BIBLIOGRAPHY

I. Persian works

A. Chronicles

Ala al-din Ata Malik-i Juwayni. *Tarikh-i Jahan Gusha.* Edited by Mirza Muhammad. 3 vols. London: Luzac and Co., 1912–37.

'Ali Muhammad Khan. *Mir'at-i Ahmadi.* Edited by Syed Nawab 'Ali. 2 vols. Baroda, India: Oriental Institute, 1927–8.

Mir'at-i Ahmadi Supplement. Edited by Syed Nawab 'Ali. Baroda, India: Oriental Institute, 1930.

Abu al-Fazl. *Akbar Namah.* Edited by Agha Ahmad 'Ali and Maulavi Maulavi 'Abd al-Rahim. 3 vols. Calcutta, India: Asiatic Society of Bengal, 1873–86.

Ansari, Muhammad 'Ali Khan. "Tarikh-i Muzzafari." Persian Manuscript Collection, Or. 466. British Museum, London.

Ashob, Muhammad Badsh. "Tarikh-i Shahadat-i Farrukhsiyar-u-Julus-i Muhammad Shah." Persian Manuscript Collection, Or. 1015.British Museum, London.

al-Badauni, 'Abd al-Qadir. *Muntakhab al-Tawarikh.* Edited by Maulavi Ahmad 'Ali and W.N. Lees. 3 vols. Calcutta: Asiatic Society of Bengal, 1865–9.

Bakhtawar Khan. "Mirat al-'Alam." Persian Manuscript Collection, Add. 7657. British Museum, London.

Brahman, Chandar Bhan. "Chahar Chaman Brahman." Persian Manuscript Collection, Or. 1892. British Museum, London.

Burhanpuri, Bhimsen. "Nuskha-i Dilkusha." Persian Manuscript Collection, Or. 23. British Museum, London.

Chaturman Rai. "Chahar Gulshan." Persian Manuscript Collection, Or. 1791. British Museum, London.

Harawi, Nizam al-Din. *Tabaqat-i Akbari.* Edited by B. De and Muhammad Hidayat Husain. 3 vols. Calcutta: Asiatic Society of Bengal, 1913–40.

Khafi Khan, Muhammad Hashim. *Muntakhab al-Lubab.* 3 vols. Edited by Maulavi Kabir al-Din Ahmed and Sir Wolsely Haig. Calcutta: Asiatic Society of Bengal, 1869–1925.

Lahauri, 'Abd al-Hamid. *Badshah Namah.* Edited by Maulavi Kabir al-Din Ahmad and Maulavi 'Abd al-Rahim. 2 vols. Calcutta: Asiatic Society of Bengal, 1866–72.

Lahauri, Muhammad Salih Kanbo. *'Amal-i Salih.* Edited by G. Yazdani. 3 vols. Calcutta: Asiatic Society of Bengal, 1912–46.

Muhammad Faiz Baksh. "Tarikh-i Farah Baksh." Persian Manuscript Collection, Or. 1015. British Museum, London.

Muhammad Kazim b. Muhammad Amin. *'Alamgir Namah.* Edited by Maulavi Khadim Hasain and Maulavi 'Abd al-Hai. 2 vols. Calcutta: Asiatic Society of Bengal, 1865–73.

Muhammad Sadik. "Shahjahan Namah." Persian Manuscript Collection, Or. 174. British Museum, London.

Muhammad Saqi Musta'idd Khan. *Ma'asir-i 'Alamgiri.* Calcutta: Asiatic Society of Bengal, 1873–5.

Muhammad Wali Allah b. Ahmad 'Ali Farrukhabadi. "Tarikh-i Farrukhabad." Persian Manuscript Collection, Or. 1718. British Museum, London.

Muhammad Waris. "Padshah Namah." Persian Manuscript Collection, Add. 6556. British Museum, London.

Mukhlis, Anand Ram. "Ahwal-i Nuskah-i Sawanih." Persian Manuscript Collection, Ethe 410. India Office Library, London.

Nur al-Din Jahangir. *Tuzuk-i Jahangiri.* Edited by Syud Ahmud. Allygurh, India: n.p., 1864.

Qandahari, Muhammad Arif. *Tarikh-i Akbari.* Edited by Haji Mu'umid-Din Nadwi, Dr. Azhar Ali Dihlawi, and Imtiyaz 'Ali Arshi. Rampur: Hindustan Printing Works, 1962.

Sayyid Nur al-Din Husain Khan Bahadur Fakhri. "Tarikh-i Najib al-Daulah." Persian Manuscript Collection, Add. 24,410. British Museum, London.

Shakir Khan. "Tarikh-i Shakir Khani." Persian Manuscript Collection, Add. 6585. British Museum, London.

Sujan Rai. "Khulasat al-Tawarikh." Persian Manuscript Collection, Or. 1625. British Museum, London.

"Tarikh-i Ahmad Shahi." Persian Manuscript Collection, Or. 2005. British Museum, London.

"Tarikh-i 'Alamgir Sani." Persian Manuscript Collection, Or. 1749. British Museum, London.

B. Insha (letter) collections

Abu al-Fath Qabil Khan, *Adab-i 'Alamgiri.* 2 vols. Lahore: Punjab University, 1971.

"Dastur al-'Amal-i Agahi." Persian Manuscript Collection, Add. 18,422. British Museum, London.

Hamid al-Din Khan. *Ahkam-i 'Alamgiri.* Persian text with an English translation by Jadunath Sarkar. Calcutta: M.C. Sarkar and Sons, 1912.

Inayat Allah. *Ruka'at-i 'Alamgiri.* Translated Jamshid H. Bilimoria. Delhi: Idarah-i Adabiyat-i Delhi, 1972.

Muhammad Salih. "Bahar-i Sukhan." Persian Manuscript Collection, Or. 178. British Museum, London.

Munshi Udairaj Tali'yar Khan. "Haft Anjuman." Translated by Jagdish Narayan Sarkar. *The Military Despatches of a Seventeenth Century Indian General.* Calcutta: Scientific Book Agency, 1969.

C. Akhbarat (newsletters) and orders

A Descriptive List of Farmans, Manshurs, and Nishans Addressed by The Imperial Mughals to the Princes of Rajasthan. Bikaner: Directorate of Archives, 1962.

Selected Waqai of the Deccan. Edited by Dr. Husuf Husain. Hyderabad: Central Records Office, 1953.

A Descriptive List of Farmans, Manshurs, and Nishans Addressed by the Imperial Mughals to the Princes of Rajasthan. Bikaner, Rajasthan: Directorate of Archives, 1962.

A Descriptive List of the Vakil Reports Addressed to the Rulers of Jaipur. 1 (Persian). Bikaner: Rajasthan State Archives, 1967.

"Akhbarat-i Darbar-i Mu'allah," Persian Manuscript Collection, no. 133. Royal Asiatic Society, London.

Delhi Affairs (1761–88), Persian Records of Maratha History. Translated by Jadunath Sarkar. Bombay: Director of Archives, 1953.

"Delhi Newsletters of 1779–82." Persian Manuscript Collection, Add. 25021. British Museum, London.

"Delhi Newsletters of 1781 A.D." Persian Manuscript Collection, Add. 25020. British Museum, London.

D. Biographies and memoirs

Abd al-Baqi b. Baba-i Kurd Nihawandi. *Ma'asir-i Rahimi.* Edited by Maulavi Muhammad Hidayat Husain. 3 vols. Calcutta: Asiatic Society of Bengal, 1910–31.

"Ahwal-i Khan Dauran." Persian Manuscript Collection, Or. 180. British Museum, London.

Bruit, Gaston. "Ahwal-i Bibi Juliyana." Persian Manuscript Collection, Add. 14,374. British Museum, London.

Gulshan 'Ali Jaunpuri. "Surat-i Hal." Persian Manuscript Collection, Add. 16,805. British Museum, London.

Hazin, Sheikh Muhammad 'Ali. *Tarikh-i Ahwal be Tazkirah-i Hal.* Edited by F.C. Belfour. London: Oriental Translation Fund, 1831.

Jahanara Begum. "Munis al-Arwah." Persian Manuscript Collection, Or. 250. British Museum, London.

Jauhar. "Tazkirah al-Waqiat." Persian Manuscript Collection, Add. 16711. British Museum, London.

Kalim, Abu Talib Khan. "Diwan-i Kalim." Persian Manuscript Collection, Add. 24,002. British Museum, London.

Khwaja Abd al-Karim. "Bayan-i Waqa'i." Persian Manuscript Collection, Add. 8909. British Museum, London.

Mirza Mughal Beg b. Muhammad Beg. "Sair al-Bilad." Persian Manuscript Collection, Ethe 3731. India Office Library, London.

Muhammad Habib Ullah. "Zikr-i Jami-i Auliya-i Dihli." Persian Manuscript Collection, Or. 1746. British Museum, London.

Muhammad Hadi Kamwar Khan. "Tazkirah al-Salatin-i Chaghatai." Persian Manuscript Collection, Ethe 395. India Office Library, London.

Mukhlis, Anand Ram. "Waqai'-i Sayr-i Ganga." Persian Manuscript Collection, Ethe 3724. India Office Library, London.

"Bada'i-i Waqai" or "Tazkirah-i Anand Ram." Persian Manuscript Collection, no. 409. Maulana Azad Library. Aligarh Muslim University. Aligarh, U.P.

Chamanistan. Lucknow, n.p., 1877.

Nawab Dargah Quli Khan Salar Jang. "Risalah-i Salar Jang." Persian Manuscript Collection, Add. 26,237. British Museum, London.

Nawab Samsam al-Daulah Shah Nawaz Khan. *Ma'asir al-Umara.*Edited by Maulavi Mirza Ashraf 'Ali and Maulavi 'Abd al-Rahim. 3 vols. Calcutta: Asiatic Society of Bengal, 1887–91.

Sharma, Ramesh Chandra. "The Ardha-Kathanak, A Neglected Source of Mughal History." *Indica* 7 (1970) pp. 49–73, 105–20.

Tahmas Khan. "Tazkirah-i Tahmas Khan." Persian Manuscript Collection, Or. 1918. British Museum, London.

E. Administrative manuals and other historical works

Abu al-Fazl. *A'in-i Akbari.* Edited by H. Blochmann. 2 vols. Calcutta: Asiatic Society of Bengal, 1872–7.

"Bayaz-i Khushbui." Persian Manuscript Collection, Ethe 2784. India Office Library, London.

"Dastur al-'Amal." Persian Manuscript Collection, Or. 1690. British Museum, London.

"Dastur al-'Amal." Persian Manuscript Collection, Add. 6599. British Museum, London.

"Dastur al-'Amal-i 'Alamgiri." Persian Manuscript Collection, Add. 6598. British Museum, London.

Jagat Rai. "Farhang-i Kardani." Abdus Salam Collection, no. 315. Maulana Azad Library. Aligarh Muslim University, Aligarh, U. P.

"Khillaq al-Siyaq." Persian Manuscript Collection, no. 314. National Archives of India, New Delhi.

Mir Abd al-Kasim. "Ma'rifat al-Sanai." Persian Manuscript Collection, Add. 16,839. British Museum, London.

Mirza Kamran, "The Mirza-Namah (The Book of the Perfect Gentleman) of Mirza Kamran with an English Translation." Edited and translated by Maulawi M. Hidayat Husain. *Journal of the Asiatic Society of Bengal,* n.s. 9 (1913).

Mukhlis, Anand Ram. "Mir'at al'Istilah." Persian Manuscript Collection, Or. 1813. British Museum, London.
"Dastur al-'Amal." Persian Manuscript Collection, Ethe 2125. India Office Library, London.
"Zawabit-i 'Alamgiri." Persian Manuscript Collection, Or. 1641. British Museum, London.

F. Geographical works

'Abd al-Rahim Shah Nawaz Khan. "Mirat-i Aftab Namah." Persian Manuscript Collection, Add. 16, 697. British Museum, London.
Amin al-Din Khan Harawi. *Ma'lumat al-Afaq*. Lucknow: n.p., 1870.
Chand, Lala Sil. "Tafrih al-Imarat." Persian Manuscript Collection, Or. 6371. British Museum, London.
Chand, Manik. "Ahwal-i Shahar-i Akbarabad." Persian Manuscript Collection, Or. 2030. British Museum, London.
Isfahani, Hakim Maharat Khan. "Bahjat al-'Alam." Persian Manuscript Collection, Ethe 729. Indian Office Library, London.
Khan, Ghulam Muhammad. "Travels in Upper Hindustan." Persian Manuscript Collection, Ethe 2725. India Office Library, London.
Sadid al-Din. "Ahwal-i Agra." Persian Manuscript Collection, Or. 1763. British Museum, London.
Sangin Beg. "Sair al-Manazil." Persian Manuscript Collection, Or. 1762. British Museum, London.
Shafiq, Lachmi Narayan Aurangabad. "Haqiqatha-i Hindustan." Persian Manuscript Collection, Or. 205. British Museum, London.
Sada Sukh Dihlavi Niyazi. "Ajaib al-Hind." Persian Manuscript Collection, Or. 1841. British Museum, London.

II. Shahr Ashob (Ruined City) poems

Mir, Muhammad Taqi. *Kulliyat-i Mir*. Introduction by S. Ihtesham Husain. 2 vols. Allahabad: Ram Narain Lal Bini Madhu, 1972.
Zikr-i Mir. Edited by Abdul Haq. Aurangabad: Anjuman-i Tarqqi Urdu, 1928.
Sauda, Mirza Muhammad Rafi. "Masnavi Dar Haji Shidi Fulad Khan, Kotwal of Shahjahanabad." *Kulliyat-i Sauda*. Introduction by Imrat Lal Ashrat. 2 vols. Allahabad: Ram Narain Lal Bini Madhu, 1971. 1 pp. 279–82.
"Mukhammas Shahr Ashob." *Kulliyat-i Sauda* 2 pp. 261–6.
"Qusida Shahr Ashob." *Kulliyat-i Sauda* 1 pp. 226–30.

III. Government and archeological reports and inscriptions

Ahmad, Bashir al-Din. *Waqiat-i Dar al-Hukumat-i Dilhi*. 3 vols. Delhi: Muhammad Bashir al-Din Khan and Muhammad Shams al-Din Khan, 1919.

Archeological Survey of India. *List of Muhammadan and Hindu Monuments in Delhi Zail.* 4 vols. Calcutta: Superintendent of Government Printing, 1915–22.

Beale, T.W. *Miftah al-Tawarikh.* Agra: Messenger Press, 1849.

Bendrey, V.S. *A Study of Muslim Inscriptions.* Bombay: Karnatak Publishing House, 1944.

Blunt, E.A.H. *A List of the Inscriptions on Christian Tombs and Tablets of Historical Interest in the United Provinces of Agra and Oudh.* Allahabad: Government Press, U.P., 1911.

Christian, G.J. *Report on the Census of the Northwest Provinces of the Bengal Presidency – 1853.* Calcutta: Government of the Northwest Provinces, 1854.

Cunningham, Alexander. *Archeological Survey of India: Four Reports Made During the Years 1862, 63-64-65.* New Delhi: Indological Bookhouse, 1972.

Delhi Museum: Descriptive Catalogue. Delhi: n.p., 1882.

Fortescue, T. "Report on the Revenue System of the Delhi Territory, 1820." *Records of the Delhi Residency and Agency, 1807–57.* Lahore: Punjab Government Press, 1911.

Foster, William. *The English Factories in India: 1618–69.* 13 vols. Oxford: Clarendon Press, 1906–27.

Grant, James. "Firhist-i Subahjat-i Hindustan." Persian Manuscript Collection, Ethe 433. Indian Office Library, London.

Horowitz, J. "A List of the Published Mohammedan Inscriptions of India." *Epigraphia Indo-Moslemica (1909–10).*

Khan, Sayyid Ahmad. *Asar al-Sanadid.* Reprint edn Delhi: Central Book Depot, 1965.

Metcalfe, C.T. "Delhi, 1815." *Home Miscellaneous Series,* 776. India Office Library, London.

Press List of Mutiny Papers, 1857. Calcutta: Imperial Record Department, 1921.

"Revenue Tables of Subahs and Parganahs in Reigns of Shahjahan and Aurangzeb." Persian Manuscript Collection, Or. 1779. British Museum, London.

Roberts, A.A. "Population of Delhi and Its Suburbs." *Selections from Public Correspondence – Northwest Provinces.* Agra: Government of the Northwest Provinces, 1849–51.

Sharma, Y.D. *Delhi and Its Neighborhood.* 2nd edn New Delhi: Director General – Archeological Survey of India, 1974.

Transcripts and Translations of Dutch Records at the Hague: Letters from India, 1600–1699. India Office Library, London.

IV. European travellers' accounts

Bernier, Francois. *Travels in the Mogul Empire, 1656–68.* Edited by Archibald Constable. Translated by Irving Brock. Reprint edn Delhi: S. Chand and Co., 1972.

Bhargave, Krishna Dayal, ed. *Indian Record Series: Browne Correspondence.* New Delhi: National Archives of India, 1960.

Clavijo: Embassy to Tamerlane – 1403-06. Translated by Guy Le Strange. London: George Routledge and Sons, 1928.

Das, Harihar. *The Norris Embassy to Aurangzeb.* Condensed and rearranged by S.D. Sarkar. Calcutta: Firma K.L. Mukhopadhyay, 1959.

"Description of Delhi and Its Environs." *The Asiatic Journal and Monthly Register* 15 (January–June 1823) pp. 551–60.

Fitch, Ralph: *England's Pioneer to India.* Edited by J.R. Ryley. London: Humphrey Milford, 1899.

Forbes, James. *Oriental Memoirs.* 4 vols. London: White, Cochrane, and Co., 1813.

Franklin, William. "An Account of the Present State of Delhi." *Asiatick Researches* 4 (1795) pp. 419–32.

Fryer, John. *A New Account of East India and Persia.* Edited by William Crooke. 3 vols. London: Hakluyt Society, 1909–15.

Gentile, M. *Memoires sur l'Indoustan or Empire Mogol.* Paris: Chex Petit Librarie de S.A.R. Monsieur et de S.A.S. le Duc de Bourbon, 1822.

Hamilton, Walter. *A Geographical, Statistical and Historical Description of Hindostand and the Adjacent Countries.* 2 vols. London: John Murray, 1820.

Hanway, Jonas. *An Historical Account of the British Trade Over the Caspian Sea.* 4 vols. London: Jonas Hanway, 1753.

Heber, Reginald. *Narrative of a Journey Through the Upper Provinces of India from Calcutta to Bombay, 1824–25.* 2 vols. London: John Murray, 1828.

Jourdain, John. *The Journal of John Jourdain: 1608–17.* Edited by William Foster. Cambridge: Cambridge University Press, 1905.

Kemp, P.M., trans. and ed. *Russian Travellers to India and Persia: 1624–1798.* Delhi: Jiwan Prakashan, 1959.

Law, Jean de Lauriston. *Memoires sur quelques Affaires de l'Empire Mogol, 1756–61.* Paris: Alfred Martineau, 1913.

Maclagan, Edward. *The Jesuits and the Great Mughals.* London: Burns Oates and Washbourne Ltd, 1932.

Manrique, Sebastien. *The Travels of Fray Sebastien Manrique.* Translated by C.E. Luard, 2 vols. London: Hakluyt Society, 1927.

Manucci, Niccolao. *Storia do Mogor.* Translated by William Irvine. 4 vols. Reprint ed. Calcutta: Editions Indian, 1965.

Modave, L.L. Polisy de. "The Delhi Empire a Century after Bernier." Translated by Jadunath Sarkar. *Islamic Culture* 11 (1937) pp. 382–92.

Monserrate, Father. *The Commentary of Father Monserrate, S.J.* Translated by J.S. Hoyland. Annotated by S.N. Bannerjee. London: Humphrey, Milford, 1922.

Mundy, Peter. *The Travels of Peter Mundy in Europe and Asia.* Edited by Richard Temple. 5 vols. London: Hakluyt Society, 1907–36.

Nugent, Lady Maria. *A Journal From the Year 1811 to the Year 1815.* 2 vols. London: n.p., 1839.

Orlich, Leopold von. *Travels in India.* Translated by H. Evans Lloyd. 2 vols. London: Longman, Brown, Green, and Longmans, 1845.

Orme, Robert. *Orme Manuscripts.* India Office Library, London.

Pelsaert, Francisco. *Jahangir's India: The Remonstrantie of Francisco Pelsaert.*
    Translated by W.H. Moreland and P. Geyl. Cambridge: W.H. Heffer and
    Sons, 1925.
Purchas, Samuel. *Hakluytus Posthumus or Purchas His Pilgrims.* 21 vols. Glascow:
    Janus Maclehose and Sons, 1905.
Querbeuf, Y.M.M., ed. *Lettres Edifantes and Curieuses Ecrites des Missions
    Etrangers.* 26 vols. Paris: n.p., 1780–3.
Rubruck, William. *The Journey of William of Rubruck to the Eastern Parts of the
    World: 1253–55.* Translated by William Woodville Rockhill. London:
    Hakluyt Society, 1900.
Sen, Surendranath, ed. *Indian Travels of Thevenot and Careri.* New Delhi:
    National Archives of India, 1949.
Tavernier, Jean-Baptiste. *Travels in India.* Edited by William Crooke. Translated
    by V. Ball. 2 vols. London: Humphrey Milford, 1925.
Temple, R.C. "The Travels of Richard Bell and John Campbell in the East Indies,
    Persia, and Palestine: 1654–70." *The Indian Antiquary* 35 (1906) pp. 130–5.
Thorne, Major William. *Memoir of the War in India.* London: T. Egerton, 1818.
Tieffenthaler, Joseph. *Geographique de l'Indoustan.* in *Description Historique and
    Géographique de l'Inde.* Edited by Bernoulli, Jean. Berlin: Chreien Sigismond
    Spener, 1786.
Twining, Thomas. *Travels in India a Hundred Years Ago.* Edited by William H.G.
    Twining. London: James R. Osgood, McIlvaine and Co., 1893.
Wilson, C.R. *The Surman Embassy.* vol. 2, part 2 of the *The English in Bengal.*
    Calcutta: Bengal Secretariat Book Depot, 1911.

V. Secondary works

Acharya, Prasama Kumar, trans. *Architecture of Mansara.* London: Oxford
    University Press, 1933.
Andrews, C.F. *Zaka Ullah of Delhi.* Cambridge: W.H. Heffer and Sons, 1929.
Athar Ali, M. *The Apparatus of Empire: Awards, Ranks, Offices, and Titles of the
    Mughal Nobility (1574–1658).* Delhi: Oxford University Press, 1985.
Ardalan, Nader and Bakhtiar, Laleh. *The Sense of Unity: The Sufi Tradition in
    Persian Architecture.* Chicago and London: University of Chicago Press,
    1973.
Bayly, C.A. *Rulers, Townsmen, and Bazars: North Indian Society in the Age of
    British Expansion, 1780–1870.* Cambridge: Cambridge University Press,
    1983.
Das Gupta, Ashin. *Indian Merchants and the Decline of Surat: 1700–1750.*
    Weisbaden: Franz Steiner Verlage, 1979.
Farmer, Edward. *Early Ming Government: The Evolution of Dual Capitals.*
    Cambridge: East Asia Research Center, 1976.
Fleischer, Cornell H. *Bureaucrat and Intellectual in the Ottoman Empire: The
    Historian Mustafa Ali (1541–1600).* Princeton: Princeton University Press,
    1986.

Frykenberg, R.E., ed. *Delhi Through the Ages: Essays in Urban History.* Delhi: Oxford University Press, 1986.

Gupta, Naraini. *Delhi Between Two Empires: 1803–1931.* Delhi: Oxford University Press, 1981.

Grunebaum, G.E. von. *Islam: Essays in the Nature and Growth of a Cultural Tradition.* Comparative Studies of Cultures and Civilizations. No. 4. Menasha, Wis.: American Anthropological Association, 1955.

Habib, Irfan. *The Agrarian System of Mughal India: 1556–1707.* London: Asia Publishing House, 1963.

Hardy, Peter. *The Muslims of British India.* Cambridge: Cambridge University Press, 1972.

Hodgson, Marshall G.S. *The Venture of Islam.* 3 vols. Chicago and London: University of Chicago Press, 1974.

Huang, Ray. *Taxation and Governmental Finance in Sixteenth Century Ming China.* London: Cambridge University Press, 1974.

Hucker, Charles O. *The Traditional Chinese State in Ming Times (1368–1644).* Tucson: University of Arizona Press, 1961.

Inalcik, Halil. *The Ottoman Empire: The Classical Age 1300–1600.* Translated by Norman Itzkowitz and Colin Imber. London: Weidenfeld and Nicolson, 1973.

Irvine, William. *The Army of the Indian Moguls: Its Organization and Administration.* Reprint edn, New Delhi: Eurasia Publishing House, 1962.

Jackson, Peter and Lockhart, Laurence, ed. *The Cambridge History of Iran, vol. 6: The Timurid and Safavid Periods.* Cambridge: Cambridge University Press, 1986.

Knizkova, H. and Marek, J. *The Jenghis Khan Miniatures from the Court of Akbar The Great.* Translated by Olga Kuthanova. London: Spring Books, 1963.

Lewis, Bernard. *Istanbul and The Civilization of The Ottoman Empire.* Norman: University of Oklahoma Press, 1963.

Malik, Zahiruddin *A Mughal Statesman of the Eighteenth Century: Khan-i Dauran, Mir Bakshi of Muhammad Shah.* Delhi: Asia Publishing House, 1973.

Metcalfe, Barbara D., ed. *Moral Conduct and Authority: The Place of Adab in South Asian Islam.* Berkeley and London: University of California Press, 1984.

Mujeeb, M. *The Indian Muslims.* London: George Allen and Unwin, Ltd., 1967.

Naqvi, Hammed Katoon. *Urban Centres and Industries in Upper India: 1556–1803.* London: Asia Publishing House, 1968.

   Urbanisation and Urban Centres Under the Great Mughals: 1556–1707. Simla: Indian Institute of Advanced Studies, 1972.

Nasr, Sayyed Hossein. *An Introduction to Islamic Cosmological Doctrines.* Cambridge: Belknap Press, 1964.

Pearson, Michael. *Merchants and Rulers in Gujarat.* Berkeley and Los Angeles: University of California Press, 1976.

Qaisar, A.J. "Distribution of the Revenue Resources of the Mughal Empire

Among the Nobility." *Proceedings of the Twenty-Seventh Session of the Indian History Congress.* Aligarh: n.p., 1967.

Richards, John F. *Mughal Administration in Golconda.* Oxford: Oxford University Press, 1975.

Rozman, Gilbert. *Urban Networks in Ch'ing China and Tokugawa Japan.* Princeton University Press, 1973.

Urban Networks in Russia, 1750–1800, and Premodern Periodization. Princeton University Press, 1976.

Savory, Roger M. *Iran Under the Safavids.* Cambridge: Cambridge University Press, 1980.

Totman, Conrad D. *Politics in the Tokugawa Bakufu: 1600–1843.* Cambridge: Harvard University Press, 1967.

Weber, Max. *The City.* Edited and translated by Don Martindale and Gertrud Neuwirth. Glencoe: Free Press, 1958.

Economy and Society. Edited by Guenther Roth and Claus Wittich. 3 vols. New York: Bedminster Press, 1968.

Wheatley, Paul and See, Thomas. *From Court to Capital: A Tentative Interpretation of the Origins of the Japanese Urban Tradition.* (Chicago and London: University of Chicago Press, 1978.

Wheatley, Paul. *City as Symbol.* London: H.K. Lewis and Company, 1969.

The Pivot of the Four Corners. Chicago, University of Chicago Press, 1971.

INDEX

Agra (*Akbarabad*), as sovereign city, 184
ahadi (single trooper), 21
Ahmad Khan Abdali, 163–5
A'in-i Akbari, analysis of, 20–4
Akbar, Emperor, 14–5;
  as man of the pen, 135
Ali Mardan Khan, 31
  builder of Paradise Canal, 64–5
  mansion of, 76
army, Mughal, in *A'in-i Akbari*, 21–3
artisans, in karkhanahs of emperors and
  great men, 105–12;
  independent in Shahjahanabad, 112–5
Aryans, 3
'ashura khanah (place where death of
  Imam Husain is commemorated),
  139
Aurangzeb, Emperor, 16;
  as man of the pen, 136

Babur, Emperor, 13;
  as man of the pen, 135
barahdari (summer house), 62, 64
bazaar, see market
begum (women of rank), builders of
  mosques in Shahjahanabad, 54, 81–2
Brahman, Chandar Bhan, 24, 133
British, capture of Shahjahanabad, 169
  administration of Shahjahanabad, 170–3
  rationalize the economy of
    Shahjahanabad, 176–7
  effect on society in Shahjahanabad,
    179–81

caravansarai (inn for travellers), in
  Shahjahanabad, 65–6
Chandni Chawk (Moonlight or Silver
  Square), 56

goods in, 118–20
chawk (square), 54
  of Kotwali Chabutra, 56
  of Sa'adullah Khan, 57, 118

darbar (audience), 26
Dargah Quli Khan, Salar Jang, author of
  Risalah Salar Jang, 150–1
darogah (supervisor), in great amiri
  household, 107, 117
darshan (showing), of Mughal Emperor,
  38, 91
Daulat Khanah-i Khas, see Hall of Special
  Audience
Daulat Khanah-i Khas-o-'Am, see Hall of
  Ordinary Audience
Delhi, cities in area, 5–13
  origin of name, 6
  list of cities, 7
  as religious center, 28–9
  Renaissance in, 180–1
Din Panah, 12
diwan (financial officer), in great amiri
  household, 107

economy, of Shahjahanabad, 1739–1857,
  175–7
  of Agra, 186–7
  of Istanbul, 188–92
  of Isfahan, 197–8
  of Edo, 202–4
  of Peking, 208–9
Edo (Tokyo), as sovereign city, 199–204

Faiz Bazaar (Market of Plenty), 56–7
  goods in, 118–20
faujdar (army captain), 23
Firuzabad, 11

223

Friday (Congregational) Mosque, *see* Jami' Masjid

Ghazi al-Din Khan, tomb of, 61
great amir, 125–30
  as man of the pen, 133–5, 138–40
  as man of the sword, 143–6
  as man of the sword and pen, 148–9
Guptas, 4

Hall of Ordinary Audience (*Daulat Khanah-i Khas-o-'Am*), in palace-fortress, 91–2
  in imperial camp, 100
  in Agra, 185
Hall of Special Audience (*Daulat Khanah-i Khas*), in palace-fortress, 92–3
  in imperial camp, 100–1
  in Agra, 185
Harappa, 2–3
harem (women's quarters), 21, 38–9, 43, 86–7
havili, see mansion
household, imperial, in *A'in-i Akbari*, 20–1
huqqa (waterpipe), 48, 56, 138–9, 160
Humayun, Emperor, 13–4
  as man of the pen, 135

imperial camp, layout, 94–9
  population, 99–100
Isfahan, as sovereign city, 193–8
Istanbul, as sovereign city, 187–93

Jahangir, Emperor, 15
  as man of the pen, 136
Jahanpanah, 10
Jai Singh Pura, mahallah in suburbs of Shahjahanabad, 58
Jami' Masjid (Friday or Congregational Mosque), 52–4, 82

khanazad (house-born), 129, 150, fn. 100
Kailughari, 10
karkhanahs (workshops), of Mughal emperors, 105–7
  of princes and great amirs, 107–8
  of merchants, 108–12
Khas Bazaar (Special Market), 57
  goods in, 118–20
Khattri, merchants in Shahjahanabad, 1639–1739, 110–12
  as men of the pen, 132
  merchants in Shahjahanabad, 1739–1857, 176

khil'at (ceremonial robe), 31, 92
khiyal (a kind of song), 157–8, 160
Kotla Firuz Shah, 11
kotwal (city magistrate), 23

Lal Kot, 9

madrassah (Islamic institution of higher learning), 51
Magadha, 3
mahallah (quarter), in suburbs of Shahjahanabad, 58–60
  caste/craft, 84
  elite, 84–5
  palace-fortress as, 85–6
  mansions of princes and great amirs as, 86–8
  social structure in elite, 88–90
  in Shahjahanabad, 1739–1857, 178–9
  in Istanbul, 190
mansabdars (officeholders), 21
mansion (*havili*), of princes and great amirs, in Shahjahanabad, 144–51
  as elite mahallah, population, 95–8
  public ritual in, 84–7
  markets in, 117–8
  in Agra, 186
  in Istanbul, 190
  in Isfahan, 196
  in Edo, 201
markets (*bazaars*), in Shahjahanabad, 55–7
  hierarchy in Shahjahanabad, 116–20
  neighborhood in Shahjahanabad, 117
  regional in Shahjahanabad, 117–18
  central in Shahjahanabad, 118–20
  in Agra, 186
  in Istanbul, 191
marsiya (Shi'i elegy on the death of the Imam Husain), 139, 154
men of the pen (*ahl-i qalam*), in Islamic history, 123–5
  in Mughal India, 125
  culture of, 130–40
  khattris as, 132
  Mughal Emperors as, 135–7
  great amirs as, 138–40
men of the sword (*ahl-i saif*), in Islamic history, 123–5
  in Mughal India, 125
  culture of, 141–8
merchants, in Shahjahanabad, 109–12
  in Istanbul, 191
  in Isfahan, 197
  in Edo, 202–3
  in Peking, 209

Ming Empire, as patrimonial-bureaucratic empire, 204–9
mir bakshi (paymaster-general), 141–2
mir saman (head steward), in great amiri household, 107
mirzai (gentility or gentlemanliness), 131–2
Mir, Muhammad Taqi Mir, 165–6
Mohenjo-Daro, 2–3
mosque (*masjid*), in Shahjahanabad, 51–5
Mubarakabad, 11
Mughal, 13
Mughal Emperors, interest in architecture, 12, 26
as men of the pen, 135–6
as men of the sword, 144–6
Mughal Empire, 13–7
fall, 17
structure of, 23–5
Mughalpura, mahallah in suburbs of Shahjahanabad, 60
muhandis (architect-planner), 28
musha'ira (literary evening devoted to poetry), 134, 139
mutiny of 1857, 172–3

Nadir Shah, attack on Shahjahanabad, 17, 162–3
Nahr-i Bihisht, *see* Paradise Canal
New Delhi, 13
Nizam al-Din Auliya, tomb, 29, 60
celebration of 'urs, 153

Ottoman Empire, men of sword and pen in, 149
Istanbul as capital of, 187–93

Paharganj, mahallah in suburbs of Shahjahanabad, 58
Paradise Canal (*Nahr-i Bihisht*), 39, 64–5
Patparganj, mahallah in suburbs of Shahjahanabad, 58
patrimonial-bureaucratic empire, Mughal Empire as example of, 17–25
economic organization of, 104
Ottoman Empire as example of, 187–93
Safavid Empire as example of, 203–8
Tokugawa Shogunate as example of, 199–204
Ming Empire as example of, 204–9
patron–client relationship, in mansions of princes and great amirs, 88–90
in palace-fortress, 90–3, 96
Peking, as sovereign city, 204–9
pishkash (ceremonial offering), 31

population, of Shahjahanabad, 1639–1739, 66–8
of Shahjahanabad, 1739–1857, 173–5
public ritual, in palace-fortress, 90–3, 96
in princely and great amiri mansions, 94–7

Qadam Sharif (Sacred Footprint), tomb, 61
celebration at, 152
Qamar al-Din Khan, map of mansion, 46
location and description of mansion, 78–9
qawwal (a kind of song), 157–8
Qila' Mubarak (palace-fortress), 36–44
population of, 85–6
public ritual in, 90–3, 96
markets in, 118
Qila' Rai Pithora, 9
qila'dar (fort commander), of Qila Mubarak in Shahjahanabad, 38

Rasail (Epistles) of *Ikhwan al-Safa* (Brothers of Purity), 34–6
Risala Salar Jang (Treatise of Salar Jang), 150–1

Sa'adullah Khan, 23, 31, 53–4
chawk of, 57, 118
mansion of, 81
Safavid Empire, immigrants to Mughal India from, 33–4
men of sword and pen, 149
Isfahan as capital of, 193–8
Sahibabad (Abode of the Master) Garden, 63
Sauda, Mirza Muhammad Rafi, poem on Shahjahanabad, 165–6
Shahjahan, Emperor, 15
interest in architecture, 26–7
as man of the pen, 136
building activities in Agra, 185
Shahjahanabad, location, 1
founding, 12–31
attack of Nadir Shah on, 17, 162–3
as axis mundi, 29–30
inauguration as capital, 31
wall around, 31–2
gates, 32
city plan, Hindu influence, 32–3
city plan, Islamic influence, 33–6
palace-fortress of, 36–44
mansions of princes and great amirs in, 44–51
mosques in, 51–5
Jami' Masjid, 52–4

Shahjahanabad (Cont.)
  markets (*bazaars*) in, 55–7
  Chandni Chawk (Moonlight or Silver
    Square), 56
  Faiz Bazaar (Market of Plenty), 56–7
  Khas Bazaar (Special Market), 57
  suburbs, 57–66
  Paradise Canal, 64–5
  caravansarai (inn for travellers) in,
    65–6
  population, 1639–1739, 66–8
  map of mansions and mosques, 71–82
  social structure, 99–103
  karkhanahs (workshops) in, 105–12
  markets, hierarchy, 116–20
  utilization of goods and services in,
    120–21
  popular culture in, 150–60
  poets of, 156–7
  singers and musicians of, 157–9
  dancers in, 159–60
  actors and mimics in, 160
  decline, 1739–1803, 161–9
  description by Sauda, 165–6
  description by Mir, 165–6
  British takeover and administration of,
    1803–57, 169–73
  mutiny in, 172–3
  population, 1739–1857, 173–5
  economy, 1739–1857, 175–7

culture, 1739–1857, 177–81
Delhi Renaissance, 180–1
shahr ashob (ruined city) poetry, 165–6
Shergah, 12
Shi'ism, in Safavid Iran, 127, 135, 193–4,
  197
sipah salar (army commander), 23
Siri, 10
subahdar (commander of a province), of
  Shahjahanabad, 30
suburbs of Shahjahanabad, 57–66
  area, 57
  map, 57
  mahallahs (quarters) in, 58–60
  gardens in, 62–4
Sufism, in Shahjahanabad, 151–6

ta'ziya (representation of the shrine of
  the Imam Husain), 154
Tokugawa Shogunate, as
  patrimonial-bureaucratic empire,
  199–204
Tughlaqabad, 10

Urbanism, pre-Mughal, 2–5
'urs (death anniversary commemoration),
  60–2, 140

Weber, Max, 17

CAMBRIDGE SOUTH ASIAN STUDIES

These monographs are published by the Syndics of Cambridge University Press in association with the Cambridge Centre for South Asian Studies. The following books have been published in this series:

1 S. Gopal: *British Policy in India, 1858–1905*
2 J.A.B. Palmer: *The Mutiny Outbreak at Meerut in 1857*
3 Ashin Das Gupta: *Malabar in Asian Trade, 1740–1800*
4 Gananath Obeyesekere: *Land Tenure in Village Ceylon: A Sociological and Historical Study*
5 H.L. Erdman: *The Swatantra Party and Indian Conservatism*
6 S.N. Mukherjee: *Sir William Jones: A Study in Eighteenth-Century British Attitudes to India*
7 Abdul Majed Khan: *The Transition in Bengal, 1756–1775: A Study of Saiyid Muhammad Reza Khan*
8 Radhe Shyam Rungta: *The Rise of Business Corporations in India, 1851–1900*
9 Pamela Nightingale: *Trade and Empire in Western India, 1784–1806*
10 Amiya Kumar Bagchi: *Private Investment in India 1900–1939*
11 Judith M. Brown: *Gandhi's Rise to Power: Indian Politics 1915–1922*
12 Mary C. Carras: *Dynamics of Indian Political Factions: A Study of District Councils in the State of Maharashtra*
13 P. Hardy: *The Muslims of British India*
14 Gordon Johnson: *Provincial Politics and Indian Nationalism: Bombay and the Indian National Congress, 1880 to 1915*
15 Marguerite S. Robinson: *Political Structure in a Changing Sinhalese Village*
16 Francis Robinson: *Separatism among Indian Muslims: The Politics of the United Provinces' Muslims, 1860–1923*
17 Christopher John Baker: *The Politics of South India, 1920–1937*
18 D.A. Washbrook: *The Emergence of Provincial Politics: The Madras Presidency, 1870–1920*
19 Deepak Nayyar: *India's Exports and Export Policies in the 1960s*
20 Mark Holmström: *South Indian Factory Workers: Their Life and Their World*
21 S. Ambirajan: *Classical Political Economy and British Policy in India*
22 M. Mufakhrul Islam: *Bengal Agriculture 1920–1946: A Quantitative Study*
23 Eric Stokes: *The Peasant and the Raj: Studies in Agrarian Society and Peasant Rebellion in Colonial India*

24 Michael Roberts: *Caste Conflict and Elite Formation: The Rise of Karāva Elite in Sri Lanka, 1500–1931*

25 John Toye: *Public Expenditure and Indian Development Policy 1960–1970*

26 Rashid Amjad: *Private Industrial Investment in Pakistan 1960–1970*

27 Arjun Appadurai: *Worship and Conflict under Colonial Rule: a South Indian Case*

28 C.A. Bayly: *Rulers, Townsmen and Bazaars: North Indian Society in the Age of British Expansion, 1770–1870*

29 Ian Stone: *Canal Irrigation in British India: Perspectives on Technological Change in a Peasant Economy*

30 Rosalind O'Hanlon: *Caste, Conflict, and Ideology: Mahatma Jotirao Phule and Low Caste Protest in Nineteenth-Century Western India*

31 Ayesha Jalal: *The Sole Spokesman: Jinnah, the Muslim League and the Demand for Pakistan*

32 Neil Charlesworth: *Peasants and Imperial Rule: Agriculture and Agrarian Society in the Bombay Presidency, 1850–1935*

33 Claude Markovits: *Indian Business and Nationalist Politics 1931–1939: The Indigenous Capitalist Class and the Rise of the Congress Party*

34 Mick Moore: *The State and Peasant Politics in Sri Lanka*

35 Gregory C. Kozlowski: *Muslim Endowments and Society in British India*

36 Sugata Bose: *Agrarian Bengal: Economy, Society and Politics, 1919–1947*

37 Atul Kohli: *The State and Poverty in India: The Politics of Reform*

38 Franklin A. Presler: *Religion Under Bureaucracy: Policy and Administration for Hindu Temples in South India*

39 Nicholas B. Dirks: *The Hollow Crown: Ethnohistory of an Indian Kingdom*

40 Robert Wade: *Village Republics: Economic Conditions for Collective Action in South India*

41 Laurence W. Preston: *The Devs of Cincvad: A Lineage and State in Maharashtra*

42 Farzana Shaikh: *Community and Consensus in Islam: Muslim Representation in Colonial India 1860–1947*

43 Susan Bayly: *Saints, Goddesses and Kings: Muslims and Christians in South Indian Society*

44 Gyan Prakash: *Bonded Histories: Genealogies of Labor Servitude in Colonial India*

45 Sanjay Subrahmanyam: *The Political Economy of Commerce: Southern India 1500–1650*

46 Ayesha Jalal: *The State of Martial Rule: The Origins of Pakistan's Political Economy of Defence*

47 Bruce Graham: *Hindu Nationalism and Indian Politics: The Origins and Development of the Bharatiya Jana Sangh*

48 Dilesh Jayanntha: *Electoral Allegiance in Sri Lanka*

49 Stephen P. Blake: *Shahjahanabad: The Sovereign City in Mughal India 1639–1739*

Printed in the United States
121659LV00002B/169-174/A

9 780521 522991